Also by **DAVID KING DUNAWAY**

Oral History: An Interdisciplinary Anthology

Writing the Southwest

Huxley in Hollywood

Aldous Huxley Recollected: An Oral History

Route 66: A Manual for Oral History

The Pete Seeger Discography

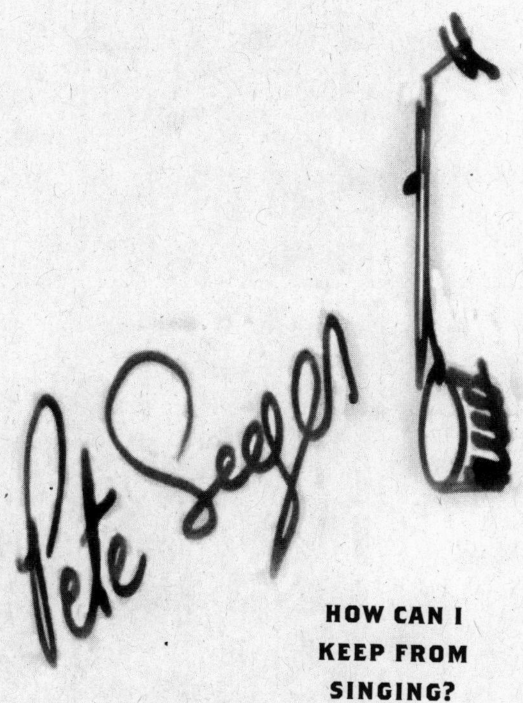

HOW CAN I KEEP FROM SINGING?

V

VILLARD BOOKS

New York

How Can I Keep from Singing?
THE BALLAD OF
PETE SEEGER
David King Dunaway

2008 Villard Books Trade Paperback Edition

Published in the United States by Villard Books,
an imprint of The Random House Publishing Group,
a division of Random House, Inc., New York.

VILLARD and "V" Circled Design are registered
trademarks of Random House, Inc.

Originally published in hardcover and in slightly different form
in the United States by McGraw-Hill Book Company, in 1981.

Acknowledgments and permissions credits are located beginning on page 493.

ISBN 978-0-345-50608-5

LIBRARY OF CONGRESS CATALOGING-IN-PUBLICATION DATA

Dunaway, David King.
How can I keep from singing? : the ballad of Pete Seeger /
David King Dunaway.—Trade paperback ed.
p. cm.
Includes bibliographical references (p. 459),
discography (p. 477), and index.
ISBN 978-0-345-50608-5 (pbk.)
1. Seeger, Pete, 1919– 2. Folk singers—
United States—Biography. I. Title.
ML420.S445D8 2008
782.42162'130092—dc22
[B] 2007041814

Printed in the United States of America

www.villard.com

2 4 6 8 9 7 5 3 1

Title page photograph courtesy of The Providence Journal
Book design by Barbara M. Bachman

TO THOSE WHO GAVE THEIR LIVES
TO SING OF FREEDOM:
"YOU MAY BURN MY FLESH AND BONES
AND THROW THE ASHES TO THE FOUR WINDS,"
SMILED ONE OF THEM.
"YET MY VOICE SHALL LINGER ON,
AND IN THE YEARS YET TO COME
THE YOUNG SHALL ASK WHAT WAS THE IDEA
FOR WHICH YOU GAVE ME DEATH
AND WHAT WAS I SAYING
THAT I MUST DIE FOR WHAT I SAID."

—*Carl Sandburg,* THE PEOPLE, YES

FOREWORD

—

I NEVER EXPECTED TO BE WRITING A FOREWORD FOR THIS book. I read the first edition only after it came out. But then I spent many days going over each page with David, pointing out what I felt were mistakes in that edition. Now I congratulate him for years upon years of research and more research, rechecking, rethinking his book.

What can I add?

Consider: The Agricultural Revolution took thousands of years. The Industrial Revolution took hundreds of years. The Information Revolution is taking only decades. If we use the brains God gave us, we can perhaps now bring about the Non-violent Revolution. If we don't, this could be the last century for the human race.

Who knows, who knows? Technology may save us if it doesn't wipe us out first. In any case, the next few years will be the most exciting years any of us have ever known.

Maybe there's room to retell my parable of the Teaspoon Brigade. Imagine a big seesaw. One end is on the ground, held down by a bushel basket half full of rocks. The other end of the seesaw is up in the air with a bushel basket on it one-quarter full of sand. Some of us have teaspoons and are trying to fill it. Most people are scoffing. "It's leaking out as fast as you put it in."

But we say, "No." We're watching closely, and it's a little more full than it was. And we're getting more and more people with teaspoons. One of these days that whole seesaw will go *zoop!* in the opposite direction. People will say, "Gee, how did it happen so suddenly?"

Us and all our little teaspoons over thousands of years.

Keep in mind that we have to keep using our teaspoons, because the basket does leak. Are you in the Teaspoon Brigade?

Thank you, David, for your years of work. As Robert Burns put it, "O wad some Power the giftie gie us to see oursels as ithers see us."

Pete Seeger

PREFACE

"I'M A LINK IN A CHAIN," PETE SEEGER VOLUNTEERS, IN A LONG American tradition of singing for reform. Abolitionists; union organizers; civil rights, peace, and environmental activists—all turned to song to make their points.

For music captures the soul in ways that few political speeches can; it has encouraged and inspired revolutions. Realizing this, governments have tortured musicians like Victor Jara in Chile and Mikos Theodorakis in Greece, hoping to destroy a song by silencing its composer or performer.

In the United States, investigations of composers take the place of thumbscrews. Pete Seeger and his popular quartet, the Weavers, in the fifties, have the distinction of being the only artists in American history formally investigated by the Senate for sedition and insurrection under Title 18, U.S. Code 2383-85.

No one is investigating Pete Seeger these days. At eighty-nine, he still lives with Toshi, his wife of sixty-five years, in a converted red barn in New York's Hudson River Valley. Though he once set Carnegie Hall vibrating with the sound of a thousand voices, he's beginning to give up singing.

Few recordings capture his way of uniting strangers in song, and few know all that his campaigns have cost him and his family—the confiscated passports, the lost jobs, the personal attacks.

Pete Seeger's life resembles his song "Abiyoyo," an African folktale he adapted. It's the story of a boy and his musician father, whom the town banishes for playing too loudly or too late at night.

Then the Giant comes, and the boy defeats him. He doesn't fight him, exactly. Instead of a stone, he uses a ukulele.

The Giant dances until he's out of breath and falls down. Then the father whisks him away with his magic wand. The boy's music saves the town.

Now the town's elders can't remember why these great patriots shouldn't be at the head of the parade.

"Come back, bring your damn ukulele!" And the crowds welcome them and sing a song in their honor.

That Pete Seeger's father was run out of Berkeley's music department; that his son would bring his banjo to sing to his inquisitors—one doesn't need to know these things to decipher the parable. That music could help save a community from fascism or McCarthyism; that it's one of the forces uniting humanity—this has been Pete Seeger's belief all along.

IT'S A CHALLENGE to write about a complex man whose motto is "Strive for simplicity, and learn to distrust it." The ideal biographer of Pete Seeger would be a musician and an ethnomusicologist, an activist and a sailor, a forest ranger, an archivist, and a political historian.

I'm not all of these things. I am not even sure I'm any of them. But a quarter-century ago I wrote Seeger's biography. When I began, Seeger cautioned me: This biography would not be authorized. He wouldn't read or censor the draft; he would cooperate with interviews and research.

In the past few years, I've consulted dozens of memoirs and histories published since this book came out. Besides the 120 interviews I deposited at the Library of Congress, I've talked with dozens more. Mostly, I've talked with Pete Seeger.

At the beginning of this century, at his request, we went through the book page by page. For three days we woodshedded reactions, corrections, and regrets. From the early morning sun till the last light off the river, we'd sit in the log cabin he'd built, until

Toshi came out from the barn and tapped at the window for lunch or dinner. We'd eat awfully healthy meals of lentils and brown rice with miso or homemade garlic butter, and an occasional nod to his sweet tooth.

Pete Seeger's reactions are now laced throughout the book. His most frequent response was a dislike of the word "career":

> To most people that means making money and getting famous, and I was not concerned about this. I've lived with this terrible contradiction. If I splurge, if I go down and buy some fancy food I don't need, that's food that could keep somebody else alive. It's one reason that I didn't want to go into the music industry and make a lot of money, why I definitely didn't want to have a career with a capital C.
>
> Now it's true, I could have become a violinist—my mother wanted me to. I could have become a businessman—my grandfather wanted me to. I could have become a journalist; if I'd had more perseverance, I might have. If I'd had a grant early to be a researcher, I could have been one. But I wasn't willing to take the discipline. To be a real researcher, you have to get that degree and fulfill all the academic obligations.
>
> Instead, I drifted into a particular niche I'd found for myself that no one else had ever found before.

His niche has so far lasted seven decades of performing. It is easy to forget, as Jimmy Collier said, that "it's the same guy who traveled everywhere playing his little banjo; who wrote all those great songs; who's on *Sesame Street*; who was singing civil rights and folk songs, but couldn't appear on *Hootenanny.*" A career—or a calling—like Seeger's may not reoccur in America, for his Popular Front patriotism belongs to a distant, less cynical era. Is America still a country where a southern farmer would call a wandering Yankee over for a glass of milk and teach him a banjo lick?

—

WHEN I RETURNED to this book, and the radio series that followed, some questions haunted me. I still wondered how he keeps up his optimism. And how he's held to beliefs some call Pollyanna-like but that he has maintained in the face of arson and bloodshot hatred in the eyes of his detractors. Could being blacklisted have actually made him stronger? Did he place politics before music? Has he come to terms with the excesses of Communist practice, including Stalin's?

LET ME START the story where it began, as I started to work with Pete Seeger at his cabin overlooking the Hudson, which stretches flat and chocolate brown below us. We'd been up to a concert at MIT the previous evening . . .

CONTENTS

INTRODUCTION

—

"THOSE WHO KNOW THE WORDS, SING OUT, SO YOUR NEIGHbors will take courage," says Pete Seeger, unshouldering his banjo. Stepping out toward the audience from the lights, he frowns. "Well, we've got a bunch of good singers here. But *some* of you are holding back. Preserving their academic ob-jeck-tivity."

In the wood-paneled college auditorium, the overeducated crowd roars appreciatively. Before them stands a rail-thin, fifty-seven-year-old in a sailor's cap, frailing his banjo nonchalantly and acting more like a concerned friend than an entertainer. It's 1976, and three thousand New Englanders are gathered to raise bail for demonstrators arrested at a nearby nuclear power plant. Eager promoters have oversold the house, and the air feels hot and thick.

The crowd is watching a musician who has been concertizing for forty years. At a conservative estimate, Pete Seeger's total audience—those in seeing, hearing, and microphone distance—might total between four and five million people in forty countries.

Seeger rolls up his sleeves and gets to work. Thick-soled hiking boots clump out the rhythm, jiggling the microphone. He swings his long-necked banjo toward the crowd, and they echo a chorus. They put their voice in his charge, confident he will not ask the impossible or try to sell them his latest album. Seeger drops his voice into a lower octave to harmonize; the room lights up, and the audience becomes a reverberating instrument in his hands.

When he sings the old ballads, his gray beard points off into the balcony and his eyes fix above it, to a point in the ether. He pours forth good spirits like a cornucopia. Before the audience has a chance to applaud, he unobtrusively changes key and introduces the next song. The audience is content. Seeger is in high form tonight, doing just what made him famous.

TO HIS FOLLOWERS, Seeger is an institution—a preacher with a banjo in place of a psalm book. If at times his songs ring flat or his music strikes a strident chord, well, the audience comes for the presence, not the show. "I go to a Pete Seeger concert for a hit of *him*," one fellow in a flannel shirt says. "He could stand up there and play the chair for all I care."

If Wayne Newton is at home in the casinos of Las Vegas, Seeger's abode is the impromptu political benefit. Over the years, he has worked with so many social movements that journalists have paid more attention to his politics than to his music. Most everywhere he sang, controversy followed. "Khrushchev's songbird," the John Birch Society called him; "a saint" was Bob Dylan's word. Writers argue over whether he is a revolutionary or a victim of red-hunting: a subversive or a patriot.

The listeners understand Seeger has been blacklisted; it adds a touch of danger to his performance, like books read under the covers. Yet for all his notoriety, despite being one of the most picketed, boycotted performers in American history, his private life remains a closely held secret. No scandal sheets report his comings and goings. No television network features him.

Even to his friends Seeger is a mystery. After having known him for thirty years, his friend Gordon Friesen comments, "He's not a man I sit and chew the fat with." Family members tell of his immense reserve, insisting they've never been close. Despite his warmth on stage, there's not much left to meet humanity one-on-one.

For a performer whose voice and instrumental skill are today overshadowed by younger musicians, Pete Seeger has a popularity as enigmatic as the rumors that circulate about him. One surprising story comes from a woman who's known the musician since he was seventeen. In the past decades, she is convinced, he secretly "doesn't think he made the right choice somewhere" and feels "his career didn't matter."

I wonder at this as I look out over the excited faces in the audience. Tuning his guitar with deliberate slowness, Seeger calms the crowd for a quiet song about living by the Hudson River. Then he closes with his tune "If I Had a Hammer," and even the hard-hearts sing. *I'd hammer out danger, I'd hammer out warning*—the song takes life; awakened from memory it rises and moves offstage, into the aisles. People stand and sway; the walls seem to shake like tent flaps at an old-fashioned camp meeting.

For the encore, Seeger does "Amazing Grace." He teaches the audience to sing it in a long-meter style, in surges of sound that roll across the hall:

Shall I be wafted to the skies
On flowery beds of ease
While others strive to win the prize
And sail through bloody seas.

As he readies himself to leave, a very attractive woman with long auburn hair waits by his dressing room. She says she wants to talk to him privately and follows him into the room. The door closes. Does Pete Seeger have groupies?

Inside, she hesitates. "I just wanted to tell you how much you've made folk music come alive for me and my friends." Hoarse from singing and interviews, Seeger nods and bends down to give her shoulder a squeeze. His timing is perfect, the touch fatherly and gentle. He smiles and ducks out of the room. Watching this familiar cameo, I notice how Seeger's eyes flick into the distance, how he listens bemused, bobbing his head. He's heard this many times. He's not quite there.

I DRIVE SEEGER HOME across Massachusetts and Upstate New York; the russet-brown Berkshires whirl by the window. Dressed in a T-shirt, he snoozes in the back seat, his glasses hanging around his neck on an elastic band. Without the sailor's cap, his thinning hair adds ten years to his looks. His knees raised to the roof, he manages to fit himself into the small sedan seat; his head bounces along on an armrest. He sleeps until the turnoff outside Beacon, where I struggle up his rocky driveway.

As we pull up, his four-year-old grandson Tao is sitting in the sun in front of the log cabin with a plastic shovel. Toshi, his Japanese American wife, gardens nearby, behind the log cabin where they live. A few years younger than Seeger, she is also a good foot shorter, with shiny black hair and dark, restless eyes. As teenagers, they met at a square dance.

His wife talks over her shoulder as she unpacks the maple syrup buckets we bought on the way home. The frosted aluminum sparkles in the sunlight. She stacks the pails with the air of one habitually well organized, then stops to look me over. As Seeger's long-time partner, Toshi has spent years shielding their privacy; she has become watchful of writers. She asks how his CBS interview went.

"Oh, I talked too much," he answers unenthusiastically. "Started to argue politics with the fellow."

She throws him a look. It's dinnertime, and we sit on cushions at a low table. Their eldest daughter, Mika, has been to the health food store, and the fusty odor of soy milk fills the room.

"Toshi's very private about her own life," Seeger later reflects. "She does not want to be a public figure and she refuses even to be photographed. It's not just with you, but with everybody. She'll be very cordial over the dinner table, laugh and joke, and as long as it's not for press she doesn't mind people knowing about her. Her ancestor chart goes back further than mine. Mine just goes back to the seventeenth century, hers goes back to the sixteenth century with members of Parliament. She does not talk about it."

As I awake the next morning in a tiny trailer, the smell of wet leaves and river fog hangs over the grounds. To my right is the cabin, forty feet by twenty, divided into three rooms. Over to the left stands the barn, with offices and archives upstairs. A terraced garden hangs over the edge of the sloping yard. At the bottom of the hill the Hudson flows like a wide highway through the mountains. In the distance, the river disappears into a gray cloud up toward Poughkeepsie.

A PERFORMER WITHDRAWN from friends and his public often confides in his journal, and with fresh hopes I pass the morning alone in the barn, poring over the files in Seeger's study. In a little office over his wife's pottery studio, Seeger spends much of his time answering mail, writing songs. On top of a stack of tapes is a prominent songwriter's new album. Hundreds demand Seeger's opinion about their songs, stories, and causes, and he initiates his own projects so rapidly they cram the wooden chests of his small, square study.

In these chests and boxes reside Seeger's dreams. Like many frustrated journalists, Pete Seeger has written thousands of pages of unpublished journals, song notebooks, and sketches—even two book-length manuscripts, including the provocatively titled *Fantasies of a Revisionist.*

"Look here," he says, pulling open a drawer to reveal a handmade flute. Reels of tape spill from their boxes. "A record on Chinese flute music I wanted to edit—twenty years ago." He points at a brown box in the corner.

"My banjo book. It's so out of date I hate to mail out copies. I wrote it in hotel rooms during Henry Wallace's campaign in 1948. 'What the heck,' I decided. 'Might as well publish it myself.' First year, I sold a hundred mimeographed copies. The ninth year, nine thousand. By now, we've sent out a quarter million. The last five years I've been trying to find a month free of mail to revise a few points. No luck," he says in frustration.

The performer's public cheerfulness sours. Mail's the root of his personal evil: requests for benefits, missing lyrics, tunes for a worthy quatrain—he feels a duty to answer them all. Writers in twenty countries have pushed Seeger's correspondence out of control, leaving him with a six-month backlog of letters.

His problems with correspondence may be a foil for deeper concerns. It turns out Seeger questions his role in a folk song revival that, according to writer Jon Pankake, had young enthusiasts rifling America's folk traditions "like so many grubby urchins grabbing at pennies thrown in the street."

Amid the mounds of paper lie Seeger's hopes and doubts about politics and fellow performers, clues to a man unfamiliar to his public.

I START WITH THE JOURNALS.

In the first of these, the sixteen-year-old noted a telling dream about music. After a performance of the New York Philharmonic, ten thousand people appear at the box office of the Roxy Music Hall to demand their money back. Although Toscanini conducted with a phosphorescent baton, "he did not wave it about enough," according to the crowd. (Seeger's violinist mother had hopes of raising a virtuoso; he didn't much care for the idea.)

Another entry reveals Seeger's precocious interest in radical politics. At thirteen, he already had a subscription to the Communist literary magazine *New Masses*; he was a "red diaper" baby a generation before Dr. Spock. Just as he'd follow in his father's journey into American folk music, so he'd read Mike Gold in the '30s, as his father wrote a column on music for the *Daily Worker.* "Fascism is the last stage of capitalism," Seeger scribed with the orthodoxy of adolescence. "The greatest danger [to revolutionaries] is the Greenwich Village type, the bohemian." Stern words from someone who'd eventually spend four years living in the Village.

In letters from his army days in World War II, he comments on the lines at boot camp and how his Yankee accent stands out in a southern regiment. Yet on his first day in the army, "New York" (as bunkmates called him) won friends and a banjo contest by picking southern tunes.

I am momentarily distracted by a sound outside the window. Seeger is standing at the edge of his garden, head tilted up to the sky. He's yodeling into the wind. "Yodl-ay-dee-ohh." I watch fascinated, half expecting to hear the river return the sound. "Ohh-dl-ay-dee-ohh." I am reminded of a tune he once composed for Shakespeare's *Tempest*: the song of Ariel, the breezy spirit who plays invisible instruments.

Turning back to the stack of papers, I come across an unfunded grant proposal. At the height of Seeger's commercial success, when "Goodnight Irene" was America's most popular song, he applied for a Guggenheim fellowship to research "Instrumental Styles in American Folk Music." Soon after the grant went in, however, Seeger's name came up before the House Committee on Un-American Activities (HUAC). He received a polite turndown from the foundation.

Seeger's thickest files are those labeled BLACKLIST. The volume of his collection is astounding—at least four hundred documents. One letter, typed on the thickly embossed stationery of the New-York Historical Society, catches my eye. According to their letter, the Society canceled a 1957 concert due to last-minute indications of "political unpleasantness." The entertainer's reply shows a self-protective irony. It was a shame, he wrote the Society, to cave in to a few threats. Not only had he and his parents lived in New York for years, but a great-uncle had been the mayor, the man who christened the Brooklyn Bridge.

There is an even larger collection of documents that Seeger has yet to see: his FBI files. To America's intelligence agencies, Seeger and his friends were a public menace; the FBI infiltrated, eavesdropped, and maintained mail and trash covers. Six years of litigation under the Freedom of Information Act has yielded ten feet of reports on informers in the folk music community, imagined cabals of folk musicians, even details of the Bureau's behind-the-scenes role in Seeger's blacklisting. But the FBI does not have all of Seeger's correspondence. For decades politicians have been writing him: Senator Fred Harris of Oklahoma promises to find a marker for Woody Guthrie's home in Okemah; in 1948, Councilman Paul O'Dwyer thanks him for helping out New York's municipal radio station; young Martin Luther King Jr., twenty-seven, warmly acknowledges his help back in 1956.

Some of Seeger's letters show an unsuspected bleakness, as in 1974, when he wrote the songwriter Malvina Reynolds:

> I guess my problem is really not too different from an awful lot of other people. It's simply that I'm weary of never catching up on a huge pile of mail. The months and years go by and I somehow never get the songs written that I intend to. It's a relief to go on a trip where all I have to do is stare at a hotel room instead of a study that has about ten unfinished jobs.

As I look around this study, the unfinished tasks are still here. The tapes sit silently, waiting for a sympathetic hand to insert them into the tape player. The past lies in scraps around the room: dreams of political change, fantasies of a quiet stint as a folklorist, frustrations at the boycotts that shadow his singing.

"You must be about drowned in all this paper." The voice startles me. "One of these days I'm going to throw all this out," Seeger laughs.

He's been chopping firewood, a favorite exercise, and his cheeks are red from effort. "Fellow my age should get out of breath once a day," he insists. A nondrinker, nonsmoker, Seeger unwinds by ice-skating, chopping wood, and playing music. "Let's get some lunch, and we'll talk afterwards. But not too much. If I talk for a whole afternoon, I can't perform for the next two nights." He stops short, wistfully. "Nowadays I sometimes have to eat by myself on nights I perform."

A harbinger of problems to come. Seeger's characteristic stance—head lifted high, forward of the body—leaves his vocal chords unsupported. In time, it will rob him of his voice.

We take a break. He lopes down the stairs and across to the cabin, where he grates a hunk of white cheddar into some eggs and the flat beer he keeps especially for rarebits. As the tasty goop steams, he spots his grandson Tao, then four years old, in the corner. Picking up his recorder, he begins a jig, softly at first. Tao looks up, and his grandfather smiles. The boy dances, and his grandfather plays faster and faster until Tao gets so excited he wobbles. Seeger slows the music and his grandson falls to the floor, giggling. Grandpa picks up Tao, swinging him around the room, and walks to the stove for a taste. He licks his finger, stirs in more mustard, and ladles it out for the half-dozen friends and relatives the smell has assembled.

At the table, there's no small talk. We discuss an article on free speech in the *New Yorker.* I ask Toshi about the fantastic stories concerning her father, Takashi, who was exiled from Japan and who once fought with Sun Yat-sen.

"Oh, Peter shouldn't have told that story," she laughed, with an edge to her voice. "That's family business. And besides, he tells it *all wrong.*" Seeger is oblivious to her comment; he sits straight as a deacon, cross-legged. Absentmindedly passing the butter, he practically drops it in midair.

AFTER LUNCH WE CLIMB the curving barn stairs to his study. Strapping the microphones in place, I wonder how to tackle the hard questions. How do you bring up the Communist Party with a man once sentenced to jail for refusing to discuss his political associations? What has he actually done to be so heavily targeted by right-wing groups?

"Instead of me, you really ought to write about Aunt Molly Jackson [a Kentucky mine organizer and balladeer]," he begins immediately, leading us toward folk music. He launches into a now-familiar disclaimer: "Too many people listen to me and not enough to the people I learned from." His words carry unselfconscious modesty, mixed with the antipsychology, anti-individual canon of historical materialism: One life doesn't count; only the many matter. "If Seeger ever wrote his autobiography," fellow songwriter "Country" Joe McDonald mused, "he'd content himself with a half-dozen entries in the index."

He was also influenced by the Anonymous movement, a fascinating group of artists in Paris in the 1920s, who refused to sign paintings. They insisted that works of art must stand on their own merits, not on the artist's personality. Thus, talking with Seeger about his past is like starting a detective novel halfway through; you're never sure whom to follow in the plot.

Not that Seeger is evasive. In our interviews he's chatty, but careful. He doesn't wait for questions, throwing off a string of anecdotes: the upper-crust boarding schools he attended; his start in music and in politics; his time bumming cross-country with Woody Guthrie; and particularly his fight against the blacklist. For the first time, Seeger volunteers information about his involvement with the Communist Party, matter-of-factly.

With the thin wire of a microphone trailing him, Seeger wanders about his study. Without his banjo, the man's arms become an instrument, as he waves them in the air to make a point. He gestures haplessly at the wire basket with six inches of today's mail. He discusses his worry that his voice will give out. His words are mesmerizing, but I can't help feeling his attention has flown away. Seeger speaks in parables. His stories are set pieces, each capped with a moral. The concern about office work is genuine but solvable; he could afford three secretaries if he wanted them, but they'd intrude.

At the end of the session, I pack up my equipment while he rests, head cradled in his palms. Eventually he perks up and stretches. He walks over to a bookshelf and pushes files aside until he comes up with a black notebook the size of a well-worn wallet. Holding it gingerly, he flips the pages for a minute, his back to me. When he turns around, he has a sheepish grin.

"Look at this, David." He turns the notebook so I can read the neatly printed song lists.

"I sat down thirty years ago to copy names of songs I know all the way though. Here they are, maybe six hundred of them." Then he looks up hopefully, pursing his lips and scanning the song titles. "Let's see how many I still remember."

PETE SEEGER WONDERS how he forgot his lyrics, and I despair of finding an avenue into his past. His communicator is set on long-range broadcast, a farsighted man who holds the world at arm's length.

AFTER OUR INTERVIEW, Seeger suggests I help out with the chores. "Sure," I nod, and he smiles broadly. He throws me a pair of cotton gloves. Backing up the pickup, we head for the dump with a contribution to the world's waste problem.

There's something democratic about garbage dumping. Everyone—the lowly and the great—creates and disposes of waste. Some stuff it down the sink and push a button. Most Americans pile it in a bag, take that out to a can, and forget about it. More and more people recycle. In garbage, like wine, there is truth. As the biographer Plutarch tells us, attention to small tasks characterizes people more truly than their heroic moments.

It is a bright and sunny afternoon as we wind down the hillside, with the wind blowing sweetly off the Hudson—the sort of fair and pleasant day when knights and pilgrims meet in English ballads. The cans rattle in the back of the pickup as Seeger stops to add a load at the Beacon Sloop Club, his home-away-from-home. He picks up odds and ends left by teenagers from the last sailing class. The tin-roofed clubhouse, with a nonpolluting toilet that produces mulch (and uses no water), sits forlornly opposite the railway station.

Here the Hudson is over a mile wide, gliding silently past the little pier. A hundred years ago, riverboats stopped in this shallow; today the project Seeger helped start, the sloop *Clearwater*, anchors here for sailing lessons and meetings, or to publicize the club's annual strawberry shortcake fest: heaping mounds of hot biscuits on icy, sweet strawberries. On these days, the club overflows. Folks promenade on the riverbank, sing, picnic under the trees, use the nonpolluting toilet, and, of course, stuff the garbage cans full.

This afternoon the river laps quietly at the Beacon waterfront as we load. The ovens for cooking shortcake lean like giant breadboxes against the clubhouse, and commuters' cars crowd the shoreline. We heft the cans up on the tailgate and drive off.

Some might wonder why Seeger bothers with all this. A half-dozen concert promoters and good causes across the country are probably trying to get through to him right now, and we're out hauling trash.

At the dump, he pulls his old truck into the loading spot with a ritualized slowness. We knock at the keeper's window, and a farmer sitting there nods. I start to tip the nearest can into the pit when I feel a restraining hand on my shoulder.

"Whoa," he says gently, "better not tilt it like that, or the whole can'll go in. And you with it." His mood is improving.

He rolls the can at an angle three feet from the edge and tilts it cautiously toward the opening. Grasping the rim, he rocks back and forth, his long arms pushing the can away, then snapping it back so a third of the contents falls out. Like salt from an oversized shaker, the heavy can empties in a few rhythmic motions. He bends over, then straightens up, pivoting until the empty can spins back next to a full one. He performs this efficient dance with the same attention he gives to audiences.

The job done, he snaps up the tailgate and quickly pulls the truck to one side, so a neighbor can get in. He turns the pickup into a long driveway with a guard's hut on one side. Seeger tells a white-haired man that someone has busted the lock behind the river park.

"It's those kids from the next town," the attendant sighs, with a boys-will-be-boys smile. "Guess it's time to put in a heavy chain." Seeger agrees, suggesting a sign telling vandals the cost of lock and fence. The other man nods; he'll get it tomorrow, or at the latest, the day after. That's quick enough for fences in Beacon, and

Seeger swings back toward home, with the empties clanging as we go up the bumpy dirt road.

"Funny thing about that man we were just talking to," Seeger says. "Not long ago, he used to gripe about the young longhairs moving into town. Now he comes to the Sloop Club. Sends his kids. He maintains the chain himself; some weekends he brings the family down to the waterfront. And you know," he grins, "twelve years ago he may have signed a petition to stop me from singing at the local high school."

I sit silently as he threads the truck expertly up his driveway. So *this* is where he has been all afternoon. While we talked of labor organizing in the forties and Czechoslovakia in '68, he's had this broken bit of chain in mind. He has moved from international to local concerns. Seeger keeps on preaching, but now he reaches local teenagers, huddled around a wood stove in the clubhouse by the river.

But why would a forty-year veteran of national campaigns turn to cleaning up a river? Seeger knows river fairs don't redistribute power or wealth. A journalist who worked with him in the forties suggested the *Clearwater* was the closest thing today to Don Quixote's horse.

As we unload at the cabin, I realize what a long day it's been. Seeger's earlier diffidence has burned off with the morning fog, and he's back ribbing academic ob-jeck-tivity like any successful college dropout. For a moment I see him on stage again, "a sixty year old smiling public man" as Yeats described himself, with thousands hanging on every syllable. Then the image of Seeger rocking the garbage cans superimposes itself. As I start to leave I notice a stone the size of a baseball cemented into the chimney. It destroys the symmetry. The more I look at the stone, the more out of place it seems. I ask Seeger where it came from.

"That rock nearly hit my son Danny," he begins softly. "Came through the car window on a strange, violent afternoon, nearly thirty years ago. I glued the rock up there so I'd never forget."

Outside, dusk is settling and mosquitoes buzz faintly in the evening air. We sit silently, both staring at the stone. I imagine the force that hurled it through his window, until Seeger breaks in on my thoughts.

"Let me tell you the story of Peekskill," he says grimly. "People threw stones at women and children, with intent to kill. At my own family. I had two little kids in the car . . ."

HOW CAN I KEEP FROM SINGING?

Chapter 1

HOLD THE LINE

—

AT DAWN ON SUNDAY MORNING, SEPTEMBER 4, 1949, THE first convoys of cars headed north from New York City for Peekskill, a summer resort town where Seeger, Paul Robeson, and others were to sing. By 9 a.m. the roads were blocked with veterans' groups and local anti-Communists who had vowed to stop the concert. New York labor unions sent a security force of two thousand to keep the concert grounds open. Outside the gates, a thousand armed police lined up in formation. Across town in the woods, down by the riverside, a half-dozen men piled rocks the size of tennis balls into a car trunk.

THE CONCERT HAD BEEN advertised two weeks earlier with a notice in the *Daily Worker.* Readers were invited for a pleasant evening in the country at the Lakeland Picnic Grounds. The name hinted at a quiet affair: beer and sandwiches, with a blanket to keep out the cool night air.

The FBI clipped the notice for their files. The *Peekskill Evening Star* called Robeson "violently and loudly pro-Russian"; their editorial was unusually bitter: "The time for tolerant silence that signifies approval is running out." A few residents wrote the editor, calling this an invitation to violence. That, for a time, was that. If the local citizens agreed with the *Star*, they weren't vocal about it.

On his newly purchased country land, Seeger didn't always see the morning papers. When he did, the news was scary. Communist

Party leaders faced jail for teaching and writing about Marxism. Radio commentators called for a war to stop Communism. Anti-Communists beat up left-wing actors outside a theater in New York. Half the cast of *They Shall Not Pass*, a play about the trial of the Scottsboro boys, ended up in the hospital. There were no arrests.

Nineteen-forty-nine had not been a good year for Seeger's causes either. That spring, right after he'd turned thirty, People's Songs—an organization he had built from scratch and had run for three years—went bankrupt. He felt responsible for its debts. His new singing group, an unknown quartet called the Weavers, was falling apart from lack of work. Neighbors in Upstate New York distrusted the Seegers as "city folks." And then in August, Seeger's prim mother arrived for a visit, but the only accommodation he could offer was a tiny trailer lacking water or electricity. He and Toshi took the tent.

They had spent the summer clearing their land by the Hudson. The work could be toilsome, such as digging the foundation by hand. But days passed and the hole grew. They hauled a cement mixer up the hill.

"It was Hi! Here's a shovel," so often, Lee Hays joked of "Seeger's slave camps." Few guests had a chance to lie back and watch the boats pass. Toshi complained about people asking her husband about songs; the whole construction line could stop as he showed them a lick or two.

In balance, this beat New York City by a country mile. Takashi, Toshi's father, and Toshi planned a garden. She looked forward to making their dinner plates and to the kids growing up in the woods.

Seeger remembers being "happy as a lark" choosing and sawing the logs for the cabin: The thick green woods saw a lot of this energetic thirty-year-old, bounding through the forest. Seeger had fewer Party meetings, which meant more time with his banjo.

Seeger's bookings were not numerous, but he survived. The night before he'd been first scheduled to sing at Peekskill, he'd led a performance of some teenagers he'd brought together, the Good

Neighbor Chorus. He'd driven into the city and set up, taken the kids home after the show, and carted off the instruments; it was probably 2 a.m. before he got to bed. Fortunately, the concert was not until eight the next night, and only ten miles away. After dinner that evening, Seeger packed his banjo in the car and, with his mother in tow, cheerfully headed south. They didn't know they were heading straight into the first full-scale riot of America's cold war.

He'd ignored predictions of violence, though Peekskill had a reputation as a center for the Ku Klux Klan. The preconcert parade organized by the Joint Veterans Council of Westchester County was already the subject of rumors. Suspecting the parade might get rough, the leader of a teenage marching band had withdrawn, telling the *Peekskill Star*, "I wouldn't want to bring my boys anywhere they could get hurt."

It was one of those seductively warm August evenings, but the road to the concert was empty. Seeger expected the concert to go on: "It *was* legal and there might be a few who'd object, but after all, there were policemen there." He planned to sing a few songs and show that people can say what they want in America.

Mother and son had a pleasant ride along the parkway. They arrived early, but at the exit from the highway, a patrol car blocked their way. Seeger pulled his car to one side and walked over.

"Officer," he said politely, "I'm one of the performers here tonight. Do you think you could help me get through?

"He looked at me rather peculiarly. 'There's not going to be any concert,' he said, striding away." Seeger was puzzled. He could see press cars hurriedly pulling up, while police idled at the entrance to the picnic grounds.

He later found out what had happened. Novelist Howard Fast was master of ceremonies, and he'd arrived an hour or so before Pete. At first, everything had gone smoothly: The sound system worked, the lights were set. Fast was relieved at how well things were going. That was at seven o'clock. A few minutes later, matters looked quite different, as Fast wrote in *Peekskill USA*.

A boy ran up to say there was trouble at the top of the road, where the veterans' parade was gathered. When Fast and his crew ran up to the entrance, veterans charged them, three hundred vigilantes with billies and brass knuckles and rocks in clenched fists and American Legion caps. It became clear why no more people or entertainers were coming into the concert. One of the forks of the road was piled high with rocks, a great barricade of stone, and the other had a Legion truck parked across it.

It was straight out of an old-time western: Fast and his friends were cornered in a box canyon with nowhere to turn. Picnic dinners were forgotten.

The veterans in the parade weren't gangsters. These were respectable folk: well-dressed real estate men, grocery clerks, and filling-station hands, men who feared losing what little they had, vets frustrated at not having a good job after the war. They blamed the city intellectuals in their summer houses, the Negroes, and the Jews.

Fast sent off a scout to find help. Not knowing what else to do, Seeger drove his car up on the grass and turned back, departing just as the scout reached the main gate. Exactly what happened next has never been determined. In the last light of the day, the veterans were bearing in, shouting, "We'll finish Hitler's job!" and "Give us Robeson. We'll lynch the nigger up!" Soon Fast and the others were backed against a truck while the crowd swung into them with bats and fence posts.

Someone aimed a blow at Fast. A friend deflected it, but the attacker leaped on the writer, tearing off his glasses. Others went down in the free-for-all. Someone yelled, "They're killing Fast, God damn it."

Fast limped up from beneath a pile of bodies, his clothes torn. Then he did something Seeger might have done in his place; he began to sing. The concertgoers locked arms to form a line and started.

We shall not—we shall not be moved!
We shall not—we shall not be moved!
Just like a tree that's standing by the water,
We shall not be moved!

The road in front of them was bathed in the glare of headlights, but all else lay in darkness. Across the beams came the "new Americans," brandishing fence rails. In the shadows, a man was stabbed.

Off in one corner, three men in suits scribbled furiously in their notebooks. They were from the Justice Department, and to them, this was a bold new experiment in red-hunting.

As the vets closed in, they met a new resistance. Emboldened by the music, the concert organizers halted their retreat. Joining arms and singing gave them an extra measure of courage. They fended off the attackers for two more hours, until the mob battered their way to the stage. Frustrated that Robeson wasn't there (he'd been warned of the attack), the vigilantes broke up wooden chairs and set fire to pamphlets and songbooks. They left behind a flaming cross, the Ku Klux Klan trademark.

At ten o'clock, the police began to help. The wounded were taken to a hospital, the buses rumbled back to the city in the dark, and the long night was ended.

Next morning, Seeger read the half-dozen stories in the *New York Times*: RIOTS STOP CONCERT. The local D.A., an ambitious fellow named Fanelli, said the audience provoked the violence by showing up where they weren't wanted. Veterans' groups denied responsibility for the attack; their parade had officially disbanded before dark. There were no arrests.

Seeger signed a group telegram urging Governor Dewey (the recently defeated presidential candidate) to investigate. The governor named District Attorney Fanelli as his neutral observer.

This was Monday. The veterans' riot had taken place on Saturday, and the furor still hadn't let up. Not content with congressional hearings or labeling subversive books in libraries, anti-Communists had opened a new front: street violence.

On Wednesday, August 31, 1949, the FBI started checking into People's Artists, a left-wing booking agency that had organized the concert. They found that Seeger served on the board of directors. The New York office questioned eight informers on People's Artists. Then a "patriotic citizen" called the FBI to complain of a mailing from People's Artists. The special agent in charge "recruited" the caller and sent off an immediate report to Washington.

On Thursday, Seeger found out Robeson wanted another chance. The Civil Rights Congress held a mass rally in Harlem. "If the police won't protect the audience," Robeson promised in his velvety bass, "we will protect ourselves." A decision was made at the highest levels of the Communist Party: The concert *would* take place—on Labor Day weekend, two days hence, half a mile from the previous violence. "From now on, we take the offensive, and that offensive begins tonight," Robeson told the cheering crowd.

It was a gutsy move. Seeger and a half-dozen others agreed to perform; they weren't giving up their right to be heard, even if it meant a fight. Fifteen veterans' groups in Westchester and surrounding counties announced a counterdemonstration. The FBI teletyped J. Edgar Hoover with the news. Seeger and the other directors of People's Artists decided to seek an injunction against the veterans' counterdemonstration.

On a Friday, the case was heard just before the court's recess. Judge John W. Clancy turned down the injunction, blandly stating, "I don't know why you think the veterans are going to disobey the law."

And so the weekend began. All over Peekskill bumper stickers appeared: WAKE UP AMERICA, PEEKSKILL DID! On street corners and in bars, local residents boasted of what they would do to Commies.

America *was* awakening, from dreams of wartime prosperity into a national shortage of jobs, houses, and schools; from hopes of united nations into cold war, a global morality play of markets and propaganda. Everything Soviet was sinister, and tolerance gave way to curses and right-wing violence.

The mood in Peekskill was grim; local citizens felt their town was being invaded. "No Parking" signs were posted, and American flags appeared outside homes. Some residents felt remorse, and others regretted the bad name the previous week's violence had given the town. The majority seemed to agree with a spokesman for the veterans: "Our objective was to prevent the Paul Robeson concert, and I think our objective was reached." According to the *Star*, the worst part of the disturbance "was that it played into the hands of the Commies." Meanwhile, the largest number of police in the history of Westchester County arrived in Peekskill. By busload after busload they came, jamming the roads, cleaning their guns, and drilling in the parks. The citizens of Peekskill had a small-town distrust of outsiders.

An apocalyptic fear of anti-Communists infected many in Seeger's circle, who increasingly expected "the beginning of a fascist onslaught," he recalled. "This was no more than Hitler did in 1933, when he burned down the Reichstag and said, 'I must have emergency power, the traitors are destroying our country.'" Many Party members seriously believed a right-wing coup was in the offing.

"Experienced older people told me, 'Pete, don't you know this is how Hitler got started in Germany? In a year or two from now people like you and me are going to be in hiding or in jail or left for Canada or some other part of the world.'"

The day before the second concert, the Klan was bold enough to write and thank Seeger (and People's Artists) for stimulating 722 new membership applications in the week since the riot.

SUNDAY, THE MORNING of the rescheduled concert, Pete and Toshi were back sleeping in their trailer, now that his mother had returned home. Outside the drafty sliding window, a gray mist covered the river. The air was moist and still, broken only by the splash of a creek.

In ten years of singing professionally, Seeger had found himself in tough spots before, but he had never brought his family into danger. Now the family argued over who should go to the concert.

"Pete," his father-in-law said, "you don't know what could happen."

"There'll be no problem with all this publicity. They couldn't get away with it," Seeger said. "They couldn't do the same this week as they did last week." He felt his children should see whatever happened. He assured Toshi that dozens of reporters would be there and thousands of people. The whole world would be watching.

"Don't be naïve," Toshi's father told him. "There'll be trouble."

"I'm going with you!" Toshi put in. "I want to make sure these babies are not hurt."

"Okay," they finally agreed, "let's do it. If one of us goes, we all go." Toshi's father joined them, and so did an army buddy, Mario Cassetta, and his girlfriend, Greta: seven of them, with Seeger at the wheel. If there was trouble, the kids would lie on the floor. He drove the stretch of the Taconic Parkway to Peekskill less cheerfully than before.

Not all his friends thought he'd made the right decision. "There's a kind of ruthlessness in the Seegers' feelings of principle," long-time friend Bess Lomax reflected. "Once he decided he was right, his course was set. He wouldn't brutalize his family, but he thought about their safety and serenity *after* he made his decision.

"There were some very scary rumors about the Robeson concert. It was going to be a real tough scene, that much was widely known. We had a year-old baby and there was no way we could justify bringing her. Toshi and Peter took the kids and talked about how important it was for the children to see this happen. I thought it was something an infant *shouldn't* see."

The Seegers approached the parking lot in Peekskill at 11 a.m., a few hours before the program was to begin. From the main gate, Seeger peered down into a bowl-shaped field where the stage was set in an empty meadow, open to attack. On the surrounding hill, he saw what looked from a distance like the Great Wall: a line of 2,500 union men, mostly veterans, elbow to elbow in a human chain around the grounds. The veterans outside were more vocal than violent, shouting curses: "Kikes!" "You white niggers!" "Go back to Russia!" And, ominously, "You'll get in—but you won't get out."

At 2:50, as Seeger began to sing, the demonstration outside was scheduled to end; if the police had dispersed the vets at the appointed time, the day might have ended peacefully.

This was the man who'd been threatened with lynching the previous week, and the stage was crowded with his bodyguards. The program was cut short to get everyone out before dark.

Seeger had time for only a few songs, including one he and Lee Hays had written six months earlier, "If I Had a Hammer." This song had been sung at a benefit for Communists on trial under the notorious Smith Act; the lyrics were considered so controversial, no commercial publisher would touch it. Neither Hays nor Seeger ever imagined the Hit Parade would find the song, or that it would eventually be attacked by both right- and left-wingers. To its composers, the song offered an affirmation of the Left's sustaining power: we *have* a hammer, and we *have* a song, and we won't back down. To the audience, it was an anti–cold war mantra.

They sang the song loudly, out past the antisniper patrols and union defenders, out across the neighboring valleys and dusty roads where local residents were gathering.

Then, fifteen thousand heard Paul Robeson sing "Ol' Man River"; he earned an ovation with the lines "I must keep fightin'/ Until I'm dyin'." After the singing and announcements, people congratulated each other on a peaceful event and finished off their picnic baskets. Cars massed at the exit. At 4:10, Westchester police began directing all traffic along a winding road, Division Street, to the confusion of those leaving. Seeger wanted to turn left toward home, but the police told him, "No. Everybody this way." It was a setup. There was a heaviness in the air and a sinking sensation, like the opening plunge of a roller coaster. Seeger described what happened next.

"We hadn't gone a hundred yards from the gate when I saw glass on the road," Seeger remembered. "And in my innocence I said to the family, 'Hey, watch out, they may be throwing stones at us.' Hell, I had no idea how well organized it was. Around the next corner was a guy with a pile of stones, waist high, each about the size of a baseball. As the cars came by, four or five feet away, WHAM! Around the next corner was another group with another pile of stones."

Seeger drove a Jeep, an unprotected car with glass all around. "Now!" he shouted at his children. "Heads *down*—here it comes!" Their windows caved in, spitting splinters of glass everywhere.

It was a battle of two Americas: the city and the country, the liberal and the conservative. Goaded by local press and radio, the attackers blamed the gadflies for the frustration of wartime dreams. The attackers were true Americans, as patriotic as the Know-Nothings who tortured the Irish and Catholics before the Civil War, as American as the 1919 Palmer raid arresting thousands of "anarchists" in immigrant communities coast to coast.

Up ahead a state trooper said, "Let's get the bastards," pointing to a car in which a man from New Jersey sat helplessly in traffic. The trooper took careful aim and shoved his nightstick, point first, at the driver's left eye. The man ducked, too late. The club missed the eyeball, but caught the corner of the lid. It began to bleed, and when the man brought his head up, the trooper aimed at the eye again.

The police ordered passengers out of the car and beat them with nightsticks. One trooper noticed a bandage on the driver's left hand, which had been burned a week before. He jumped on the hand and ground his heel into the bandage, fracturing a burned finger.

Hysterical cries and the sound of breaking glass spread panic along the line of trapped cars. Seeger couldn't stand it. Despite stones raining in his Jeep's windows, he stopped the car abruptly, pale and shaking with rage.

Such moments didn't happen often. Even in the middle of violence, Pete Seeger maintained his New England reserve. Songs were his chosen weapons, not baseball bats. He fought with symbols—a union, a tall, thin banjo—for the causes of others. For years he'd sung about the downtrodden and abuse he'd never experienced; now he was getting his own taste of the lash.

Until the car stopped, he'd managed well, if one "manages" driving a terrified family through acres of blood and broken glass. "I don't remember shouting," he said later. "When there's a real crisis I get very cold." About a hundred feet beyond the next pile of stones stood a police officer, arms folded across his chest.

"Officer," Seeger shouted at him out the window, "aren't you going to do something? What are you *waiting* for?" The trooper just hollered "Move on, move on!" and took a step back.

"I look around and the guy in back of me is getting it. Because I'm stopped, he's got to stop. And he's getting stone after stone right through his window. So I moved on."

His friend Mario Cassetta was caught in the back of the Seeger car: "The veterans stood on an embankment and heaved a small boulder from up there. It hit the windshield like a cannonball. The highway was strewn with these rocks; steering through them was like crossing a minefield. We could feel the buffeting and the rocking and the terrible noise of these huge stones ringing against the car.

"I was scared to death. I expected any moment that damned car would roll over. Then I heard this terrible noise, a crack. Somebody said, 'My God, Greta's been hit.' A rock had come through the window and hit her just above the eye.

"We got to the end of the run and there was a clearing. We stopped. Some people were sitting. We asked, 'Do you know the nearest hospital?' And they all started laughing and cackling. *Cackling.* I remember one woman rocking back and forth slapping her knees, like she'd heard a good joke. It was unbelievable, like I imagine Nazis would have been in those early street gang days in Berlin. All the way into the Bronx—more than twenty miles—you could see the injured, a long bloody alley."

When the Seegers arrived in Beacon, glass covered their clothes. They could barely move without cutting themselves. Pete knelt by his three-year-old son, calming him as he pulled slivers of glass from his hair and skin: "We turned off at a nearby camp because where we were staying, we didn't have water. Hundreds of people went to the showers and carefully washed broken glass out of their hair." Obviously the rock throwers, whoever they were, existed everywhere, even in Beacon. Whom could he trust? Seeger knew almost nobody in town, not even the grocery clerk. The next day, he spread out a newspaper and methodically hammered every bit of glass from his car windows: "Unless somebody looked closely, they didn't notice we didn't have windows." Only one neighbor stopped by to see if they were injured. Seeger resolved to win his neighbors' acceptance—though it would take him decades.

A well-known guitarist, Bob Gibson, later told Seeger, "You know, I was raised in Peekskill, and I know the whole story behind that riot. The Klan organized it."

"How?" Seeger asked. "I never knew for sure the Klan was up there."

"Oh, yes," Gibson replied, "and they were in cahoots with the police. They had that place surrounded with walkie-talkies, just like a battlefield. You didn't have a chance."

"How do you know?"

"My father was on the Peekskill police force."

The Peekskill riots were an unsubtle threat that drew leftists together. "The people in Peekskill were calling out to the rest of America," said Seeger, remembering his alarm. "Whenever you find a Commie around, do something about it—don't wait for the long process of the law, do it right away, because our country is in danger."

Two weeks after the event, Lee Hays, Pete Seeger, and friends had worked up a new song, "Hold the Line."

Let me tell you the story of a line that was held,
And many men and women whose courage we know well;
As they held the line at Peekskill on that long September day,
We will hold the line forever till the people have their way.
Hold the line! Hold the line!
As we held the line at Peekskill we will hold it everywhere.

Which line was really held? The one separating radicals from the rest of America? The Party's? Or perhaps the barrier separating civil liberties from mob rule—but this line had broken down.

At first glance, "Hold the Line" seems a bluff. The cold war was heating up, and only a few months later the junior senator from Wisconsin, Joe McCarthy, would begin waving his list of secret Communists. But Seeger was terribly serious about the song; optimism and perseverance were the bedrock of his art, a music born of political adversity. His songs were blunt weapons, but he lanced them with all his might.

BOTH SIDES CLAIMED Peekskill as a victory, but neither won. Yellowed newspaper photos still show the hate-filled faces and terrified concertgoers, the air frozen about them in great, still blocks. On that day, the observer in Seeger departed and the activist burst forth, only to retreat as he urged a policeman to enforce the law. He inhabited Tocqueville's America, alternately violent and pacifist, naïve and worldly wise. Yet, in the name of patriotism, conservatives would attack Seeger in every way short of assassination.

"I thought I was fighting in the right way," he reflected. "I was not getting angry, I was singing songs: funny ones, sad ones. Robeson had the crowd singing 'America the Beautiful.' How could they be attacked for that?"

Seeger's character manifested itself in optimism and the stubbornness of principle that made him bring his children to a riot. He was a stubborn man, a tall skinny fellow who didn't like to be pushed around. The stones thrown at Peekskill (and the pickets and blacklisters who followed later) couldn't penetrate his shell of idealism. Peekskill only forced him *toward* those who throw the first stone, a passion that led him over and over to a cycle of confrontation and controversy and, eventually, to discontent.

Chapter 2

WASN'T THAT A TIME

—

THE STONE-THROWERS AT PEEKSKILL MIGHT HAVE BEEN SURprised to learn that Seeger WAS actually a local boy, who'd spent summers at his grandparents house thirty miles away, or that his family considered itself "enormously Christian, in the Puritan, Calvinist New England tradition." By background, Seeger had more in common with local conservatives than with the immigrants, blacks, and Jews he sang with.

"When I was a teenager, I was not much interested in any of my ancestors," Seeger once told an audience in introducing the song "Wasn't That a Time." "My grandmother, a member of the Mayflower Society, told me a funny story about a man who came to address them once: 'Ladies,' he said, 'those who come from common ancestors, let us remember that most of them were very, very common.'"

"My ancestors came to this country because they didn't want to answer questions put to them by the then *un*-English committees. One of them, Elder Brewster, was on the *Mayflower* with Governor Bradford, one of the leaders of the Plymouth Colony. His descendants that came my way were staunch upholders of independence among the colonists. Not one was a royalist."

Seeger's Puritan ancestors inhabited a world of callings and righteousness and moral uprightness, of Good Works to edify their brethren. Part of this doctrine was to bear witness, to oppose that "oppression which the Lord groaneth under," and to condemn pride, worldliness, and want of truth. It was a social duty Seeger was ready to accept.

"One of my ancestors is said to have walked down Bunker Hill backward because he wouldn't turn his back on the redcoats. One was a quartermaster and another a major on General Putnam's staff. He might have been at Valley Forge."

Our fathers bled at Valley Forge
The snow was red with blood
Their faith was warm, at Valley Forge
Their faith was brotherhood.

Wasn't that a time
Wasn't that a time, a time to try the soul of man
Wasn't that a terrible time?

These lyrics later gave Seeger trouble before an investigating committee; the implicit patriotism of "Wasn't That a Time" infuriated conservatives. "The nerve of singers like Seeger," they would say, "to try and claim they are a part of the American story."

"These ancestors of mine," Seeger continued, "were all subversives in the eyes of the established government of the British colonies. If they had lost the War of Independence, they might have each and severally been hung. . . . Later, my ancestors were abolitionists. My great-grandfather Seeger was a doctor like his father; he lost many patients in the town of Springfield, Massachusetts, because of his abolitionist stance. One of my great-great-grandmothers died as a result of having to escape from Charleston after the firing on Fort Sumter in the Civil War."

And brave men died at Gettysburg
And lie in soldiers' graves
But there they stemmed the slavery tide

And there the faith was saved . . .
Wasn't that a terrible time.

"I spent much of my life trying to forget my antecedents, I confess it. I tried to ignore them, to disparage them. I felt they were all upper class." One relative he did admire was his father, Charles Seeger, "the one person that all my life I was able to talk and argue with." Yet the man closest to him also cast a shadow that Pete dodged as he grew up. "The biggest danger for Peter," his brother John said (with the insight only a sibling possesses), "was whether he'd be swallowed up in father's dreams."

In 1919, when his third son, Peter, was born, Charles Seeger had become as much of an outcast as the radicals in Peekskill. Yet Charles was brought up not as a radical, but as a gentleman scholar: erect and precise. Growing up on Staten Island, Charles traced his ancestors back to Gebhard von Seeg of the Crusades and divided the world into three categories of worth: "the Seegers, friends of the Seegers, and everyone else." The Seegers had four servants and a plot of land large enough for twenty houses. Pete Seeger's grandfather had made a small fortune in sugar refining in Mexico, and he lived in semiretirement, writing his memoirs and playing Wagner by ear. The family took pride in being Yankee: Probity, self-control, and strict table manners were expected. Like the rest of his family, Charles had the hard, slim nose and high cheekbones of New Englanders who speak when spoken to. He wore a trim mustache and spectacles with gold frames. In Europe, his speech had acquired a Germanic clip. Proud, fastidious, he nonetheless had a mischievous sparkle in his eye, as if warning people not to take him too seriously.

Charles had studied music at Harvard. As an aesthete, he'd scorned politics until 1914. Then, age twenty-five, he had an experience that shaped his (and his son's) life. At one of those faculty wine-and-cheese evenings, an economist quietly joined his circle. As Charles Seeger and a friend finished diatribes against socialism, the newcomer laid into them.

"You don't live in a real world, sitting in your libraries. You could talk your heads off and it wouldn't make *any* difference to *anything*," he admonished.

The young economist, Carlton Parker, stayed afterward to introduce himself. He hadn't meant to offend, he explained, and if they were willing, he'd show them what he was talking about.

His remarks surprised Charles, who thought himself worldly. He had, after all, conducted the Cologne Opera before becoming the youngest full professor in the history of the University of California. In New York, Charles had been introduced to an equally slim violinist of excellent family, Constance de Clyver Edson. Their courtship was quick and musical; the couple played parlor concerts in high society. In 1911 they'd married and soon afterward set up their household in what seemed another continent: Berkeley, California.

Constance was a shy but headstrong girl, raised in Tunisia and trained at the Paris Conservatory, blond, with linen-white skin and a delicate, sweet smile. Grime wouldn't stick to her. Her grandfather had run one of the most fashionable schools in New York, the Charlier Institute. Though related to the wealthy Curtises of Philadelphia, she grew up with more noblesse oblige than money; her mother was an incurable spendthrift. In response, Constance practiced extremely hard and watched the family finances. She was a student (and eventually a teacher) at what would be the Juilliard School, alongside Charles.

Classical music dominated her life. She communicated through her violin; in person, she sometimes struck people as prim and self-conscious, with a poor sense of humor. Patient with her students (less so with others), she'd been raised to be self-conscious about class and position. She'd hesitated to exchange her New York social life and her antiques for California's primitive comforts, but the financial security of Charles's job had made the sacrifice worthwhile.

Berkeley was not then a city of coffee palaces and health food stores. The Seegers lived in a quiet town surrounded by farmland and tall eucalyptus forests; wildcats and packs of dogs roamed the hills behind the house. Their windows looked out on San Francisco Bay, a flat glassy table of blue. The couple gave dinner parties and recitals; after the birth of their two sons, Charles III and John, they hired a governess. Constance hated housework, and Charles refused to be disturbed in the morning before he was ready. "Father liked things just so: the table napkins, the settings, everything had to be perfect," Charles III remembered.

TWO WEEKS AFTER that faculty party where Charles had been challenged, he and the economist Carlton Parker drove up the long, dusty driveway of a hops ranch in the San Joaquin Valley. The wagons of migrant workers lined the road; off to one side were tents, farm animals, a lot of children, and a latrine—nothing but a board over a ditch. Charles had never seen anything like it.

This was an unlikely spot for a political conversion. Everyone over the age of six picked busily. In the middle of this activity, Charles spotted a double of his son John, with the same color eyes and hair. After days in the field, however, this boy looked wretched and pockmarked: "We talked to some of the workers, and they told us the miserable wages and the hard working conditions," explaining how they walked for days through hot, dusty valleys—only to find the promised jobs gone when they arrived. Charles returned to Berkeley a changed man.

"Deeply shocked, Seeger was giving a speech about what he had seen," his son reported, "when a burly voice from the audience said, 'Sit down, you lily-livered bastard. You've just found out about these things. We've known them all our lives.' "

The fellow who said this probably belonged to the Industrial Workers of the World (IWW), then organizing in California's fields. This union of bindle stiffs, miners, loggers, and rebels had an enthusiastic (and musical) membership out west; when songs wouldn't get them better working conditions, they weren't shy about sabotage. Charles stopped by their office, and before he knew it, he was a regular on the ferry linking Berkeley and the San

Francisco waterfront, near IWW headquarters. He tried to juggle his newfound radicalism and his academic career, a precarious balance Jack London described in a short story, "South of the Slot."

His first years of teaching had gone well. Charles had coauthored a respectable book on harmony and built up enrollment in his courses. He'd composed a half-dozen pieces. His dean was pleased. His one eccentricity was his insistence on approaching music from a historical and social perspective, as historical musicology. "He asked the head of the American Musicology Society if they had a place for him. He said he didn't think so," Pete Seeger recollected in 2006. His father largely introduced the discipline of ethnomusicology, folk music, into America in the '20s.

His attempts at linking music and society produced good-natured chuckles among his Berkeley colleagues, who underestimated the self-confident, nattily dressed intellectual. Charles was a scrapper. In faculty meetings, he could be fanatically stubborn. When a professor sponsored a concert that included whistling, Charles insulted his choice "in no uncertain terms" and later panned one of his concerts without hearing a note. (He claimed he was listening in the hall.) Eventually his elderly opponent fell ill and left; Charles Seeger triumphed but left enemies behind. He had an infuriating way of tuning out: If he didn't want to see someone, when that person walked into the room, Charles simply walked out.

Some of this haughtiness softened after his conversion in the San Joaquin Valley, but the Seegers kept up with society via letters of introduction to San Francisco's prominent families. When Charles was not visiting the IWW office on Market Street or stalking the docks with longshoremen, he hobnobbed on Nob Hill. Between his lectures on music in the Renaissance he found time to compose an opera and pass out leaflets. His contradictions amused him, but his balancing act could not continue for long. The war in Europe upset this equilibrium.

Since 1914 news of European war had steadily increased, but in California, so far from the front, people had remained neutral. By

1917, though, the university community was becoming solidly pro-Ally—except for the Music Department, which revered Germans from Bach to Wagner. Not one to shy away from controversy, Charles told his dean (an Englishman) that Germany and England were both imperialist powers, and as far as *he* was concerned, they could fight each other to a stalemate. Rather than sounding principled, his stance came off as imperious.

Charles opposed World War I as fervently as his son would oppose wars in Vietnam and Iraq. Charles's IWW friends complained about the government's Committee on Public Information, which had launched the most extensive pro-war advertising campaign in history. After 1916, being antiwar was unpatriotic. Even Constance moved to the Left. "She called herself a socialist, but she was not really a political person," her son reflected in 2006.

The growing pro-war sentiment only drove Charles closer to the IWW. Once he arrived to give a lecture to them and found a police cordon and a huge crowd surrounding the entrance. Plainclothesmen filled up the standing room, "down to the last square inch." Seeger spoke about Bertrand Russell, who'd recently been jailed for six months for public opposition to the war. At the end, the moderator asked him to join the IWW. Charles declined, ironically claiming that he was unworthy "of mixing my bourgeois background with your proletarian ancestries."

Word traveled back across the Bay: That young professor was "going a bit beyond the bounds of decency." A biologist, formerly friendly, cut him dead when they passed on campus. Charles turned sharply and caught his arm, asking, "What's the matter?"

"I do not recognize people who approve of bayoneting Belgian children to barn doors," the biologist replied. Charles turned on his heel.

HE IGNORED THE STARES as best he could. To escape the campus, he bought a gleaming black Model T Ford. Adding a primitive camper with a hammock, Charles, Constance, and their two boys traveled the open wilderness that was prewar California, up the dirt roads and canyons to the waterfalls of Yosemite. The trailer bumped along back roads to cross the Sierras at Tioga Pass, two miles above sea level. Below stood a forest of sequoias, the oldest in the nation: dark, leafy giants, tall as skyscrapers. The hostilities of Charles's life in Berkeley fell away among the rivers and snowy mountains.

At other times Charles Seeger sought music in the wilds. The anthropologist Alfred Kroeber had played him Indian music recorded on phonocylinders, and the Seegers hunted songs among the Hoopa Indians on the foggy northern coast of California, where the Klamath River churns to the sea.

Each time the family returned to Berkeley, however, they found their situation worsened. The university administration began hinting that it was time for a sabbatical, to be followed by a permanent leave of absence. Then, in April 1917, war was declared. President Wilson signed the Espionage Act, and a wave of sedition trials began against war resisters. Vigilantes calling themselves Sedition Stompers cursed and attacked pacifists, particularly those with German-sounding names like Seeger. Brass bands played "I'd Like to See the Kaiser with a Lily in His Hand." Everything German became taboo, and sauerkraut had a new name: "liberty cabbage."

In September 1917, Charles's IWW friends in San Francisco were arrested as part of a national raid against "un-Americans." Local anarchist Tom Mooney was sentenced to death on highly suspect evidence. In Boston, a mob of sailors broke into the headquarters of the Boston Socialist Party and wrecked the offices.

AS THE UNPOPULARITY of his position grew, Charles Seeger only hardened his opinions, showing the love of a worthy fight that his son would later emulate. Charles's friends warned him he would get into trouble. Uniformed student-soldiers were loudly parading outside the offices of "unpatriotic" professors like Seeger. His savings were few, his kids young, but instead of backing off, Charles grew intransigent. Asked to buy a war bond on campus, he answered hotly, "I don't approve of war and will *never* contribute voluntarily." Remarks like this spread quickly.

When his draft board asked him to register, Charles declared himself a conscientious objector. In WWI, alternative military service was not widely accepted, and the first reaction of many draft boards was to slap COs into prison or call them traitors. A confrontation could have been avoided. Charles was thirty and underweight. In the past trying year he'd lost twenty pounds; his suit jacket drooped on him like clothes on a hanger. All in all, Charles didn't look like much of a soldier. The judge taking his deposition begged him to change his application—there was no need for the CO business, for the army would refuse him anyway. But Charles Seeger was in no mood to make life easy for the authorities.

His parents were disappointed with Charles's attitude. He was an embarrassment, unlike his older brother, Alan, who couldn't wait for the United States to join the war.

Thin, effusively idealistic, Alan Seeger used to say life was not worth living past thirty. Everything was in the moment for him, and this war attracted him like a beacon. Alan had Byron's genius of merging poetry and life; change itself seemed glorious, "the older order irrevocably vanished." Like Siegfried Sassoon or Rupert Brooke, Alan Seeger saw WWI as a chance for a generation to prove itself.

After graduating from Harvard, he'd lived among those dread bohemians in Greenwich Village, writing poetry and sleeping on the couch of his pro-Bolshevik classmate John Reed, author of *Ten Days That Shook the World*. Charles was the family's intellectual and Alan its adventurer.

Alan volunteered for the French Foreign Legion when the war was only a few weeks old. On July 4, 1916, just before he was to have read an ode at a public ceremony in Paris, Alan Seeger was shot down by machine guns. "I have a rendez-vous with Death" he wrote in his *Last Poems.* Alan became a legend in the family; his flamboyant courage made a high standard to match. "Pete [who bore a striking physical resemblance to his uncle] once said that if he could play one person in a film, he wanted to play Alan," Toshi would later remark.

IN BERKELEY, a young economist Charles knew was ordered to report to military camp in the Sierras. Like Charles, he was a CO, and rumors traveled about what happened to war resisters in these camps. Not everybody who went came back, and those who did return told of suffering and even torture. In one camp Charles heard of, COs were lined up twenty-five at a time and blasted with fire hoses. The force of the water broke bones and dislocated backs. At Fort Riley in Kansas, COs had ropes "put about their necks, hoisting them off their feet until they were at the point of collapse. Meanwhile officers punched them in their ankles and shins."

As a full professor, Charles might have avoided this fate, but why wait to see if he was called up? Charles and Constance decided to leave California. The departure was overdue; the president of the university, "a properly chauvinistic Britisher," had all but fired Seeger. On a hot September afternoon in 1918, the Seegers left their house keys with a tenant and headed east. Charles's "sabbatical" from the university would last forty years.

Losing his professorship for activism affected Charles profoundly. He wouldn't bow to expediency, but he "retreated," as his eldest son put it, feeling "a bitter defeat." On the other hand, the experience led Charles to encourage his sons to do the things he had been afraid to do, and to hold fast when challenged. He hoped his children would see the point of principles.

Riding a slow train across the country, Charles and Constance had plenty of time to take stock of their shattered lives. Charles's health had begun to fail; Constance had only one skill, her violin. The couple had no income, and Constance fretted over how they would live; Charles, exhausted, didn't seem to care. All her life she'd been pressured: as a prodigy, a debutante, a professor's wife. Now she had two kids to take care of and a husband who'd thrown over his job for his conscience. The strain told on her, and she developed a "deep, dark, dyed-down pessimistic" streak where money was concerned. The marriage began to drift and then fray.

Charles's medical problems turned out to be serious. His physician said he was headed for a nervous breakdown from the strain he'd suffered in Berkeley. He was a sick man, shot to pieces: "I didn't think I would last long."

On top of all this, Constance discovered she was pregnant.

Chapter 3

ABIYOYO

—

IN THE WINTER OF 1918, THE FAMILY ARRIVED AT CHARLES'S parents' estate in Patterson, fifty miles north of New York City. They had come to a land thick with woods and creeks, where the towns had the names of Indians and Dutch settlers. Thirty miles away, the Hudson River glistened and slapped at its rocky banks. Charles's parents lived on fifty quiet acres near the Taconic Mountains, with big barns, an expanse of lawn, and a main house with a balcony of wood carved to resemble wrought iron. Charles and Constance settled into separate bedrooms, and on May 3, 1919, a month before the treaty ending World War I, Peter Seeger was born.

Fatefully, Pete's birth coincided with that of the Red Menace, as Attorney General A. Mitchell Palmer called it. Before the baby had his first birthday, Palmer arrested in a single day in thirty-three cities some four thousand alleged Communists and Anarchists. In New York, a few hundred miles from the child's crib, the legislature expelled five duly elected Socialist legislators because it didn't like their politics.

Charles Seeger felt defeated by the events of his time: "I couldn't write. I couldn't compose music. I couldn't earn a living. I couldn't do anything." He lost his taste for performing; repeating the same pieces at parlor concerts bored him. Charles hit on the idea of a trip "to bring music to the poor people of America, who didn't have any music." He and Constance would take a trailer and explore the musical back roads of America. The trip would be a needed tonic: "The doctor said I wouldn't live very long, so my wife and I staked everything that we had—and our marriage too—on that trip."

Charles borrowed money from his folks and built a trailer in the most meticulous way: brass screws into tongue-and-groove maple boards, with wagon wheels and tires of solid rubber. Stuffed into special compartments were gallons of local maple syrup, pumpkins, and sacks of potatoes—all of New York they could carry into the unknown. In November 1920, with Peter a year and a half old, the Seegers set out for the South, "trailing music."

DRIVING THROUGH New York City, Charles couldn't resist showing the sophisticated set a mobile home, 1920-style. The Ford's custom transmission roared down Broadway pulling their one-ton trailer through the wide streets of midtown Manhattan. Peter and his brothers peeped out from inside. Their elegantly dressed mother rode in front, and beside her was their father in a new beard and wire-rims, tooting at the horse carts.

Across New Jersey, Pennsylvania, and Maryland they rolled, the folding spinet piano bouncing heavily in the back. In Richmond, Virginia, the weather was so hot, the trailer left grooves in the asphalt streets. Back into the Virginia hills they climbed and out across the coastal lowlands, green from winter rains. Finally they came to rest in Pinehurst, North Carolina, twenty miles from the present site of Fort Bragg.

On the road the children got restless, and Charles made up stories and songs to keep them in bed. Peter, his blond hair falling about like a thatched roof, adored his father's "nutty stories," particularly one about a little trailer in a long, wet puddle.

"One *very* rainy day, the road was covered with water. But the trailer wouldn't back up, so the driver figured, well, the puddle is probably not too deep. They kept going. It was raining so hard they couldn't see the end of the puddle. It just got deeper and deeper.

It was up to the hubcaps. The rain kept coming down, and a mist settled around them.

"They stayed on the road by seeing the telephone poles or the fences on either side. No one knew how deep it was going to get. Finally, to their relief, the road emerged from the puddle. They reached solid ground, and off they went."

Peter bounced along in his cradle, listening to the story over and over, as the rhythms of the wheels blended into the tale. Charles made "quite a suspense out of it," but always the road reemerged, and the child drifted off to sleep.

After settling in, the Seegers hiked through the fragrant hills of North Carolina, inviting local residents to free classical music concerts. Amazingly, the mountain folk came out, and went away in awe: imagine a fiddle making sounds like that! After the show, Constance would do the wash by campfire; it wasn't the most comfortable situation. "She wasn't enthusiastic about having to scrub my diapers with her violinist's hands." Pictures show Peter dancing by the fire to his father's music.

These were golden days for the Seegers, but their musical social work had little effect. The family opened the ears of their newfound community, but they were more a novelty than an inspiration, and novelty fades. Peter's parents brought their culture as an ennobling gift, but they touched off no Handel revivals in North Carolina. Music transplants poorly, they discovered, especially in the name of civilization. The failure at Pinehurst continued for Charles a long, lonely period, trying to join music and the social concerns born that hot afternoon in the San Joaquin Valley. He knew music could shape society. He could almost touch the connection, but its form eluded him.

On the Seegers' last day, the wagon was packed and ready to go, except for their fold-down stage. At nightfall, the hollow was crowded as the North Carolinians wished their odd friends Godspeed. Charles played Chopin etudes; Constance, a violin concerto. That evening's concert had an unexpected finale: The locals actually *did* have music. They produced fiddles and guitars and played the surprised Seegers hillbilly music. By accident, Peter heard his first authentic folk music when he was two.

SIX YEARS LATER, on a clear morning in the summer of 1927, Peter woke before anyone else and wandered through the grounds of his grandparents' home in Patterson. He was eight, with long, silky blond hair and sky-blue eyes. He left the barn where his brothers and father slept and lounged under the elms that separated the outbuilding from the main house and his grandparents.

"We'd bounce tennis balls up against the wall and call it barn squash—like father, who occasionally played squash at the Harvard Club," Seeger said. "Afterward we'd close off the door to the courtyard, take off all our clothes, and pail water over ourselves."

In 1927, while the Seeger boys chased tennis balls in the country, the headlines followed Babe Ruth, headed for his sixty-home-run season. Charles Lindbergh had just returned from the first transatlantic flight. In rural communities like Patterson, families gathered around the new wonder box, radio. Wind-up gramophones were still a novelty; the Seeger boys, in their grandparents' absence, listened to pop tunes like "Red, Red Robin" and "'S Wonderful."

The radio also brought lesser known tunes, particularly at night, when its waves bounced off distant clouds and the fiddle tunes of John Carson and Eck Roberts drifted up from southern stations. Soon the Carter Family and Jimmie Rodgers would be heard—but not at the Seegers', where only classical music was welcome.

Once a week the boys came in from the barn for a sit-down dinner. Dressed up in sailor suits, they were careful not to sprawl on the sofa and to use their finger bowls, as grandmother had taught them. Grandmother Elsie looked like a *New Yorker* cartoon. She entered the room like a galleon in full sail; her feet didn't seem to move, she just swept in. Sometimes she would look at Peter and exclaim, "You come from very good stock. Don't *ever* forget it—very good stock."

Grandfather Charles was equally proud. He'd gone to Mexico as a business journalist and made his money first in sugarcane and then in rubber. Now he cultivated a continental mustache. He looked like dukes are supposed to look, but rarely do, steeped in family tradition from the days when the Seegers circulated a family newspaper modestly titled *The Prophet*.

After the Pinehurst trip, Charles and Constance had had a terrific row over money. Constance had taken a job as a music teacher and set up a secret bank account; when Charles found out, he exploded.

"'I have a right to my own money!' Constance told him. She was smiling as she said it. For my dad it was the last straw," Pete Seeger recalled.

After their fight, Charles put the three boys in the car and took them to his parents' house. Divorce split the allegiances of the Seeger boys: John and Charles hewed to mother. To them, Charles had walked out, or Constance had thrown him out for good reason. But nothing was discussed. At one point Peter burst out, "We're having such a nice time—where's mother?" No one told him his parents had separated. In Peter's case, neither really had custody; he was always off at school. The closest he came to a home was the barn in Patterson.

Peter had been sent off to boarding school at four, an unusually early age. Like many children of divorce, Peter was caught between parents and developed an aversion to family quarrels. Constance felt wronged by Charles, who still hadn't found a full-time job. She had her smooth, milky complexion, but ever since Charles had been fired in Berkeley, the pressure of supporting a family had soured her inside. The couple also had radically different ideas about music; Peter's musical education was "the last big fight" the couple had. Was Peter to be trained properly, Constance demanded, or was he going to grow up a musical illiterate?

Charles's laissez-faire answer reflected the changing currents of music in the twenties. While Constance remained faithful to the three Bs (Beethoven, Brahms, and Bach), Charles was intrigued by musical experimentation: the twelve-tone compositions of Schoenberg and Webern, Bartok's experiments with folk music in orchestral settings, Shostakovich's New Symphony. At this point, John Seeger reflects, "Charles was no longer tied, hooked, hand and mouth, to the classics; and mother never moved that far." These currents propelled Charles on his search for a social dimension to music, and Peter absorbed his new interests.

Of the three sons, Peter was the only one who refused piano or voice lessons. Yet he wasn't unmusical, just undisciplined: "Whistles, anything that made music I banged on. I didn't want to study, I was just having fun . . . The idea of reading notes was as boring to me as painting by numbers." Another problem was Peter's foot. According to the way Constance taught, the whole body was kept motionless, so that the energy would pour out in the music. But no matter what he did, Peter couldn't keep his foot from tapping. In his eighth year, his parents gave him a ukulele. The uke seemed daring, with its light, unelaborated sound. Peter played it constantly, till his brothers lost their patience; then he would sneak up on them from behind the sofa and start again.

Years later, Seeger made up a story-song about a boy who played the ukulele. The boy lived happily with his magician father, whom the townspeople shunned. Then one day a giant appeared, Abiyoyo, a monster as tall as the sun. With the help of a song and his father, the boy saved the town from destruction. In the end of the fantasy, based on a Bantu legend from South Africa, the boy became a hero. A close friend later called this tale of ukuleles, magical fathers, and victorious songs "the key to Pete Seeger's imagination."

AFTERNOONS, WHEN the wooden boats had all been carved and the vegetable plot tended, Peter often disappeared into Patterson's thick woods. He loved to play Indian, creeping through the bushes in a loincloth. He made himself a sixteen-foot-high tepee, meticulously sewing canvas with a steel needle and shoe laces. Other times Peter stalked rabbits with his homemade bow and arrow. The best he could do was to scare them, hissing like a rattler. Then, surrounded by the rich, hot summer smells, he would dip his feet in the stream and read his favorite books by the Canadian naturalist Ernest Thompson Seton, whose romances of woodcraft and Indian lore fascinated him.

The boys in Seton's books make music by stretching a calfskin drum, Indian-style. They cook over a wood fire and make their own tepee. When the boys finally huddle inside, lighting a fire without matches, they have a reward Peter craved: "the pleasure of achievement in the line of great ambition."

"Seton was one of the big influences on my life. I read every one of his books. I came across a picture of Seton saying, 'Could you survive in the woods with just yourself and an axe?' Seton—a founder of the Boy Scouts—thought boys should pattern their ideal on the American tradition: self-reliant, strong, moral, and clean. Whatever you had you shared."

Seton's teachings offered Seeger dual ideals: the independent axman, who survived outside society by his strength, and a tribal communism of uncompromising moral purity. In time Peter became both: the woodsy, self-sufficient craftsman and a communalist, looking for his tribe.

"Talk about ivory towers, I grew up in a woodland tower. . . . I knew all about plants and could identify birds and snakes, but I didn't know that anti-Semitism existed or what a Jew was until I was fourteen years old. My contact with black people was literally nil. . . . If someone asked me what I was going to be when I grew up, I'd say farmer or forest ranger. Maybe an artist. I'd always loved to draw." A slim, dreamy child, he would rather hike in the snow to sketch animal prints than sip tea in his grandmother's parlor. He would spend rainy afternoons poring over romances by a British author, George Henty: tales of jousting for honor and the quest for the Holy Grail. Between this medieval chivalry and Seton's Indians, Peter steeped himself in absolutes.

Only through music did he come out of his shell, like the time he and his roommate, Bob Claiborne, led a group sing at their progressive-education boarding school, Spring Hill, in Connecticut. Peter's mother gave him a book of sea chanteys, and the pair rigged up a blue backdrop and a ship's railing. Another friend held a bottle while they sang "What Shall We Do with the Drunken Sailor"; by the last song, they had the whole auditorium singing. With his uke Peter easily became the center of attention, no matter how awful he sounded. For a half-hour his shyness would melt, and he would bask in the attention. Then it was back to feeling alone and hiking off by himself. Part of his isolation came from his isolation from his family. From his seventh till his seventeenth year, he saw his family only at Christmas, Easter, and summers. One of his schoolmates, George Draper of the *San Francisco Chronicle*, described what separations like these mean to a child: "No tears allowed at family separations—that you get used to early. You have this emotional blindness. . . . You don't grow up to see all the compromises of a family."

John Seeger watched his kid brother grow up far from the family, without emotional support, terribly independent. Family life, when he had it, was never warm. "In the second and third decades of this century, when I was brought up," Peter recalled, "the modern way to think was 'Don't baby your child. Give him a good schedule and obey it strictly.' . . . There wasn't any cuddling in our family; they held our hand, yes, but a lot of people would think it a very cold childhood—Pop was the only one I hugged.

"When I graduated from Spring Hill, at thirteen in 1932, I came home to my father's place.

"'Has anybody told you that Ruth and I are married?' Charles asked me. They'd driven out to Reno and Charles was divorced from Constance and remarried. She was already pregnant with Michael." Learning about the divorce through an aside was typical of his hands-off upbringing.

The next Christmas, in 1932, Peter tromped through the frozen grass in Central Park. Only policemen on their horses ambled through the icy meadows. Peter, thirteen, felt out of place. He spent half the vacation with his mother and the rest with his father, wandering like Holden Caulfield in a city he recognized but barely knew.

He had arranged to meet his father and new stepmother at their new apartment on East Eighty-ninth Street, a good walk from his mother's studio on West Sixty-fifth Street. Peter enjoyed the fresh air. After listening to Constance's pupils play scales, he felt suffocated. Before he could leave, Constance sat him down for a talk: "You must take lessons. You've got the hands that can do it. I'm sorry, but we're going to insist." Then, in the hallway, his mother quizzed him on ways to save money. He'd practically leaped out the door.

"My father was the one person I really related to. For good or bad, I had very few relationships with anybody else. I was cordial with everybody—I didn't like to fight and I didn't like to argue. My brothers? We got along; but they were much older than me—six and seven years older—and in a different world." He might have gone on to say, as his distant ancestor Henry Adams did, that "his education was chiefly inheritance, and during the next five or six years, his father alone counted for much."

Arriving at the apartment of Charles and his new wife, composer Ruth Crawford Seeger, Peter found them leaving to hear Aaron Copland speak at the left-wing Pierre Degeyter Club, named after the composer of "The Internationale."

The couple took the boy to an unheated loft downtown. As Peter watched from the back of the room, two dozen New York composers arrived, dressed in corduroys and leather jackets, carrying scores and instruments. Trained in the best music schools in the country, they were the renegades of the Philharmonic, passionately political. "The social system is going to hell," they told each other. "Music might be able to do something about it. Let's see if we can try. We *must* try."

Charles had finally found a way to mix music and activism. He belonged to a group within the Degeyter Club, the Composers

Collective, which tried to write songs for picket lines and unemployment demonstrations. As devotees of the new dissonance, however, the musicians sought to uplift workers' musical tastes while stirring up revolution. The Composers Collective was probably the first group in the world to attempt a twelve-tone protest song.

Peter did his best to follow Copland's address, but neither the politics nor the music made sense to him. He did realize how important the Collective's mission was to his father; Charles was now writing "The World of Music" columns for the *Daily Worker* under a pseudonym, Carl Sands. Peter later heard about his father's entry in a contest for the best May Day song. When submissions were played through, the Collective chose Copland's "Into the Streets May 1st," with its loud, rhythmic chords on the piano. Charles agreed that musically, Copland's song was better, but his was more singable, he insisted. These were marching songs, after all, and how were workers going to carry a piano on a march?

This was the heyday of Tin Pan Alley, and Cole Porter's "Night and Day" and Rodgers and Hart's "Isn't It Romantic." Folk music meant old hillbilly tunes or rural blues. Charles's colleagues disliked folk music, which they called "defeatist melancholy, morbidity, hysteria, and triviality" because the music predated Marx. Doctrinaire radicals like Hanns Eisler thought folk songs "a badge of servitude"; Charles himself called them "dead relics." Ironically, Peter heard these sentiments at a time of tremendous American musical growth. Gene Autry, "America's Number One Singing Cowboy," was captivating the nation with his movies and "western" music (later called "country and western"). In Kentucky and the Midwest, the Monroe brothers had developed a sound later named after their band, the Bluegrass Boys; Bob and Johnny Lee Wills broadcast "western swing" over KVOO in Tulsa.

Like his father, Peter knew nothing about traditional music. He was caught between musical eras; his choices were among classical, experimental, pop music, jazz—and none of these interested him. He left Copland's talk confused, but thrilled by the composers' high passions: "I got the feeling that here were people out to change the world. The world might be corrupt, but they were confident they could change it." Charles's experiments in protest songs were too highbrow to succeed, but at least he was out challenging tradition, not hiding from it in the woods.

On this vacation, Peter went away with one of his father's radical rounds, which he and John sang on hiking trips:

Oh, Joy upon the earth
To live and see the day
When Rockefeller Senior
Shall up to me and say:
Comrade, can you spare a dime?

His father's radicalism actually fit Peter as well as Seton had, different as the two were. Resistance was part of the New England nature; his great-grandfather, a Huguenot preacher, would have been proud. Peter could look back on the generations of predecessors who viewed the world as a thing to be reformed. The duty to keep at that battle continued, endlessly. The Depression swept in on Peter's woodland tower like a tornado, shattering its isolation. In the next months he began reading radical newspapers, watching Eisenstein's films, and generally soaking up the radical education New York offered in the 1930s.

For a firsthand look into the Depression, Charles walked his son through New York's Lower East Side, telling him, "The streets aren't so well lit as where we live." Skeletons of buildings stood empty, the floors covered with broken glass. Shutters fell off their hinges. Father and son walked for miles until their feet ached. The Lower East Side stretched endlessly, compared to the sliver of well-to-do life on Fifth and Madison Avenues. The garbage-filled alleys were so different from Peter's school in New England that he visited them as a conscience-stricken tourist.

If the Lower East Side was poor, by 1932 the rest of the country was hard on its heels. Banks called in loans and foreclosed farms by the thousands. With mortgages gone and the dust bowl blowing, families wandered the land. One in four was out of work—and the country had no unemployment insurance, no Social Security.

Through the Composers Collective, Peter met many people who called themselves Communists: "It was quite different from the cartoons of a person with a beard and a bomb. I found these were very organized, highly intelligent, and argumentative people."

His new comrades told him of textile strikes in Gastonia and Marion, North Carolina; of the Scottsboro boys, blacks falsely imprisoned for rape on weak evidence; of songs and coal strikes in Harlan County; and of Norman Thomas, the Socialist who received 900,000 votes for president in 1932. The Communist Party (CP) had captivated Charles and his friends; joining the Socialists, as John Dos Passos said, had about the same effect "as drinking a bottle of near-beer." In the streets, Peter watched volunteers from the CP-led unemployment councils restoring the furniture of evicted tenants; to him, these people were *heroes*.

Soon Charles was taking Peter to his first May Day demonstration. They crowded in line on Fifth Avenue singing IWW tunes like "Pie in the Sky" and Maurice Sugar's "Soup Song." New York's finest rode by, their nightsticks slapping against the horses' flanks. A delicious defiance floated in the air. The singing and laughing made Peter feel part of a high-minded family, far different from his own. He didn't notice that a few blocks away, another contingent paraded separately from the Communists—the Socialists. The "family" Peter had joined was not on speaking terms with its relatives.

Back at school, Peter came across a Bolshevik children's book in the library, *New Russia's Primer.* Written with a Whitmanesque grandeur, it promised a new world in the next Five Year Plan: new brigades to hasten production and cut pollution. Futuristic tales of

Russian scouts in uncharted forests were not lost on Peter, who saw the pioneer spirit of Seton's *Two Little Savages* harnessed to a socialist ideal.

It was a heady moment when Ernest Thompson Seton met Lenin's Young Pioneers on Peter's bookshelf. But for this Depression-born radicalism, he might have become like his brothers: a teacher, like John, or a scientist, like Charles III. Yet any connection between strumming his uke and the *Daily Worker*'s politics escaped Peter's notice, even as father and son heard their first urban folk songs.

This happened at an opening of the murals of Thomas Hart Benton, Charles's fellow instructor at the New School (where Charles had been teaching part time since he'd left Juilliard). Home on vacation, Peter drank in the bohemian crowd of composers and painters sipping wine and chatting noisily. In one corner of the gallery, Benton amazed the boy and his father with "John Henry." Peter's foot started tapping immediately. This was the stuff—much better than mother's dreary violin exercises. Even in a room echoing with conversation and overshadowed by fifteen-foot murals, the music cut right through him. Peter didn't understand what attracted him; later he decided it was the rhythm. Afterward, Benton lent Charles some records, but the music didn't take. When Peter first heard the folk banjo—Dock Boggs's version of "Pretty Polly"—he thought the melody sounded Chinese, it's modal harmonies escaping him. Yet he was a fast learner; only a year later he'd sit in on tenor with Benton and his friend Jackson Pollock, his first musical group.

IN THE FALL of 1932, Peter entered high school at Avon Old Farms. Avon trained boys to take their place in the company of men, to preserve "the elite of the well-ordered mind," as their brochure promised. Peter was going as a scholarship student, but Avon's dress code—Brooks Brothers suits with starched wing collars and bow ties—were required for supper.

When he arrived at the school Peter could scarcely believe his surroundings, which resembled an English manor in the 1500s. The school's patron, an eccentric steel heiress, had spent five million dollars creating a Tudor village in the Connecticut woods. Peter couldn't help admiring this fortress. After unpacking, he explored the three-thousand-acre park; the woods delighted him. He wondered at the red slate roof and ran his hands over rough, red-stone walls, two feet thick.

It was a schizophrenic new life. One moment he read about Russian Communism and the next he sang in a chapel of hand-hewn oak beams and leaded glass. The boys teased him about his "sweet girlish complexion," as schoolmate Bill Leonard, later president of CBS News, remembered. Even at fourteen, Peter's long curls made him a natural for the female roles in Avon's theatricals, including "Consuela, the Bare-backed Tango Queen." Being a scholarship student puts one in one's place. He earned pocket money by blacking classmates' shoes, like Charles Dickens. He barely entered the camaraderie of boarding school life; and scholarship, the refuge of the antisocial, never held his attention; he earned mostly Bs and Cs.

One of his more memorable events at Avon occurred soon after his arrival. Peter met a teacher, Charles Langmuir, who owned a four-string banjo he wasn't using. (The four-string, or tenor, banjo was popular for Dixieland jazz.) Peter toyed with the banjo and decided he *must* have one. It was an easy step from the uke; both instruments are strummed. His strategy was to ask his mother; she'd prefer a classical instrument but would be happy to have him playing anything.

Constance had written, "Did you receive the package with the shirts, the wing collars, the patent leather shoes?" She got no answer. Her next letter ended, "Please check what clothes you received." Still no answer. With the third letter came another checklist. Peter answered, "Mother, please, nobody wears those patent leather shoes, they're awful—and a complete waste of money."

In between he wrote, "There's a master here who would like to sell his banjo to me for ten dollars. Please may I have it?" His mother's letters never mentioned the banjo. Finally, near the end of the term, she sent a checklist of all the things he was supposed to have written home about: "Did you receive my package, the sweater, and underwear?" and Peter doggedly replied, "Yes, yes, yes"; then he made his own checkbox: "Please, mother, can I have that banjo?"

Peter got his instrument, and music gradually caught his fancy. He started playing in Avon's five-piece Hot Jazz Club, learning tunes like "Night and Day," "Blue Skies," and "I Got Rhythm." In this, he was exposed to one of the melodically richest periods of American pop music. Even in later years, when his musical tastes had changed, he found himself doodling on Gershwin tunes, like "Blue Skies."

"I liked rhythmic music. Even when my mother played Bach, it didn't have incisive rhythm. One of the things I latched onto with the banjo was the rhythmic quality."

As a child Peter had banged away at the autoharp and ukulele; as an adolescent he came to appreciate how music frames a mood and affects people. His Glee Club instructor, Dr. David Boyden, who worked with Peter's clear but ordinary soprano voice, remembered his talent as "unfocused." Boyden taught him fundamentals of harmony, but music was still little more than a game to Seeger, something to tease with or provoke authority. Singing harmony was frowned on in chapel, but when Peter had an anti-authority impulse, he stepped to the back of the group and harmonized during vespers.

LONG BEFORE RECEIVING his first banjo, Peter had decided on journalism as his career. In elementary school, he'd published a penny paper, the *Spring Hill Telegraph*. At Avon he started another, the *Avon Weekly Newsletter*. He had read muckraker Lincoln Steffens's autobiography with excitement; he quickly earned a reputation for overworking his contributors. "Watch out for Pete," his sports columnist Dan North was warned. "He'll have you doing his own work if you're not careful." As an editor, Seeger occasionally ran afoul of the school administration; once he wrote a devastating story about a snake loose in the dorms, the property of poet Archibald MacLeish's son, Kenneth.

"It was one of my funniest stories," Seeger chuckled later, "and they censored it out. MacLeish had a big snake, which had broken a rib. He'd taken the animal to his room to nurse it, but the snake escaped. Kids in the dorm said, 'I'm not going to live in that building with an eight-foot Texas bull snake loose.' Well, they looked everywhere and couldn't find it. Commander Hunter, the assistant provost, got upset. 'MacLeish,' he said, 'you'll stay in your room until that snake is found.' Of course how could the boy find the snake when he's in his room?"

The incident gave the aspiring journalist his first lesson in politics. He typed up his story, but Commander Hunter told him not to publish it. When the young editor protested, Hunter insisted, complaining that the publicity would ruin the school. Peter naïvely agreed, all the while developing a vehement distaste for censorship. Next time, he promised himself, he'd stand on his rights.

He didn't wait long for a second round. A Jewish student wrote the *Newsletter* a letter on anti-Semitism: "There's a lot of talk about democracy and freedom in this country and in the school, but when it comes down to the way people actually act, face it, they don't always live by their pretty words." The student told Peter he could print the letter—if he dared—but he had to keep it anonymous. He agreed, running off the paper himself on the mimeograph.

In the early thirties, anti-Semitism was growing in America. The pro-Hitler Liberty League raved about Jewish bankers; Peter's classmates—and ten million others—heard Father Coughlin attack President Roosevelt's "Jew Deal" on the radio. When the next edition of the *Newsletter* came out, "The guys who'd been making anti-Semitic cracks were furious," Peter remembered. These were husky fellows, and they cornered Seeger one afternoon: "Who wrote that letter?" He refused to say.

Commander Hunter asked the same question. Peter again refused to name his source. Hunter, an ex-Navy man who took pride in discipline, called the boy into his book-lined study and gave him hell. Peter sat there and fumed. He walked away in a slow burn, hating the "bluff old phony" but uncertain what to do. He had given his word, but the provost was threatening to take away the paper, or expel him.

His situation paralleled that of later, unfriendly witnesses before the House Committee on Un-American Activities. Resistance was symbolic, for the provost undoubtedly guessed the letter writer's identity—there were only a few Jews at Avon. The point was apparently to humiliate Peter publicly. Had he been self-serving, he might have negotiated an exemption from academic requirements in exchange. Had he more political cunning, he might have exacted limits on future censorship.

Instead, Seeger gave in without conditions. The decision still rankles him.

"I guess I showed a talent for compromise," he said wistfully forty-five years later. "I didn't want to be a *cause célèbre* and figured okay, I wouldn't butt in on the provost headfirst, I'd try and find some way to get around him or ignore him." Seeger had tried his character and found it wanting; the decision haunted him. These disputes over censorship returned throughout his adult life, and each time the stakes would grow higher.

In the next few years, Peter had an ever harder time keeping his woodsy isolation. He remembered one conversation as the turning point when he began to leave Seton behind. He and his mother were visiting two of her students, the Kantrowitzes. Adrian Kantrowitz remembers Constance as attractive, "with a sense of the power of music as a personal language. But she was too gentle, the type people and society will run all over." While Constance and her long-time student Dorothy Kantrowitz practiced inside, the three boys sat out on the porch of their house in rural Connecticut in the summer night, talking over the drone of crickets. A few months after his fight with the provost, the censorship still rankled, and he vented his frustration.

"With all the dishonesty in the world, how can anyone lead an honest life?" Peter asked.

"Come on, Pete, not everyone's dishonest," replied one of the Kantrowitz boys.

"No, but society sure is. The only ones who can be honest are those who don't have to compromise: the hermits. I wouldn't mind being one." He stared into the warm darkness, shielded by mosquito netting.

"But, Peter," his friend replied, "what kind of morality is that? Be pure and let the rest of the world go to hell?"

In the 1300s Pete Seeger might actually have become a hermit. He yearned for a morally consistent life; complications and compromises only made him want to retreat. Yet he'd always had another side, which felt a duty to stay and fight. His friends' arguments and his father's commitment slowly swayed the fifteen-year-old: "I thought about that conversation for some time, and finally decided the Kantrowitz boys were right." That fall, 1933, Peter returned to Avon with a subscription to the Communist literary magazine *New Masses.* Unfortunately the magazine publishing Dreiser, Anderson, and Dos Passos was once censored by the Party for, in a wonderfully arcane phrase, "a lack of political intransigence." The presence of such authors represented the massive turn to the Left of artists and intellectuals. As Sherwood Anderson commented, on being asked the difference between Socialists and Communists, "I guess the Communists mean it."

Peter quickly became a devotee of a *New Masses* firebrand journalist, Michael Gold. Gold was everything Peter wasn't: Jewish, working class, and politically committed. The author of *Jews without Money* grew up on the Lower East Side, quit school at twelve to work, and hung out with New York bohemians like John Reed and Peter's uncle, Alan.

There was another road Seeger could have taken into politics but didn't: that of anti-Communist Socialists like Norman Thomas, whose popular appeal exceeded anything the Party ever received. If Communism was associated with Peter's father, Socialism was his mother's choice. She voted for Thomas because he drove an old car and wore worn suits. What a world of difference Seeger's life would have taken if he'd joined up with the Socialists.

Peter kept his radical sympathies secret. A favorite English teacher lampooned *New Masses* while Peter sat in the back of the class, never saying a word. He had become a closet radical, lounging in a herringbone suit—which never fit his scrawny frame—and smiling superiorly while his dorm mates discussed the Harvard-Yale game or their fathers' cars. Their wealth had a flaccid, decadent quality. Peter kept to his room, working on the newspaper. To others he seemed a goody-goody; he thought himself a rebel. At night in the dorm, the precocious journalist had to put aside his typing at lights out, but he wasn't worried: "It was against the rules to have lights on past a certain hour, but no one said anything about getting up early."

When Peter needed rest and isolation, he used Verne Priest's log cabin for a trailhead, disappearing in the woods for a day at a time with two apples and a book.

An earthy logger from Maine, straight out of Seton's pages, Priest knew the land surrounding Avon as if born there. He needed fuel for his pancake suppers, and Peter was the one who chopped it. On fall afternoons when the leaves turned yellow and red and the air smelled like bitter chocolate, few activities exhilarated him more than cutting and stacking a five-foot pile of logs. One of his many afternoons there, Peter finished chopping and swept up the broken bark. He slid into a favorite chair, where his back found a notch it fit perfectly. Rain fell lightly on the wooden roof, and the firs stood tall, outlined by the drops as the wind rustled the wet branches.

Nearby stood his teepee, where he'd cook Sunday breakfast by himself over an open flame.

BUT JUST AS Charles had failed to balance his academic career and his social concerns in Berkeley, his son Peter could not remain a radical in the woods. He might have been isolated at Avon, but as the economy hit its deepest trough, hundreds of thousands were committing themselves to Socialist and Communist campaigns.

Long after the thirties passed, this formative decade would mark Seeger's repertoire. By the midthirties, intellectuals had "discovered" American folk music; a handful of folklorists were trying to give this music a wider audience—Robert Gordon, Ben Botkin, John and Alan Lomax, and now, surprisingly, Charles Seeger. Their movement combined nationalism and patriotism, a sense that here at last was America's *true* music. This occurred during the Popular Front era, when Communists united behind President Roosevelt and tried to sink roots in American tradition. Radicals turned a new ear to traditional folk tunes; the hostility of groups like the Composers Collective softened. It was a chorus-filled era, in politics as well as music.

Music was bursting through and around Seeger. The struggle for what kind of music Seeger would identify with paralleled that of his parents' differing political leanings. On the one hand, he'd learned to keep his taste for popular music to himself; he'd plunk out the tunes to George Gershwin's "Girl Crazy" only when Grandmama wasn't at home in Patterson, for she found it "dreadfully vulgar." His mother still hoped he'd take classical training. Charles encouraged him to play anything he liked.

In the end it wasn't ideology, but musical taste that drove Seeger into folk music: the honesty and simplicity of old ballads of heartbreak and despair; the pure, clean ring of a banjo; the dreamy emotional moods of a well-played guitar.

In this development, Peter's mentor played an important part. After leaving New York and the Composers Collective in 1935,

Charles administered music programs for the Resettlement (later Farm Security) Administration. Peter spent the summer of his graduation, 1936, with his father, one of those languorous stretches near the end of adolescence when seventeen-year-olds stand between childhood and adulthood, with the privileges of both. With Senate investigations of labor spies and railroad monopolies, New Deal Washington was an exciting place for leftists and a welcome change from Avon. Peter visited with Charles's new friends, including Alan Lomax, a wide, bluff fellow a few years his senior. Already famous for his song-collecting expeditions with his father, John, Alan talked like he was shouting into an imaginary microphone. Older, better-read, Alan Lomax became a concerned older brother to Seeger.

Seeger was meeting Party members debating the new slogan "Communism is twentieth-century Americanism"; Paine and Jefferson were resurrected as American radicals. The Seeger boy fit right in to this new patriotism, with his all-American stock and wholesome habits. He came of age in one of the rare moments when American radicals succeeded by working in coalitions rather than in sects. He never forgot this convergence: Folk song, radicalism, and patriotism blended in his mind.

At Charles's new home in Silver Spring, Maryland, Peter visited with his stepmother, Ruth, and relaxed by the oversize fireplace in the living room. It was like living in the office of a great cause; he had only to sit still, and raw, field-recorded music came his way. No raja's son could have had better access to America's musical treasury, a privilege he later shared with Ruth's children, Mike and Peggy Seeger.

With nothing better to do on the long muggy evenings, flies buzzing in the Maryland heat, he listened as Dio (Ruth) transcribed Library of Congress recordings for the Lomaxes. Dio fascinated Peter; she warmed the house with her presence; she was round-faced and laughing, but extremely serious about music. As a young composer she had already produced her eerie and dissonant "String Quartet No. 1" and received a Guggenheim grant to study composition in Berlin. By the midthirties, she had become as fascinated with folk music as Charles had; she transcribed with maniacal precision, sometimes listening to a song dozens of times to see if a note was closer to C or C-sharp.

But when Peter sat down to learn these tunes on his four-string banjo, he found he couldn't do it. These "simple" tunes escaped him. He didn't realize that everyone on these recordings played a five- rather than a four-string banjo. At the end of one particularly browbeaten session, his father walked in: "Peter had the four-string in his lap, and I asked 'What are you playing that for?' (I was quite new in the field, and convinced the five-string was *the* proper one.) Peter looked up at me and asked, 'Well, father, what *should* I play?'" Charles suggested they talk it over with banjo picker Bascom Lamar Lunsford in North Carolina. A few weeks later, father and son packed up their big blue Chevy and drove South.

Soon the mountainous Piedmont again stretched before them. The North Carolina hills "were lordly, with a plan," as Thomas Wolfe wrote. "Westward, they widened into the sun." Nestled among the Blue Ridge and Smoky Mountains, Asheville's clean air attracted three thousand guests to the Ninth Annual Folk Song and Dance Festival in 1936. To Peter, the scene was as exotic as a market Sunday in the Middle Ages; crowds of mountain people jostled past them to fill seats in the bleachers of a baseball field. Sellers hawked steaming corn on the cob and sarsaparilla. In sessions running late into the night, old-time string bands played for dance teams from towns named Rattlesnake Knob and Greenbriar Creek. Two banjoists impressed Peter: Samantha Bumgarner from Dillsboro, and Lunsford, the master of ceremonies.

From the first banjo tunes, he was transfixed. The crisp rhythms and rippling notes clamped him to his seat. Lunsford carried his instrument like a favorite coat; sitting down to pick, his banjo became an extra arm.

Seeing the five-string banjo on its native ground made an instant convert of Peter. His ukulele wouldn't do. The tenor banjo's

Dixieland plunk-plunk-plunk paled. "I discovered there was some good music in my country which I never heard on the radio. . . . I liked the strident vocal tone of the singers, the vigorous dancing. The words of the [folk] songs had all the meat of life in them. Their humor had bite, it was not trivial. Their tragedy was real, not sentimental. In comparison, most of the pop music of the thirties seemed to me weak and soft, with its endless variations on 'Baby, baby I need you.' "

In England, pioneer folklorist Cecil Sharp had experienced a similar moment in 1910, when he looked out a window near Oxford and saw a procession of men in costumes on a snowy country lane. Sharp watched with astonishment as they broke into song and did a Morris dance; he dated the English folk music revival from that moment. So the search of Charles Seeger and his youngest son for an authentic American music had its predecessors: Sharp's song collecting in Appalachia; the folklore schools of John Campbell, which interested Henry Ford in folk dance; John Lomax's early ballad hunting; and the research of a colleague of Charles's at Berkeley, Robert Gordon, who was setting up a collection at the Library of Congress. It would be years before Peter heard of any of his forerunners on the folk music trail.

Peter's third passion, after his woodland tower and the radicalism inherited from his father, was for rural, working-class music—in some ways a combination of the first two. By the end of the summer, he burned to find out more about this odd five-string banjo. He couldn't figure out how musicians got that rhythmic, percussive effect. (Because of the extra string halfway up the neck, the instrument is played differently: plucked or frailed instead of strummed with a pick.) Charles considered it the most dramatic folk instrument, but by the time Peter heard the five-string, the instrument had all but disappeared from the public eye, particularly in the North.

"Lunsford's style—plucking up on a note and then brushing down on the strings—is much rarer than frailing and brushing down, or brushing up while you're plucking notes," said banjoist

Michael Cooney. "It was just the first person Pete saw play that way, and Pete assumed it was universal."

As Charles Seeger's son—and the cousin of Natalie Curtis, a field recorder of Indian music—Peter had immediate access to recordings at the Library of Congress. Besides, who could turn him away—a ruddy-cheeked, gangly kid so eager to learn? The banjo surprised him with its long history: Egyptian dancers played similar instruments for pharaohs, slaves brought banjos to America from West Africa, and Thomas Jefferson described the "banjar" as a chief instrument among Negroes in the 1700s. The fifth string, he discovered, developed in the 1800s and gave the banjo a Scottish drone, integrating British and African heritages into a truly American instrument.

Next Peter traced contemporary banjoists with a reporter's zeal. Through their recordings and songs he entered a world vastly different from his boarding school life.

Bascom Lamar Lunsford, who lent Charles the five-string Peter first practiced on, lived like Johnny Appleseed, selling fruit trees before becoming a teacher and lawyer. He'd learned two-finger picking by playing banjo at apple-butter stirrings and house raisings. Kentuckian Pete Steele, whose clean, crisp up-picking style Peter admired, learned on a squirrel-skin banjo. Peter listened again to Dock Boggs, but now the modal scales he heard on Tom Benton's records made sense. From Uncle Dave Macon on the Grand Ole Opry, Peter learned different tunings and topical country songs. Buell Kazee, Wade Ward, Lilly Mae Ledford, the Coon Creek Girls—the list goes on for pages; one day he hoped to meet them all. The seventeen-year-old practically obliterated what records he could find, putting his thumb on the edge to slow them to a growl. He played the discs over and over until he got the hang of it. This took several years, during which he continued on the four-string.

Despite all this work, Seeger wasn't interested in music as a profession. "It was better just to play for fun." While these were beautiful tunes, as a journalist he could support himself *and* change the world.

DESPITE DEPRESSION-STRETCHED RESOURCES, the family was determined that Peter should receive a proper education—which meant attending Harvard, as his older brother John, his father, and his uncle Alan had. He started in the fall of 1936 with a partial scholarship and a job washing up in a boardinghouse. His brothers chipped in, and so did his grandfather. Lunch money was in short supply.

He didn't like Harvard; the life that pleased his ancestors didn't work for him. The college didn't teach journalism, so he studied sociology, which bored him. He was easily distracted: One minute he studied, and the next he put down his books to work on a play or redesign the furniture in his dorm room. He began to write tunes, including one he was too shy to send in to the Hasty Pudding Club Show.

In the journal he kept, ambition surfaced continually—a hunger not for wealth, power, or girls, but for distinction. "What makes a man great?" Pete Seeger repeatedly asked himself, answering: "When he is at the top of the value scale of the majority; when people think him great." Fame or fortune could not fulfill these aspirations; they led to worldliness, a sin for Puritans. He prided himself on having a "temperament that looks forward," even admitting: "You know damn well, Pete Seeger, that the only reason you are writing in these notebooks is that you want future people to read them and say, 'There's an OK guy.'" Seeger's hopes for posterity seem extreme for an acne-faced eighteen-year-old too shy to ask a girl out.

College life was more than textbooks and the Tenor Banjo Club. It was bicycling along the Charles River with autumn leaves blowing, jotting down thoughts in his sketchbook, listening to the thunder of the stadium on football afternoons. Nights in his dorm room, playing banjo or trying to read Spengler, his thoughts swirled in vast historical currents, and he missed classes and supper. When he read Goethe, he was awash in romance and sexual frustration. He rushed through his assigned readings for those he cared about, like Carl Sandburg's *The People, Yes.*

The summer of his freshman year, Seeger worked at a summer camp run by friends of the family. His fellow counselors were far more politically involved than he: Midsummer, one quit to join the Abraham Lincoln Brigade in Spain; a friend from Avon also volunteered. Like the abolitionists who streamed into Kansas to keep the state free of slavery, Seeger's generation of radicals were challenged to commit themselves by the Spanish Civil War. The fighting in Spain became a testing ground of World War II. Three hundred American volunteers had already fallen outside of Madrid, fighting Italian troops. Before Seeger returned to college that fall, an older counselor took him to task for his political reticence: "What? You're not a member of the student union?"

Seeger promised to consider signing up: "But as far as politics, I was keeping my distance. I liked the idea of not actually being involved myself, but observing the action. . . . If someone had offered me a job as a reporter, though, I'd have jumped at it." Observing was one thing, and participating another. Just as his father had refused to join the IWW, his son hedged about Spain. He used his age as an excuse, but by now he'd matured physically. He was nearly six feet tall and thin as a stick figure, the sort who sits alone at parties. People mistook his aloofness for conceit. Acquaintances argued politics with him, but they didn't invite him to their rooms to drink and talk about girls.

Seeger wasn't the only unsocial journalist Harvard had seen; thirty years before, John Reed had been every bit as lonely. Seeger and the chronicler of the Russian Revolution had much in common: Both turned to art and revolution from upper-crust backgrounds; neither managed studies or dating well. And both were romantic radicals, with a bit of Don Quixote in them. But Seeger lacked Reed's self-assertiveness, and Reed tolerated contradictions that

Seeger's Puritanism would never allow. Reed could comfortably leave a benefit for striking IWW workers to weekend on a yacht; a tall beer after the show would have been Seeger's extravagance.

GRADUALLY, BY HIS sophomore year, politics overtook Seeger's other interests. On winter afternoons, he passed out leaflets for Spanish war relief in front of Widener Library, stamping his feet in the cold. Wrapped in greatcoats of Scottish wool, the Harvard men passed him by. Seeger started yet another paper, *The Harvard Progressive*, with Arthur Kinoy (later a radical lawyer who defended the Chicago Eight). Trading the Banjo Club for the Young Communist League, he started reading Lenin's *Imperialism*. The YCL represented a good-natured extremism, advertising themselves with appeals to sports and clean fun. Joining meant a commitment.

"As an individual," Seeger wrote in his journal, "what do I count for? In the YCL, I have the Comintern behind me." The YCL leadership was then fighting for control of the liberal American Student Union; YCLers joined the ASU and formed secret caucuses. Seeger ran for and was elected secretary of Harvard's ASU chapter—without discussing his more radical affiliation. The politicking gave him moral indigestion. "I am not a politician, a fighter, an organizer," he noted in one of those acute self-realizations later ignored.

Ironically, the year Pete Seeger joined the Party was the year his father quit: "When I was fourteen, I remember asking him, 'What are the bad things about Communism? Aren't there good and bad things about everything in the world?' He took all of ten or fifteen seconds away from his work and said, 'No, it's all good.' Then he went back to his desk.

"In 1937, he backed away from the Party when he read a manuscript of the Moscow trials: 'They're obviously tortured confessions!' He wasn't going to become a Trotskyist or an anarchist. He wasn't going to be a dutiful, loyal member anymore. But I think he wanted to let me find my own way.

"It's impossible to explain to young people today why we in the YCL felt such allegiance to the Soviet Union" Seeger said. "In those days it was the workers' fatherland—the only socialism on earth."

At eighteen, Seeger's politics were a strange mix of revolution and *Robert's Rules of Order.* His political activity was confined to Harvard Yard, though he once led an expedition to leaflet Grant's department store in the wilds of Boston. Neither black, Jewish, nor Catholic, Seeger didn't face discrimination of his own. He empathized with other people's causes. "Where *is* Peter going?" his grandparents asked, confused at the radical turn he'd taken. His aunt told him he was "a damn loafer" for getting Cs in college, but Seeger shrugged it off.

Returning from a crowded recital one night, Seeger wondered why formal concerts bored him. He noted the reasons in his journal: The instruments were strained to their loudest; hot, stuffy concert halls put him to sleep; and "the audience should be a great chorus." This last phrase is a curious and prophetic one. What did he expect of audiences? Did he imagine he could change them?

School only stood in the way of Seeger's interests. He found the professors pompous and his readings irrelevant. His interest in his studies withered like the renowned organs of the state. Soon a letter from the dean's office notified him of academic probation. "If you ever decide what you want to study," the dean of students said, "we'll be glad to have you back." Seeger decided he had more important things to do. He lost his scholarship because of poor grades and left Harvard in April 1938; he hadn't bothered registering for spring semester. He took leave of the Charles River and his few friends. One afternoon before he left, he passed John F. Kennedy bustling across the yard with his personal secretary. If JFK became the most famous graduate of the Class of '40, Pete Seeger was its best-known dropout.

Chapter 4

66 Highway Blues

—

SEEGER LEFT HARVARD FOR NEW YORK CITY, HOPING, LIKE generations of eighteen-year-olds before him, for a job in the city. He imagined himself a hard-writing reporter for the *Times* or, perhaps, on muckraker Gilbert Seldes's *In Fact*. Before he tried his luck, however, he wanted a vacation. He visited his mother in Sarasota, Florida, and helped her move back to New York City. Rather than stay in her new apartment, he hit upon an original idea: to paint his way across New York State by bicycling from one farm to another and trading his watercolors for a night's lodging. His bike was an old, broken-down affair, but it would have to do. Prudently waiting until the nights were warm enough to sleep outside, Seeger left for his first summer by himself, pedaling across the Berkshires in 1938.

He still had that rosy-cheeked, long-legged look. He'd grown so much that the seat on his bicycle rode sixteen inches high, with an easel and canvas frames strapped underneath. He would choose a pretty house and approach it from behind, painting a landscape of cows and barns. He supplied plenty of pretty clouds, even on a gray day. Then he would knock on the front door.

"Hey Mary, come look at this," the astonished homeowner would say. "Some guy's painted a picture of our house!" Once a farmer caught him in the cow field before Seeger had finished. "My barn, you make it look too short," he scolded.

After overintellectualized Harvard, Seeger was relieved to

wind through the mountains on his bike: "College was fine for those who wanted it, but I was just not interested; I wanted to be a journalist." Years afterward when his name appeared in the headlines, he received letters asking if he was the same Seeger who painted the barn the wrong color.

After a couple of months, he returned to the city thin enough to slide through the subway turnstiles without paying. Without funds of his own, he moved into his brothers' apartment, where he slept on a couch and washed dishes for his share of the rent.

Autumn made its brief New York appearance, and the leaves in Central Park turned orange and brown before blowing away in the wind. New Yorkers paused on the street to marvel at the new season. The city whirled around him; he would call a paper in the morning, take a subway to the editor's office that afternoon, and find there was no job for him—all in the same day. He sat on subways with clerks in suits and housewives with sagging shopping bags from Macy's, all rocking together anonymously through the musty tunnels. After Connecticut and Cambridge, New York loomed exotic. The Seeger boys lived on the Lower East Side, at 118 East Eleventh Street, and Seeger shopped the ethnic stores and bakeries, sampling piroshki, bagels, and sour cream for the first time. He peered in at Ukrainian churches and Irish bars. With so much to explore, he thought he'd never tire of the city. His imagination hopped from one project to the next. On the same page of his journal he discussed the ideal tenure for elected officers and remarked how saving thirty cents a day yielded a hundred dollars a year.

To make ends meet, he picked newspapers from the trash bins and read books at the library. He joined Youth Arts, a branch of the Young Communist League, and painted signs for marches.

One day, his brother Charles's wife, Inez, dared Seeger to perform in the streets. Painfully nervous, acne blooming on his face, Pete Seeger stood on Park Avenue with his four-string banjo. (He still hadn't mastered the rhythm of the five-string.) A small crowd gathered when the reedy-looking boy opened his case and started plunking "Ol' Man River" and "Cindy." Seeger's voice cracked, his Adam's apple bobbed up and down, but he kept on singing. Passersby on New York's fanciest boulevard left little in the way of donations—seventy-five cents for three hours. If Seeger had ideas of being a professional musician, that experience put a match to them. Music ran a poor third, behind painting and journalism. When he wasn't visiting newspaper offices, he took classes at the American Artists School. He had always loved to sketch, from his earliest expeditions tracing animal tracks; now he studied oil and watercolors. His greatest talent was for the latter, he decided; besides, oils were costly.

TO HIS DISMAY, Seeger discovered that newspapers weren't hiring college dropouts, even Harvard-educated ones. He wrote a friend of a friend on the *Times;* no luck. Part of his problem was his presentation. His wrists poked out from his jackets; his trousers were too short. Interview after interview passed without an offer. Though his paintings showed promise—particularly to anyone fond of barns—no exhibitions came his way. Dead broke and frustrated, he visited his aunt Elsie Seeger, for many years principal of the Dalton School. She helped him out with a gig playing there, which brought in five dollars and invitations to sing at other schools, and at Margot Mayo's folk dance group on Thirteenth Street. One Sunday in 1939, the troupe was supposed to have a work party and wash the skylights of their loft. Pete Seeger and a pretty girl named Toshi Ohta were the only ones who showed up.

Toshi—the name means "beginning of a new era"—had luxuriant jet-black hair and an adventuresome streak inherited from her mother, the radical in an old Virginia family that included Jim Bowie of the Bowie knife. Peter shyly asked her about herself. She told him how, over her grandparents' wishes, her mother had married a Japanese exile and then went to Europe, to bear her baby in peace. Because of the Oriental Exclusion Act (which prevented children of 50 percent or more Oriental blood from entering the United States), she would not have been allowed in the country had not her mother smuggled her in, lying to the customs officer that the vivacious baby was 100 percent Caucasian.

Toshi grew up in the art colonies of Provincetown and Woodstock and attended "progressive" schools, including Greenwich Village's Little Red School House. Both had canvassed for Republican Spain, they discovered. Seeger was attracted to her, but reticent; they went out for hamburgers a few times. The friendship drifted as Alan Lomax—now in New York on business—introduced Seeger to a fascinating world of musicians. Lomax brought him into the Lower East Side apartment of Aunt Molly Jackson, an Appalachian who wrote "I Am a Union Woman (Join the CIO)" and "Pity the Coal Miner." Aunt Molly knew Seeger's father from the Composers Collective; the musicians there had gracelessly called her a "living anachronism," a coal mine organizer who wrote songs without even reading music.

Despite these memories, Molly received him warmly. Her rough clear voice bowled Seeger over, the first live "protesty" songs (based on folk tunes) he heard. Her songs had fire and direct, everyday lyrics, and Seeger immediately sat down and transcribed them. Lomax had an even greater success in introducing Seeger to the "King of the Twelve-String Guitar," Huddie Ledbetter.

Born on a Louisiana farm the same year as Seeger's father, Ledbetter learned play-songs and African American spirituals at home. His musical training was in juke-joints on the seamier side of Shreveport, where he had periodic conflicts with the law. Alan told how he and his father had discovered the African American singer, who called himself Lead Belly on a song-collecting trip to a southern jail in 1933, and how they helped him out of prison. Huddie and his wife had joined the Lomax household—as servants, by one account—then moved to New York. Despite his gentle side and a tenderness for children, a reputation for violence followed

Ledbetter onstage like a sessionman no one paid. Seeger didn't know what to expect.

ONE AFTERNOON—the date's unclear—the young banjo picker had his chance; when Alan called, Seeger grabbed his banjo and took off out the door. When he got to Ledbetter's apartment, he marveled at the musician's square frame and arms as thick as stove pipes. He was barrel-chested, with close-cropped salt-and-pepper hair and eyes as bright as porcelain. He had no use for the overalls Seeger affected, and he loved liquor and high times. Until Lead Belly pulled out his guitar, the pair didn't have much in common.

"Huddie was not trying to show off his excellent guitar playing. 'This is life,' he seemed to be saying," Seeger said.

Lead's music spellbound the city boy. In "Goodnight Irene," "Midnight Special," and other songs, Huddie revealed a rhyming, improvisational genius. Seeger couldn't always understand his Louisiana twang, but he caught the infectious joy of his music and its powerful rhythms. Huddie talked to his guitar as he played—and he meant it. His twelve-string guitar with its doubled bass strings boomed merrily or cried thinly in a child's moan. Sometimes it whispered like the wind.

To Seeger, who'd met only a handful of blacks in his life, Lead Belly was a sensation whom he compared to Beethoven. Huddie was also living proof of the power of song, a dark-skinned Orpheus. He had composed a song to soften the heart of Texas governor Pat Neff and literally won his freedom with a song. This was a momentous meeting.

"There I was, trying my best to shed my Harvard upbringing, scorning to waste money on clothes other than blue jeans. But Lead Belly had on a clean shirt and starched collar, well-pressed suit, and shined shoes. . . . I was proud he accepted me. Perhaps he wondered at my earnestness, trying to learn his music."

Afterward, Seeger returned to his brothers' couch, and to worrying about his modest expenses. Finding a job in Depression

New York was more difficult than anticipated. In May, he took a job as a porter at the 1939 World's Fair, sweeping up cigarette butts and watching the jitterbug contests. Painting remained his ambition until one day when an art teacher, Arthur Stern, casually asked him what else he did.

"Well, I play the banjo," Peter answered brightly.

"I've never heard you play the banjo," the instructor said, "but I'd suggest you stick to that."

AND SO, AFTER YEARS of ambivalence, after chance encounters with an art teacher, a Louisiana farmhand, and a coal miner's wife, Pete Seeger began to look to music as a profession. A friend asked him to play with a summer music-and-puppet troupe, the Vagabond Puppeteers. Weary of looking for a job, he agreed. There was no money in it, but the project sounded like fun. The group bought a 1929 Oldsmobile, built a collapsible stage on the car's back flap—as his father had done in Pinehurst—and made puppets out of papier-mâché. The idea came out of rural education campaigns of postrevolutionary Mexico, where two members of the group had trained. After writing tentative scripts, the foursome booked themselves by poster across Upstate New York, passing the hat as they went.

"Pete had a single-mindedness that belied his appearance," remembered a member of the troupe, Mary Jimenez. "Under the painfully shy, modest, seemingly self-effacing exterior was a will of iron. Nobody could make him do what he didn't want to do, though his manner appeared ever so acquiescent and agreeable.

"If there was a 'leader' in our group it was he, because he always had the single solution and was adept at mediating our silly arguments."

The puppeteers played church socials and union halls for three months in mid-1939, sleeping in barns or beneath the stars on folding cots. By chance, the troupe ran head-on into the most serious milk strike in New York history. Independent dairy farmers were fighting the low milk prices paid by Borden and Sheffield, the large chain dairies. In bloody clashes with scab drivers, farmers poured thousands of gallons of milk onto highways. The puppeteers met with Dairy Farmers' Union officials, who accepted their services. The trip went fine until Seeger announced he wouldn't step out in front of the stage to perform while the others remained in the back, a telling gesture.

He offered all sorts of arguments. Nevertheless, farmers kept coming up to ask who the banjo player was, and Seeger had to come out. He fumed, though; it wasn't right to make him the "star"; he didn't enjoy solos. Eventually he agreed to step out at the end and coax people to sing with him, as he had when he was eight at Spring Hill.

Seeger remained as ascetic as a monk. In his journal, he wrote, "A person shouldn't have more property than he can squeeze between his banjo and the outside wall of his banjo case."

ONE AFTERNOON IN August 1939, the Vagabond Puppeteers were performing for pickets outside a dairy in Ithaca. The men watched with one eye on the puppets and the other on the highway. Strikers had heard about a load of scab milk heading their way.

The skit opened with a farmer arguing with his fussy cow. "Repaint my barn," the cow (Seeger) mooed, threatening to tell the state milk inspector. The farmer sulked. Then the cow berated him for selling milk so cheaply. The farmer brought on mustached Mr. Shorden Beffield, milk dealer, to explain his prices. At "Shorden Beffield," mutterings of "What the hell is this—a puppet show?" turned to guffaws. Their attention distracted, no one noticed the distant line of dust slowly crossing the dry valley.

On stage, the cow exposed Beffield as a gouger and goaded the farmer into joining a strike. Beffield threatened to boycott the cow's milk, then hit the now-subdued farmer on the head and exited. (Boos from the crowd.)

Just then, a neighbor happened by to explain about the Dairy Farmers' Union. The farmer signed up. The cow was happy, the farmer's wife was happy, and everyone sang the topical finale, "The Farmer Is the Man Who Feeds Us All." The puppeteers left amid congratulations; pickets mooed at each other, and sandwiches and coffee were made for the night shift.

Under the cover of darkness, the scab trucks waited. The first one rumbled up the road to the dairy a few hours later. The pickets jumped to their feet.

The truck rattled along slowly, lights extinguished. The milk cans clanged as the truck swayed over the bumps. The pickets stood in a human chain across the road. At the entrance, the driver threw on his lights, down-shifted, and started to honk. The men blocked the road, motionless. Then the truck hit the line, hurling a union steward eight feet. That night, he died from internal injuries at a local hospital.

"We heard the news when we came in for breakfast next morning," recalled one member of the troupe, Jerry Oberwager. "We couldn't believe it. Night before last, that same steward had put us up. We were pretty shaken." The incident made personal the deep commitment needed for social change.

Yet even as he began to turn to music for a living, he remained divided between the two impulses of his youth: the woodland path that stretched from the teepee at Patterson to Verne Priest's woodshed, and the worldly road of Mike Gold and his father's radical friends in the Composers Collective. For the rest of his life, Seeger searched for the meeting of these two ways; involved in political campaigns, he yearned to sit by the river with his banjo, and even into the woods, he carried hopes of political change.

Returning to New York City, Seeger finally admitted to himself that he hadn't become the reporter he'd pictured at Harvard. By now, he was spending more time practicing banjo than calling up editors, but he couldn't shake the feeling that music was for fun, not a job; after earning seventy-five cents his first day out, who could blame him? He was just another twenty-year-old singer in a city of would-be crooners. He picked up a few extra dollars grading aptitude tests at Scholastic Publications. Mostly he needed to succeed at *something.* One afternoon Charles III came home and found his youngest brother sitting at a spinet harpsichord. After a few passes, Peter did a fair job of picking out jazz tunes. Then he stood up in frustration and scowled at his brother: "God damn it, I've got to stop playing so *many* instruments and learn to play one of them well."

Alan Lomax came to his aid. He had been listening to Seeger improve on the banjo. Finally he pointed out the inevitable: "Pete, what do you want to be an artist for! You ought to learn more about folk music." Alan invited Pete to join him at the Archive of American Folk Song at the Library of Congress—a natural consequence of Charles Seeger's influence and Seeger's talent. The pay wasn't great, but it beat sweeping up after tourists.

"ALAN WAS ONLY four years older than me, but way more sophisticated. He was very much a Communist, but a secret member, or he would have lost his job. He knew a *lot* of folk songs and I didn't know nothing. He was very much my mentor.

"He'd inherited his job at the Library of Congress from his dad. My father was a surrogate father, till they split over copyright: father thought no one should copyright a folk song." In the fall of 1939, Seeger worked for the Library of Congress, before returning to the Village.

"I went down to Washington to work at the Archive for fifteen dollars a week," Seeger remembered. "I lived in an old rooming house around the corner and kept to myself. Saved money and bicycled out to see my father and stepmother occasionally for a grand meal." His idea of luxury was a new set of banjo strings—which he often needed, as he experimented with different tunings. Seeger's duties at the Archive were untaxing, but he handled them conscientiously: cataloguing the dusty archives and transcribing songs. In the process, he absorbed repertoire. The songs lived for him; rather than notes on paper, like those his mother had offered him, these were new friends. He got to know Old Joe Clark, Casey Jones, the Arkansas Traveler, Joe Bowers, and Jesse James; he even met girls: Pretty Polly, the Buffalo Gals, and Jennie Jenkins.

"I remember visiting Pete at Alan's house that winter," said Bess Lomax, Alan's sister. "He had begun to play the five-string almost continuously. One night Alan had to throw him out; Pete just never shut up, and it was driving everybody mad. Oh, he was *terrible*. It was very definitely practicing, and it got to be intolerable. He played all night, and he played all day, and after a while you wanted to ship him off somewhere.

"One morning, I had to catch the train to Philadelphia at a very early hour. Pete was sitting outside on the radiator of Alan's car, playing the recorder very quietly at 4:30 a.m. He said he didn't want to disturb anybody." At length, Lomax booked him for a fund-raiser in New York.

Alan Lomax was as brash as Pete was timid. Both had quit Harvard, but the *wunderkind* of folk music, Alan, had his B.A. (from Texas) and mentioned it more. As a teenager, Alan had gone on his father's recording trips. At twenty-two, he was head at the Archive of American Folk Song. And while still in his twenties, Lomax produced two major radio series on folk music, including CBS's *School of the Air*. His many abilities did not include tact, however, and Lomax rarely let people forget his position. Alan had connections and a reputation as an activist and a folklorist. He finally decided Seeger was ready to perform on stage.

IF AN OBSERVER from another world had trained his eye on a two-mile-square area bounded by Greenwich Village to the south and Times Square to the north, with the participants drawing together from Louisiana, New York, and Oklahoma's dust bowl, he would have witnessed an art form—the modern protest song—in the making.

Topical rhymes and songs were nothing new, of course. During the early Middle Ages, defrocked monks sallied about with anticlerical songs, called goliards. "Little Jack Horner" was originally a protest over Henry VIII's scheme to take over church lands. Labor songs by the hundreds were sung in nineteenth-century America, and IWW songwriter Joe Hill wrote his parody of "Casey Jones" twenty-five years before Lead Belly set foot in New York. Yet the widespread public association of folk music and social causes dates from the mid-1930s Popular Front era. Wobblies had rewritten hymns in their *Little Red Songbook*, and labor musicals like *Pins and Needles* had used show tunes for social commentary. But traditional folk tunes had gone unexplored, except by a few scholars. No political commissar decreed folk songs in vogue; the change came about through trial and error—and through the negative example of the Composers Collective. It was as spontaneous as musicians sitting down together to sing, among them a Louisiana guitarist; a New England banjo picker, bouncy as a kid in new sneakers; and soon, a wandering Okie.

By themselves, these three could not have moved American musical history. But their tastes coincided with the New Deal's radical patriotism and folklore activities and works like Earl Robinson's "Ballad for Americans" (so nationalistic that the Republicans actually asked Paul Robeson to sing it at their 1940 presidential convention). As Arlo Guthrie, Woody's son, later wrote of draft resistance, "If one person does it, they may think he's really sick . . . if two people do it, in harmony, they won't take either one of them. And if three people do it, they may think it's an organization—a movement." This *was* a movement, the All-American Left-Wing Folk Song Revival Movement.

ON MARCH 3, 1940, Pete Seeger waited backstage for his first concert performance. The occasion was the "Grapes of Wrath" benefit for California migrant workers at the old Forrest Theatre—by coincidence the same cause that had sent Charles to the Industrial Workers of the World back in California. Seeger waited nervously in the wings for hours, for the show was crowded with America's leading folk song performers: Burl Ives, Josh White, Richard Dyer-Bennett, Aunt Molly Jackson, and Lead Belly. People milled around him, tuning guitars and peering out at the audience. The lights hummed faintly amid the backstage aromas of sawdust and spilled whiskey. Performers entered and exited past Seeger till the audience yawned from the lateness of the hour.

Finally he heard his name, and he walked out in front of the crowd, blinking at the lights. He couldn't see anyone beyond the first row. He retuned his banjo (though it was already in tune) and began. He couldn't play. His fingers twisted out of his control and hit the wrong strings. Then he forgot a verse.

"I was a bust," Seeger grimaced later. "You see, I didn't know how to play the five-string banjo. I tried to do it too fast, and my fingers froze up on me. And I forgot words. It was the 'Ballad of John Hardy'; I got polite applause for trying and retired in confusion."

He had made a poor beginning of what turned out to be one of the important nights of his life. Fortunately, Seeger was not too disappointed to appreciate the evening's surprise star: "Woody Guthrie just ambled out, offhand and casual . . . a short fellow complete with a western hat, boots, blue jeans, and needing a shave, spinning out stories and singing songs he'd made up." He sang in a dust-dry voice made of tires on hot asphalt, the midnight howl of a coyote, the rhythm of a train clacking across the plains. The effect was stunning. "Well, I just naturally wanted to know more about him. He was a big piece of my education."

Woodrow Wilson Guthrie was born on Bastille Day, July 14, 1912, in Okemah, Oklahoma, later moving to Pampa, Texas, before making the dust bowl migration to California. He came from a more middle-class family than many imagine; his maternal grandmother was a schoolteacher. Despite a hard childhood, with his mother in an asylum, his sister burned in an explosion, and his father bankrupt, Woody had an optimistic, come-what-may spirit. Yet a hard loner sound colored his voice; he could never really belly laugh.

Like Seeger, he had little home life, and he earned attention through music. He followed his father Charles's footsteps: as a Democrat, a political columnist, a musician, and a free-love advocate; he had started singing as a boy, quitting school early to pick grapes and haul wood. What licks he didn't learn from his father or his fiddling uncle Jeff, he picked up off Carter Family and Jimmie Rodgers records. As with the Russian writer Maxim Gorky, barbershops and saloons were his university.

A few years before meeting Seeger, Woody had landed in Los Angeles, where he'd made a reputation with his dust bowl ballads on the radio. There he also met Communist organizers, who saw in Guthrie a native proletarian; he toured the migrant workers' camps, where the treatment of the Okies and Arkies—his people—infuriated him. As his fame grew, radical actor Will Geer (whom Steinbeck cast in *Grapes of Wrath*) mailed Seeger a book of Guthrie's songs. Guthrie arrived in New York only two weeks earlier, having stopped to record with Alan Lomax at the Library of Congress. Though curious to meet Woody, that night in New York Seeger didn't push his way through the crowd around Guthrie. Only later, at one of those cocktail parties where patrons meet performers, did Alan finally pull him forward and say, "Here. Woody Guthrie, I want you to meet Pete Seeger."

The next morning Seeger scanned the papers, perhaps expecting to see himself denounced by the *New York Times* music critic. He found news of everything except what he was looking for. Seabiscuit looked like a sure bet for the $100,000 Santa Anita purse. In Atlanta, the Ku Klux Klan was campaigning to outlaw the Communist Party "and other un-American activities." A snowstorm swept across Finland, slowing the Russian infantry's advance toward the Nazi border. At last Seeger found the review: JOHN STEINBECK COMMITTEE TO AID DUST-BOWL REFUGEES. The *Times* ran a list of entertainers—his name was not there—and one comment: "The house was almost full." So much for his concert debut. New Yorkers preferred Frank Sinatra in Tommy Dorsey's new band.

If Seeger was disappointed, Alan Lomax thought it a momentous occasion: "Go back to that night when Pete first met Woody Guthrie. You can date the renaissance of American folk song from that night. Pete knew it was his kind of music, and he began working to make it everybody's kind of music. . . . It was a pure, genuine fervor, the kind that saves souls."

Alan invited Woody and the young soul-saver to join him in a cherished project; for years, Alan told them, folklorists had omitted songs they considered political or obscene from published collections. Though Guthrie distrusted Lomax's "toothy smile and overwhelming self-confidence," the three agreed to compile a book of political songs in April. *Hard Hitting Songs for Hard Hit People*, as the manuscript was called, had Woody working feverishly. For two months, he sat at the typewriter, day and night, writing head notes to the songs, while Seeger transcribed melodies. Lomax contacted publishers, who found the book politically hot. (Twenty-six years would pass before the manuscript was published.)

Through Lomax's connections, Guthrie was invited to sing on CBS's *School of the Air* and into a studio at the end of the month, April 26 and May 3, 1940, where he recorded *Dust Bowl Ballads*. Then, in mid-May, Woody said, "Pete, you want to come West with me?" Seeger agreed, overcome by wanderlust.

"When I first met Woody, I'd hardly been west of the Hudson River. Like most Yankees, I really didn't see why it was so very important to go West. But Woody said, 'It's a big country out there, Pete, you ought to see it, and if you haven't got money for a ticket, use the thumb.' Woody came driving through in a car and said he was going to visit family in Oklahoma and Texas. The car was not paid for by a long shot. Woody called the trip 'hitch-hiking on credit.'"

At the time, Seeger was sharing a place in Arlington, Virginia, with Alan and Nicholas Ray (later, the director of *Rebel Without a Cause*). He didn't have anything to hold him; he was ready for his adventure, ready to discover folk music no one else had found.

He said goodbye to Ruth and his father—who initially dismissed Woody's accent and cowboy manners as "affected"—and the pair took off for Oklahoma by way of Tennessee.

They made an unlikely pair. Seeger had just turned twenty-one; he stood a head taller than Woody; he had innocent eyes and an unquenchable enthusiasm. "That guy Seeger," Woody once told a friend. "I can't make him out. He doesn't look at girls, he doesn't drink, he doesn't smoke, the fellow's weird." Woody, on the other hand, acted hard-bitten. He ate with his cowboy hat on and didn't bother taking off his pointed boots in bed, massacring the sheets. His reputation as the "Dust Bowl Balladeer" preceded him.

Woody's element was fire, and Pete's air. Guthrie burned across the roads of America; volatile in his moods, he walked around in heat. "Ya got me plumb on fire," he tells a woman in his novel *Seeds of Man*. "Melting clean down, blazin', burnin'." His humor was the dry, crackly kind, and few were warmer with children.

Seeger was Guthrie's opposite, down to his tall, airy frame. He was Ariel in a guitar case. His head pointed skyward as he frailed his banjo; his passions rarely settled down to earth. For the next few years, the pair would need each other as a flame needs oxygen.

They started down through Virginia and then across to Nashville, picking up every hitchhiker they saw until the car couldn't hold any more. After dropping off their riders, they stopped to play at the Highlander Folk School, a rural labor college. Seeger breathed in the America he had dreamed of: road trips, bumming meals, jamming with strangers, doing everything Americans do while searching for the national soul. A decade before the Beats and twenty years ahead of the hippies, Seeger and Guthrie breezed across the hot asphalt, spring turning to summer as they traveled south. Like the characters of *On the Road*, there was no state that bored them, no town that did not call out a rhyme or song. They savored motion itself and new faces and streets and songs.

No sooner would they stop the car and pull themselves out, wiggling their toes after the long drive, than someone would ask if they could play those instruments. "Sure," they'd say, and despite promises to make good time, they were soon sitting on a porch swapping licks. They needed no letter of credit; their songs were always good for a round of drinks and a bowl of chili.

They made a game of how far they could stretch their musical credit, with Seeger once getting his hair cut for a song. On May 28, 1940, they were hungry in a river town in Tennessee. They sauntered into a café, two strangers asking for coffee (Guthrie) and two glasses of buttermilk (Seeger). As their eyes got used to the darkened lunchroom, they noticed they were the only whites there. They were hungry, though, and the smells of gravy, red beans, cornbread, and beef-rib stew were irresistible. The counter girl avoided them for a while, then told them to go. If they stayed, racists would tear down her café. Seeger was learning about racism firsthand.

They left. Seeger was learning about America the hard way, as the characters in the film *Easy Rider* did thirty years later. He was finding what he had left New York for: an unfiltered water glass of Folk.

From Memphis they headed for Woody's home in Texas. They drove Route 66, the migrant's road, the Okie trail, the road of Tom Joad in the *Grapes of Wrath*. U.S. 66 was recently paved, a high-riding trail to California. It was the road to a better life, a road of dreams. Day and night different dreams rumbled by each other on "the long concrete path across the country," as John Steinbeck called it. The car radio blared Gene Autry, Bob Wills, and Mexican stations. The gospel stations roused them Sunday mornings, after a long all-night drive. Gas money was scarce, but that made things more exciting.

"Woody, let's stop at a saloon, already. Make some change," Seeger would pester him.

"Let's drive on," said Woody, always a man to postpone necessity. "I think we still have a little cash."

And drive they did, across hilly and dust-dry Oklahoma and Texas at the tail end of the dust bowl. Hamburger stands lined the road, and wooden shacks with two gas pumps in front and living quarters above. Inside were pies on wire racks, steaming coffee urns, and corn flakes. They'd walk in yodeling and come out with cheeseburgers with all the trimmings.

ALL THIS SINGING made a musician of Seeger. From 1939 to 1941 he learned his basic musicianship from Guthrie and Lead Belly. Lead taught him bass runs for the 12-string's doubled bass notes tuned an octave apart; Lead patterned them after the piano breaks in Louisiana boogie-woogie. From him Seeger also learned the importance of rhythm. Woody taught him to play simple and straight, sometimes playing a ten-verse song with just two chords. Seeger and Guthrie differed in vocal color and tone, the qualities that distinguish two voices singing the same notes together. Woody's voice had a flat, clear resonance in it; he'd reach up and lay his voice on a note, covering it completely, and sustaining it like a kid with a newfound quarter, until he tired of it. On those sad cowboy ballads, the effect was as hypnotizing as the lonely stars. Try as he might, Seeger never duplicated it, or Woody's other mannerisms. One time, Pete tried, unsuccessfully, to tell a story to introduce a song.

"Pete," Woody said, "I can't stand it when you just keep on talking like that! Can't you cut it short sometimes?"

"Well, why don't *you* ever cut it short?" Pete asked.

"Ah, well. That's different," Woody said.

Woody knew what he was talking about; it *was* different. Seeger didn't have the same timing. Woody grew up with the country music of Oklahoma and Texas; when he opened his mouth everything just poured out: all the dust and beer halls and flop houses, everything.

"Now Pete thinks he sings Woody's way," a former singing partner said. "He professes not to believe in dynamics or effect—yet he's one of the most contrived, dramatic performers I've seen." Seeger's musical genius would prove interpretive rather than imitative: knowing when to flat a seventh or how to slow a tempo at the right moment to move an audience to sing. He eventually paid Woody back for his teaching by exposing millions to Guthrie's music. Woody was awfully rich ore, but without the miner and the mill, many would never have seen the gold.

Music was not all Guthrie taught Seeger. He absorbed Woody's healthy disinterest in commercial success, from episodes like Woody's contract with the Model Tobacco Company, which had paid him a princely two hundred dollars a week to sing on a radio show, on condition he keep his radicalism off the air. Woody decided he liked freedom better than Model Tobacco, and the two parted ways. Guthrie wasn't above commercial work, so long as it didn't disturb his lifestyle. Seeger, more of a moralist than his friend, made a credo out of noncommercialism.

TWO HUNDRED MILES east of Pampa, they put up at a flop house in Oklahoma City. Though exhausted from driving, they made up a song, the first complete tune Seeger remembers composing: "66 Highway Blues." The song eventually appeared in *Hard Hitting Songs*, with Woody's fanciful introduction: "I had part of this tune in my head, but couldn't get no front end for it. Pete fixed that up. He furnished the engine, and me the cars, and then we loaded in the words and we whistled out of the yards from New York City to Oklahoma City, and when we got there we took down our banjo and git-fiddle and chugged her off just like you see it here. She's a highroller, and easy rider, a flat wheel bouncer and a tight brake lady with a whiskey driver."

There is a highway from coast to coast,
New York to Los Angeles,
I'm goin' down that road with troubles on my mind,

I got them 66 Highway Blues. . . .
Been on this road for a mighty long time,
Ten million men like me.

You drive us from yo' town, we ramble around,
And got them 66 Highway Blues.

Sometimes I think I'll blow down a cop,
Lord, you treat me so mean,
I done lost my gal, I ain't got a dime.
I got them 66 Highway Blues. . . .

I'm gonna start me a hungry man's union,
Ain't a gonna charge no dues,
Gonna march down that road to the Wall Street walls
A singin' those 66 Highway Blues.

The next day they met Bob and Ina Wood, who told Woody, "Isn't it about time you wrote a union song for women?" By morning, he was typing away at "Union Maid." The Woods, local organizers, recruited the pair to sing at a meeting of striking oil workers.

"There were hardly 50 or 60 people present," Seeger later wrote, "but it included some women and children who evidently couldn't get babysitters. It also included some strange men who walked in and lined up along the back of the hall without sitting down. Bob Wood leaned over and said, 'I'm not sure if these guys are going to try and break up this meeting or not. It's an open meeting and we can't kick them out. See if you can get the whole crowd singing.'"

This was quite a challenge for a twenty-two-year-old on his first trip west. For centuries writers have claimed that music tames the savage instincts, but few writing this were musicians, and fewer still had to practice it before a gang of union busters.

"Woody and I got the crowd singing, and you know, those guys never did break up the meeting. We found out later they had rather intended to. Perhaps it was the presence of so many women and children that deterred them—perhaps it was the singing."

This was Seeger's first time using music to avoid violence, a lesson in the unifying power of song.

FINALLY THEY ARRIVED at Woody's home in Pampa to see his three kids and his wife, Mary, a blonde with the lean flat face of a plains woman. The pair looked so raggedy, Mary's parents almost turned them away. Mary had been taking care of their family since Woody had disappeared for New York, and she was furious. "When is Woody going to get a job and settle down?" she complained. "He can't travel forever!" After this disastrous reception, Seeger—uncomfortable in the gritty poverty of Woody's family—headed back to Oklahoma City. Woody was under pressure to stay with Mary and the kids, which he did—for a few days.

Just before departing, Seeger asked, "Woody, what kind of songs will get me some coins if I sing them?"

"Well, try 'Makes No Difference Now' or 'Be Nobody's Darling but Mine.' And a few Jimmie Rodgers blues can't go wrong." This was exactly the sort of tip Seeger needed.

"Now don't start singing right away," Woody continued. "Just keep that banjo slung on your back. You nurse a nickel beer as long as you can, sooner or later somebody's gonna say, 'Hey kid, can you play that thing?' Don't be in too big a hurry. Say, 'Well, not much.' And keep sipping your beer. Pretty soon they'll say, 'Come on, I'll give you a quarter if you'll play me a tune.' *Now* you unlimber it."

Though they rarely talked about style and presentation ("We just sang; if it came out right, it came out right"), Seeger had quietly absorbed Woody's repertoire. Guthrie himself borrowed freely, without regard for tradition or copyright. "Aw, he just stole from me," he once admitted, "but I steal from everybody. Why, I'm the biggest song stealer there ever was."

Seeger looked to Guthrie for authenticity, and Woody in every way fit the definition of the hillbilly or regional singer: His musical modes, casual performances, the way he made no concession to dynamics, everything functioned on one level—love, war, death, politics, hoboes, freight trains. In the 1920s, Woody had grown up on country music and Seeger on pop tunes, two distinct musical cultures. (When the same company had both pop and country releases, it issued them on different labels, in different areas.) From this union of Seeger and Guthrie came a new music: citybilly meets hillbilly—a blend of politics, country music, and ballads.

After returning from his first trip, in the summer of 1940, Seeger was eager to set out again, this time hitching cross-country alone. His father escorted him to the edge of Washington, DC, where he thumbed a ride carrying a small knapsack and his banjo.

"Now Peter, have you got some money with you?"

"Ah . . . no," his son said petulantly. "Father, I'd just spend it."

"Come on, take five dollars."

"No."

"Well, how much *do* you have?" Silence.

"Here's five dollars. Take it."

Peter tried to be civil, but his patience gave way. He said he had some change in his pocket and *please*, that would be enough, he'd manage on his own.

Charles was actually far more supportive of his son's collecting than he let on. Only a year before he'd published an article that could have been a blueprint for his children, "Grassroots for American Composers," where he urged them to go out and learn America's vernacular music and enrich our musical treasury.

But when Peter admitted he'd been thinking of riding the rails, Charles exploded.

"For God's sake. There's a sheriff just this side of Scottsboro, Alabama, that's retired and lives next to a cemetery. He sits on his front porch and takes potshots at the hoboes riding the rails." Enough. Pete got in a passing car and waved goodbye.

He kept right on moving, searching for the America of the songs he loved. As one folklorist described his journey, "He saw the little old sod shanty in the west, hopped the midnight special train from Sourwood Mountain to the dreary Black Hills, walked out in the streets of Laredo and beyond the Red River Valley." Out of these adventures, Seeger fashioned art.

"I still run into people who remember meeting Pete in those days," said Mike Seeger. "'Hey, I met your brother,' they tell me. 'We called him Slim, and he hopped off a freight train. He introduced himself to my husband and me, and told us that he was out trying to meet the people of the United State, the real people. So he came and stayed with us. We had lots of music, stayed up talking till late hours of the night.'"

Without Woody, however, traveling didn't turn out as smoothly as before. Preparing to jump off his first freight, banjo in one hand and knapsack in the other, he lost his balance. He didn't position his feet right, and when he landed, he knocked his breath out. Behind him there was a loud *crack!* He'd smashed the neck off his banjo. He had no money in his pocket, and no way of earning more with music.

The August days were hot, but the nights got cooler as he traveled north across the plains. Just as in the Vagabond Puppeteers, he bent over backward to travel light; instead of a sleeping bag, he slept in a floppy Salvation Army overcoat.

"Finally in Rapid City, South Dakota, I did it. I'd had to pawn my camera—worth sixteen dollars and hocked for five—to get a cheap guitar, because I'd broken my banjo. There I was, a thousand miles from home. I had to earn some money right away, so I hit the saloons. The first night I made five dollars and got the camera back with the song 'Makes No Difference Now.'

"Gene Autry had a big hit from it. A woman bartender gave me a whole silver dollar and said, 'Sing it again.' I had to sing it five times, but I got five silver dollars. I never had quite such good luck anywhere." He floated out the smoky saloon doors, deliciously satisfied with himself. The evening breezes gave relief from the August heat, and the heavy dollars jangled in his pockets. He wandered out to the edge of town, where the hay fields began: "There were piles of straw, and I just buried myself and slept like a kitten."

—

SEEGER FINALLY FOUND a train going east, landing in New York at the beginning of September 1940. Travel had toughened him, and he knew he'd never go hungry if he held on to his banjo. He came back bubbling with Americana: Folk music was patriotic. But New York City radicals, many of them Eastern European immigrants, couldn't share his enthusiasm. When a friend applied for a job as a music director in New York, radicals criticized him for being "too American" in his music, "just like Pete Seeger."

Seeger played at a few "cause parties," evenings where someone gave over their house to fund-raising, but this didn't cover the rent. He shared his problems with Lead Belly, who, despite his enormous talents, eked out a bare living in New York. While Guthrie and Seeger had traveled Route 66, Huddie had been in prison on Rikers Island on an assault charge, an embittering experience. The big city tantalized him with a recognition that was never his. He played the few dates that came his way and stuck close to home. It upset Seeger to realize that, with less experience, he could get more work than Lead Belly—because he was white and talked the "right" English.

He received an invitation to sing a few months later with Guthrie at a peace rally in Washington, DC. At this point the Communist Party—and most of Seeger's friends—had broken with Roosevelt over his refusal to support the Spanish Republic and over his preparations for war. All summer Seeger had read about the fat defense contracts given to Ford and other companies; tanks rolled off Detroit's assembly lines. Seeger had never been enthusiastic about fighting, even in Spain. Now, like many Communist radicals in 1940, he opposed Hitler but denounced the war as "imperialist," a ploy to get Nazis to fight the Soviet Union. Though it was easy to imagine Winston Churchill gloating over a Hitler-Stalin confrontation, overlooking Hitler's crimes was not easy. Seeger focused on the evils of war, though this no more allowed him to escape the nation's war fever than it had his father at Berkeley, before World War I. An unpleasant, irrational violence moved through the land.

SEEGER'S APPETITE FOR TRAVEL approached gluttony. In October 1940, he took off again to visit Alabama. He was all legs in those days, full of Yankee stiffness and working-class affectations, such as refusing to wash. "I was worried about my beds, he was so dirty," recalled his host, Mrs. Joe Gelders. To get him to clean up, the family had to promise washing would help the purplish-red acne that persisted in patches on his face.

He tried to lose his Yankee ways. On arriving in Birmingham, he had walked into a department store and bought a set of overalls. He envied Woody's ability to fade into a working-class bar; the only way he could be accepted by a southern railway worker was to play the banjo. He worked this for all he could, walking up to a farmhouse on a hot day, his banjo on one shoulder, and asking for some water. "Say, can you really play that thing?" the farmer invariably asked. "Well, I try," Seeger would answer and play a few tunes.

He kept a journalistic distance from his experiences; the *Southern News Almanac* published his first article in a paper not his own, about visiting a family of musicians in rural Alabama.

"An old man came to the door. 'Yes, I'm Mr. Smith. . . . Hey Bill. There's a young feller here to see you!' This was all the introduction I had. We became acquainted right off when he saw I was carrying a banjo. 'Well, what do you say, we'll rattle off a tune together.' So the instruments came down off the walls, and out of the dresser drawers.

"Well, you can have your Radio City Music Hall, your Hotel Savoy, your Hollywood Klieg lights, and your tuxedos, but as far as I'm concerned some of the best music I ever heard came out of that old shack in Townley, Alabama. We played all that evening, and the next day went the rounds of the neighbors, swapping songs, and me getting acquainted.

"But before I go on, I want to give you a picture of this place. The coal mine which used to support everybody at Townley closed down several years ago, and since then half the town has moved away. . . . Stores closed down, grass coming through the sidewalks, houses falling into disrepair, and a general gray color to everything. . . .

"[The next morning] I was watching the design made by a hundred glowing cracks in the top of the ancient stove. Joe mixed some biscuits. . . . We hear a train whistle down the tracks that run straight through town. 'There's your train callin' you!' I gobbled down my breakfast, grabbed up my banjo and my hat.

"'See you next Wednesday!' I shouted at the door, and lit out in the early morning darkness, just in time to catch the blinds of the fast passenger express as she started to roar down the tracks to Birmingham."

Seeger was reading Lincoln Steffens's letters, and these inspired a columnist's eye for local color. But longer pieces didn't hold his attention. He was adopting Guthrie's view: "There is something too slow and too plowy and ploddy for me to spend my time at fooling around with long novels. . . . I've never heard nobody yet get a whole room full of friends and enemies both to sing and to ring the plaster down singing out a novel."

Coming back to the city in November 1940, Seeger looked and sang country. Rural values (and music) inspired him as Seton's tribal communism once had: Here were honest ideals, far from city slickness, unspoiled by commerce. Seeger's association of folk music and antimaterialism may have come from mistaken notions of country living, but he nonetheless made it his life. He was becoming a Greenwich Village character, traipsing down Broadway in overalls and bending his friends' ears with tales of life Down South.

Soon after his return to New York, someone who knew about *Hard Hitting Songs*—probably Peter Hawes—told him that a fellow named Lee Hays was also putting out a collection of labor songs. "No sense having the books repeat," said Seeger, arranging a meeting. Hays turned out to be a down-home Falstaff, and they spent a pleasant evening together, trading tunes. "How about teaming up?" Lee suggested. "I know some songs, and you know that banjo." Seeger immediately liked the tall, heavy-set fellow. He'd gone from an itinerant preacher's son to a cook and song leader at a radical labor school, Commonwealth College, in Arkansas. As a result of postsurgery complications, he'd gained a lot of weight. At 6 feet 3 inches, his pearlike frame comically contrasted with Seeger's, a sort of Laurel and Hardy of the musical Left. Later on, Hays would become his closest friend and lyricist, and his biggest problem. Seeger couldn't resist his wry way of telling a story. In a bar, Lee could engross his listeners so thoroughly they didn't realize he'd drunk half their whiskey in the telling.

"We had a cow at home used to get drunk," he would say. "Find her way over to these mash barrels a neighbor had, and she'd get so drunk she couldn't come home by herself. We'd have to get about two dozen neighbors to carry her home on a barn door. If you ever saw a cow with a hangover, it's a pitiful sight. Poor thing had a sad end. One day she commenced to give milk bourbon punches, and we milked her to death."

Hays grew up religious but irreverent, "a renegade expatriate southerner," as one of his biographers put it. He had two assets: a deep, loud voice and a profound knowledge of the southern songs Seeger had heard at the Library and in his recent travels.

The partnership percolated while Seeger considered other possibilities, among them jobs Alan Lomax might find him on radio, playing banjo. It would be a small but important break. In the days before TV, a coast-to-coast radio appearance was unsurpassed exposure. Plenty of professionals had waited years for just such an opportunity. Unfortunately, Seeger wasn't ready for the major leagues.

"I couldn't sing with the banjo; I had to either play the banjo or sing, but couldn't do both." Alan knew this as well as anyone. When Seeger returned, Alan had asked, "What have you learned?" Seeger showed him a few things on the banjo.

"Well, you haven't learned much on the banjo," Lomax replied with characteristic bluntness. But then he heard Seeger sing and complimented his voice.

Yet CBS balked. They weren't convinced Seeger could make it as a pro. "In those days, radio was all live," Alan's sister Bess pointed out. "They'd point at you and say 'Now' and you had to perform instantly." On the other hand, Seeger was one of the few people in New York who could play old-time banjo. Alan and Nick Ray, the show's director, prevailed. Seeger just didn't have the skills, however, and he was let go after a few sessions.

He didn't let this become a setback. He saw more clearly than ever the connection between music and society that had eluded his father in Pinehurst. His notebooks were stuffed with song ideas and snatches of tunes written in his thin, elegant hand. He and Lee started rehearsing. This time there wouldn't be any problem about Seeger stepping in front of the stage; travel had made him audience-wise. He'd even helped stop a near-riot in Oklahoma with his singing.

In December 1940 Hays and Seeger sang at the Jade Mountain Restaurant in New York City, their first booking. Seeger gave Lee the five-dollar fee: "You need it more than I do." Soon Lee's roommate, Millard Lampell, started coming along. The trio kidded around a lot, but Seeger was serious. Having traded his woodsy ideals for the life of a city radical, he was tired of drifting. Seeger tied his ambition to causes larger than himself; he meant to Change the World, as Mike Gold called his column. Two months later the group had a repertoire and a name, the Almanac Singers.

Chapter 5

TALKING UNION

ONE HOT, MUGGY EVENING IN LATE MAY 1941, NEW YORKERS crowded the stoops of brownstones. Inside Madison Square Garden, Pete Seeger and the Almanac Singers tuned up backstage. At this, their first big rally, twenty thousand striking Transport Workers Union members waited impatiently for the performers. Over the echoing conversations, the Almanacs could barely hear themselves tune.

They made a strange-looking ensemble. Instead of wearing tuxedos, the Almanacs had come from Greenwich Village in their street clothes. Pete Seeger was twenty-two, and the others weren't much older. After eight years of playing banjo, he'd begun to resemble his instrument: long and straight-necked, with a topknot of hair. Lee Hays, a burly, joke-cracking southerner, sang bass, and Pete Hawes, a radical with a taste for breeding horses, added a tenor. Mill Lampell stood out in a clean shirt and suit jacket, an athletic, all-American sort. None of them knew what to expect. The striking subway workers had brought their families, and the kids squirmed in the heat, fanning themselves with the programs. The crowd looked awfully big, and union chief Mike Quill underestimated the controversy of the Almanacs' songs.

Two weeks before, Seeger had been attacked while singing at a party in Greenwich Village. He'd been finishing up an antiwar song poking fun at Winston Churchill when "a drunk guy came up, and WHAM, the next thing I know, he'd socked me right in the eye. Banged my head right against the mantelpiece. His friends pulled him away, and he said, 'I like Churchill!'" The assault only made Seeger more outspokenly antiwar; he hated to be told what to sing.

A drunk was one matter, and an audience the size of tonight's was quite another; a run-in here could lead to more than a black eye. The group walked on stage nervously, to mild applause and snickers at their casual dress. Seeger took a long breath and started "Talking Union":

If you want higher wages let me tell you what to do;
You got to talk to the workers in the shop with you;
You got to build you a union, got to make it strong;
But if you all stick together, boys, it won't be long
You get shorter hours, better working conditions.
Vacations with pay, take the kids to the seashore.

The crowd perked up. No one had ever sung them a song about *unions.*

'Course the boss may persuade some poor damn fool
To go to your meeting and act like a stool;
But you can always tell a stool, though, that's a fact,
He's got a rotten streak a-running down his back;
He doesn't have to stool—he'll make a good living—
On what he takes out of blind men's cups.

The audience laughed and hooted; Seeger grew more intense.

Suppose they're working you so hard it's just outrageous,
And they're paying you all starvation wages,
You go to the boss, and the boss will yell,
"Before I raise your pay I'd see you all in hell."

Well, he's puffing a big cigar and feeling mighty slick
'Cause he thinks he's got your union licked.
He looks out the window, and what does he see
But a thousand pickets, and they all agree
He's a bastard—unfair—slavedriver—
Bet he beats his wife.

The audience roared in appreciation. Only a year before, Seeger had left the stage in defeat; now, after his cross-country travels, he received an ovation. The Almanacs had done a good job for "the only group that rehearses on stage," as Woody called them. They didn't want all-expenses-paid trips to Hollywood; union rallies were what they craved. They opposed war and promoted unions the way early Christians believed in the Church.

Next they did a song from their new antiwar album, *Songs for John Doe,* a number that often shocked audiences by ridiculing the president (to the tune of "Jesse James"):

Oh, Franklin Roosevelt told the people how he felt.
We damned near believed what he said.
He said, "I hate war and so does Eleanor, but
We won't be safe 'till everybody's dead."

The Almanacs weren't entirely alone in these opinions. The audience was of an age to remember relatives killed or wounded in World War I. Yet by 1941, most Americans supported sending troops to fight in Europe. Of those opposed, many were Communists who'd been denouncing war since the 1939 Hitler-Stalin pact. The Almanacs boosted this antiwar campaign with songs so militant their record company, Keynote, refused to stamp its name on the discs.

At the Garden, their union songs brought the loudest applause. The Almanacs swayed enough of the audience that when Mill

Lampell approached Quill and Saul Mills of the N.Y. Congress of Industrial Organizations, they agreed to help them set up a national tour of CIO unions, a royal invitation.

THE GROUP HAD not been together six months when all this happened. Mill and Lee had recently moved from a small dark room in Chelsea to a forty-five-foot loft on Twelfth Street and Fourth Avenue, within spitting distance of the Bowery. They were an odd but vital combination: Lee Hays brought southern hymns, an understated, country wit, and his religious-organizing background. Following the example of radical minister Claude Williams of Commonwealth College, he'd started adapting traditional lyrics to union songs. As a roommate, Lee could be grumbly and tended to pit people against each other; Seeger, eager to learn song leading from him, made allowances.

Mill Lampell came from a liberal Jewish family in New Jersey; short, quick-witted, and dapper, he was a radical Joe College. Mill was also a born operator, hustling publicity and engagements for the group. The Almanacs teased him about his fondness for dress-up clothes, but they appreciated his remarkable ability to improvise verses, sometimes producing a whole song in minutes. Women were often on his mind, and it may have been he who introduced Pete to Ellen Moskowitz. Pete and Mill would double-date, and at the end of the evening, Pete would hem and haw out on the stoop with Ellen, while Mill and his date casually marched up the stairs and into bed.

Pete Hawes grew up in Massachusetts, a baritone who loved sea chanteys and political theory. He had inherited money from one of the Boston Houghtons and enjoyed discussing the proletarian dictatorship out on a sundeck with a tall drink in hand. His contradictions were no less pronounced than those of Bess Lomax, Alan's sister and daughter of the renowned folk song collector and banker, John Lomax. Bess was a proper, auburn-haired Texan who took weekends off from Bryn Mawr to partake of New York's fringe Left. She had an infectious, throaty laugh and a sparkly quality, like a woman in love.

"My contribution was trying to hold things together. . . . I was always trying to find common ground, whether it was music or food or politics," he later recalled.

Pete Seeger was the disciplined musician of the group, the central element that the others needed to function. "When Woody and I were together," Lee said, "nothing much happened; we drank wine and talked a lot, had a great time, but no sparks flew."

Everybody pitched in to fix up the loft. They added an extra-high sink so their long-armed banjoist could do the dishes. A friendly carpenter built them a fourteen-foot picnic table with benches. Soon, hungry musicians were dropping in for dinners from a stew pot long on potatoes but short on beef. They held Sunday afternoon rent parties, which packed in a hundred people at thirty-five cents a head, and their peace songs got them so many write-ups in the *Worker* that other left-wing musicians grumbled. The group's specialty was improvising verses to old tunes, which was how they wrote "Talking Union." One afternoon Mill and Lee were tossing around verses to a traditional talking blues.

If you want to get to heaven, let me tell you what to do
You got to grease your feet with mutton stew
Slide out of the Devil's hands
Ease on into the Promised Land.

In an hour, they had two-thirds of "Talking Union" worked out. Finding a positive ending stumped them. That task fell to Seeger, who worked it out on the roof in his undershirt, with his banjo and a bottle of pop. He came up with a moral, something he was always good at: "Take it easy, but take it."

In time, "Talking Union" was itself parodied by anti-Communist musicians on the Left as "Talking Management Blues":

If you want higher profits let me tell you what to do,
You got to talk to the people who work for you,
Got to bust up the unions. They're much too strong,
Fire anybody who dares belong!
Get rid of the agitators,
Hire friendly people
Willing to work for an honest wage.

Seeger had his hands full before the CIO tour. The group had agreed to provide their own transportation, but they had no car, nor money to buy one. With the help of Henrietta Yurchenko, Seeger arranged to record an album of cowboy songs and one of sea chanteys for a small, jazz-oriented label, General Records. With the $250 from the session, Mill bought a roomy 1929 Buick and enough gas to get to their first booking. Seeger and Lampell charged around writing letters and polishing songs. Seeger would schedule early-morning house meetings, which the others slept through.

His zeal for unions was near religious, and many of the Almanacs tunes had a gospel flavor, appropriate to an era when labor organizing had the evangelical fervor of born-again Christians in the 1990s. The thirties and forties, when unions became Seeger's obsession, were some of American labor's finest hours. Talented and bright radicals went broke organizing the CIO, but they got results: Henry Ford negotiated with a labor union for the first time; every week another major factory got CIOrganized. Riding this wave, the Almanacs hoped to be the songleaders of American labor.

Seeger had come a long way since 1938, when the Harvard Jazz Band had turned him down for not reading notes fast enough. "Pete was absolutely absorbed in his banjo," Mill Lampell remembered.

"He would get up in the morning, and before he'd eat or anything, he'd reach for the banjo and begin to play, sitting on his bed in his underwear." He also practiced the guitar, and when there was no one else to play with, the recorder. "Even at that early age, there was a charisma about Pete Seeger," a journalist commented. "The feeling was: Here's a young guy who's not just singing for everybody, he's singing especially for *us*." Audiences trusted him. At twenty-one, he'd already had a record out, and its title song, "The Ballad of John Doe," was his solo. "Back then, Pete had enormous energy," Mill continued. "He wasn't the greatest banjo player, he didn't have the greatest voice, but there was something catchy about him. . . . It was a time when the left wing was very romantic about America; in literature, these were the days of Carl Sandburg, Archibald MacLeish, and Stephen Benet. Then suddenly it was as if the *music* of America had arrived," carried on the shimmering strings of a young Yankee banjoist.

Pete Seeger was "the original of the fresh, untempered youth who . . . projects out of his heart the adventure by which he'll season himself . . . or court the self that, if he's worthy, will accept him," wrote one psychodynamically oriented folklorist.

"Pete was superb with that banjo," added Earl Robinson. "I saw then what came out later: Pete would stand up in front of an audience and really get them going, and in the enthusiasm of the moment, he'd tear off about twelve seconds of totally brilliant cadenza-type banjo; music that would stand up on any concert stage. Then he'd pull back and say, 'Well, let's all sing a song, shall we?' He didn't want to act 'long-hair,' didn't want to be taken for a classical musician."

Seeger stood out from the group, a situation the Almanacs hadn't expected and resisted as best they could. Inspired by the Anonymous movement in Paris, in which artists didn't sign their works, they copyrighted their songs collectively and took turns singing lead. The Almanacs even refused to list their names on album covers. Despite these efforts, newspaper writers spotlighted Seeger's "technically brilliant, haunting solos." *Time* noticed his "bitter sincerity": "Lanky Pete Bowers [a name Seeger took to protect his father's government job] talks union with plenty of persuasion."

Yet as a profession, songwriting was on the rise; technological advances in record production had lessened the music industry's dependence on sheet sales; and while formulaic, Tin Pan Alley–style songwriting still dominated the industry (20th Century Fox alone employed twenty-five songwriters for its films). Records had become less expensive to produce, thus opening opportunities for independent songwriters. "Anyone could write a popular song," said Irving Caesar (who, with George Gershwin, wrote "Swanee"). "That's no great shakes. But to be able to write a song any time of day and night, that's what a pro had to be able to do. I wrote my songs *any* time, on a bet."

In reworking folk songs, the Almanacs involved themselves in a different process. They put their lives and politics into songs. Sometimes it cost them jobs, sometimes their reputations.

A COUPLE OF WEEKS before their scheduled departure, on a warm Sunday afternoon, June 22, 1941, the Almanacs were holding a rent party. As usual, the crowd clapped and sang, dropping nickels in the can for cups of coffee. All of a sudden Alan Sloane, a friend of Mill's, burst into the room. "The Nazis have invaded Russia," he said, and the singing stopped dead. For a moment there was silence, as people tried to imagine what would happen next. Then everybody started arguing. For two years the Communist Left had followed Russia's lead in opposing the war. Now, partisans of the Soviet Union were cut adrift, hesitant either to go to war or to desert Russia. How could the Almanacs go on singing peace songs while the Soviet Union fought for its life? Maybe they'd have to give up their tour.

Skilled as the Almanacs were at rewrites, history had changed faster than their songs. Political singers have always been the pinch hitters of the musical world, able to field a political position on short notice. But the Almanacs lacked the true politician's facility for changing overnight, and the group soon found themselves in trouble with their radical colleagues, particularly with the Socialists and Trotskyists, who gloated over the Party's ill fortune. Even friends such as Dorothy Millstone, progressive journalist for the *New York Post*, grew uneasy. "After hearing that Russia had been invaded, I hung up the phone, and the first thing I did was break my Almanac records."

Two years before, when the Hitler-Stalin pact had been signed, Seeger had been touring New York State with the Vagabond Puppeteers. He'd had a hard time believing his ears. There was no *Daily Worker* for guidance, and he'd been shocked that the Nazis and the only Socialist nation on earth should suddenly become allies. The Jewish members of the troupe were horrified. In the city, other Party members had had a similar reaction. "There were those who said, 'Well, what're you going to say about this one,'" reported Alvah Bessie. "There were those who claimed to know immediately what it meant and were sounding off. But they didn't sound too convincing. Then there was the cautious voice which said, 'We haven't got all the facts. Let's wait and see. I'm willing to give the Soviet Union the benefit of the doubt.'

"At that point one guy got up and said, 'Well, I'm *not*! You can explain it all you want, but no matter how you slice it, it's still baloney!'"

Seeger had been in the wait-and-see camp. On his return, he had heard the Party's side: that the West hoped Hitler would attack Russia, but Stalin had outfoxed them and bought time for defense.

"I scratched my head in wonder. Was this the guy who'd in 1920 said 'We must strangle the Bolshevik infant in its cradle?'

"'Yes, Pete,' people told me. Churchill has changed his mind. He's no longer trying to persuade Hitler to attack the Soviet Union."

Seeger was both antifascist and antiwar.

He didn't know whether to believe his own gut reaction or the *Daily Worker*. Opposing the pact would have cut him off from friends and jobs in New York. The Soviet Union's *Realpolitik* was hard to overlook, but Seeger had forced himself.

Now that bargain was off. The invasion of Russia put him back where he'd started, with the Soviet Union and Nazi Germany in warring camps. Only in 1941, twenty-two-year-old Seeger had a national reputation for singing "Franklin D. You Ain't Gonna Send Me across the Sea."

Underlying his political back-and-forthing was the basic truth of the Almanacs' antiwar songs: A good cause didn't make war any less horrible. Many would later criticize these flip-flops as cold-hearted, which overlooks the deep roots of both anti-Nazi and antiwar instincts in the thirties. Then, radical youth seesawed between pacifism and antifascism, first taking the antiwar Oxford Oath, then pledging to fight for Collective Security in Spain. In these contradictions Seeger was by no means alone, even if other New Yorkers his age were more interested in Joe Louis's next title fight or Joe DiMaggio's hitting streak with the Yankees. Seeger had understood both sides. Now, with Russia in the war, all he got for giving up his dreams of hermithood was a conscience that hurt like a broken tooth. Glenn Miller could play the same sweet tunes no matter what happened to the world, but Pete Seeger faced the occupational hazard of political singers: song obsolescence.

Meanwhile, war spread from country to country, and nothing, not the threats of statesmen nor pleas of the church, could stop it. Though America wasn't at war, "We aren't going to let neutrality chloroform us into inactivity," Secretary of State Cordell Hull insisted. Scientists at the National Defense Research Committee began investigating a new field: atomic energy. Said one, "I hope they never succeed in tapping atomic power; it will be a hell of a thing for civilization."

"Woody was also continually frustrated (and amused) by the curves of history which were wiping out our repertoire," said Bess Lomax. "He really wanted to write songs that would last. To express this, he parodied a song he knew . . . and called it 'On Account of That New Situation'":

I started to sing a song
To the entire population,
But I ain't a' doing a thing tonight,
On account of this new situation.

To make matters worse, Harvard professor Carl Frederick called the Almanacs "Poison in Our System" in an article in the June 1941 *Atlantic.* "These recordings are distributed under the innocuous appeal: 'Sing out for peace.' Yet they are strictly subversive and illegal. . . . You can never handle situations of this kind by mere suppression." The words "mere suppression" had an ugly ring, but Seeger wasn't about to change what he sang to please the professor.

Whenever he tried to bring politics and music together, it was like practicing woodlore in the city. He wanted to sing on the right side, but this kept changing; the problem with topical songs is *keeping* them topical. Seeger grew more adept at this in later years, but now he struggled with the contradictions.

IN THE BEST of times, communal living can be tense; among impoverished musicians trying to agree on politics, blowouts were inevitable. Lee claimed he had bronchitis, undiagnosed because no one had money for a doctor; the Almanacs accused him of "malingering" and "divisionist tendencies." Once, as the group left for a booking, Lee said he was too sick to sing and draped himself over a couch, one hand falling dramatically over the edge. Seeger reached into his back pocket and pulled out his trusty recorder. He played "Taps," and everyone howled with laughter, except Lee. Hays's "sicknesses" came so often, the others asked Seeger to expel him from the Almanacs in October 1941, replacing him locally with Arthur Stern.

With Russia attacked and half their repertoire "inappropriate," everyday strains burst out. Hardly a day used to go by without a new song, but the group grew unproductive, dissipating energy in political debate rather than music. A day before their tour began, Seeger shepherded everyone over to record again for General, whose advance they'd already spent. Fortunately, Woody Guthrie breezed into town just in time for the recordings, half-shaved and road-weary from a month writing songs for the Bonneville Power Administration. Asked if he wanted to record and tour in the west, he scratched his chin and said, "Well, I just *came* from there . . . but I don't guess I mind if I join up with you."

These were one of the few sessions Seeger recorded with Guthrie. In *The Soil and the Sea* (originally two sets of 78s titled *Sod Buster Ballads* and *Deep Sea Shanties*), Guthrie's tastes for simple accompaniment went to extremes, but his voice made up for it, rolling out in eerily sustained waves, half drone, half wail. Seeger studied his friend's vocal control and phrasing, how he reached up and laid his voice on a note, covering it completely. Seeger had none of this self-possession. His voice cracked nervously on the first phrases, but at least he could now sing and play banjo together. And where his voice hadn't quite knit, he knew how to cover himself with his instrument.

On July 3, having agreed to perform only folk and union songs on the trip, the Almanacs left New York on tour. Illness plagued them from the beginning. Pete Hawes contracted pneumonia as they were leaving, and they'd gotten only as far as Philadelphia when he quit. Some CIO officials greeted them with open arms, but others were unfriendly or downright hostile, treating the Almanacs more like cheerleaders than consciousness-raisers. The young radicals looked to unions as a golden stairway to decent pay and safe housing conditions, and they never understood why they had to battle union leaders for the privilege of singing for pennies. When the Almanacs reached San Francisco, having sung for radical groups and striking CIO locals in Detroit, Chicago, Milwaukee, and Denver, they had their grand finale, which Seeger later described: "When we walked down the aisle of a room where one thousand local members of the [San Francisco] longshoremen's union were meeting, we could see some of them turning around in surprise and even disapproval. 'What the hell is a bunch of hillbilly singers coming in here for? We got work to do.'

"But when we finished singing 'The Ballad of Harry Bridges' for them, their applause was deafening. Standing ovation. We walked down the same aisle on our way out and they slapped Woody on the back so hard they nearly knocked him over."

Seeger didn't know it, but among those pounding Woody was an FBI operative. He didn't enjoy the show. In his report, he characterized the Almanacs as "extremely untidy, ragged, and dirty in appearance." Their song-leading technique couldn't fool the FBI. "After going through the song once, the majority of the audience joined in the singing," noted the informant. "They joined in not from their own desire, but were led into it through mass psychology and apathy toward the utter control of the meeting by Communist officers and members." FBI headquarters took particular exception to one line in "The Ballad of Harry Bridges": "The FBI is worried, the bosses they are scared." Undaunted by such criticism, Washington sent out three communiqués warning field offices to watch out for any Almanac singers in their midst. From this point on, Seeger's singing held great interest for intelligence agencies. Each time the *Daily Worker* mentioned his name in an ad, the clipping found its way into a growing file eventually turned over to Seeger's enemies.

THE STRAINS OF TRAVELING fragmented the group. Lee Hays rode a bus home, too sick to keep up. Lampell met an old girlfriend in Los Angeles and returned separately. The Almanacs were reduced to Guthrie and Seeger, who were to make their way east via Portland, Seattle, and Butte, Montana. One host described the pair in that summer of 1941: "Pete was a slat of a lad, all Adam's apple and large trusting eyes, with sudden attacks of embarrassment that reddened his cheeks. . . . Woody was as light and wiry as one of the early planes made of sticks and canvas, and he was as light on his feet as a cat avoiding trouble."

They started their return in Portland (disappointing) and Seattle (where they attended a singing party called a "hootenanny"). Seeger did the shopping, stowed their gear in the car, and reminded Woody of their schedule for the day. Woody usually ignored him and pounded on his typewriter, when he wasn't teasing him about Ellen. Traveling together was like old times, except when they swung through Butte, Montana, where for a change Seeger knew his way around and Guthrie didn't. The Oklahoman wrote out his memories in a long, unpublished account:

> Pete Bowers and myself had just started back across the country from California to New York, singing in all kinds of places in all kinds of towns. . . .
>
> We pulled out through the hills north of Butte, and the sun was just about the middle of the afternoon, and when we got about forty or fifty miles out of town, the sun went down, and we hit the high winding mountain roads, full of all kinds of short turns and quick curves. We didn't have extra good brakes, so we didn't drive very fast. But as we drove on higher and higher up into the mountains, the weather got colder and colder, and we finally hit a big snowstorm, and the wind was blowing ninety miles an hour, pushing our old car all over the road, and the snow piled up in the highway and covered it over so we couldn't see it, because the ice got so thick it broke our wiper, and we had to stop about every mile or two and scrape and hack and dig the ice off. We couldn't see the road because it looked just like a big white herd of sheep out in front of us. So we just barely oozed along. And driving this slow, our motor first got too hot and started boiling our water out, and the steam

flew like a train engine, and we wondered what in the devil was going to happen next.

The steam froze all over the front of the car and all over the radiator, and the wind couldn't get through to cool the motor off, so it kept boiling worse and worse. The whole thing seemed crazy, because it looked like everything in the world that could go wrong was doing it.

We got to the tops of the mountains and coasted down faster, and the motor was running slower, and the whole works froze tight and solid. Like one big icebox under our hood. We had icicles a foot long all over our car, and the wiper and the lights not working, no brakes, and about 27 hundred and 50 miles to go to get back to New York.

The snow stayed with us all of the way across Montana, North Dakota, the big wheat and farming country, and on till we come to Duluth. . . . Minnesota gets awful, awful cold. I remember that it was so cold that it just seemed to pop and crackle in the air. The trees would crack and pop and it would ring out like guns, and it always sounded like the men were out there somewhere swinging their axes.

At this point, Seeger picks up the tale, providing a clear contrast between his journalistic style and Guthrie's more naturalistic one.

An organizer for the lumberjacks union asked us if we would be willing to go around and sing in some of the camps, and we said, "Sure." He was on a routine inspection tour to make sure that the union contract was being obeyed by the bosses. . . . He introduced Woody and me. We walked up to the center, sang a song. There was dead silence. We sang another song, there was still dead silence. We looked at each other and said, "Suppose we ought to sing another?" Well, we sang one more. There was still dead silence when we finished. We thanked the men for listening to us, and walked over to the side. One of the men said, "Aren't you going to sing any more, boys?" A little reluctantly we went back and sang a couple more songs, again to complete dead silence, and then we figured we better not push our luck any more and said good night.

The next morning one of the men said to us, "Boy, that music sure was wonderful. Wish you had sung a lot more, we could have listened to it all night."

Seeger and Guthrie left the ice behind as they coasted toward New York. Thrown together in a car for weeks on end, the odd couple thrashed out their differences. "I can't stand him when he's around," Seeger later told Lee Hays, "but I miss him when he's gone."

According to the woman they stayed with in Duluth, Irene Paull, "Pete was having a lot of trouble with Woody on that trip. Pete was the most patient guy in the world, but Woody! . . . If he wasn't in the mood to talk, nothing could make him do it. He'd sit, play the fiddle, and say, 'Dance.'"

"Woody kind of jarred Pete's regular way of life, made Pete feel unnerved when he was around," Lee recalled. "Woody was hard to take; he was not housebroken. If he drank too much, he was obnoxious and rude, at best an unruly child."

As a young man, Pete Seeger was drawn to his opposites: working-class heroes like Mike Gold, Lead Belly, and Guthrie. In Woody, Seeger had found a companion and a teacher, but he no longer needed him as a role model.

WHEN THE PAIR reached New York in the fall of 1941, they found the Almanacs in disarray. No one mentioned antiwar songs; they had literally changed their tune. The group had learned a lesson in politics: To survive in closed-drawn organizations like the Party, one has to read the wind (or the *Worker*). Giving up his peace songs reminded Pete of the difficulty of keeping ideals pure; looking back, the best he could say of this period was that he hadn't "stood on any false consistency."

Their first day back, Seeger had wanted to see Ellen, to whom he'd written love letters every other day for months. Mill Lampell took him off to one side and explained that in his absence, Ellen had fallen for Pete Hawes, and the couple were planning to be married. "Pete jumped up, wearing those big farmer's shoes, and took off into the night. He didn't say a word—but he was gone for hours or a day. He never told anyone where he went, either," Mill said.

At the end of September, the Almanacs gathered at a house on the New Hampshire–Vermont border, Stone Pond, which Hawes was caretaking. They were getting some sorely needed political education from the Party and deciding what to do next.

"That was when the Communist Party decided they should give us a little instruction," Seeger recalled. "'We know you're too busy to go to the average meeting—how about a weekly session?' They had a nice man come down from the Bronx. Once a week he'd say, 'What do you think of the news of the week?'"

"We'd give our interpretation. He'd say, 'Well, have you thought of this?'"

"Oh, no, we didn't think of that."

"'Well, you should. Marx pointed out the class basis of things.'"

"We met him five or ten times. Now we read the *Worker* every day."

They'd moved into a townhouse at 110 West Tenth Street and turned it into a frat house of musical revolutionaries. Woody stayed on the second floor, and the others bunked where they could. Mill took a place nearby for more privacy with his dates. Show-business people, journalists, and guitar pickers gathered for suppers, feasting on bread and salad. Music was always coming out of one room or another, and the living room was cluttered with song sheets, instruments, and debris. Bess would come downstairs for breakfast and find Woody asleep over a typewriter on the dining table, a bottle of wine at one side and sheets of manuscript scattered over the floor. She sometimes overlooked the romance of the situation as she hunted for a clean cup.

At the end of the day, Lead Belly or Earl Robinson might drift in for a late-night jam session. A pint of whiskey would go round, and everybody would sit on the floor and whoop it up, sometimes singing "John Henry" for hours as people tossed out new verses. Once in a while someone would replenish the bottle or wander into the kitchen for a snack; all they'd find was salad or bread crumbs from Lee's homemade loaves.

On nights they had bookings the group raced through what they called "the subway circuit." Around nine, they went off to their first booking (worth perhaps ten dollars for a twenty-minute set); then they rode the subway to the next one, returning home at 3 or 4 a.m., after as many as five appearances. The Almanacs learned to tune fast; if they overstayed, they lost the next booking. They were picturesque; in those days walking around with guitars and banjos was like leading a giraffe. Seeger loved the echoey subway stations; when they had some nice harmonies ringing in the station—to the surprise of their fellow riders—he would get so giddy, he would dash up the down escalator, clomping around like a kid.

To pay the ninety-five-dollar rent for their three-story house, the group held "hootenannies," named after the ones Seeger and Guthrie had attended in Seattle. On Sunday afternoons, audiences assembled in their basement; those in the know brought old coats or cardboard to sit on.

Generally, the Almanac House ran on turmoil and music, the only items the group had in excess. Theirs was the poverty of rebellious intellectuals. Nights, the group sang protest songs, such as "Jim Crow":

Lincoln set the Negroes free
Why are they still in slavery?
Jim Crow!

By day, their house was cleaned by Ethel, their black maid who earned four dollars for her twice-weekly labor.

AS THE MONTHS rolled by, an underlying frustration crept in on their work; the Almanacs weren't taken seriously—or heard—by working people. They played in an occasional union hall, but all too often Seeger and the others were cheap, midmeeting entertainment on the Party circuit, a situation as frustrating as that of a Bible-thumping revivalist unable to hold a crowd long enough to preach. The Almanacs mainly blamed this on a capitalist plot: "Bosses have hired fake songwriters . . . but the people know inwardly that these 'hits' are no part of their working, slaving, worrying." Actually, the problem went far deeper: the Almanacs assumed working-class immigrants would identify with folk songs, the way they did. Unfortunately, most city dwellers didn't know "John Henry," and even if they did, the song might have sounded "country" to those emigrating from the South. Instead of union songs, New Yorkers listened to their own ethnic music, or to the show tunes and pop hits the Almanacs scorned.

"I think we were in the wrong city," Bess said. "In New York, we sang Appalachian songs to Central European or Irish immigrants in the International Ladies' Garment Workers' and the Transport Workers Unions." The traditions mixed as smoothly as an outing of Rotarians at a roller disco.

Except for Woody, the Almanacs sang in the name of a class they didn't belong to: the People, who stubbornly preferred Harold Arlen's "Blues in the Night" or the "Chattanooga Choo-Choo" to "Talking Union." If the Almanacs had wanted to reach local audiences, maybe they should have played saxophones or zithers instead of guitars. But they couldn't have. They worked with folk songs because they loved them—particularly Seeger, who had become so absorbed in the banjo that even simple conversations grew difficult. He played for hours at a stretch, his back against the living room wall and his long legs jackknifed across the floor. Coming home from a night of bookings, he would play a few more tunes before bed.

Seeger began to develop his signature style: using the banjo to punctuate lyrics by adding a strum off the beat, or by varying soft and loud strokes to build musical tension. He began strumming underneath his song introductions, evolving a folk *Sprechgesang* (speech-song) where introduction and song flow seamlessly into one another.

"He played three-fingered on the banjo: 'bump-ditty,' with the 'bump' the index finger, going up; the 'dit' is the middle finger and the 'ty' is the thumb going down," banjoist John Cohen said.

"The idea of plucking up on a note and then brushing down on the strings is much rarer, as it were, than the style of plucking up on a note and then brushing up on the strings with the same finger. Bascom Lamar Lunsford was just the first person Pete saw play in that way, and Pete assumed it was universal. It's still not a widespread banjo style. Commonly, it's either frailing and brushing down or brushing up when you're plucking."

"By nesting a resonant chord between two precise notes, a melody note and a chiming note on the fifth string, Seeger gentrified the more percussive frailing style," one critic wrote, "with its vigorous hammering of the forearm and its percussive rapping of the fingernail on the banjo head."

He learned from the musicians who later brought folk music to mass audiences: Burl Ives, Sonny Terry, Josh White, and others. The greatest influence was still Woody, at the time working on his vocal delivery off blues records of Blind Lemon Jefferson and T-Bone Slim. "Woody had his own little record player upstairs with about eight records he listened to absolutely continuously," Bess said. "Sitting in the kitchen you could hear him play the record, and at the end of the cut, he'd pick up the needle and move it back to the beginning. He'd play these songs maybe a hundred and fifty times, until he drove us crazy." (Woody told everybody he wanted to marry one of the Coon Creek Girls—or two, or three of them.)

There was a big difference, however, between listening to the masters and capturing their style. Compared to Jim Garland (the Kentucky labor organizer now living in New York, who wrote "I Don't Want Your Millions Mister"), Pete Seeger was out of his depth. He could sing, play, and make up songs that pleased urban audiences, but because Garland's political songs came from his experience as a coal miner, they had a solid feel; Seeger's attempts resembled furniture made of plywood with a folk veneer. He was a citybilly, destined to be a middleman between rural singers and city audiences accustomed to crooners like Bing Crosby.

The Almanacs sang mostly for members of or close kin to the Communist Party and suffered the fate of most artists in political organizations: They were either ignored or suspect. The singers themselves vacillated between trying to make workers into unionists or unionists into revolutionaries. And Party functionaries couldn't help clarify this, for cultural politics are nonquantifiable; music and drama touch emotions, rather than dogma. Thus the hard-working Almanacs found themselves judged on their support of current slogans. One time Party representatives stuffily complained because a chorus ended with the words "Jim Crow" rather than the more militant "Jim Crow must go."

Why did the Almanacs put up with this, and why did Seeger now finally join the Party itself, graduating from its youth organization? To be radical meant many things, but to many in the thirties to be committed meant joining the Party: Talk was cheap. "Can a sunrise or a revolution create a poem you don't live?" asked Seeger's friend Walter Lowenfels in a poem, "On Joining the Party."

"Fellow travelers" supported the Party but didn't join up; that was like standing outside a Students for a Democratic Society meeting in the 1960s, while the insiders targeted the next demonstration. Being approached about membership carried a feeling of being chosen, of becoming a tough, sacrificing comrade; not everyone was invited.

The pleasures of belonging brought unpleasant side effects, however, such as those interminable political discussions. Occasionally they got to discuss topics like "How to Write a Good Worker's Song," but mostly the agenda concerned the Party's new campaigns. But even forward-looking musicians needed a break from gab, and the Almanacs' meetings often degenerated into impromptu hoots as people hauled out instruments to illustrate a point.

Ideology didn't hold Seeger's interest; he had to fight a tendency to get up and stretch every half hour. "If Pete went to a lecture on Leninism, he's the type that would stop and think about it, and eventually come up with a creative observation on how the idea works for the subway system," Bess said. His fingers would find an instrument, and he'd drift off into another world, leaving the comrades discussing Earl Browder's *The Way Out*. Seeger had his own way out, and somehow it always came back to music.

"I remember driving with him one time," Bess continued, "and we went over a long section of metal grating. We hit this road and the pitch of the tires went way up. Pete started speculating on how [an engineer] could grade the surface of the road so that you could play a tune on coming into a city—the right song to put you in the right mood, with a sign that said 'Hit this at 42 miles per hour and you'll hear . . .' "

No one in the Party knew what to do with a mind like this. Partly because of his value as a fund-raiser, administrators tended to let him have his head, reminding him to look at the *Worker* when they disagreed with one of his comments. On his part, Seeger viewed the Party the way suburban mothers sometimes regard the PTA: an organization worthy of support, but not great fun—in a word, duty.

ON DECEMBER 7, 1941, Pearl Harbor was attacked, and America finally entered the war. Though a relief, the declaration of war actually worsened the Almanacs' situation; the Party soon asked unions for a no-strike pledge, and class-consciousness songs like "Talking Union" were put to pasture "for the duration." Six months before, the Almanacs had lost their peace songs, and they fell back on union songs. Now these, too, were obsolete. Prisoners of their own talent, the Almanacs discovered that their songs would not disappear. Rank-and-file unionists (and Ku Klux Klan members, bent on embarrassing the Almanacs) kept asking for "Get Thee Behind Me Satan," which equated bosses with the devil. Here was a strange profession. No sooner did they write a good song and make it popular, than they stopped singing it. Seeger might have fared better as a plumber; at least no one tore up the old pipes when it came time to begin a new line.

In their next apartment, on Sixth Avenue, Seeger felt the pressure of their situation. Few jobs came in, the rent was due, but to his frustration, no one seemed to care. Woody laughed and answered the phone "Almanac House and Barn Shelter," but Seeger didn't see the humor. Pete and Bess shared a room, a curtain demurely dividing their beds. They lived chastely, though Bess had a heavy crush on Pete: He was so all-fired innocent and cute, if scrawny. The Lomax and Seeger families wouldn't have minded if the friendship became something more; Bess was one of Ruth's favorite people. At times the singing got so loud, the landlord complained about "the continuous stamping that seems to be going on at certain times during the day or night." Bess—the only Almanac who punched a time clock—lost her job as a secretary, and finances careened toward disaster. Seeger withdrew. "The only time Pete seemed to come out of his shell was during our work meetings," said Bess. "In the middle of an argument, Pete would simply get up and walk out. He was such a rock, everyone would try to fix it up by the time he got back."

One day toward the end of December 1941, two members of the Almanacs, Gordon Friesen and Sis Cunningham, came in from a booking. As they passed the office, they found Seeger sitting at his desk with his head in his arms. "Damn it, it's terrible," he sobbed. "Nobody cares about the Almanacs anymore."

The landlord cared very much about the Almanacs. He had gone to court to evict them for nonpayment of rent. Neither the landlord nor the utility company—now threatening to shut off service—showed much compassion for down-and-out singers.

"Pete Seeger, diligent fire builder and stoker, finally had no fuel left to feed the furnace," wrote Gordon Friesen. "All efforts to keep the house heated on weekdays were abandoned; frigid temperatures took over; windows frosted; pipes froze; icicles grew like stalactites in the bathroom. The only source of heat (really quite feeble) was the gas oven in the kitchen, lit and turned up full force. Those huddled around the open stove door could hear the chattering teeth of guests fool enough to stay overnight. . . . Woody, always ready to record in song what went on around him, wrote a blues, one verse of which went:

"I went into the bathroom and I pulled upon the chain,
Polar bears on icebergs came floating down the drain,
Hey, pretty mama, I got those Arctic Circle Blues."

"We were struggling, always," Seeger said later. "We hoped to sing for lots of unions. Instead, just a few left-wing unions would have us, and masses of right-wing unions thought we were dirty Commies . . . and a whole lot of Social Democrat unions, like David Dubinsky's, didn't like us either. It wasn't like we hit bottom—we never went up!"

In January, Alan Lomax and Nick Ray warned the group to change its name; in wartime, they reasoned, the anti-Roosevelt, antiwar songs were not merely inappropriate, they were treasonous. Seeger fought the change as a sellout, convincing the group not to hide their past. Like many of Seeger's decisions of principle, this one eventually landed him in hot water. Lomax was proven right; the Almanacs' name would be a liability when they least expected it.

Seeger usually kept himself aloof from arguments, but the Almanacs' reputation and house finances preoccupied him. The group kept their communal fortune in a box on the kitchen shelf; everyone was allowed a dollar a day, on the honor system, which didn't always work. Personal conveniences were the stumbling block, for one person's necessity was another's luxury. And Seeger's spartan habits made anyone's indulgences look wanton. "Pete was at that time quite puritanical. He didn't approve of liquor, cigarettes, coffee, even sex. Woody (and Lee) loved them all," Bess laughed. "Now Pete didn't come on about this all the time, but if you drink, it costs money. He just couldn't approve." Sometimes Pete would come home and find the cupboard bare. Woody and Lee would be sitting in a corner with a pint, looking like two cats who'd pulled a chicken out of the refrigerator. Seeger would blow up. "God damn it Woody," he'd yell, "you can't buy whiskey when we need new strings." Then he would stomp from the room, calling after him, "We just don't have enough money for this stuff! And don't do it again!"

"Oh, go on, Pete," Woody and Lee would taunt him. "You don't have a hair on your chest. Why, you're just a little boy. When you grow up, you'll learn to like a drop or two."

After an exchange like that, Seeger would storm off around the corner to the Jefferson Diner where, Bess recalled, Woody had somehow convinced the owner that in his home state hamburgers came with all the free lettuce and tomatoes he could eat. Pete Seeger would sit there by himself, wolfing "Oklahomas" until a delegation came to soften him up.

Whether urging them to clean up or cut down on their drinking, Seeger was the kind of roommate whose vacations are occasionally welcome. But for his politics, he might have been at home in a church choir or a 4-H Club. Though he still shared a bedroom with Bess, apparently nothing more racy occurred than his playing banjo in his underwear. Besides, he already had a sweetheart. There was one problem: Toshi was half Japanese in an era when Japanese Americans had become the enemy within, a "yellow horde" herded off to detention camps in California. "We'll stomp their front teeth in," *Time* reported Americans saying after Pearl Harbor. When the

Tennessee Conservation Department received a request for a hunting license for six million "Japs," an official returned the application with the note "Open season on Japs, no license required."

Even the Party agreed on preventive detention for Japanese Americans. Toshi's situation grew even more tense because her father, Takashi Ohta, was not one to hide his background. An adventuresome exile from a highly respected family in Japan, Takashi had traveled the world as a soldier of fortune, fighting under Sun Yat-sen, hiking the Gobi Desert, and serving in the British Merchant Marine. He fascinated Peter; his life was the stuff of romance. If Toshi's father had been on the West Coast, he would have been rounded up and put in a camp; in New York, the FBI came and took his binoculars, camera, and bread knife. The controversy only made Toshi more desirable. The first time Seeger brought her to meet his parents, his sister Peggy rushed into the bathroom, not knowing Toshi was there: "She stood there with nothing on and her hair all the way down her back. I'd never seen anything like it. She was really exotic, beautiful."

Ruth and Charles accepted her, though Constance had her doubts. Once Seeger told one of his brothers he was thinking about getting married. "You're getting married?" his sibling reportedly said. "She's got to be either Jewish or Negro—which is she?"

"She's Japanese," he answered.

Toshi visited Almanac House regularly, and her teasing often brought the young banjo player down to earth. When he was performing in blue jeans and hiking boots, Toshi told him not to put on airs: "Look, you're not a working man, you're just pretending. Everybody sees through it."

AS WINTER THAWED, the Almanacs dug themselves out of the ideological hole where they had been since the previous June, when Russia had been invaded. Popular outrage at Japan and their own hatred for Hitler led the Almanacs to write war songs in earnest. The most successful of these was "Reuben James," the story of the ninety-five people drowned in the first American ship torpedoed in World War II. On first try, Woody had turned the passenger list into an impossibly long ballad, listing everyone who went down. Seeger doubted anyone would listen to the end. The Almanacs discussed it in a circle in the living room. Woody was adamant and ready to spend a week memorizing the verses. Finally someone asked, "What *were* their names?" and that became the chorus. This was Almanac songwriting at its best: direct, non-rhetorical, focused on people instead of statistics.

Pro-war songs filled the hit parade; the pitch was irresistible. Radio and the newspapers portrayed a country in wartime unity. Unions and manufacturers met in Washington to plan the economy. Seeger wanted to do his bit and wrote "Dear Mr. President," a singing letter to Roosevelt in "expiation for those 'John Doe' songs," according to Earl Robinson. "Dear Mr. President" was the title song of the next Almanac album, released in February 1942. The song is an artful mix of patriotism and social protest; two of the verses demonstrate how Seeger liked to think of himself:

I'm an ordinary guy, worked most of my life,
Sometime I'll settle down with my kids and wife.
I like to see a movie, or take a little drink,
And I like being free to say what I think,
Sorta runs in the family . . . my Grandpa crossed the ocean
For that same reason . . .
I never was one to try and shirk
And let the other fellow do all of the work
So when the time comes, I'll be on hand.
And I can make good use of my two hands.
Quit playing this banjo around with the boys,
And exchange it for something that makes more noise.

He sang all this in the most heartfelt voice; he was now as devoted to war songs as he had been to peace and union songs.

—

AFTER SEVEN MONTHS of heatless nights and watery soup, the Almanacs' fortunes began to rise. Gifted songwriters from the start, the Almanacs now played on the government's side, and that made all the difference. Even the most unmusical administrator at the Office of War Information understood the value of songs in building morale. When the Almanacs had sung peace songs, critics had called it propaganda; now that they sang war songs, the government styled it patriotic art. After "Reuben James," word got around that they were hot again. Their hootenannies became stylish; at the beginning of February 1942 a photographer from *Life* visited one. On February 9 the prestigious William Morris Agency offered to manage the group. The Almanacs' moment of success had come. The rift between the Party and Roosevelt closed up after the Pearl Harbor attack, and Popular Front patriotism reflowered. War bonds sold like popcorn at a Sunday matinee, and the nation wanted fighting songs.

The Almanacs did their best. One evening a delegation of firemen invited the group to learn how to put out fires in case of an air raid. Seeger insisted everyone go. The singers soon discovered how out of shape they were from their erratic diet and unusual hours. "About all they learned," wrote Gordon Friesen, "was to distinguish between the male and female couplings of a fire hose (one goes into the other, but it doesn't work vice versa)."

Fortunately, they were better at singing than firefighting. When the government needed publicity about air-raid shelters, the Almanacs worked up a song about a romance between a young couple who met in a shelter, "Taking It Easy." A few weeks later the phone rang, and the Almanacs almost lost another song. "The Civil Defense people said they didn't like the song . . . people were getting too casual about air raids—people shouldn't be taking it easy, they should get the heck into the bomb shelter," one of the Almanacs laughed. They had better results with radio. Woody, Bess, Sis Cunningham, and Seeger sang for a CBS program, *We the People*, and were promised another spot. One success led to another, until the

Almanacs were invited for an audition in the Rainbow Room, one of New York's swankest nightclubs high atop Rockefeller Center. A successful showing there could have started them on a nationwide concert tour and their own radio series. The agent at William Morris imagined the Almanacs singing headlines for fifteen minutes every day on CBS. They could be the first left-wing entertainers to reach a mass audience through electronic media, no small achievement.

The audition date was set, and one afternoon an elevator whisked the group high above Radio City, then the world's largest office complex. Only a year had passed since their Madison Square Garden appearance, but the Almanacs were far better musicians—though no better dressed.

Walking into the nightclub was dizzying. Manhattan stretched out before them, dropping away on all sides; the room resembled an enormous airplane cabin, empty except for the management. Rows of tables on pedestals spread out in a horseshoe, and matchbooks covered in glossy rainbows were displayed in a cut-crystal bowl. The opulence drove Woody wild.

"There was big drops of sweat standing on my forehead," he wrote, "and my fingers didn't feel like they was mine. I was floating in high finances, sixty-five stories above the ground, leaning my elbow on a stiff looking table cloth as white as a runaway ghost."

The Almanacs had never even seen a place like this. "We were absolutely unprepared for success of any kind," said Bess Lomax. "We were awfully young and green. The Almanacs made it on sincerity. That was part of the difference between us and the workers we tried to reach. They were poor and didn't want to be. We were poor and didn't notice it. . . . The people running the club were sharp businessmen; they thought of us as an act, and treated us as one. . . . But if we were anything, it was *not* an act."

"The man that had been our guide and got us up there in the first place," Woody continued, "walked across the rug with his nose in the air like a trained seal, grinned up at us waiting to take our tryouts, and said, 'Sssshhh. Quiet, everybody.'"

The Almanacs began singing their most popular anti-Nazi song (to the tune of "Old Joe Clark"):

Round and round Hitler's grave
Round and round we go,
We're going to lay that poor boy down
He won't get up no more.
I wish I had a bushel
I wish I had a peck
I wish I had old Hitler
With a rope around his neck.

The club owners loved it. Maybe the group lacked showmanship, one said. Another suggested the men wear overalls, and the women sunbonnets.

That did it for Guthrie. Seeger tried to steady him, using his banjo to even out the rhythm. Mill and Woody would not be calmed; they took the next song, Lead Belly's "New York City," and improvised:

At the Rainbow Room, the soup's on to boil
They're stirring the salad with Standard Oil

It's sixty stories high, they say,
A long way back to the U.S.A.

The managers thought this was hilarious—a clever part of the act. The Almanacs continued, even madder than before.

The Rainbow Room, it's mighty high
You can see John D. a-flyin' by.

The Rainbow Room is mighty fine
You can spit from there to the Texas line.

The more insulting they became, the more the owners laughed. It was a devastating experience: "I don't think Woody ever got over it. He'd finally gotten to a territory where he couldn't be outrageous enough," said Bess.

To play in nightclubs or on the radio, the Almanacs had to accept a new identity: entertainers. The owners of the Rainbow Room allowed themselves to be insulted—as long as it sold drinks—but Seeger (and the others) refused to be turned into vaudeville. Seeger left the room humiliated, suspecting, "They'd never let us sing our songs anyway." If the management had their doubts, they also saw commercial potential; they made a tentative booking, to begin in two weeks. Once started, the Almanac bandwagon was difficult to stop. The labor singers finally joined a union, Local 802 of the American Federation of Musicians, after the William Morris Agency paid their dues. Bookings arrived and the Almanacs began rehearsals for another tour and for the next big radio broadcast.

The way they got on radio is itself fascinating, involving internal changes in the music industry. Ever since the "talkies" began in the late twenties, the Hollywood film industry had dominated music publishing through the American Society of Composers, Authors and Publishers (ASCAP). When radio began making inroads on movie receipts, film companies simply doubled ASCAP's royalty rates, the fees stations paid for broadcasting music. The move backfired. On January 1, 1941, a coalition of radio stations set up their own publishing organization, Broadcast Music Incorporated (BMI). Stations began searching for previously unrecorded singers, anyone with talent and no ASCAP contract; these changes (and a bitter strike by the musicians' union) further opened up song publishing to nonprofessionals. Previously only 125 writer-composers accounted for most of the songs published and played on American radio. By 1941, when Seeger's career as a songwriter luckily began, everyone was looking for new musical talent.

On February 14, 1942, the Almanacs played for nearly thirty million listeners at the opening of a new series, Norman Corwin's

This Is War. The show was broadcast in prime time, Saturday night, on all networks from Maine to California. The Almanacs' beat-Hitler songs made a sensation. Decca Records called to propose an exclusive contract on favorable terms.

IF THE FBI had had a say in the matter, the Almanacs wouldn't have received that contract—or any other. A bit behind the times, the Bureau had just discovered *Songs for John Doe* and decided the peace songs threatened wartime mobilization. But because the albums bore only the imprint "Almanac Records," the Bureau didn't know where to turn. J. Edgar Hoover sent out a memo, eventually forwarded to a Bridgeport, Connecticut, police chief, asking if anybody knew about the Almanac gang.

On September 1, 1942, the special agent in charge of the FBI's New Haven office drove a hundred miles to a record-pressing firm in Newark and discovered the masters of *John Doe* belonged to a company long extinct. Six months later, hot on the trail of the out-of-print records, the agent drove across Connecticut and New Jersey to interrogate officials of the Radio Corporation of America (RCA), one of the most commercial record companies in the world. They'd never heard of the Almanacs. When the FBI agent asked them for a list of all the small record companies in the United States, frustrated RCA executives suggested the FBI try reading *Variety* or *Billboard*.

While the FBI hunted the Almanacs' past, reporters in New York had done their own research, which soon hit the front pages. Seeger's insistence on keeping the Almanac name turned out to be a disaster. Three days after the *This Is War* show, Seeger picked up the *New York Post* and read PEACE CHOIR CHANGES TUNE. The *World-Telegram* proclaimed: SINGERS ON NEW MORALE SHOW ALSO WARBLED FOR COMMUNISTS. The stories rehashed the *Atlantic* article "Poison in Our System," published before the Nazi attack on Russia.

The Almanacs' commercial career crumbled as suddenly as it had begun. The William Morris people dropped their negotiations for a tour. Decca canceled its record offer. Seeger made a flurry of calls and sent angry letters, but soon even he resigned himself: "We weren't willing to change, and the Rainbow Room and the others weren't willing to take us on our own terms. Besides, we were very busy singing at rallies." According to their booking calendar, however, jobs were few. Days and even weeks went by without a paid performance. Seeger still didn't care much about wages, fans, or free drinks—all the liquor he could drink wouldn't fill a medium-size tumbler. And he didn't like nightclubs; he was just as happy helping the war effort by turning in early and getting up at 6 a.m. to scavenge tires for the rubber drive.

Underneath his bravado at losing radio work, however, lay a mild concern that in time ripened into a mania: finding an audience for his music. At age twenty-two, Seeger had no family to support and a fierce antimaterialist streak that wouldn't have allowed him to enjoy fame even if it arrived without effort on his part. What mattered to him was the audience, and now that was gone.

What frustration he felt at their lost chance, he kept under wraps. In the rare instances when he let it out, Seeger had a violent temper, as one incident showed.

Once, coming back from a group retreat to plan their future, the Almanacs began to argue among themselves. "We had taken down the seat of the station wagon and Pete was lying there, stretched out. It had been a very strenuous week, and there'd been an awful lot of bickering—were we going to stop for supper now, or drive on through? This had gone on for about an hour and everybody was very tired and antsy," Bess Lomax said.

"What the Almanacs need is a manager," Pete Hawes said, ignoring Seeger's attempts to act as one.

"I'd been knocking myself out trying to do the best job I possibly could and felt that no one was appreciating it," Seeger said.

"All of a sudden there was this crash from the back," Pete Hawes continued. "Pete had put his foot through my mandolin. Smashed it completely. Nobody said a word—complete silence for the rest of the trip. When Pete breaks out, it's very scary."

—

THE ALMANACS' FALL CONTINUED. The William Morris Agency gave up on them. After the incriminating headlines, even friendly club owners hesitated to hire them. Their calendar lists bookings in Seeger's fine hand, later crossed out with equally neat strokes. Finances looked like a corporate sales chart in a bad year; at first, twelve-dollar bookings predominated, then ten-dollar ones; finally they were down to seven-fifty. The proceeds of one benefit came to twenty-eight cents. The inequality of talent within the group reemerged: Only Seeger and Guthrie had solo bookings. In February, they were about equal. By June and July, dates marked "Pete" took up half the Almanacs' bookings. As the summer of 1942 began, notations in the margin read "if possible Pete." Seeger didn't pull rank or expect everybody to do his laundry now that he brought in much of the commune's income. In fact, his responsibility increased. "Other people could miss a meeting and we would go on," Bess said. "For Pete, we had to wait."

Woody still teased him about his hairless chest, but Seeger had matured and even outgrown his mentor. On commission, Woody wrote the rousing "Boomtown Bill" for the Oil Workers' Union. "But in the studio," Seeger said, "either I pronounced the words clearer, or had more stamina for rehearsal after rehearsal. After a number of takes, Woody said, 'Pete, you better try this. I can't seem to do it.'" From this point on, Seeger rarely took second billing.

He had slowly reconstructed his personality to suit a performer's life, learning to tolerate his friends' minor vices. Yet his performances still had that sense of mission Alan Lomax had noticed. Whatever Seeger sang, he turned it into a cause. "In May 1942," wrote Gordon Friesen,

> a friend got Woody, Pete and Sis Cunningham a booking at the Waldorf-Astoria for a national conference of big business executives and managers. Pete was leaving for the army in a few weeks.

It was late in the evening when the three Almanacs began. The five hundred conventioneers were drunk, relishing the fat war contracts on the way. They were eating hurriedly, impatient for the next round of pleasure—the girls. The Almanacs sang a few anti-fascist songs but no one listened over the hub-bub. Pete's temper exploded. He grabbed the mike and said, "What are you, human beings or a bunch of pigs? Here you sit slobbering whiskey, and hollerin' for whores. Don't you care that American boys are dying tonight to save your country for you? Great God Almighty, haven't you got any shame?"

Frankly it was like shouting against the wind; a drunk millionaire at one of the front tables bawled: "Aw shut up, and play some music. How about 'She'll Be Coming 'Round the Mountain'?" Woody's guitar and Sis's accordion took up the song, and Pete cooled off by concentrating on the strings of his banjo. After a few minutes, Woody said: "Let me take the next verse."

Stepping real close to the mike so his voice filled the room, he sang to the bosses:

She'll be coming 'round the mountain when she comes,
She'll be coming 'round the mountain when she comes,
And she'll be wearing a union button,
She'll be wearing a union button,
She'll be wearing a union button when she comes.

The Almanacs picked up their instruments and walked out.

They were no longer a novelty among left-wing New York audiences. Without peace or union songs, their repertoire—in its third generation in a year—had stretched thin. The Almanacs also suffered the fate of many successful (or persistent) musical groups:

hangers-on who wanted to sit in. In an excess of democracy, the group decided anyone could be an Almanac. One admirer from the Bronx sang quite loudly, in the Polish fashion; her Bronx-Polish accent made their Appalachian songs bizarre. Then there was one of Woody's girlfriends, who knew one chord on the guitar, D. "He used to take her out on bookings," Lee remembered, "and all of a sudden everything we were playing was in the key of D—and she wasn't even playing the other chords. But every time we'd come around to the D-chord, she'd wham the hell out of it."

Another time an organization fond of Pete Seeger booked the Almanacs months in advance. On the night of the concert, the only ones free to perform were Sis Cunningham, Sonny Terry (blind and led on stage carrying a cane), and Brownie McGhee. Afterward, one of the sponsors asked Brownie in an irritated voice, "Who are the Almanacs, and how many are there?"

"Well, I don't know," Brownie answered. "We ain't counted them lately."

Seeger received his draft notice in June 1942; he wrote in his journal that he was "almost glad" to get out of the Almanacs before they fell apart. He griped about leaving Toshi, but figured he'd find a way to be with her again.

Parting was still difficult. It wasn't only friends he left, but the team that he'd hoped would reach America's working class through music. Woody was joining the Merchant Marine along with two singing buddies, Jim Longhi and Cisco Houston. Half the Almanacs were leaving New York for Detroit to work in war production.

Meanwhile, as the Almanacs said their goodbyes, the FBI stepped up its efforts to find the traitors behind *Songs for John Doe*. After the RCA interview, various field offices tried to avoid jurisdiction; the New York office lost, and the file labeled "Gramophone Records of a Seditious Nature" was reopened there. At this point, a year and a half had passed since the antiwar records had been issued. When the FBI finally walked into the office of Keynote Records, the manager baldly told them the discs were collector's items: "Things have changed since those were recorded."

Satisfied that subversion had been checked, on April 28, 1943, J. Edgar Hoover wrote the New York office to call off the chase. Hoover was irate because the three records that had started the investigation were now broken. "See to it," Hoover sternly noted, "that records are more carefully packed, in order that incidents of this type will not reoccur."

RIGHT BEFORE ENTERING the army, Seeger was playing a booking with Sis Cunningham at a summer resort near Monticello, New York. The day before, Gordon Friesen had boosted Pete's self-confidence by telling him of a conversation with Bob Miller, the Almanacs' publisher. "Gordon," Miller had said, "do you realize Pete's the second best banjo player in the country?" Gordon smiled. "Seriously," Miller continued, "there's only one better—Uncle Dave Macon of the Grand Ole Opry. And Macon's seventy-one." In Monticello, a string broke on Seeger's banjo, curling up around his shoulder. "Ooooh," the audience murmured. He smiled sweetly. "Now don't worry," he told the crowd, "I can play this thing without strings."

Four months earlier, on "Dear Mr. President," Seeger had promised to trade his banjo for something that made more noise; after basic training began, he was less sure. He planned to keep talking union, but he worried that he might not live to return or might come back "wounded, crippled or blind."

Chapter 6

UNION MAID

—

ON A HOT, STICKY DAY ALONG THE GULF COAST, PRIVATE PETE Seeger was bored. His regiment had shipped out without him, and he sat in the orderly room, picking up cigarette butts and watching the soldiers drill. The new recruits marched better than he did.

In army fatigues and crew cut, Seeger looked young. Army chow didn't agree with him, and he'd grown almost as lean as the broom he pushed around. This wasn't how he'd imagined army life. Seeger had thought he would fight fascists instead of singing about them, do a little organizing, and get the boys singing progressive tunes. Down in steamy Biloxi, Seeger found out different. Classified as a mechanic, he couldn't work as a musician.

In his first months at Keesler Field in 1942, Seeger studied the hydraulic system of the B-24, graduating second in his class. He had disappointed himself by not volunteering for combat duty, but hell, that was dangerous. Anyway, he'd be shipped out at any moment, he told himself. But week after week went by without a word. Everyone else had gone, but his orders never came through. "What happens to a dream deferred?" Langston Hughes once asked; Seeger was finding out.

Lonely for his Almanac singing partners, he began leading strangers in impromptu songfests. At dusk, in the half-hour between supper and his evening classes, he sat outside the barracks and sang. People wandered over, a new audience—one that didn't know a manifesto from a manifold. He soon had a chorus going, and he wrote the Almanacs about his method for rousing both New Yorkers and southerners with "common denominator" songs. In a postscript sideways on the page, he added fatefully: "Even though the song may not be the greatest, when the audience feels sure of themselves, then they really sing out with confidence, and it sounds swell."

Years later, he discovered why he'd never shipped out with his regiment. Toshi had written him on stationery of the Japanese-American Committee for Democracy, to which she and her father, Takashi, belonged. "The military started to investigate me and opened my mail. My outfit went on and I stayed behind, picking up cigarette butts."

"FINALLY, AFTER SIX MONTHS I decided, for all I knew, I was going to spend the entire war there. I wrote Toshi: 'Let's get married on my furlough.'" They wed the summer of 1943 in a little church in Greenwich Village. Toshi proved herself indispensable: When Pete didn't have the money for a wedding ring, she wore her grandmother's. Toshi paid the two dollars for the license. After the ceremony, they walked back to Toshi's parents' house on MacDougal Street. The Ledbetters and the Lomaxes came over, and their singing echoed up the steep brick walls in the July heat.

Toshi's parents tried to dissuade her from moving to Mississippi with her new husband. Anti-Japanese sentiment was still high, and in Mississippi, she'd be "colored" and subject to laws forbidding interracial marriages. Toshi forced the issue and told her parents she could take care of herself. "We moved our suitcase into a room off-base, put towels on the racks in the bathroom, and cooked supper." After a few delicious days, the new groom reported for duty. "Seeger!" they cried. "Where've you been? We've been looking all over for you. You're shipping out tomorrow."

"We heard later that an order had come through that no left-winger was to be near the sea coast. So I and another guy were to be sent to Amarillo, Texas. Toshi was all set to head for Texas when three days later they said, 'Seeger! You're being transferred to Fort Meade, Maryland.' I quickly called Toshi and told her not to get on the train." Seeger used his father's Washington contacts to transfer into the Special Services Division (for performers). A month later, he was stationed close to his family, and his wife had a job wrapping packages at Garfinckel's department store in Washington.

Seeger felt "far away from our old work," as he wrote Ben Botkin at the Archive of American Folk Song, hungering for news of the Almanacs. In his new Special Services unit, he found himself surrounded by show business pros unimpressed by his talent: "I wasn't looked on as a serious performer. 'It's fun sitting around the barracks singing old-time songs with Seeger,' the pros thought, 'but this isn't what makes a fast-paced show.' I was a kind of freak. I didn't perform in any of the shows: I remember being rather hurt by it.

"One time, at a party, they said 'Oh, Pete's here. Let's ask him to do a song.'" Before they could ask twice, he had his banjo out for Uncle Dave Macon's "Cumberland Mountain Bear Chase." Seeger pulled out all the stops, trilling the strings to imitate a hoot owl and a hound's bark and frailing furiously. But when he finished and looked up expectantly, "a little polite applause" was all he received. "I felt so terrible—and Toshi was there!" It was more than he could bear.

Seeger lived at full tilt. It wasn't enough to be talented; he needed an audience, a community, a cause. "Though I don't drink or smoke, I have got one helluva dissipation," he wrote Toshi, "and that is music. I can get quite drunk on it—I hope you are a patient wife." Toshi proved more than patient. Her new husband sent her a tax receipt from a recording session to hold for him. She kept that receipt and the thousands that followed.

"You want to know the difference between Seeger and some of

the guys back then?" a friend asked. "Between him and Josh White? Maybe the biggest is having Toshi Ohta behind him—for seventy years!" Eventually, she'd question that role, but for now she had only one receipt to guard for her music-drunk husband.

HE WROTE MOE ASCH of his plans to do "more Almanac work after the war." But the move to Fort Meade proved a boost: New York was just a train ride away. During 1943 and 1944 he appeared at three recording sessions: Earl Robinson's "Lonesome Train," a cantata based on the death of Abraham Lincoln; an album of songs of the Spanish Civil War (Seeger later wrote the producer worrying if he'd slandered Generalissimo Franco); and then, in March, he recorded with Guthrie and Cisco Houston, Burl Ives, Tom Glazer, and Josh White—an all-star group called the Union Boys. He recorded a talking blues aimed at the 1944 election:

It's a mighty long time since the early days
When it took a bunch of pickets to get a raise
We've built a union—stand millions strong
We taught the bosses how to get along
With the working class . . . more respectful like
Friendly conferences and mutual understanding . . .

The man who'd sung "Talking Union" now saw "friendly conferences" between bosses and the working class; perhaps he was being ironic.

While Seeger moonlighted from the army, the Federal Bureau of Investigation continued to be his most active follower. The FBI added Seeger's first mention before HUAC to their file. For the moment the FBI had nothing on Seeger except his songs, but they kept after him; they weren't done yet.

Before leaving for overseas to the Pacific Theater, in the summer of 1944, he wanted one thing in good shape: his banjo. Seeger's musical intuition kept reminding him of the instrument's limitations; he couldn't play in F sharp, and other keys required constant retuning or placing a capo so high on the neck that he lost his bass notes. He persuaded master instrument maker John D'Angelico to saw off his banjo neck and extend it three frets. The extra-long banjo eventually became Seeger's trademark. Decades later, his innovation is still used by manufacturers and musicians.

On the troop ship overseas, Seeger found, to his surprise, that he had more to offer the enlisted men than the colleagues who'd snubbed him: "I had an advantage over the pros, with their limited amount of material. A juggler had his one act. Once you'd seen it, you'd seen it. Even the clown had a limited number of jokes. But I had three hundred songs in my head. . . . The first night it was 'Down in the Valley' and 'My Little Margie' and 'Tea for Two,' my common denominator songs. . . . For two weeks, I sang every night for half an hour without repeating myself: Latin and calypso songs, blues, old pop tunes and hillbilly songs."

Seeger had his audience, and the pros marveled. Even his reputation among the men improved; previously, Seeger was known as the prude of the barracks. A musician who kept a mistress had once called his relationship "liberating"; Seeger stood up and called her a whore. This might have done for a boys' school, but not the army. He must have been the only guy in the barracks who didn't talk about sweethearts and sex. Crossing the Pacific, though, he loosened up. In a skit, he shuffled on stage with a straw hat on, carrying a jug. He upended it to whistles from the crowd and played "hillbilly" banjo.

On Saipan island in the South Pacific, Seeger felt needed. He was put in charge of hospital entertainment, with an office and a borrowed jeep. By mid-1944, he had learned the basic skills of an organizer: coordinating schedules, jollying administrators and secretaries, spending hours on the phone. He wasn't terribly proud of himself, though; the only enemy he fought was army red tape.

Watching the wounded pour in made him feel guilty; in his dreams oversize telephones rang, and huge, uniformed hands grabbed him, as he wrote Toshi: "A dozen times in the past year and a half, I have seriously thought of transferring to the infantry and losing myself in the war. . . . I have decided against it for many reasons; the first is fear of getting my head shot off. . . . I'm not proud of it, but it's true. I'm not volunteering for death—yet." He consoled himself by hard work and by experimenting with music-rehabilitation therapy: healing patients by getting them singing.

Evenings he traveled the unpaved jungle roads with the entertainers he booked: a barbershop quartet, some Frank Sinatra imitators, and a string band he played with, the Rainbow Boys. They would rumble along in a truck with broken springs, singing in officers' clubs or as a warm-up act for an open-air movie. Soldiers accustomed to the Andrews Sisters or Bing Crosby had a surprise in store when Seeger pulled out his banjo. The union songs, the barracks' songfests, the music rehabilitation—these were linked. Pete Seeger was discovering music as an elixir for the body politic.

ONE NIGHT ON WXLD, the base radio station, he attracted the attention of an old Almanac fan, Mario Cassetta, listening in the compound.

"I thought to myself, my God, this guy is right here, a few yards from me. I literally ran pell-mell to the station and peeked through the glass. I saw this skinny guy with his head up, frailing away."

Seeger and "Boots" Cassetta became fast friends. Together they commiserated about the offensively patriotic discs flooding the airwaves, jingles like "Good-bye Mama, I'm Off to Yokohama," "Little Bo Peep Has Lost Her Jeep," or the offensive "Don't Be a Sap, Mister Jap." They pulled together an informal singing group. Off in the abandoned hospital barracks, officers swapped songs with enlisted men, taking off their bars to avoid breaching army discipline:

Fuck 'em all! Fuck 'em all!
The long and the short and the tall
Fuck all the admirals in the Com So Pac
They don't give a shit if we never get back;
So we're saying good-bye to them all
As over the gangplank we crawl
There'll be no promotions
This side of the ocean
So cheer up my lads, fuck 'em all!

Or they sang about the time the enlisted men broke into the officers' beer stash (to the tune of "Who Broke the Lock"):

Who broke the lock on the forward hold?
We'll find out before we go.

Took it by the can and they took it by the case
Everybody had a smile on his face.

A first lieutenant came snooping around
And boy was he surprised at what he'd found.

Who broke the lock, the question was asked
As far as I'm concerned, they can kiss my ass.

These songs held an important lesson for Seeger, though perhaps he was slow to learn it. Propaganda becomes unnecessary when inequality is obvious; no one had to write a song, for instance, to motivate GIs to break into the officers' beer. This distinction—between songs created *by* people instead of *for* them—would prove crucial to his continuing hopes of inspiring singing in unions.

—

ON A WARM NIGHT in 1944 Seeger and his friends were having a party under the coconut palms. Boots was there, a friend named Felix Landau, and a USO singer new to Saipan, Betty Sanders. A cook bootlegged some food, the officers brought the beer, and everybody sang their lungs out in the balmy tropical air. After a while, the conversation turned to the Almanacs, and to what would happen after the war. According to Cassetta, Seeger sketched out "a loosely knit organization, some structure where people could get together to exchange and print songs. He told me, 'Boots, you could work with Earl [Robinson]! I'll do it in New York and you can do it in L.A.'"

Out of this casual beginning came a new organization, People's Songs, Inc. (PS), which would publish union songs in a national network, singing on picket lines and demonstrations. In their year and a half, the Almanacs had been great as far as they went, but labor needed a larger effort.

It was too late. Seeger overestimated labor's interest in this goal in his unquenchable enthusiasm for a movement of songs that could improve society. While Seeger sang anti-brass songs on Saipan, Greek and French partisans also sang—but few Greeks imagined defeating the enemy by songs alone. Seeger's chosen medium was only entertainment to most Americans. To him, singing helped people fight, and fighting gave them power; thus, the gift of song is a gift of power, and time and again, the social glue of community. Yet, as he would painfully discover, the chain linking song to action is not so simple or so direct.

In the nineteenth century, labor songs typically came from laborers themselves, or from nonprofessional songwriters. By the 1940s, however, the United States had more listeners and record buyers than singers, and labor audiences liked or knew few of Seeger's cherished Appalachian tunes. Though he associated the "folk" with the working class, he would have an uphill struggle convincing American workers.

There was another problem: His hopes for a singing labor movement rested on two organizations, the CIO and the Communist Party, which had gone through wartime developments that Seeger, in his isolation on Saipan, did not fully understand.

The Communist Party U.S.A. had its greatest influence and success during the thirties and forties. In these years, the CP fought for unemployment benefits, campaigned against lynching in the South, and sponsored the heroic (if unsuccessful) American participation in the Spanish Civil War. The Party had Americanized itself out of its isolation of the 1920s. At the same time as the Soviet party was becoming despotic under Stalin, its American counterpart was opening up. To be a socially conscious writer, actor, or musician in the Depression meant contact with the Party's cultural fronts, even if one disagreed with its tactics.

Back in 1937 Seeger had found a wholeness in the Young Communist League, with "the Comintern behind me." As one of Seeger's contemporaries expressed it, "Marxism was the transforming stuff, the new color, the new space, the new texture, the one that brought to the surface the life until then obscured. Do you know what that means? That's what the artist waits a lifetime for. . . . But the tool with which to shape the stuff of Marxism . . . that was the Communist Party."

Yet American Communism in 1944 was quite different from that of 1937. With nearly a hundred thousand members—56 percent of them trade unionists—the Party represented America's wartime ally, the Soviet Union. The Sunday *Worker* boasted a national circulation of a hundred thousand. Communists held rallies in Madison Square Garden, ran four political/labor schools, a publishing house, and a host of weekly, daily, and monthly publications. The price of this success was collaboration with the Party's previous enemies, such as the National Association of Manufacturers.

The same was true for the CIO. When Party leader Earl Browder announced support for a no-strike pledge for unions—which Russia needed to keep the United States fighting at its hardest—the CIO went along. Labor leaders sat down with manufacturers at the feast of war profits. In exchange for speed-ups and overtime and a salary freeze, unions built up their postwar benefits: health care, sick leave, vacations. This seemed a fair trade-off for national unity—at least in the beginning. But as war profits doubled and tripled, CP and CIO leadership in the plants was discredited; rank-and-file unionists grew disaffected with "radicals" who avoided strikes. Even singing ones.

In the summer of 1944 Seeger ill understood these changes; he expected to return and find the Left-labor alliance unchanged: "I just assumed we were all coming back with long-deferred projects, and I would dive in to pick up where we left off." Of course, Seeger had other things on his mind. He was about to be a father.

WHEN NEWS OF the birth of Peter Ohta Seeger reached Saipan in August 1944, Seeger was so proud of Toshi and "Pitou" that he gave in to tradition and passed out cigars. For Toshi, he drew an "Album of Daydreams" in cartoon form, all about his postwar hopes: a large vegetable garden, a fully equipped tool shop, instruments hanging on the wall, and "a kitchen full of good crockery." To pass the time till his return, Seeger tried his hand at ethnomusicology, like his dad, starting with the bawdy songs his group sang. Sundays, a folklorist in fatigues, he crossed the island to the security camps where Saipan's native Chamorros and Kanakas lived. They sat around trading songs; the islanders loved "You Are My Sunshine." In the barracks, people would come up and sing him their favorite tunes for the pleasure of having Seeger sing them back. He would learn from anyone: Roy Acuff tunes from the hillbillies, blues from the hipsters. He made friends through music and discovered the side effects of community singing: the trust between song leader and singers, the chesty warmth that comes from strangers resonating in harmony.

All this only made him ambitious for a larger organization than the Almanacs. "After the war," he wrote Toshi, "I want to organize a very large chorus of untrained voices."

A film biography of George Gershwin, *Rhapsody in Blue*, cut into him like a whip. Any film about a songwriter would have fascinated Seeger, but he'd admired Gershwin since learning his tunes on the ukulele at Patterson. At one point in the film, a character tells the young songwriter, "George, you can give America a voice!" This touched a hidden nerve; Seeger immediately wrote one of his most introspective letters of the war years. Feelings of inadequacy, of not getting anywhere, flooded in on him. He had never quite overcome his mother's bias in favor of classical music, and now he worried that his lack of formal musical training would keep him from ever writing "serious" music: "I used to think there was nothing in the world I couldn't do if I wanted to. I've since learned some limitations: an overlight and nervous physique and other things. . . . Now I know [my profession] won't spring from intuition and unschooled genius, but take hard study and perseverance and concentration."

"There have been so many failures," he wrote to Toshi. "You don't know. Every song I started to write and gave up was a failure. I started to paint because I failed to get a job as a journalist. I started singing and playing more because I was a failure as a painter. I went into the army as willingly as I did because I was having more and more failure musically."

At twenty-six, with four albums, a national tour, and appearances on coast-to-coast radio, Seeger felt like a failure. No worldly success could satisfy his ambitions. As William Perkins wrote in 1612, "A vocation or calling is a certain kind of life ordained and imposed on Man by God, for the common good." Seeger might not have chosen these words to characterize himself, but they're apt. He also suffered from the emotion his Puritan ancestors called humility: the modest pride that let a John Brown rouse a congregation against slavery, then weep quietly at his own unworthiness.

Humility and uprightness emerged in other ways, in what a fellow soldier called Seeger's "personal intransigence," citing one legendary incident.

One evening Seeger and his string band were driving across Saipan in a jeep. They'd just given a concert of country music for the native settlers of Saipan; the islanders had loved the show, particularly Seeger's yodeling. As they rode back to the barracks, the band talked of their lives back home, as Seeger relaxed in the warm breeze: "I was feeling proud that I'd gotten these otherwise prejudiced Southerners to change their opinions. Because originally they'd said, 'What do you want to sing for those gooks for?' I'd answered them, 'Oh, you'll like it. They're nice people.'"

It started getting dark. Nightfall made Saipan bleak and menacing; several hundred Japanese survivors still hid in caves, coming out only at night. The soldiers had been warned more than once not to stop the jeep for anything. Enemy soldiers were known to set up roadside ambushes, with one man pretending to be wounded.

They got to talking about the "jigs": "The niggers this, and the niggers that," Seeger remembered. Then the lieutenant from Texas told him, "You know, back home we have to string one up every now and then, just to keep the rest of them in line."

"You just let me out of here," Seeger said. "I can't stand this any more." He insisted on walking back to camp, across the fearsome island. The men worried that Seeger would turn them in. He didn't. He never reported the conversation (though news of it spread through camp).

A few months later he learned that his six-month-old son had died, born without a bile-duct tube. From nine thousand miles away, there was nothing he could do. He rarely mentioned the death in his letters, didn't complain, blame, or soothe his wife. All he wrote in his journal was one matter-of-fact line: "Over a month ago my and Toshi's baby died." The words that comforted him most were his father's: "Something good that has happened cannot be made to unhappen." The pain drove him toward home and his new projects: "The whole last year," he wrote the following April, "has been a bit of a nightmare. Weeks rush by with disconcerting speed and yet time drags horribly. . . . I only want to go home home home."

"WHEN PETE CAME BACK from the war," Bess Lomax recalled, "he was a very different man. He had matured physically and become a stronger singer. Now he was physically vibrant. He'd always been tense, lean, and bony, but the years of physical activity had put some weight on him. He was as hard as nails. . . . He'd worked for all kinds of audiences and come back with People's Songs in his head and the same burning intensity. He had a national idea in mind now."

In short order Pete Seeger scheduled meetings of musicians, CIO representatives, and others (including FBI informants). By the end of December, he'd collected $155 to start the new organization. He was president of People's Songs, Lee Hays vice president, and they began to edit the *People's Songs Bulletin*. In an article about their "back from the war party," Woody gently poked fun at Seeger's new seriousness: "We will print up a bulletin, a little bulletin," Toshi said, explaining Pete's dreams.

> "Not too little," Pete put in.
>
> "Anyhow, a bulletin, either by mimeograph or photo offset."
>
> "Or off the presses of the *Daily News*," Pete said again.
>
> "Well, not just overnight, anyhow." Toshi smiled, lit up a cigarette, and knocked the ashes off into an incense burner. . . . "Of course later on, we will buy out the *Daily Mirror*. . . . Me, I want to raise children for Peter to sing to sleep. But maybe I can find some sort of organizing career here working with People's Songs."
>
> "Your job is to keep me organized," I heard Pete laugh.

This she did, providing him the guidance he accepted from only one other person, his father: "Toshi played a very strong role in Pete's political education," one friend pointed out. "She was responsible for much of Pete's staunchness of approach and political direction."

In one respect, though, he needed no direction. Asked about his purpose in life in January 1946, he answered, "Make a singing labor movement. Period. . . . I was hoping to have hundreds, thousands, tens of thousands of union choruses. Just as every church has a choir, why not every union?" He assumed unions would need the same thing they had before the war: singers for picket-line duty, publicity, and building attendance at meetings.

Seeger's isolation in the South Pacific had built up a tremendous emotional charge, which now burst forth. In 1946 alone, he helped run People's Songs, Inc., edited the *Bulletin*, taught courses in radical songwriting, spoke at conferences on folklore and civil rights, made a film, composed music, and set up and performed at People's Songs hootenannies. After two months, People's Songs, Inc. boasted a thousand paid members in twenty states. The more the organization grew, the higher his hopes rose.

If the people of People's Songs wanted to hear "No Business Like Show Business," however, they'd have to find another people's songster. Seeger still associated the folk with an urban proletariat or a rustic peasantry. He was torn between his desire to sing or compose and his duty to political discipline. Playing the banjo or hiking in the woods, he'd remember the destructiveness of racism, but sitting in on a discussion on colonialism in the South's Black Belt, he sometimes wished he was home with the banjo.

To resolve his ambivalence, Seeger again turned to the Communist Party. Reports of Stalin's crimes fell on deaf ears still echoing Lincoln Steffens's report from Moscow thirty years before: "I have seen the future, and it works." "Back then, the Party held no conflicts for musicians," Seeger's friend Earl Robinson ingenuously commented: "I was following the Party line for guidance in my composition—particularly 'Communism is twentieth-century Americanism.' I had that pasted up on my piano."

This was when Woody was closest to the Party (which had become the Communist Political Association during wartime). Guthrie was reading Lenin on the Agrarian Question; he boasted he'd memorize *Das Kapital* in a week. (Already there were signs he was drifting afield; Woody proposed to Seeger that they move in together and restart the Almanacs.) Whether he ever actually joined the Party, no one seems to know.

After the war, Seeger tried to enlist the Party in his efforts, unconscious of the tensions following the recent denunciation of CP leader Earl Browder for collaborating with big business. In January 1946, a few days after PS began, Seeger met with a representative of the Party's cultural section and showered him with ideas: progressive songbooks for every union, workers making their own culture and spreading it through People's Songs. Apparently embarrassed at such an outpouring, the functionary asked Seeger to step around the corner for a cup of coffee. "It was a young guy I met, not V. J. [Jerome, unofficial cultural consultant to the Party]. He said 'Sure, fine, great idea, put us on your mailing list'—but he didn't seem to care much one way or the other."

The meeting disappointed him; he'd tried to go through the right channels, but the Party representative was more preoccupied with surviving internal power struggles than supporting a singing labor force. Seeger might well have heeded the CP's indifference; People's Songs saw itself as more than "red" entertainment, but cultural officials only nodded and tapped their toes to the music. This forced Seeger (and others of the lyrical Left) to compartmentalize their art, producing songs alternately for specific campaigns and for more lasting (and more fulfilling) ones. The Communist Party did not "use" People's Songs, because PS believed in the Party more than the Party ever believed in it. On the other hand, Party organizers felt free to criticize: Once, when Seeger played Kentucky banjo tunes alongside topical songs at a fund-raiser, a Party dignitary took him aside and said, "Pete, here in New York hardly anybody knows that kind of music. . . . If you are going to work with the workers of New York City, you should be in the jazz field. Maybe you should play the clarinet."

This cheeky comment—as if Seeger would change his repertoire because some ideologue preferred the clarinet to the banjo—had its grain of truth; New York's ethnic audiences knew jazz, Yiddish, or Slovak tunes better than Appalachian ones. Still, Seeger was a musician first, and a politician second. He continued to keep up his ties, however, and when the Party organized a "club" composed largely of PS staff, Seeger joined. His cross-country travels excused him from most responsibilities. He never had to sell the *Daily Worker*, never handed out leaflets on the street. Everyone was asked, repeatedly, to recruit new members into the Party; though Seeger started to draw up a list, he never got far. Because of his independence—and musical taste was only a part of this—Seeger had a reputation as an "unreliable"; at least one committee on "backsliders" chided him for not having the right attitude. But to make PS succeed, Pete Seeger would listen to their counsel, even when he didn't follow it. He would need all the allies he could find.

IN THE BEGINNING, there was no stopping People's Songs. Favorable publicity on the group appeared in *Time*, the *New York Times*, even *Fortune*. Circulation on the *Bulletin* rose weekly and was up to two thousand members. A wild idea: a union but not a union.

The organization seemed to float on Seeger's enthusiasm: "When a bunch of people are seen walking down the street singing, it should go almost without saying that they are a bunch of union people on their way home from a meeting," he wrote in *New Masses*, paying a debt from his boarding school nights.

No sooner had People's Songs set up offices near Times Square than the FBI opened a file on the group. All this talk of peace, unions, and racial brotherhood sounded suspicious. At first, the collection amounted to only a few flyers in a scrapbook.

The FBI notwithstanding, events in 1946 seemed to favor People's Songs: America had its greatest labor unrest since the midthirties. Two million went out on strike in January 1946; before the year ended, five million had laid down their tools. Just like old times—in the papers Seeger saw that the National Association of Manufacturers was back to denouncing labor unions. Despite fiery rhetoric on both sides, however, the worldwide expansion of U.S. commerce satisfied manufacturers, unions, and government alike. Labor settlements produced a now-familiar pattern: Union leaders got regular pay increases for their members, and employers recouped these through inflated prices, automation, and government subsidies. The last thing either unions or manufacturers wanted was labor disorder.

The decline in labor militancy had begun with the war. While Seeger had stumbled in close-order drill, the ingredients of a multinational postwar economy had been readied. The twenty million war workers would need employment after the war ended, and this many jobs, as even Earl Browder predicted, would require foreign markets for American goods. While Seeger had wandered through Saipan collecting songs, Walter Reuther was preparing an attack on leftists in the United Auto Workers, both to fend off outside pressures and to assume the power and seniority of the "reds." As Seeger shipped out for home, formerly radical unionists like Joe Curran were purging progressives from the National Maritime Union.

After the war, as PS opened shop, red-baiting in the unions increased with a vengeance. At a United Steelworkers meeting in May 1946, Philip Murray used the term "outside interference" to describe the Communist organizers who had set up his union. Six months later, after a fierce battle, the CIO passed an anti-Communist resolution. It seemed like decades since Roosevelt, Churchill, and Stalin had pledged postwar cooperation in Teheran;

since Walter Winchell had remarked that "the fear of Russia" was a "bogey"; since *Life* had devoted an entire issue to Soviet-American cooperation—but that was just four years ago. The cold war sun was rising steadily, and though early in the day, the heat had begun to build.

Then came the Taft-Hartley Act in 1947, which allowed employees to sue unions for damages from strikes and required union leaders to take loyalty oaths. Soon, President Truman extended these loyalty oaths to all federal employees.

People's Songs thus began at a dramatically inappropriate time. Its successes would be those of its founder: good musical taste, originality, and dedication. Unfortunately, its grandiose aims and its ambivalence between organizing and musicianship also characterized Seeger: a man with his mind in the clouds, his fingers on an instrument, and his head a long way from the ground.

In September 1946, the couple made the gossip column in *New Masses*: "The Pete Seegers are expecting a young folksinger." Danny Seeger was born on Labor Day. Pete and Toshi Seeger managed well together. Toshi was very smart and more savvy than her husband in organizations. She held her own in meetings of People's Songs held in their basement. Her style was to listen carefully before saying a word, then passionately leap in. The couple lived traditionally; Toshi took care of the children and filled a salad bowl the size of a horse trough for hungry guests, while Seeger came and went "like a boarder."

In the army, Seeger couldn't wait to be a father; now he put work before family life: "I felt shot through with adrenaline as I dashed around from appointment to appointment. Just think of getting so much done in a short time! . . . Poor Toshi. She stayed home changing diapers and I'd get home at 1 a.m. from one committee meeting, then be off at seven the next morning to another. It was a real case of the male supremacist organizer who expects the wife to run the house while he's changing the world."

The initial success of People's Songs kept Seeger on the run. In its second year, PS opened western and midwestern branches. Boots Cassetta and Earl Robinson played at strikes in the Hollywood studios. Members sang at a Westinghouse strike in Pittsburgh, on street corners in New York to protest the end of price controls, and in a California housing caravan. The *Bulletin* had more songs than they could print; Malvina Reynolds (who later wrote "Little Boxes") couldn't get a song in against competition like "Picket Line Priscilla":

She could make those vigilantes
Run like ants was in their panties . . .

As 1947 wore on, it was People's Songs that ran a race against time. The Party's "must" demands multiplied as its membership shrank, and Seeger noticed a hardening since his Almanac days, when meetings had flowed into hoots. Union leaders were unenthusiastic. In the beginning, People's Songs had worked not just with the CIO but with a few locals in the more conservative A.F. of L. But toward the end of 1947, even CIO education director Palmer Webber quietly severed his ties. Once Seeger traveled to Washington to ask a union official to sponsor a songbook. "Well, no," the union man hedged, "we're working on our own."

Alan Lomax (who now had a Guggenheim fellowship and a well-paying job with Decca Records) tried to round up support. Radio personality Studs Terkel sent his greetings, and a "Board of Sponsors" blossomed on the *Bulletin*'s masthead: Aaron Copland, Leonard Bernstein, John Hammond, Oscar Hammerstein II, Dorothy Parker, and Harold Rome. Though the PS staff disagreed about the value of such luminaries, no one denied the list looked impressive.

It's doubtful many of these notables wandered into the ramshackle office off Times Square. If they had, they'd have found four people crammed into one room, the People's Songs library on one side, a front desk, and a file cabinet spilling over with graphics. In one corner Wally Hille, music editor of the *Bulletin*, would transcribe songs, sitting on his desk with a guitar, a pencil stuck behind his ear. Pete Seeger spent his time on the phone, trying to convince groups to pay the musicians, for goodness' sake. Volunteers in jeans straggled in, the phone rang constantly, and the hubbub of Times Square filtered up. The office had more in common with a draft resistance center in the 1960s than a music publisher in the 1940s.

One noticeably missing from this scene was Woody; though he'd signed onto the People's Songs board, he didn't take an active role. He was writing songs and hard at work on a long novel eventually published as *Seeds of Man*. The pair were still close; Woody planned to name his next boy Pete. The first symptoms of the disease that later paralyzed Guthrie began to appear, though these were mistaken for drunkenness.

In May 1947 Irwin Silber, a short, energetic fellow with thick glasses and a commanding, nasal voice, joined People's Songs as executive secretary. Irwin ran the Party's musicians' club, and he soon made the office shape up. Unlike Seeger or Hille, Irwin was not a musician. Fresh out of Brooklyn College and the American Folksay Group of dancers, he enjoyed folk music, but organizing was his calling. Irwin had quite a reputation in the Party. Ex-comrades still flinch at his name, recalling him as "a dedicated-but-not-brilliant worker, a Jimmy Higgins type." Silber had a keen, incisive mind, always ready to leap into political arguments. Unfortunately, his pronouncements were edged by theory rather than compassion.

Some disliked his heavy-handedness. One West Coast member called him "a sectarian personality. . . . I had a lot of confidence in Pete, but after a while I got the feeling Irwin was running things." Irwin minded the store while Seeger toured, and according to Hille, a neutral party, the two argued over which songs to print. Silber favored the politically correct songs and Seeger the more musical. Silber had files for everything and he put in long hours; Seeger had the spark that drew members. For the next twenty years, their friend-adversary relationship would continue, as Irwin Silber went on to edit the folk song magazine *Sing Out!*

Silber wasn't the only one Seeger had trouble with at PS. Lee Hays joined People's Songs expecting equal billing, but times had changed; Seeger's prominence was incontestable. In fact, friends wondered if his head would swell, if he'd be the same old Pete. Lee Hays was one of the few who teased him, joking about his "arrogant modesty." Lee would sit in the office, typing out his column, and chat with whoever dropped in. He'd joke about his 250-pound frame and tell funny stories about Arkansas. After a while, old habits returned. He had a way of talking about people behind their back.

When tipsy, Hays could be genial and fascinating, but Seeger had too much at stake to let a bad situation last. He complained to Alan Lomax of Lee's "sectarian maliciousness" and apologized for an incident when Lee insulted Alan (the two had never gotten along). Seeger avoided it as long as he could, but finally he asked Lee to step down as vice president. Reflecting on how he showed Hays the door, Seeger admitted, "Occasionally Toshi reminds me of something we've gone through that's been very unpleasant, but I haven't the faintest memory of the occasion. It's as if I have some protective device inside my brain; instead of causing grief by remembering it, I simply erase it. Maybe I've got a little mental eraser that just blots things out."

An interesting and handy device. Puritans in colonial America believed in something similar, a "reprover," which kept a lookout for wayward impulses and pride. Seeger's "little eraser" let him float over office politics, trusting that the good cause would keep people working together. "Pete never liked to say no," Earl Robinson once said. "He'd much rather you didn't ask him twice."

"I feel very optimistic and confident," Seeger had written at the close of 1946, with the exuberance simultaneously his strength and flaw, "that we will keep growing for a long time to come." Not all of New York's Left was as excited. Anti-Communist radicals outside the Party would poke fun at PS and Seeger (to the tune of "The Wreck of the Old 97"):

Well, they gave him his orders
Up at Party Headquarters,
Saying, "Pete, you're way behind the times.
This is not '38, this is 1947,
And there's been a change in that old party line."
Well, it's a long, long haul
From "Greensleeves" to "Freiheit,"
And the distance is more than long,
But that wonderful outfit they call the People's Artists
Is on hand with those good old People's Songs.

Seeger brushed such jibes aside as his work took off in two directions at once: as a People's Artist and as a nightclub entertainer. He had just completed his first solo engagement at the Village Vanguard, and *Billboard* had praised him as the "trim, slim Sinatra of the folksong clan." The *New Yorker* called his singing "fresh" and "contagious." In the first years of People's Songs, Seeger could afford the exquisite luxury of holding a commercial career at bay; he turned down nightclub jobs to teach nights at the Marxist Jefferson School. It didn't disturb him to play for the same small union that could pay him no more now than it had in 1941. He wasn't worried about being "overexposed"; he did not push himself to play ever-larger halls. In his own quiet way, he had balanced a professional reputation with keeping his friends and his convictions, much as Charles had balanced university life and the IWW. Many of his friends were growing tired of living from hand to mouth and ached for a family and a house, but Seeger seemed content. He had no pressing need for money; his father could support himself, and anyway, he had no other profession to fall back on for an income. He also never seemed to age; though his peers fretted about receding hairlines, Seeger had barely gotten over his acne. In a film that year, *To Hear Your Banjo Play*, Seeger appears in a work shirt, his hair swirled back into a pompadour. He resembled a nineteen-year-old farm boy fresh from a hay ride; his front teeth stuck out, and he banged his foot so hard the stage shook.

In the postwar years, Seeger lived with Toshi's politically progressive parents. "For twenty-three years Peter had one family. Then, after the war, he adopted mine," said Toshi. The Ohtas had more in common with Pete than his own parents (Toshi's grandfather had translated Marx into Japanese). Though often summering in New York, Constance Seeger had now retired to Florida, where she gave violin lessons and hoped for Peter to establish himself as a respectable musician. The Seegers visited regularly, but Constance got on their nerves with occasional anti-Semitic or prejudiced remarks. Once they all decided to drive to the beach. In a fit of pique, Toshi turned off at the entrance marked "Colored." Constance recoiled. "Where are you going!" she asked. "Well, down here," Toshi answered, "they call me and my children colored, you know."

Relations with Charles had also attenuated, though they visited him regularly. As close as the pair had been in Peter's childhood (and considering both worked with folk music, Charles now at the Pan American Union), their distance was unexpected, perhaps triggered by Charles's growing political troubles in DC.

IN OCTOBER 1947 People's Songs held its first national gathering: in Chicago, at Hull House. Publicity began a full three months before the event.

Before the delegates could gather, however, FBI Director J. Edgar Hoover received an urgent telegram on the convention from his New York office, which had been watching the organization since March 1947, when the Bureau received an Army report on Seeger, dating back to his days at Keesler Field. The FBI followed this up with a visit, concluding, "They play folksongs . . . where the hoity-toity red intellectuals gather." In April, the Los Angeles office had sent an agent to investigate PS's West Coast operation, discovering the organization was run by one "Peter Suger." The agent chatted with Boots Cassetta, a slim, energetic man persuasive enough to sell ice cream to Alaskans. This time Boots outdid himself. Before the agent could get out the door, Boots had extracted a small contribution and thrust the *Bulletin*'s first-anniversary issue in his hand. In May, in the U.S. Army's weekly *Domestic Intelligence Summary*, the Bureau had cited People's Songs as a Communist front. On July 21, the FBI met Walter Steele, who gave himself the exotic title of chairman, National Security Committee of the American Coalition of Patriotic, Civic and Fraternal Societies. Steele's HUAC testimony—that People's Songs performed for Communist-led groups—landed verbatim in FBI files.

Unaware of this investigation, Seeger publicly spoke of opening a new international division. On the eve of the People's Songs convention, he flew into Chicago from Los Angeles, trailing success. A writer for the *Los Angeles Examiner* had somehow sensed the Seton in Seeger, describing his singing as "a refreshing excursion out of the mental and physical smog of urban life." Seeger, in a suit and tie, accepted the pretentious title of chairman of the board. Big Bill Broonzy, Earl Robinson, Woody Guthrie, Seeger, and Alan Lomax put on a bang-up hootenanny. And, to Seeger's delight, CIO locals in Chicago sent representatives. The new chairman went away thinking, "New branches will open in cities in the United States and Canada. . . . Performers will leave the big cities and head out over the countryside." Seeger didn't seem to mind that only sixty people had attended—at least one of them an FBI agent.

Despite their urgent telegram to Hoover, the FBI had decided to keep a low profile at the convention. Attending the gala hootenanny, the Bureau's informant noted the program "had a definite 'pinkish tinge'" and reported the convention was arranged "by some group of Jewish women." What the FBI lacked in accuracy they made up in bulk. In the next two years the Bureau compiled five hundred pages on People's Songs, including stolen and photocopied documents, phone calls recorded without warrants, and infiltration of PS board meetings. The FBI took People's Songs more seriously than the Communist Party did.

In its humdrum way, the Bureau was an accurate critic: Its analysts realized (more fully than Seeger did) the limits of song in producing change without a mass social movement. They understood that Seeger sang for "red intellectuals" rather than any sector of the working class. Yet the FBI concluded that PS threatened national security, for songs nourished the radical community.

THE FBI WAS NOT the only agency worried about People's Songs. In Canada, the provincial government of Quebec seized copies of the new *People's Songbook* (edited by Wally Hille), declaring the song "Joe Hill" subversive (also confiscated in the raid were Tolstoy's *War and Peace* and Whitman's *Leaves of Grass*). Seeger issued an unusually rhetorical statement: "Do you think, Mr. Duplessis [Quebec's governor], you can escape the judgment of history? Long after the warmakers are relegated to the history books . . . people's music will be sung by the free peoples of the earth."

"For People's Songs, 1948 was the year of the Progressive Party and Henry Wallace," Irwin Silber said. "Today it seems like a footnote to history, but there's no way to describe the importance attached to it by the Party and people on the Left. . . . The wartime alliance was over. There was an excitement that gripped our organization and Pete stood in the thick of it. In the beginning, we thought Wallace would get ten million votes."

Henry Wallace had been Roosevelt's secretary of agriculture and vice president (and later, Truman's secretary of commerce). He was a midwesterner known for his folksy editorials and his Pioneer Hi-Bred Corn. Passed over for renomination as vice president in 1944 because of his liberal views (and Democrats' need to appease conservative southerners), he made anti–cold war speeches a major part of his 1948 presidential bid.

Seeger could have predicted the costs of supporting the candidate. Given the Party's support, working for the campaign was both inevitable and a bad bet; nothing was surer to sever People's Songs' ties to unions. Nevertheless the cause was right, and Seeger stood with Wallace from the beginning, singing at the Philadelphia convention where he was nominated (probably the singingest one in U.S. history). Through Alan Lomax, People's Songs contracted to provide music for the Progressive Party; Boots even had a desk at Wallace headquarters. The Progressive Party so frightened President Truman and his advisers that they set out to tar Wallace's Communist allies. Two days before a Wallace rally in Yankee Stadium (where Seeger was scheduled to sing), a federal grand jury issued indictments against key leaders of the Communist Party under the Smith (Alien Registration) Act. Seeger and his friends sang that much louder:

A VISIT WITH HARRY
(to the tune of "Oh, Susannah")

I went up to the president
And this is what he said,
"This fellow Henry Wallace
Is a rantin' Rooshian Red!
We've got to jail the communists
To keep this country free,
And everyone's a communist
Who doesn't vote for me. . . ."

THE SAME MERRY-GO-ROUND

The donkey is tired and thin,
The elephant thinks he'll move in.

They yell and they fuss, but they
Ain't fooling us,
'Cause they're brothers right under the skin.

It's the same, same Merry-go-round,
Which one will you ride this year.
The donkey and elephant bob up and down
On the same Merry-go-round.

Pete Seeger and Paul Robeson were asked to tour with Wallace. Sometimes Toshi came along, bringing Mika ("more than beautiful," their new baby) in a bassinet. The campaign made a clean test of the power of song. "There were times when a song lightened the atmosphere," Seeger later reflected. "I think it probably helped prevent people from getting killed. It was a very touch-and-go proposition, that tour. A number of people thought Wallace was going to be assassinated. . . . The police allowed some of the Ku Klux Klan to get away with throwing things. Once they found out they could get away with that, then they really descended.

"I remember a courthouse in Mississippi, where an absolutely livid white southerner stood in front of me and said, 'Bet you can't sing Dixie!' I said, 'Sure I can, if you'll sing it with me.'" The Dixiecrat stood there furious, unsure whether to sing or not, while Seeger sang not one, but three verses he had learned in the army.

By the end of August, the campaign was clearly sinking. HUAC had just finished a brutal attack on the Progressive Party; Harry Dexter White, a former Wallace aide, had a heart attack and died from the strain. Most of the CIO unions had fled the campaign, leaving the CP virtually alone in its support. Then Wallace decided, against his advisers' pleas, to campaign through the South, bringing Seeger to warm up the crowds and a black woman as his secretary.

Monday morning, August 30, 1948, fifteen cars in Wallace's

contingent brought Seeger and the candidate to the textile town of Burlington, North Carolina. A grim mood hung over the entourage: The night before, a supporter had been stabbed twice by anti-Wallace crowds. A hostile throng was waiting for the caravan. It took four policemen to clear the road for the automobiles to reach the public square.

"Mr. Wallace," one of them said, "I hope you're planning to leave soon. I don't think we can handle this crowd." A Klan truck had preceded Wallace, passing out eggs and tomatoes.

The driver of the lead car, Marge Frantz, was an immediate target. The sight of blacks and whites in the same convertible (the top fortunately rolled up) sent a shock wave through the already excited crowd. A few cars back, Seeger sat guarding his banjo and guitar. The angry southerners crawled onto the hood of his car and peered down inside as it slowed to a halt. The mob started banging on the car doors, and the shell of metal must have seemed thin.

He waited coolly as the crowd pressed in, yelling obscenities and "Go back to Russia!" No one seemed to be in the mood for a sing-along. According to plan, Seeger was supposed to leave the car, wait while a mike was positioned, and lead the crowd in group singing. But when he stuck his head out, the eggs started to fly. One hit Wallace, spattering his white shirt. It was clear no mike would be set up. Seeger hurriedly introduced Henry Wallace.

"Whenever Wallace attempted to speak, he was greeted by an unfriendly roar and had no chance to make himself heard above it," historian Curtis Macdougall wrote. "He waited as an occasional egg or tomato splashed on the street near him. Then he suddenly committed an act which, in retrospect, seems comparable to putting one's head into a lion's mouth. He reached out and shook a bystander by the shoulder.

"'Are you an American?' Wallace shouted. 'Am I in America?'"

"Take your filthy hands off me," was the tense reply.

"The man was absolutely furious," Seeger remembered. "It was a very close call to a lynching—only one policeman and about a thousand angry men. Not a black person, or a woman in sight." Eventually the situation cooled, but the divide in America was not so easily healed.

Seeger and Wallace shared a vision of an America of rustic virtue, where people helped strangers and their union brothers, where black and white sang in church together and sat down to Sunday dinner afterward. In a land of honest woodsmen, confrontations like this were foreign. "Am I in America?" Wallace had to ask, waves of hatred roiling around him.

What keeps a performer cool when the audience is climbing on his car and pounding in the doors? Obstinacy, perhaps, and conviction: Seeger trusted music so much he would stand before an angry crowd and try to connect. And, incredibly enough, sometimes he pulled it off, and a thousand strangers found themselves disarmed and singing the "Star-Spangled Banner" together. Then there were the other times, when the magic failed and there wasn't even time to tune up, when no amount of banjo picking was going to stop the cold war.

SEEGER WASN'T ALONE in going all out for Wallace; People's Songs had invested heavily. For almost six weeks, the campaign became its principal activity; no one noticed how the stipend from Wallace headquarters had taken the place of members' dues.

"We knew the price we would pay," Irwin said defensively. "We were losing out with the unions. If some of our friends who saw us as a folklore outfit were unhappy, well, that was too bad." Seeger might have been irritated at Irwin's dismissive comments; he had fought both right-wingers and the Party for his right to sing folk music. On tour with Wallace, while the candidate's advisers clustered in hotel rooms writing speeches, Seeger sat in his room writing an instruction manual for the five-string banjo, the first of its kind.

He could work on it only in snatches, but he carried the manuscript with him everywhere, stuffing it into his banjo case; after an evening dodging missiles from the crowd, he would return to his hotel and polish off a few pages. The book and his campaigning represented two instincts, side by side: his need for political engagement and his belief that music itself had social-curative powers.

Downstairs in the bar, his fellow campaigners thought Seeger a queer duck. The first year he sold only a hundred copies. It didn't matter. He was proud of both, the book and his dangerous evenings with Henry Wallace.

AS THE MONTHS wore on, Seeger spent more time on Wallace's campaign than he'd expected. The singing flourished at Wallace rallies, but few unions were leading the chorus. In the end, Wallace could joke as satirist Tom Lehrer did about the Spanish Civil War: "They may have won all the battles—but we had all the good songs." When the votes were counted in November, there were long faces at People's Songs. Wallace had not only lost, he'd received barely a million votes, finishing fourth behind segregationist Strom Thurmond.

Coming back to the office, Seeger discovered what he should have known for months. While he was out on tour, PS had slipped to the edge of bankruptcy. Desperate, the group tried a go-for-broke concert, but the concert wasn't professionally organized and cost money. The office remained glum, except for one officiously cheerful fellow, Harvey Matt, who'd wandered in earlier and offered to set up a book-and-record-buying club. He already had a reputation for selling the *Worker* in record time, and everyone figured fine, let him help People's Songs. It turned out Harvey wasn't much of a businessman. He ordered huge stocks of records, which disappeared, leaving a pile of bills. In December 1948, Lee Hays finally wrote to Seeger: "The times which led the Almanacs to live and make good songs are no longer here."

When Seeger notified members of the bankruptcy, he struck an optimistic note: "We filled a great need and filled it well." The gala third-anniversary edition of the *Bulletin* shrank to four pages when the printers wouldn't extend their credit. PS ended so fast board members on the West Coast never even had a chance to vote. On March 6, 1949, the *Daily Worker* ran a special feature on PS, calling it "a lusty baby of three with a long future." On March 11, the group disbanded. One of the last songs published was "Swinging on a Scab":

A stool is an animal with long hairy ears,
He runs back with everything he knows.
He's no bargain though he can be bought,
Though he's slippery he still gets caught.
But if your bargains are like the rear end of a mule,
Go right ahead and be a stool.

Opposite this was a birthday greeting from Harvey Matt.

"Thus ended a chapter of my life," Seeger wrote, but the full realization of the failure of PS was months and years away. One thing was settled: That was the last office job he ever wanted for the rest of his life. His dreams of being a music organizer persisted, but he made an unwritten decision to leave the desk work to the Irwin Silbers—or perhaps to the Toshi Seegers—of the world. "In these years, the biggest pressure on Pete," said Silber, "was his proximity to People's Songs—we counted on him to be a full-time participant in organizational affairs." Seeger felt his contribution should be in making music. "His basis in Marxism was so sketchy I couldn't imagine Pete as a Party organizer," Silber continued. "What Pete does onstage is a marvelous act of communication, but there are very few people he can sit and communicate with—very difficult for him. There are times when you feel that the man's real life is in public life."

The ideal Seeger struggled for in People's Songs was captured in a song Woody had written on their first trip west together, "Union Maid," a hymn to women in the labor movement: "Pete and me was fagged out when we got to Oklahoma City, but not too fagged to plow up a Union Song. Pete flopped out acrost a bed, and I set over at a Writing Machine, and he could think of one line and me another'n until we woke up with a great big fifteen pound blue-eyed Union Song, I mean Union, named 'Union Maid'" (to the tune of "Redwing"):

There once was a Union Maid who never was afraid
Of goons and ginks and company finks
And deputy sheriffs who made the raids.
She went to the Union hall when a meeting it was called
And when the Legion boys came 'round she always
stood her ground.

This union maid was wise to the tricks of company spies;
She couldn't be fooled by a company stool,
She'd always organize the guys,
She'd always get her way when she struck for better pay;
She'd show her card to the national guard,
And this is what she'd say:
Oh you can't scare me
I'm sticking to the Union
I'm sticking to the Union . . .

At first, Seeger hadn't thought much of the song; the lyrics were sappy. But the chorus was good-spirited and catchy ("sticking to the union" had a percussive effect when sung quickly). When the Almanacs recorded the song, they'd wanted another verse; Mill went off for twenty minutes and came up with one feminists later criticized:

Now you gals that want to be free,
take a tip from me:
Get you a man with a union card,
and join the ladies' auxiliary
Married life ain't hard when
you got a union card
And a union man leads a happy life
when he's got a union wife.

After People's Songs folded, the song took on a bitter irony; Seeger hadn't meant to be the unions' maid, but that's what PS was reduced to, as they begged for labor audiences. The lyrics belonged to another era, when unions were more maidenly; by the late 1940s, many felt the Union Maid had developed myopia, and "company stools" looked like friends. The anti-Communist Left underscored this in a parody:

There once was a Union Maid who always was afraid
Of Socialists and Anarchists
And the games the C.P. factions played . . .
You gals who want to be free, just take a tip from me;
Don't marry a man who's a union man,
Might as well buy stock in the company.

The reason "Union Maid" and PS didn't ignite a singing labor movement was not mysterious: "When we went on the picket line to sing," commented PS's San Francisco director, "we became aware that we were looked at as entertainment. The message we were singing was being tolerated or not listened to. We were under the illusion that somehow we were educating them. We weren't educating them, because we didn't talk to them in their language. . . . Their main interest was economic." Most working folks sang together in churches or bars, not in union halls.

People's Songs had been born too late. The scheme Seeger and his friends dreamed up on Saipan *might* have worked in the Almanacs' days. Unions had different needs then: to garner publicity and to persuade members to join a labor organization for the first time. This is what the Almanacs had done. But after the war, when unions had a good foothold in the plants, picket lines largely disappeared in favor of contract bargaining—and picket-line singers vanished as well. It was a time of business unionism, as the labor movement evolved from the IWW's One Big Union for All to the AFL's "We represent our members." Industrial workers wanted refrigerators and washers, not labor conflict.

These were blue times for a song agitator. Seeger searched for an explanation, but as People's Songs faded from view, he saw only its minor failings. In an April 1949 letter to Earl Robinson about the end of People's Songs, Seeger blamed musical arrangements: "PS banked too goddamned much on soloists." In the same note, he offhandedly mentioned receiving a songbook "of the Viet-Nam rebels."

Seeger slowly reached a long-resisted conclusion: "Even unions with left-wing leadership felt they had to concentrate on pork chops to the exclusion of songbooks and choruses."

THE SIX MONTHS after Wallace's defeat and the bankruptcy of People's Songs took a toll on Seeger. "Shortly after the election, I was hired to sing at a birthday party by a wealthy person. I didn't really want to do it, but she said, 'Oh Pete, I've just been married and it's my birthday party. My husband knows I'm a great fan of yours. . . . Come sing, and show him what I mean when I talk about folk songs.'

"So I went, and her husband had a whole lot of conservative friends there. One was about as insulting as she could be to Henry Wallace. She didn't know I'd ever been a Wallace supporter. I demurred a bit, but she kept going. Finally I just lost my temper. My hand was shaking in front of me, and I threw a whole glass of Coca-Cola up and down her entire dress. I walked out of the room shaking all over. The host brought me my banjo and mailed my hat back the following week."

This violent streak burst out only in his most trying times. Seeger had lost the self-confidence that had propelled PS through its early days. Wally Hille remembered one unhappy evening at a "wingding" in Seeger's basement, where his friends had gathered. Time after time, Seeger was passed over as the crowd called for "Huddie" and "We want Huddie" (Lead Belly). Finally, Seeger stood up and looked around. Competition hung awkwardly in the air. "I guess you don't need me around here," he told the gathering and huffed upstairs, two steps at a time. By the time Toshi had calmed him down, the party had ended. There's nothing harder for an idealist than losing his vision. Take away his livelihood, and he takes up art. But take away his dreams, and you have his heart.

SEEGER'S ENTHUSIASM FOR New York City had died: "By 1949, I could see the disadvantages of city life. My health wasn't any good. I got no exercise except by running up and down stairs. Each day was a list of phone calls a foot long. We had a pay phone in our house and I did a sneaky trick of pinching two needles together to avoid paying the nickel for the call. . . . In those days, I didn't quibble about stealing money from Bell Telephone."

In a few months, he would turn thirty. He had two young children and no job. He would have to start over, with a strike against him: his red reputation. Seeger couldn't live off Toshi's parents forever; they had little. He wanted to figure out what to do with his life, but all he managed was to get by, teaching music at private schools and taking any booking that came in. (One of the strangest of these was on April 13, 1949, at the Thursday Evening Club, where Seeger sang to a group of executives, including the forty-one-year-old Nelson Rockefeller.)

The year 1949, when much of the Left stopped whistling in the dark and ran for cover, was a poor time to begin again. Casting about for work, he considered folklore; after all, Alan had made a good living at it. Seeger wrote the Library of Congress proposing they film his banjo techniques in slow motion for the Archive of American Folk Song. Unbeknown to Seeger, Duncan Emrich (then head of the Archive) was collaborating with the FBI; as soon as People's Songs ended, he offered the Bureau his file of complimentary copies of the *Bulletin*. He told the FBI of his alarm "at the efforts of Communists and Communist sympathizers to infiltrate and gain control of Folksinging." Emrich worried that these singers "might be unpatriotic"; he eventually wrote Seeger "regretting" that he had no resources to spare.

Everywhere he turned, Seeger found barriers that hindered his singing. It wasn't until the afternoon of his first commercial television job, a children's program, that he realized the price of working for People's Songs and the Wallace campaign: "A sharp-faced man glanced at me as I waited in the lobby. In a few minutes, the director came out and said he was sorry, but plans had been changed and there was no room for me on the program. I found out later that the sharp-faced man had been the owner of the station. 'What's that young fellow doing in the lobby? He's the son-of-a-bitch who was singing at the Wallace convention. Get him out of here.'" This was only the first of Seeger's many problems with television.

Another problem was Seeger's dissatisfaction with the CP. He was pressured to attend more meetings at the moment they interested him least. In its growing isolation, the Party's discussions focused inward on issues such as "white chauvinism." The Party's democratic centralism—a process in which all apparently contribute to a policy and all agree to carry it out—had become far more centralist than democratic. No one incident precipitated it, but Seeger began to think it was time to separate from the Party.

One day a friend stopped by and found Seeger sprawled across a couch and despondent: "I guess I ought to think about getting a job in a factory." Yet in the middle of this slump, Seeger wrote songs as a kind of self-medication. Just when things looked bleakest, he turned to music to remind himself of the better times ahead, if only he could hold on. Afternoons, he would sit by himself at the piano, his oversized heron legs pushing out the sides of the upright. Lee Hays would leave a set of lyrics taped to the piano and Seeger would work out tunes. In the background, sounds of shoppers would distract him, and long shadows flickered across the basement as he worked on "If I Had a Hammer" and another Hays-Seeger collaboration, "Tomorrow Is a Highway." An underground spring nourished his hopes for a new and brighter dawn:

Come let us build a way for all mankind
A way to leave these evil years behind
To travel onward to a better year
Where love is and there will be no fear,
Where love is and no fear.

Tomorrow is a highway broad and fair
And we are the many who'll travel there
Tomorrow is a highway broad and fair
And we are the many who'll build it there
And we will build it there.

Seeger's wartime dreams of a handmade kitchen and tool shop beckoned. His children deserved better than the city streets. He hadn't forgotten his own childhood: stalking the woods at Patterson, playing barn squash and eating garden-fresh vegetables. In a time of crisis, the musician returned to the self-sufficiency of Seton's world: Chop wood yourself, and you'll never be cold; learn to plant and build a house, the Seegers now reasoned, and we'll survive.

The couple began to take trips upstate to Dutchess County in early 1949, looking for an old farm. Everything with a building on it cost too much. Finally, after a concert, a real estate agent proposed raw land, at a hundred dollars an acre. Seeger decided to build a log cabin. In the spring of 1949, he and Toshi borrowed $1,700 from family and friends for a down payment on seventeen hardy acres overlooking the Hudson River. Youthful admirers in the Young Progressives bought him a pick and an ax, and he was ready to begin.

Chapter 7

If I Had a Hammer

—

SEEGER STARTED HIS HOUSE WITH THE EAGERNESS HE BROUGHT to new projects. With an ax he cleared land and chopped down a few trees to produce a view of the river and space for a garden. Then he went to the New York Public Library and looked up "l-o-g-c-a-b-i-n" and took careful notes. Using wood from their land he began the foundation of their new home.

If he thought the pressures of the city were behind him, though, he was mistaken; he had barely dug his first trench when he sang at the bloody concert in Peekskill. The cold war had come up from the city for a visit and proved an intransigent guest.

The Seegers' problem was not just the cold war but cold itself. "The fall weather's getting cool for sleeping outside," Seeger wrote to Rockwell Kent, the artist who'd lent him a tent: "It was literally a life saver."

Duchess Junction, near Beacon, New York, was a sleepy village on the east bank of the Hudson, opposite the bridge to Newburgh. Its major attraction was an incline railway billed as the world's steepest, "The Eighth Wonder of the World," Lee Hays joked. In 1663 the wooded banks were settled by the Dutch; centuries later only a few trains a day bothered to stop.

The chill fall winds blew in off the Hudson, which tossed red and yellow oak leaves into heaps like a parti-colored comforter. At night, campfires added a bluish smoke to the cinnamony smell of burning leaves. Green turned to gray in the forest, as Seeger divided his time between rehearsals and rallies in the city and forays to the land. "The place is so much isolated that there's some question about how he is going to get in and out when the snow falls," Lee Hays wrote a friend.

The Peekskill riots cast a dark shadow. Friends were still in the hospital; a man had his skull cracked open; another woman had her finger sliced off; the rock that smashed in the Seegers' car window, showering their son with glass, also tore open the eyebrow of their friend Greta Brodie.

For Seeger and the others, the months after Peekskill became a round of hospital visits and committee meetings. Veterans' groups threatened more anti-Communist violence, and a roundup of leftists might begin any day.

Two months after Peekskill, in November 1949, the blood and beatings still fresh in mind, Hays and Seeger rehearsed one afternoon with their quartet, the Weavers.

The Seegers hadn't yet moved out from the Ohtas' house in Greenwich Village, and the basement where they discussed their future was long and damp, with rotting floorboards. In one corner stood Seeger's upright piano.

Going around the room, there was Ronnie Gilbert, an attractive brunette from Brooklyn in her early twenties, with dramatically arched eyebrows. Ronnie was a voice student now turning to folk songs for her brio. Next to her sat Freddy Hellerman, twenty-two and, like Irwin Silber, fresh out of Brooklyn College. Fred had hung around the Almanac House, one of those eager youngsters who'd hauled mattresses down the staircase for the Sunday hoots and foraged for firewood. He'd learned guitar by literally sitting at Lead Belly's feet.

Freddy had a smooth baritone and a quick smile; his receding hairline and prominent nose made him look like a jaunty rabbinical student. The senior members of the quartet were the lean tenor and Hays, whom nature had endowed with the bass (and physique) of a tuba.

Just as the Almanacs had assembled from compass points of America, so the Weavers represented diverse ages and experience. Hays, drawn first into radical labor colleges and then Manhattan, merged with Seeger, who'd barely left New England before his travels with Guthrie. Ronnie and Fred, meeting at a Communist summer camp in New Jersey, had a different, Jewish take on social conscience but a shared destination, that Better World A-Coming. Together the quartet would sing their way there, and change their country's popular music in the process.

Hays and Seeger had the greatest stake in keeping the group together; the others, almost a decade younger, had alternate plans: Ronnie was ready for a family, and Fred wanted an MA in English. Even Lee was casting his eyes at a new career as a short story writer.

The quartet had started informally a week after the end of the Wallace campaign, with its first performances at People's Songs concerts at Thanksgiving and Christmas. On January 23, 1949, they'd appeared on Oscar Brand's *Folk Song Festival*. But paying gigs were few; the unions had lost interest. So now the scarcity of progressive bookings forced Seeger and his friends toward surviving commercially, not their first choice.

"This is where we're abandoning our main job," Hays told Seeger.

But the violence at Peekskill made progressive audiences hesitate to gather in public. Dispirited, the group wanted to cut their losses and disband. "We were ready to break up," Seeger said. "We had never intended to be a commercial group. We were dead broke and about to go our separate ways." Why rehearse when no one dared come hear them?

Seeger wanted them to continue. He had begun refusing solo bookings in hopes of rekindling the group spirit of the prewar period. "No," people told him, "we'll take you, but not the Weavers."

By the end of 1949, the Weavers had developed a small following from the rallies and benefits where they'd sung. They also had a record out, produced by Seeger's old Saipan friend Boots Cassetta: "If I Had a Hammer," a song they'd recently performed at a benefit for the eleven Communist Party leaders now on trial. The song's lyrics and majestic, rising melody characterized many Seeger-Hays collaborations:

If I had a hammer
I'd hammer in the morning,
I'd hammer in the evening,
All over this land.
I'd hammer out danger,
I'd hammer out a warning,
I'd hammer out love between
All of my brothers
All over this land.

If I had a bell . . .
If I had a song . . .

Well I've got a hammer
I've got a bell
And I've got a song
All over this land.
It's the hammer of justice,
It's the bell of freedom,
It's the song about love between
All of my brothers
All over this land.

"We wrought better than we thought," Seeger said later; neither had any idea how far the song would travel. A decade later, Peter, Paul and Mary would have their first big hit with a streamlined version of "If I Had a Hammer." To Seeger's delight, the two versions of "Hammer" harmonized. At his concerts people would sing in unplanned harmony; he couldn't stop talking about this, insisting politicians could learn from it.

Sing out danger, *sing out warning*. Some found the song subversive: "When the song was first published in the *Peoples' Songs Bulletin* in 1950, one man wrote: 'Cancel my subscription: all you left out was the sickle.'" Tolerance was in short supply, and the Weavers found themselves surrounded not only by anti-Communism, but by growing anti-Catholic, anti-Semitic, and antiforeign emotions of the sort the Seegers had met on a recent trip.

Before buying the land, they'd visited Constance in Florida, where they basked in the sun and ate their fill of fresh fish. They'd left with dark tans, especially Toshi's father, Takashi, and the kids: Danny, a year and a half old and Mika, their nine-month-old baby. The trip home had started out pleasantly, as the family roamed back roads with a trailer, chugging slowly up the hills. They'd rolled north through the flat coastal marshes of Florida and Georgia, lush green with fall rains; then they drove the Blue Ridge Parkway through North Carolina.

Seeger had threaded through his past; Constance and Charles had traveled this way twenty-seven years before, also in a trailer, also carrying their young children. Approaching the foothills of Appalachia, the Seegers passed near Asheville, where he'd first met the five-string banjo in the crisp mountain air of the Piedmont. They'd been in no hurry. They'd wanted to show their kids America and camp with them, letting matters at home slide out of mind. The last thing they'd expected was trouble with the police. In Salem, Virginia (near Roanoke), they were eating lunch at what they'd thought was a public picnic ground when a policeman came over, waving his pistol.

"'You folks gotta get out of here,' he said.

"'What's wrong?' I said.

"'This park's for Americans only,' the policeman said.

"'We're all Americans,' I told him.

"'Not them,' he said, pointing at Seeger's tanned and Oriental wife and children. 'Them's gypsies.'" The family drove off, upset, wondering how anyone could *look* un-American. It was a sign of the times.

BACK AT THE MUSTY Greenwich Village basement, the Weavers' discussions continued. Seeger suggested, more forcefully, that if they didn't find new audiences—even trying nightclubs, like professional singers—they might as well quit. Lee disagreed: "Our main job is not in nightclubs."

Seeger had been stewing about this for months, even ending his new project, the Good Neighbor Chorus. He wouldn't give up easily. He explained their duty, as he saw it: to reach out to the faces behind the rocks at Peekskill. Then he tossed out an idea of Toshi's.

"Look, I think Max Gordon would have me back at the Village Vanguard. Rather than go there by myself, let's go in as a group. If we split my salary four ways, we'd each get fifty dollars a week." Lee was still opposed, with Ronnie and Fred undecided. The gathering broke up as they agreed to think matters through.

Actually, another incident motivated Seeger, one he later spoke of as a crossroads in his life. One afternoon in 1949, Irwin Silber had been called by the left-wing American Labor Party, who wanted to set up a benefit concert with Richard Dyer-Bennett, a singer of traditional ballads.

"Perhaps I can help you get him," Irwin had answered. "But in case he can't make it; how about getting Pete to do the concert?"

"Oh, we know Pete," the caller from the ALP had replied. "He's sung on our sound truck for years. We need someone who can bring a mass audience. We need to raise money."

On hearing this, Seeger got really angry. He remembered long winter nights when he had sung outside for the ALP: "Here I was, trying to follow what I thought was a tactical, strategic course, and yet Dick Dyer-Bennett—who was making a career in a traditional fashion—was more use than me. That taught me something." It was a story he'd tell hundreds of times. For years he had avoided commercial bookings, content with local, progressive audiences. If it takes a "name" to bring in a large crowd, Seeger figured, that's what I'll have: "I decided to stop congratulating myself on not going commercial."

Trying their talent in the marketplace tempted Ronnie and Fred; furthermore, Seeger's point about political isolation was brutally driven home when the Weavers did campaign for an American Labor Party candidate, Vito Marcantonio (probably the closest to an advocate the CP had in Congress). They went out on an open sound truck. Gordon Friesen from Almanac days ran the affair well, but the crowds didn't respond. The Weavers sang their left-wing repertoire and songs made up for the occasion. From a nearby window, tomatoes started splattering the unprotected truck. Seeger looked up anxiously:

"What do we do now?"

"Be glad they're not bricks," Gordon answered with a grim smile.

The Weavers' initial failure, like Wallace's, was not musical so much as political. Hays and Seeger, in the Almanacs, didn't sing for candidates (even ones as close as Marc or Ben Davis); they sang more abstractly, of unions and peace. Timely or timeless—that's the choice for political songwriters: The more immediately usable a song for a march or rally, the less it seems to endure.

EVENTUALLY, THE WEAVERS' nightclub premiere was set. Toshi volunteered to be the group's temporary manager. In her level-headed way, she took charge of the changes necessary to sing in nightclubs: She marched them all down to Robert Hall to buy green corduroy jackets (for fifty dollars a week, they weren't shopping at Brooks Brothers). "Lee kept complaining, 'It isn't comfortable, it doesn't fit,'" Hellerman remembered. "What wasn't comfortable, what didn't fit was us wearing uniforms!" Then she negotiated the contract with the Vanguard. "Part of our agreement was two hundred dollars a week plus free hamburgers," Seeger laughed. "Max Gordon once came in and saw the size of the hamburg I was making—I'd put half a pound of meat in, and eat three or four a night. He said, 'Let's rewrite the contract; two hundred fifty dollars a week, but no free hamburgers!' "

Singing carols, the Weavers opened in Christmas week, 1949. After the novelty wore off and their friends had all come, business dropped. One night in February, only a half-dozen customers visited the once-bustling club. Max Gordon liked the music, though, and he carried them. Every night was a rehearsal. By reworking and rearranging, they wove the songs into a dense harmonic tapestry, trading parts midsong. Alan Lomax brought Carl Sandburg to hear the group, and the poet's praises roused newspaper editors: "The Weavers are out of the grass roots of America. I salute them. . . . When I hear America singing, the Weavers are there." Before the Weavers understood what had happened, crowds were packing the Vanguard.

Harold Leventhal introduced himself backstage one night. They shook hands all around, and Seeger asked the song plugger if he wanted to be the Weavers' manager.

Leventhal agreed on the spot. He was a child of Orthodox Jews from Eastern Europe, had joined Zionist youth groups and, like Seeger, the Young Communist League. Working for Irving Berlin, he'd gotten a start in the music industry. Now he was ready to move into management. He had a kindly, soft-spoken way. Hays's biographer remembers him as "short, a bit round [with] a high, raspy voice."

At a typical Weavers show, Lee Hays would tell the story of a preacher who thought music was the devil's invention:

"Preacher," I argued, "how can you not like music? Music is the language of the soul: It expresses the inexpressible. . . ."

"I don't care if it unscrews the inscrutable," the preacher declared, "it's sinful, and I'm agin' it."

Next Ronnie sang a love song, "I Know Where I'm Going," with Pete's recorder coloring the melody and Fred doubling up the bass notes on his guitar. Ronnie's intense, clear voice sent a shiver through the crowd. Finally, Seeger stepped up to the microphone:

"We'd like to sing a song from South Africa by Solomon Lindy—about the lost king of the Zulus, Chaka the Lion. The legend arose that he didn't die, he simply went to sleep. Someday he would wake up and lead his people again. The African people, slaves in their own land, sing that the lion is not dead but sleeping. Well, all you lions out there. . . ." Seeger strummed the banjo and started a musical chant: "Way-up boy, Wimoweh, Wimoweh," repeated by the audience. Against this rhythm, Seeger's falsetto rose and bounced off the ceiling.

The Weavers closed with "Goodnight Irene," with Fred striking up a waltz rhythm. They hedged on the more controversial lyrics, dropping a verse about taking morphine, and changing the chorus from (Lead's version) "I'll get you in my dreams" to "I'll see you in my dreams." No matter: In 1950, singing a song by a black ex-convict made a political statement by itself.

AFTER A SHOW like this one, a dapper fellow walked up and introduced himself. "You guys are wonderful," he said. "My name is Gordon Jenkins and I work for Decca Records. We're exactly the company you ought to be with."

Seeger said yes, not really believing him. He'd heard of the bandleader Jenkins, who worked with Louis Armstrong and Frank Sinatra and had a record in the top forty every week. Most singers would have treated Jenkins like visiting royalty, but Seeger couldn't bring himself to care about pop music. Jenkins, on the other hand, was insistent. He invited them to visit Decca, where he'd introduce them around.

What interested Decca in an unsexy folk song quartet? The Weavers had musical verve and the genius of simplicity. In every era, a few musicians simplify the art of their time, producing a sound often called refreshing. This streamlining instinct underlay the Weavers' better arrangements. Quartets classically feature a tenor, bass, alto, and soprano. The Weavers had a baritone, a bass, a brilliant alto, and Seeger—who, because of his falsetto, described himself as a split-tenor. The group profited by being everything pop singers were not; they had casual arrangements and untrained voices and they downplayed vocal effects in favor of content. "They sang straight out, straight ahead," recalled the young Arlo Guthrie, whose father carried him to Weavers' concerts at age three. "A few embellishments here and there to make things funny, but basically it was songs and stories—communication, not hype. . . . They interpreted the Lead Bellys and Guthries, who were too foreign for mass tastes."

ACCORDING TO SEEGER, the Weavers' record audition was a failure: "Dave Kapp was head of Decca. He took one look at me and said, 'Oh, I know these guys, they're not commercial.' He knew I was a Lefty." But on the way out Jenkins whispered, "I'll get you in on my next recording date." Kapp had to swallow his words when the songs became some of the biggest hits Decca ever had. The Weavers again visited the William Morris Agency, but when they walked in for an audition, Seeger was greeted by the same man who'd booked the Almanacs: "I felt like I'd been here before."

Seeger hoped to do better this time, telling Lee, "Performing commercially is something that makes you want to see if you can do it as well as the next fellow." It might sound strange for Seeger to champion freedom of the marketplace, but deep down, he believed in very American symbols: log cabins, the nuclear family, the Bill of Rights. By venturing into the music industry's arena, Seeger was saying, let the best song win, just as folk songs are themselves products of a musical Darwinism.

He need not have worried, for the Weavers had no competition. In 1950, rhythm and blues was just spreading from New Orleans, where Fats Domino pounded out boogie-woogie on his piano; in Memphis, Howlin' Wolf and Sonny Boy Williamson played on KWEM radio, and the teenage B. B. King sang in bars. The Weavers ignored these trends; while young Elvis Presley stayed up nights listening to R & B on his radio, Pete Seeger was singing South African freedom songs.

On May 4, 1950—a day after his thirty-first birthday—Seeger and the Weavers recorded "Tzena, Tzena," a catchy Israeli soldiers' tune, and "Goodnight Irene." After years of drifting from one left-wing cause to another, Seeger had turned thirty at a bleak time, four months after People's Songs' bankruptcy, but a year later, he'd landed on his feet.

On his birthday, Seeger received a letter from Lee Hays. "You've been showing signs of overwork," Hays told him; he worried about the strain on Seeger's "innermost soul," growing out of performing commercially. Only Lee, it seemed, understood the toll singing in ties in nightclubs was taking on his friend. Yet Lee was also a big part of this stress. Pleading laryngitis, and drinking way too much brandy, Lee was propelling the quartet steadily toward a trio.

"We may have to take the bull by the horn," Seeger said. "If we have to, we have to. I've done it twice before."

Lee Hays heard this comment and straightened out. And then the summer of 1950 belonged to the Weavers. Their first mention in the trade journals came in *Downbeat*. The article focused on Decca's difficulties in slotting the Weavers: Were they country, pop, or what? At the end of May, *Variety* first reviewed their gig at the Vanguard; by June 28, the Weavers were mentioned in five articles in the same issue. The Weavers suddenly had their choice of the country's top nightclubs, and crowning it all, they were offered a weekly national TV spot on NBC.

Starting in June, the Weavers' first record climbed so far and so fast that disc jockeys didn't know which side to play. They turned over the exotic "Tzena, Tzena" and found "Goodnight Irene"; soon that was played more than "Tzena." Frank Sinatra launched a comeback with his cover version of "Goodnight Irene" in July. Decca couldn't press records fast enough.

"The summer of 1950, no American could escape that song unless you plugged up your ears and went out into the wilderness," Seeger said, revealing his mixed attitude toward their success.

Technological developments again favored Seeger's career. The Weavers were radio stars, at a time when the medium was more concerned with ratings than the blacklist. Sponsors looked forward to increased TV programming, "ready to abandon radio like bones at a banquet," as Fred Allen put it.

Success surprised the Weavers almost as much as it did the FBI and blacklisters, in the few glorious weeks before the blacklist in 1942. "It was too unexpected," Seeger said. "I remember laughing when I walked down the street and heard my own voice coming out of a record store. Once I was up in a publisher's office and speaking about some other musician, Don Cherry, and I said, 'Well, he's one of those Decca stars.' And they looked at me funny and said, 'Don't you realize that *you're* one of those Decca stars?'

"I'd never thought of it. People came up to me and asked, 'How does it feel to be a success?' I felt kind of silly. To me, I was a bigger success nine years before, when the Almanacs sang for the Transport Workers Union in Madison Square Garden." Peekskill and a Greenwich Village nightclub were only fifty miles away from each other, but worlds apart. Seeger suddenly found himself a pop entertainer, complete with late-night temptations.

The Weavers headlined at Ciro's in Hollywood, the Shamrock in Houston, and the flashy nightclubs of Reno. In Reno the maniacal bustle and metallic clanking of the slots proved too tempting, and the group decided to try their luck. Only Seeger refused to play: "My Puritan background was just revolted. Some of the Weavers got in over their heads, began to get nervous; instead of winning back what they'd lost, they lost more." Seeger acted like a prig. He had a silver dollar in his hand and said, "I don't mind wasting my money," and tossed the dollar into the pool. "I didn't realize how I'd insulted them," he said fifty years later.

The Weavers tasted success without understanding it; the drug called fame affects each user differently. Hays, initially hesitant about playing nightclubs, now reveled in the experience. In Nevada he discovered room service; when he found out that as a performer he could get anything he wanted, he ordered the works. Looking at the pile of half-full dishes, Seeger was nauseated. His problem was finding some useful way of passing his days. In L.A. he located a craftsman who taught him to hammer silver; in Houston, he collected songs at a black prison; in Chicago, to the dismay of the hotel management, the musician turned his room into a studio and made plaster casts of Eskimo sculpture.

"Pete just had so damn much energy!" Lee Hays wrote in his journal. "While the rest of us were sleeping off the work (or excesses) of the night before, Pete would go out to historical sites. He once bought a trumpet at a pawnshop, but management at the Palmer Hotel requested he stop playing it; and he found himself blowing it into the wind, lakeside."

The group used to tease the Seegers about their beat-up Jeep wagon, the same one they'd driven through the barrage at Peekskill. When they were at Ciro's in Hollywood, an impish idea struck the Seegers. They were staying with a black friend who owned a beautiful Cadillac, and one night they borrowed it. They drove out to the club, and Toshi told the others, "Peter finally gave in. He's decided you're right. Look what we've got!" Ronnie, Fred, and Lee sat in amazement as Seeger wheeled them out for a drive. "We don't believe it," one said. "Oh, Pete! Are you really not kidding us?" "No, great car, isn't it?" Seeger smiled.

Success also had its sobering side, and after the excitement paled, Seeger considered how long this would last, and what their new fame meant. The Weavers began throwing in radical material, Spanish Civil War songs. No one noticed. In fact, the wealthy patrons liked the Spanish tunes so well, they would ask for them as encores. The Weavers' music operated on two levels: commercial pop songs, accessible to all listeners; and a symbolic, encoded music (available only at live concerts) that reminded the Left of its existence: calypso, peace, topical songs.

The tours, the write-ups in *Variety*, all these showed that Seeger was winning his competition with success, but he often wondered if he was changing anything. Gradually he and Lee traded places, and Seeger's initial enthusiasm faded. Though more experienced at touring than Ronnie or Fred, he also had the most family responsibilities. When he was away too long, he missed the kids and felt stabs of guilt at leaving home.

Toshi, in her late twenties, was taking care of their two children, building a house while living in it: fixing the gaps between the logs where the wind whistled in and running errands for her parents. In addition, she took Seeger's messages; the phone rang from the first day it was installed, even before they had a proper floor in the cabin.

When he'd come home from the road for a month at a time, there were moments of stiffness, when he seemed practically a stranger to his family. The homecomings had their warm and tender moments, too, such as one Seeger sketched in his notebook. Toshi sat across from Seeger in one of their few chairs, rocking and staring into the fire with two-year-old Mika in her lap. The child slept in the warmth, her arms around her mother's neck. Seeger sketched with a thick lead pencil: the daughter drowsing, Toshi rocking gently in the candlelit darkness, the logs from their backyard sputtering in the fire.

This tranquillity vanished on the road, where people kept pressing drinks in his hand and offering him after-hours revels. Seeger preferred to sit around the hotel and noodle on his banjo. Once the Weavers shared a program with a man named Tiny Hill. Tiny weighed over three hundred pounds; he made even Lee look skinny. Backstage after a show, fans clustered around Tiny and the Weavers, plying them with booze. "Aw, Pete," they wheedled, "have a drink."

"They just didn't know how serious I felt about liquor," Seeger later said, shaking his head. "I don't like to be forced to drink. If I don't want to drink, I don't want to drink! I'm not a very sociable person anyway, and their urging was making me a lot less sociable.

"'C'mon Pete,' they said, 'unbend, unwind, have a little drink.'

"I picked up my banjo and I said, 'You know how I feel about this?' and WHAM, there went one good banjo. I slammed it down on the table, broke it in half." Seeger broke the very tools he had worked so hard to develop.

Despite his misgivings, the Weavers continued, doing four and five short sets a day and commanding $2,250 a week at the Strand Theater on Broadway. They opened the Blue Angel, a chic nightclub; the audience loved them. Among the listeners was New York's young district attorney, Thomas Murphy, who would in the next decade face Seeger in court as a federal judge.

NOT EVERYONE WAS PLEASED with the Weavers' triumphs. Hidden in the applauding crowd, toward the back of the room, stood an FBI informant, Harvey Matusow, who later shattered the Weavers' career. On June 16, 1950, he suggested that though the Weavers weren't actually doing anything wrong, the FBI should keep an eye on them. It wouldn't be the first time the FBI had investigated cultural workers; the Bureau had been chasing groups of anarchist writers as far back as 1919, even before the left wing of the Socialist Party gave its name to the Communist Party.

The Bureau needed no prompting. They already had a file on the Weavers, complete with army intelligence reports; all that was necessary for an FBI file was a mention in the anti-Communist magazines the Bureau religiously clipped, such as *Counterattack*.

Founded by three ex-FBI agents who hinted of access to "confidential" files, *Counterattack* was half gossip, half conspiracy newsletter—the FBI's unofficial leak. In the 1950s anti-Communism was a big business. Senate and House committees flew in ex-Communist "consultants," paying by the day to stretch out testimony. At twenty-four dollars per subscriber, *Counterattack* netted a hundred thousand dollars yearly. The editors operated a "clearinghouse" on the side, American Business Consultants (ABC), which specialized in internal investigations of large corporations at five thousand dollars yearly. In his book *The Golden Web*, Erik Barnouw, historian of radio and television, uncovered how these investigations worked.

The editors of *Counterattack* would call a company, telling them they had heard actress Y, of questionable background, was employed on their television series. As a public service, they would study her loyalty, and that of the supporting cast—for one thousand dollars. If the offer was refused, three weeks later the editors would run a story about how actress Y was not a Communist but a "fellow traveler"—almost as bad. Using these tactics, *Counterattack* drew in General Motors, Du Pont, Woolworth's, Reynolds Tobacco, and many other patrons. Criticized for employing "pink" entertainers on his new variety show, Ed Sullivan invited the *Counterattack*ers up to his living room to meet "performers eager to secure a certification of loyalty," as he wrote in the *New York Post*.

The Weavers were favorite targets for those investigating the entertainment and broadcasting industry; their visibility made them extremely vulnerable to attacks and provided blacklisters with headlines. Lawrence Johnson was one of these red-hunters; in 1951, he led an unsuccessful effort to stop the Weavers' records from being broadcast. A supermarket owner from Syracuse, New York, Johnson claimed to represent the National Association of Supermarkets. He labeled "Communist" any soap advertised on shows mentioned in *Counterattack*. Because broadcasters received 60 percent of their ad revenue from household consumables, Johnson became one of the networks' excuses for blacklisting.

As the Weavers grew more popular, some former friends attacked them. This was the period of the Communist Party's "white chauvinism" campaign against racial prejudice, and Irwin

Silber took the Weavers to task in a column entitled "Can an All-White Group Sing Songs from Negro Culture?" The Weavers were now "'chasing the bitch goddess Success, falling into a rut with their music to please their upper-class nightclub audiences.' Pete heard this kind of fault regularly from Irwin," according to Lee Hays's biographer. "Furious, Pete scribbled these notes":

> Perhaps he is right; perhaps it is a rut. But his methods remind me of a neighbor of mine in the country. I was carrying a typewriter across a field when it fell in a post hole, and got wedged in the soil so I couldn't seem to pull it out. My neighbor came up with a crowbar, and said, here, I'll get it out for you, and commenced prying and poking, until b'gosh, he did get it out—so mashed and torn by the crowbar that it was quite useless as a typewriter from then on. I was naturally quite angry, and after first feeling that he was a stupid irresponsible fool, that possibly he knew it would break the typewriter, but didn't care. This led me never to trust him again.

Silber also criticized the Weavers' lyrics as "male supremacist." At one concert, women from People's Artists told the Weavers to change the chorus of "If I Had a Hammer" from "love between all of my brothers" to "love between my brothers and my sisters."

"We don't have to," Seeger said. "You can sing it any way you want. Anybody can change a folk song."

"No! *You* change it."

He argued a bit, saying, "Well, 'My brothers and my sisters' doesn't flow off the tongue quite as nicely as 'All of my brothers.'"

"No, there's just been too much of this," they insisted.

Lee joked about it on stage: "All of my siblings, how about that?" The women didn't think that was funny.

People's Artists was the CP-oriented successor to People's Songs, run as a booking agency by Irwin Silber and Betty Sanders.

At his manager's insistence, Seeger kept his distance. The spirit of People's Songs was there, but after years of red-baiting, the body was weak. Initially the group had only a few dozen members, a far cry from the two thousand that PS boasted at its height. People's Artists started a topical song magazine, *Sing Out!*, which took its name from the chorus of the song on its first cover, "If I Had a Hammer."

Since People's Songs, Seeger had been changing his focus: "As the labor movement kicked out the radicals, I settled for 'Let's get America singing'; maybe the basic democratic philosophy in these folk songs will filter out subliminally to the American people."

He also left the Communist Party in this period, due more to his living in a rural setting than political differences. By 1950, the Party was slipping into an isolation Seeger could not accept; its membership had plummeted and its ties to unions all but vanished. To the Party, it was five minutes till midnight; revolution was just around the corner. A paramilitary spirit emerged, far different from the high-spirited bunch Seeger had met in New York in the midthirties. All these factors—combined with the paucity of Party members in the Beacon area and the Party's halfhearted support of People's Songs—caused Seeger to drift away, though friends remained in the Party. There was no dramatic break, no denunciation. He just stopped going.

When he did run into former comrades from People's Songs, he'd occasionally see a strange mix of envy and scorn in their eyes. The rumor went around that "Seeger's got a fifty-thousand-dollar estate up the Hudson now!" Meanwhile, Toshi was feeding the family on beans because none of the song royalties had come in. When they did, the Weavers received three-thousand-dollar checks, the most any had earned in their life.

Some radicals openly attacked the Weavers' success, taking on names like the Grievers and the Unravellers. Silber even published an article in *Sing Out!* accusing the group of abusing Lead Belly's music, and then had the poor grace to run this soon after Huddie's death at the end of 1949. (Huddie died in neglect and on relief. The Seegers visited him in the hospital and paid some of his bills, but his widow had to take a job as a laundress until the royalties to "Goodnight Irene" arrived.)

Seeger had hoped to sing for both left-wing friends and wider audiences. It was on this very point that he had his first censorship wrangles with Pete Kameron, a childhood friend of Leventhal, who had brought him on, seeking to keep his valuable clients away from controversy. "A breath of old show business," as Ronnie called him, Kameron talked and dressed to the limits of the latest style, without overdoing it.

"Pete," Kameron said in his office after a booking was canceled, "you can't sing at [those left-wing] hootenannies right now. A few years from now, you'll be in a position to do anything you want. Right now we've got a real problem to get you cleared and give you a good reputation. A brand new one. Your old reputation has got to go."

Kameron's nerves must have been strong. That was his talent; the manager always talked softly, as if he didn't want to insist.

"I don't see what's wrong," Seeger answered. "I've always sung at hoots." He couldn't believe he'd have to give up such an innocent pleasure.

"Now isn't the time," Kameron repeated. "You don't want to jeopardize the position you're in."

Seeger let himself be convinced, as he had at Avon when the headmaster chewed him out for an article critical of the school administration. "Well, all right," he told himself. "If I'm going to do this, I might as well do a commercial job," "Don't push it," his more loyal (and optimistic) friends urged, "you're in a position where you can get on the air." At last Seeger had his hammer—his songs were on the radio and on people's lips—but with it he could do little. Now that his name could draw the audiences his left-wing friends desired, he was a "property" under contract. He had less freedom to sing *with* fame than he had without it.

In negotiating with success, he also lost control over his music. Some of the Decca recordings sound cheesy: At the beginning of "Rock Island Line," trumpets go "toot-toot." Decca liked Gordon Jenkins's sound; the company seemingly forgot that it was the Weavers, not Jenkins, that topped the charts.

All in all, Seeger (and the other Weavers) were fish in strange waters. To reach audiences, Seeger had to dress up and sing the same harmonies, night after night. This sort of compromise was never his strong suit; one evening he insisted on wearing one green and one red sock with his tuxedo.

ON JUNE 25, 1950, just as the Weavers' first records appeared in the shops, the Korean War erupted. The casualty lists made Communists into America's mortal enemies and jeopardized the tenuous East-West division of Europe. Julius Rosenberg was about to be arrested for allegedly selling atomic secrets to the Soviet Union. And at the end of June, *Red Channels: Communist Influence on Radio and Television* appeared from the publishers of *Counterattack*.

Bound in red with no authors listed, *Red Channels* destroyed hundreds of careers in a single edition. On the cover, below the title, a microphone leaned left as a crimson hand seized control. In phrases like "Where there's red smoke there's usually Communist fire," the book listed artists and entertainers with alleged "Communist-front" associations: Lee J. Cobb, Lillian Hellman, Dorothy Parker, Louis Untermeyer, and 147 others. Much of the material came from *Daily Worker* clippings similar to those in FBI files; the "associations" were as incriminating as signing a petition to support Henry Wallace for president. In the name of Americanism, the book damned writers for writing and musicians for playing for the wrong audiences.

As a result of *Red Channels* mentions, many musicians (including folk song performers Burl Ives and Josh White) were pressured to testify before HUAC and clear their names. Oscar Brand, a longtime programmer of folk music on WNYC radio in New York, was called by one of HUAC's counsel. Brand had known Seeger for over a decade; he had included the Weavers on his show before they had a name. With his job shaky, he visited the Seegers' half-finished cabin for advice. "You know they're after me to try and cooperate with HUAC," Oscar told them. "What do you think I should do?" When Seeger answered, he must have realized he might one day have to make the same decision: He told Oscar that he had more to lose by cooperating than he could ever gain. Brand, however, "suspected" the Party's interest in folk songs, and in October 1951, at a speech at Cooper Union in New York, he broke with the left-wing folk music world. He then met privately with a representative from HUAC. Oddly (and fortunately for him), he was never subpoenaed. Burl Ives *did* testify eventually on subversion in folk music circles and named names.

In fighting their blacklist, the Weavers had an uphill battle. This was a time when *Billboard* insisted the music industry was riddled with subversion: "The Communists are hell-bent on taking over." Instead of "On Top of Old Smokey," the editors were more comfortable with "The Red We Want Is the Red We Got (In the Old Red, White, and Blue)."

The only Weaver listed in *Red Channels* was Pete Seeger; with thirteen citations he placed somewhere between Aaron Copland and Lillian Hellman. *Red Channels* reached a lot of important desks. The contract for the Weavers' TV series was canceled within the week; the timid sponsor was Van Camp's Pork and Beans. A less controversial group played opposite *The Lone Ranger*, and Lee Hays ate his way through the Weavers' only payment: twenty-four cans of pork and beans. "If a large company is not free to select the material it needs to sell its products to the American public," Hays wrote the company, "then we are indeed in a bad way."

Yet despite the best efforts of the editors of *Counterattack*, the Weavers had hit after hit. In September 1950, when the Internal Security (McCarren) Act was passed into law—including provisions for "detention camps" for leftists—"Goodnight, Irene" was number one on the jukebox and "Tzena" fourth. In October, they appeared on Milton Berle's *Texaco Star Theater*, the number one TV show of its era. In November, as Douglas MacArthur's troops reached North Korea and Congressman Nixon became Senator Nixon, "Irene" was the best-selling record in Britain. During 1951, the *Counterattack*ers couldn't turn on the radio without thinking of millions duped by the Weavers' licentious "Kisses Sweeter Than Wine" or the sinister "So Long, It's Been Good to Know Yuh." The record-buying public never read the blacklists that spoke in its name. Those situating the Weavers as part of a Communist plot, one researcher points out, fail to explain why non-Communist, even anti-Communist, audiences flocked to their concerts even as charges were hurled at them.

In the summer of 1951, the FBI stepped up its activity against the Weavers. The Rosenbergs had been sentenced to death, and Americans were in a frenzy about subversion. HUAC had successfully blackballed most of the New Deal radicals; now conservatives turned outward with a "cold clinical but deadly bureaucratic repression": throwing radicals out of public housing and civil service; barring suspect organizations from public meeting rooms and from receiving critical tax exemptions; even denying Communists old-age pensions. Libraries pasted red dots on books considered subversive.

With the help of *Counterattack*, the Bureau scored direct hits on the Weavers. First a scheduled spot on the Dave Garroway Show melted away; a month later Garroway had Connie Russel and the Songsmiths on to sing what *Variety* called "a rousing version" of "Tzena, Tzena." Garroway soon forgot the incident. "I was talent," he claimed, "and talent had no control over anything. Ask my producer." A slick NBC release said the Weavers "had asked to be relieved of their commitment because of conflicting rehearsal schedules."

Then, on August 9, 1951, the governor of Ohio, Frank Lausche, wrote the FBI for confidential information on the Weavers, who were scheduled to appear at the Ohio State Fair. His request put J. Edgar Hoover on the spot. The requested files were clearly "confidential"; no private individual, not even a governor, could legally examine them. Hoover's zeal got the best of him, however, and he passed along the information. The Weavers were canceled so fast there wasn't time to take their names out of the programs.

When they reached Ohio, Ronnie Gilbert recalled "walking down the street with these two guys following us behind. . . . I stopped and turned around and confronted them."

"'Well, do you want your subpoena here or at the club while you're performing?'

"'I'll take it now!' I said." The Weavers ignored it, uncertain of its legal status. "They let us go and said they'd pick up on us later."

They were tailed everywhere they went. When they rehearsed in their hotel rooms, they were warned not to close their doors, or the vice squad might burst in. Governor Lausche promised Hoover not to reveal where he got his facts; he also offered to circulate the materials to reporters, if needed. A week later, Frederick Woltman of the *New York World-Telegram* published an "expose" of the Weavers, using much of the same information that was in the FBI files. At this point, Senator Pat McCarren (D-Nevada) joined the hunt. The FBI turned over a basketful of informer reports and clippings to his Senate Internal Security Subcommittee, which decided the Weavers' "Rock Island Line" paralleled the Communist Party's. The McCarren Committee actually investigated whether the Weavers had violated Title 18 of the U.S. Code, sections 2383–85: Rebellion, Insurrection, Advocating the Overthrow of the Government, and Seditious Conspiracy. The Weavers may have been the first musicians in American history formally investigated for sedition.

Perhaps what disturbed McCarren and the FBI most was that the

Weavers—or any such menace—survived efforts to subdue them. In itself, the Weavers' music wasn't threatening, but by their persistence, they had become a rallying point for beleaguered radicals.

Yet only a handful of leftists publicly supported the Weavers' bridge building, and Irwin Silber was again not one. People's Artists set up their own quartet as an alternative to the Weavers: two men, two women, two black, two white—a singing Socialist version of Noah's Ark. After a heated discussion with Silber, Seeger told a young banjo student, Ron Radosh, "Irwin's a literary figure: he's not a singer and doesn't know much about music."

Haggard from legal battles, and sensing, perhaps rightly, a new belligerence toward social change, the Communist Left sought political purity over the mass support of its Popular Front days. Seeger didn't—or wouldn't—get the message. Fortunately for his psyche, he received word that the Party supported the Weavers: "Keep working, put away as much money as you can, and sooner or later you'll end up singing for progressive audiences." Once Seeger had compartmentalized his ideological and performing lives, the Party accorded him more respect.

Other left-wing groups were less understanding. In Detroit, the Weavers had a job in a nightclub no black had ever entered. Asked to explain this, Seeger limply quoted Paul Robeson's statement that a reputation as an opera singer let him be a more effective spokesman. The younger radicals walked out of the meeting, insisting, "Robeson would never do what you're doing. You are appearing in a lily-white club; now you know it's lily-white—are you going to refuse to appear?" Seeger swallowed his principles, and the quartet went ahead with the show.

The Weavers' blacklisting emerged in the press. *Variety* awarded them the distinction of "the first group canceled out of a New York cafe because of alleged left-wing affiliations," an honor the Weavers could hardly refuse. *Downbeat* acknowledged their ban, dryly suggesting, "If the Communists happen to come out in favor of milk for babies, go on record immediately as being squarely opposed to it." Pete Kameron visited *Counterattack*, pleading with the editors to call off their dogs. In his enthusiasm, the manager wishfully claimed the Weavers "were filling engagements with the American Legion and Daughters of the American Revolution." Kameron even staged a press conference where, according to *Variety*, Seeger hedged about his past, claiming he was not "sponsored" by People's Songs ("I was playing with words," he later admitted, "I sponsored them"), but "he did know members of the organization and sang with them." "Singing is all the Weavers do," said Lee Hays, in a superficially accurate statement. The publicity photos of this time show Seeger stiff-necked and ill at ease with this posturing.

"I'll go along with it, but I'll feel like a prisoner," Seeger told Lee Hays. "And all during the rest of our time he felt and acted like a prisoner," Hays wrote in his notebook. "Life became very uncomfortable for all of us. . . . He was bored. Having made the point that a quartet could do certain things a soloist couldn't, he was ready to move on."

ALL THE COMMOTION made Seeger's life chaotic. Every day, his home grew less like the quiet homestead he'd pictured during the war. Seeger had waited impatiently for the spring thaw in 1950 as the cabin began: "I had dragged Toshi up there just to hike up the hill, sleep in a freezing cold trailer, and then walked around the next day and realized there wasn't any work to do. Everything was frozen solid. . . . But in March, as soon as the snow was gone, we moved into a better tent, and we had a better fireplace. Toshi's brother Alan helped us start putting in a little driveway."

The walls went up. By September or October 1950, they had the walls and the roof on and windows and doors in: "It wasn't much fixed up, but we'd built a house."

Fortunately, Toshi found a job nearby for her parents as caretakers for a summer camp, and when the Weavers had gone on their first tour, they'd left the kids with her parents. Toshi hadn't wanted to leave Mika and Danny. She said they were too young. But the Weavers needed her organizational skills and couldn't bear to part with her for four months. She hadn't meant to be a road manager, but no one would let her stop.

Throughout the trip she worried: Six months is a long time for a four-year-old.

"We drove back to Beacon and there, by the road, was Toshi's father and the two babies. Her father said, 'There they are!' We stopped the car and got out and Danny says, 'Ta-papa said, "These are your mother and father," but you know, I didn't recognize you when you got out.'" Toshi never quite forgave her husband. This was the last tour *she* made with the Weavers.

Partly in penance, Seeger refused bookings for a while and poured his energy into their house. "Now I built the bed and the shelves. We got a cook stove. The following winter, Danny and Mika slept out on a little porch outside. I took a photograph of the snow all over them when they woke up once. Our heat came from a fireplace. When we wanted a hot bath, we went to Toshi's parents' place, two miles away."

Seeger wanted to win the respect of his new community; he wanted to prove they were not some young couple from the city who'd only last a few months. His chance came when Danny began school. When the local fathers were out clearing land by the school, Seeger came down and surprised them by holding his own. He made his reputation with his ax, like one of Seton's characters. Seeger must have been an odd addition, with his Japanese wife and foreign friends, but their community gradually accepted them as usable members.

Following her return from the Weavers' tour, Toshi worked long hours to strengthen those ties. She started the local PTA; in 1952, she was president. Working against this acceptance were the visiting bohemians.

From 1959 on, visitors had taken part in what Lee Hays had wryly called "voluntary forced labor." Summers, people would camp out, helping to build the cabin. Peggy Seeger, who spent her teenage summers there, remembered it as one long folk festival: "You'd have all the New York types coming up. They'd forsake Greenwich Village for the weekend to come scrape logs or run up and down the hill for water." Occasionally someone would sit and just play the banjo all weekend.

When Seeger was not out on tour, he labored alongside his friends under the cooling shade of tall oaks. Toshi'd grumble because every time anyone would ask Pete for a banjo lesson, the construction line would stop. Work filled their days, and the long, warm nights could barely contain the singing. When the last songs were sung, the bodies wriggled down in their sleeping bags. In the morning, they'd wake in the fragrant woods, and the work and songs resumed.

An eight-year-old visitor thought the place mysterious, compared to life in the city: "There was no electricity or running water." Everyone ate dinner outdoors, around an open fire, and they sang away the last of the daylight. Instead of chasing down MacDougal Street, Seeger dug up the garden on his hill overlooking the Hudson. His life had a lulling calm; for once no one seemed to be after him. He had more time to be a father, and to notice the first leaves that turned color in the woods. Yet even the most peaceful days would change, as the river darkened suddenly and a gray cloud swept down, the wind striking roughly at the water. Thunder rattled the cliffs as a storm shook and tore at the river's glossy surface. Lightning flickered toward the hillside where Seeger and his guests worked. The rain came in drops, then sheets, until visibility fell to a few feet, and the soil drained in streams of clay-colored water.

For that short time, the group huddled inside, singing rain songs or tending a fire. Seeger would gaze out the window at his drenched foundations.

One afternoon, in a loft on Forty-second Street, a storm of a different kind was taking place, one that would disturb Seeger's woodland sanctuary. In their efforts to defeat the Weavers, the editors of *Counterattack* had found a trump card in their match against the Weavers: Harvey Matt, the guy who'd saddled People's Songs with bills for records they never sold. A short, pudgy fellow from Ohio, whom schoolmates nicknamed "Kid Nickels" because he hunted small change, Matt turned out to be Harvey Matusow, an ambitious informer. Harvey had just won a twelve-day trip to Puerto Rico for selling *Daily Worker* subscriptions; many were later found to be duplicates. Out to satisfy his material needs, the young anti-Communist, who'd joined the Party in 1949, moonlighted as a loyalty consultant to New York's Board of Education and Police Department. He was a lonely, frustrated man, delighted by headlines with his name, and visiting *Counterattack* was a step up for his career.

"It was there that I got my first training in how to use the names of well-known people in the theatrical world to my advantage as a moneymaking witness," Matusow later wrote. "We discussed the careers of the well-known quartet who, at the time, had the top-selling record in the U.S. One of its members [Pete Seeger] was listed in *Red Channels*, but there was nothing that could be pinned on the group specifically. . . . Having known all four of them, not as Communists, but as friends, I triumphantly said, 'I know them, and they are Communists.'

"Both [editors] gave me rewarding glances, as if saying, 'Keep that up and you'll make out all right.'"

"I think I remember Harvey," Ronnie Gilbert reminisced in 2006. "He was always walking up to people in a cafeteria and selling *Daily Workers*. We didn't take him seriously." They should have, for in the next months the brash Mr. Matusow wreaked havoc on the Weavers.

AFTER LEAVING THE CITY, Seeger had more time for music. He no longer had trouble coordinating voice and banjo, as in his first, shaky recordings with the Almanacs (in the Army) a decade before. He'd learned how to hold audiences, but now, in the Weavers, he was learning show business, arranging, and stagecraft in sharing the stage with a group. From the years of performing solo since the Almanacs, Seeger was listening to his own meter, beat out by his left foot. On his own, he managed fine; with the Weavers, he needed help keeping time.

The Weavers' talent for breathing life into old songs distinguished the quartet *Time* had called "the most imitated group in the business." When the group first rehearsed a song from a book, the song wouldn't come alive. After they went through it a second and third time, Seeger's banjo picked up subtle syncopations and elisions that filled in the tune. Lee's song "Lonesome Traveler," for example, "just sort of lay there," he considered, "until Pete changed one chord, from the minor to the major. It just popped out of Seeger's hands and gave the tune new character altogether."

Seeger couldn't have explained what he did any more than a jazz improvisationist could. He was so steeped in folk music that he acted as a filter between the folklorist's field recordings and mass audiences. Never in history had folk songs moved so quickly from a dusty volume to national broadcast. A folklorist might complain that once Seeger "filtered" a song, his version was the one millions sang. Before electronic recordings and broadcasting, ethnomusicologists could tell where a singer came from by the verses and tunes he or she sang; versions were mapped like highways.

The Weavers sang songs from many lands, opening up American musical tastes. But there was a subtle danger in this song mixing. For those whose identity stems from the old song they'd learned growing up, regional accents and local versions are treasured. Making songs more singable meant they lost that distinctness.

When Seeger processed a song like "The Fortunate Rake," his ear for easily sung chords and harmonies produced a version that eclipsed variants that had taken centuries to evolve.

Later, reflecting on the Weavers' amalgamation of folk and popular music, Seeger pointed out, "Borrowing from folk material didn't start with the Weavers. The Andrews sisters sang 'Bei Mir Bis Du Schoen' in the 1940s. In the twenties, minstrel show banjo tunes of the nineteenth century imitated older plantation music."

And so it went, wave after wave of American musical discovery. The second stage of the folk revival of the 1930s had begun: not collecting songs, not conserving them, but popularizing them, finding an avenue into TV and radio.

ON FEBRUARY 6 AND 7, 1952—after meeting with Joe McCarthy's aide, Roy Cohn, and coaching in the *Counterattack* office—Harvey Matusow testified under oath that three of the Weavers were members of the Communist Party (Lee, he reported, had quit). Carried away by the lights and the attention, he almost buried the Weavers' story by adding that Communists were preying on the "sexual weaknesses" of America's youth to lure them into the Party.

Matusow's testimony "burst like a bombshell."

"It was like one of these movies from the thirties," Ronnie Gilbert recalls: "You know, the criminal or the hunted person comes into a hotel lobby, and everybody's reading the papers: 'So and so wanted.'

"That actually happened to us. We were playing in Ohio and we come into the lobby and people were reading the newspaper and it said, 'Weavers Named Reds.'"

After Matusow's testimony, a minor commotion broke out at People's Artists: No one could remember who this informer was. Silber sent a new assistant to find Harvey's picture, but he too turned out to be an FBI informer and reported in to the Bureau. That afternoon the Associated Press called the Yankee Inn in Akron, Ohio, where the Weavers were performing. Taken aback by the testimony, the manager canceled the Weavers' contract, effective immediately.

The Weavers became untouchables. "We had started off singing in some very flossy nightclubs," Seeger said. "Then we went lower and lower as the blacklist crowded us in. Finally, we were down to places like Daffy's Bar and Grill on the outskirts of Cleveland." Even there, the American Legion tried to get Daffy to cancel. "Hell no," dauntless Daffy replied. "It's just music. Quit hassling me or I'll get my boys on you." Though their single record sales now amounted to four million discs—the most folk songs have ever sold—the Weavers could barely find a hall to book them. On May Day 1951 Pete Seeger had marched down New York's Fifth Avenue with a placard: THE CENSORED MIKE.

In his later autobiography, *False Witness*, Matusow recanted; in gritty detail, he admitted committing perjury and conspiring with U.S. attorneys to give false testimony. His conscience had caught up with him, but the price was that no one, Right or Left, trusted him. For his scruples, Harvey the ex-ex-Communist received five years in Lewisburg Federal Penitentiary.

The Weavers struggled through 1952, but by the following spring they realized they had lost the battle. After their last session under the Decca contract, the company complained that stores wouldn't stock their records. The group took a sabbatical, which, as Lee Hays joked, "turned into a Mondical and Tuesdical." Yet in the community where they'd started, their reputation remained high. When the Rosenbergs were executed a few months later, they asked to hear "Goodnight Irene" on their way to the electric chair, Lee Hays was told.

Counterattack and the FBI had succeeded in blacklisting the Weavers, but "If I Had a Hammer" proved unconquerable. The song had a radical context. When Seeger suggested the Weavers perform it on bookings, Kameron had answered, "Oh, no. We can't get away with anything like that. That song just inflames blacklisters."

"Why was it controversial?" Seeger reflected. "In 1949 only 'Commies' used words like 'peace' and 'freedom.' . . . The message was that we have got tools and we are going to succeed. This is what a lot of spirituals say. We will overcome. I have a hammer. The last verse didn't say 'But there ain't no hammer, there ain't no bell, there ain't no song, but honey, I got you.' We could have said that! The last verse says 'I *have* a hammer, I *have* a bell, I *have* a song.' Here it is. 'It's the hammer of justice, it's the bell of freedom, the song of love.'" No one could take these away.

The Weavers never had the opportunity to make a hit of "If I Had a Hammer"—that fell later to Peter, Paul and Mary—but they had the satisfaction of seeing that no edict and no committee could kill a song. Songs, like revolutions, must often outlive their creators to take root. The great ones—whether commercialized, lost, or rediscovered—have a life of their own.

WITH THE WEAVERS DISBANDED, Pete Seeger was on his own again. He could sing for whomever he pleased. One of the first engagements he accepted was a People's Artists hootenanny in the spring of 1954. A thousand people jammed into New York's Webster Hall and sang their heads off. "I haven't been as far away as you might think," he told the cheering crowd.

Seeger's problematic relationship with Irwin Silber reemerged when he stepped back into the sectarian world of People's Artists. He respected Irwin's commitment, for Silber had adopted the organizer's life Seeger once fantasized about, entering the third circle of Party leadership. Seeger overlooked past attacks on the Weavers. The journalist in Seeger itched to start a column for *Sing Out!*

He named his new column after a folk legend, a Yankee who'd attended Harvard and adopted Indian ways: Johnny Appleseed (John Chapman, 1774–1845). As a boy, Chapman loved to hike through the rocky forests of Massachusetts and western Pennsylvania. At Harvard, he (like Seeger) was moved by the Swedish writer Swedenborg's antimaterialism. He earned his living by an invented profession: supplying farmers with apple seeds. Chapman would trade seeds for a night's lodging, just as Seeger had traded his paintings—though Chapman, unlike Seeger, had a head for business. "Many thought him eccentric, thousands loved him," Seeger wrote, "but all recognized the practicality of his system." In his later years, Chapman helped slaves escape along the Underground Railroad. Leading a spartan personal life, he never married, and early sold the only home he ever had. Johnny Appleseed had a calling: social worker at large, a man responsible only to his principles.

This column wouldn't bring in any money, however, and Seeger was now one of America's best-known, unemployable musicians. Thousands of less famous people suffered the same pressures and gave up their professions: Journalists went into advertising, professors drove cabs. He might have taken the road his friends Earl Robinson and Mill Lampell had: dividing himself between commercial and progressive gigs in Hollywood. Seeger preferred to keep singing his own tunes, even if he starved.

If no jobs were open to him, he would create his own; a few places still knew him as a singer rather than the Red Menace of American Music. The Seegers decided to barnstorm the country, playing in small colleges and churches; he made up a brochure, laid out with Toshi's help. She licked the stamps, and they sent out hundreds of them. They hired an agent, Paul Endicott.

"Pete went underground," singer Don McLean explained. "He started doing fifty-dollar bookings, then twenty-five-dollar dates at schoolhouses, auditoriums, and eventually college campuses. He definitely pioneered what we know today as the college circuit. . . . He persevered and went out like Kilroy, sowing seeds at a grass-roots level for many, many years. The blacklist was the best thing that ever happened to him; it forced him into a situation of struggle, which he thrived on."

"Thrived" may be optimistic. Seeger survived the early fifties, but only as a man forced to trudge across America, carrying his banjo into forty states. He eventually found an audience for his music where none previously existed. These peripatetic years steeped him in the life of America's small towns and bustling cities. From this point on, he had a never-say-die glamour for liberals, which only increased with attacks on his music.

In the early fifties, Seeger began what he called his "cultural guerrilla tactics." With no possibility of arranging formal radio or TV appearances, he turned to the surprise attack.

"I'd call up a local TV or radio station, and say, 'Is there a TV show I can come on?'

"'Who are you?' they'd ask.

"'Pete Seeger.'

"'Well, what do you do?'

"'I sing folk songs. I'm at the college tonight.'

"'Oh, you were with the Weavers. Sure, I remember, "Goodnight Irene." Come on up, we'll chat a moment. I'll play your record. Singing at the local college tonight? Good.'

"I'd go up there and we'd talk for five or ten minutes. Then he'd play some songs, and I'd be away before the American Legion could mobilize itself to protest this Communist fellow on the air."

Seeger worked effectively, but "guerrilla tactics" are a grandiose name for his efforts. In the 1950s, an underground did exist in the United States, including Seeger's former comrades. The Communist Party, expecting its leaders to be assassinated in an armed fascist uprising, had set up a clandestine network of cadres "in deep freeze." These tactics unfortunately reinforced the impression created by anti-Communist "I Spy" films and television programs. In June 1954, a Harvard poll found that 52 percent of Americans favored imprisonment for Party members. Previously, the government had charged Party leaders only with advocating—not organizing—revolution; now, under the Smith Act, it appeared that all who had been Party members in 1948 would be eligible for prosecution and ten years in prison, including Pete Seeger.

For an entertainer, the gravest worry was keeping an audience.

Seeger had been driven first from nightclubs, then from the music industry into his own circuit of schools and summer camps. Even to children, he sang subversive songs: "Be Kind to Your Parents" ("though they don't deserve it") and the "Children's Declaration of Independence" ("I will just do nothing at all, I will not eat my vegetables"). The limiting of Seeger's audience to children in the 1950s had a profound (and largely unnoticed) effect: His discourse became that of a schoolteacher and his message childishly idealistic. What else was he going to sing: "It's a bad world out there"? "Nobody can stop war"? No, he sang his young audience the ancient bedtime story of a world without war and a planet whose people heal it, of brotherhood and sisterhood all over the world. His listeners wanted to believe this, even after they grew up. And they would hold him to these sentiments, and insist on his optimism and these unselfish dreams, like the ones wished for on blowing out the candles on a birthday cake. When he later tried to change this message to something more adult, more nuanced and realistic, many would not have it.

Children found Seeger's concerts a novelty. Not only did he sing music different from what they heard on the radio, but he had this way—others might have made it a gimmick—of getting them singing. For the unprepared, even adults, it could be startling. "The concert was like none I've ever seen," said a writer for the *Providence Journal* in 1953. "He let us sing the ballads with him."

Despite his growing popularity, Seeger's media blacklist lumbered on. Apparently his only nationally syndicated TV appearance in the 1950s was on Hugh Hefner's Playboy Penthouse series in 1958, where he did his best to play banjo surrounded by jiggling "co-eds." His steady work came from teaching; folklorist and camp director Norman Studer hired him for music assemblies at Camp Woodland and at the Downtown Community School, a liberal humanist school in Greenwich Village. Seeger earned twenty-two dollars a week for singing with seventh and eighth graders: "I was glad to get it." One summer in the early fifties, he sang regularly at a summer camp in Lenox, Massachusetts; he and Toshi happily discovered that a nearby hotel would pay him an additional twenty-five dollars a night. "Those were his bookings for the summer," Toshi said dryly. "Forty-five dollars a week." To earn this sum, he had to drive two hundred miles, round trip.

He had alternatives, even if he'd have abhorred them; except for the blacklist, he might have done commercials and jingles, where the musicians were anonymous. He might have worked at the nearby textile mill. Except for his unquenchable need to sing with people, he could have become an executive, who serenaded the family on holidays with an old but treasured guitar. "Not a chance!" Toshi later remarked.

FORTUNATELY, SEEGER FOUND a patron in Folkways Records and his old friend Moses Asch, son of Yiddish writer Sholem Asch and visionary of the folk song set. Despite mikes falling off rickety stands and people opening the studio door and spoiling his recordings, Moe Asch and his assistant, Marian Distler, documented an American folk song revival long before anyone cared to buy the records.

"He was always the same old reliable sweet Moe," Bess Lomax said. "He went bankrupt and started back in again. He never paid us a cent of royalties, but if you were really flat—and most of us were—you could always drop by to see Moe, and he would invite you to lunch. Always the perfect gentleman, Moe would give you a couple of dollars, saying, with a twinkle in his eyes, 'Just so you can take a taxi home.'"

Others called Moe paternalistic. When Earl Robinson complained about not receiving royalties, Moe threatened to drop his records from the catalogue. Asch had an explosive temper and was not above manipulating artists; depending on where one stood in his hierarchy, he was a benevolent or a callous godfather.

To Seeger, Moe was sweetness and light; he kept the Seegers

eating throughout the fifties by paying him regularly. Asch's generosity would prove a bonanza for his company in later years.

Every few weeks, Seeger would visit Moe's cluttered studio, with its tapes spilling out of boxes and papers heaped in a corner with unanswered mail. There he would record an album in one or two days. On the first, Seeger would bring in instruments and a list of songs. He'd play one through, and if Moe liked the take, they went on to the next. The following day, they listened to the tapes. Seeger never knew which songs would be used; Moe issued them as he saw fit. By 1955 Folkways had released twenty-nine Seeger albums, including two excellent ten-inch records, *Darling Corey* and *The Goofing Off Suite*, both of which show his mastery of traditional Appalachian banjo and his experiments in fusing classical and folk styles. On *The Goofing Off Suite*, Seeger scored for banjo a duet from Beethoven's Seventh Symphony, the Chorale from his Ninth Symphony, and "Jesu, Joy of Man's Desiring" from Bach's Cantata 147 (selections that must have pleased his mother). It was in its way a tribute album to her and to his family's love of classical music.

If *The Goofing Off Suite* is homage, *Darling Corey* is arguably Seeger's most preservationist album. Here he plays the songs he'd picked up from the Lomaxes at the Library of Congress largely as he heard them. He frails furiously on Walter Williams's "East Virginia Blues." His banjo medley of "Old Joe Clark" and "Ida Red" led Alan Lomax to call him "a really fabulous virtuoso" in the liner notes. This recording is distinctive not just for Seeger's banjo pyrotechnics, but for his sincerity. Each ballad is sung as if it happened to him: A lumberjack's tragedy, hard times in the country, even a cowboy lament—all are embedded with expressive power. The way Pete Seeger won over a record buyer, even when singing whoopee-ti-yi-yo or a hobo song, foretold his later magic with listeners.

"Pete created his own style on the banjo," commented half-brother Mike Seeger, also a banjo virtuoso. "It's primarily to accompany songs that the banjo wasn't originally used for. His strong points as a banjoist are a strong touch and good rhythm; his weak point, subjectively, is that he makes the banjo very much his own. He wants to do it his own way, instead of the traditional way. Which really isn't a weak point."

His record producer was flexible and completely loyal. He didn't care what anybody said about Seeger or Communist-front politics. He didn't even care much about making money. Moe allowed Seeger his own projects, such as the impractical idea of reissuing the Almanacs' "Talking Union" in a time when no more than a half dozen unions would purchase a copy.

In these recordings from the late forties to mid-fifties, Seeger sought a sound far closer to the original tunes than his big-band numbers with the Weavers. This coincided with a renewed interest in folklore, mostly dormant since his collecting trips in Alabama and Saipan in the early forties.

Seeger had presented at a folklore conference in New York in 1946; in 1949, he'd asked the Library of Congress for equipment for field work (no luck). In 1951, he'd recorded prison songs in Texas as part of a Weavers tour. Now, to begin the transition from performer to researcher, he applied for a Guggenheim fellowship in 1953 to make a "Survey of Instrumental Techniques in American Folk Music." The grant was to underwrite expenses for field trips to film guitar, banjo, dulcimer, fiddle, and harmonica styles. The films were for "composers of the future"; the musician foresaw "a whole generation of young amateur musicians turning to folk music," to produce "handrolled, homemade music." Though Seeger lacked a university degree, he clearly knew his field. Why shouldn't he receive the opportunities Alan Lomax had? (Lomax had received his Guggenheim in 1947, before leaving the United States for Great Britain, where he maintained unofficial residence until blacklisting abated in the late fifties.)

If the Guggenheim Foundation hadn't rejected Seeger's application following Matusow's testimony, he might have become a folksong collector rather than a folksong performer. The decision was a lucky one for American music.

Despite this turndown Seeger pursued this new impetus, publishing articles in *Music Library Association Notes* and the *Journal of American Folklore*. In 1955, he wrote a pamphlet on the chalil, an Israeli shepherd's flute. But no matter how scholarly his work, his singing and politics remained too controversial for universities. No foundation came forth to sponsor his research. When Irwin Silber received a commendation from the Soviet Union calling him "the great American musicologist," Seeger could only laugh.

"I was interested in ethnomusicology, but I didn't want to go that academic route . . . I just wanted to reach people. When I decided I was not going to be a journalist, I decided I'd really try to see how music could help the world get to a better state."

BY 1955, POLITICAL CONTROVERSY overshadowed his scholarship and performances. In January, he sang at Pennsylvania's Bucknell University and chatted with a reporter from the *Sunbury Daily Item*. When the interviewer pressed Seeger to explain Matusow's allegations, the exchange grew strained. Then Seeger pulled a guitar onto his lap and strummed as they talked, "and the tenseness left the conversation."

"I am a loyal American," Seeger sighed. "It's a terrible thing to be accused of being a Communist. You can never prove that it is not true, and it follows you everywhere." Seeger won over the reporter by being disingenuous. Obviously he could never disprove charges of Party membership, because he *had* been a member. Woody also dodged questions like these, insisting, "Left-wing, right-wing, chicken-wing: I'm not a Communist, but I've been in the red all my life."

Seeger had hundreds of similar discussions, where only the details of his Party affiliation were raised, and never its meaning: Was Party membership supposed to make him a worse singer? Did political involvement turn his austere moralism to hypocrisy, as driving a Jaguar might? Seeger often considered revealing his Party relationship, but knew this would invite legal (and physical) attacks—perhaps on his family. Yet evading questions produced an increasing internal pressure; he felt he ought to speak out, but everyone cautioned against it, as limiting what his fame might later accomplish.

"Seeger is probably the Reds' most highly advertised entertainer," wrote Herbert Philbrick, the most famous anti-Communist columnist, in an invitation to censor or cancel his performances.

At times, Seeger booby-trapped would-be censors. In April 1955 he was scheduled into the Chicago Art Institute, which asked him for an advance list of his songs. Seeger was an old hand at surly challenges; he answered that his feeling for an audience determined what he sang, but he'd send them a list of possible songs.

The Art Institute rejected three as too controversial: "UAW-CIO" (an Almanac tune from 1942), "Lincoln and Liberty" (an 1860 campaign song used not only by Lincoln, but by Horace Greeley and Henry Clay), and another campaign song, "Rejoice, Columbia's Sons," whose chorus goes:

Rejoice, Columbia's sons, rejoice
To tyrants never bend a knee
But join with heart and soul and voice
For Jefferson and liberty.

Seeger didn't sing the offending songs. On the other hand, he had never promised not to talk about singing them. He treated the audience to a blistering recital of his correspondence with the Art Institute. The censors succeeded in bringing their censorship and Seeger's name to the front pages.

At least he no longer had left-wing censors, for after the Weavers disbanded, Irwin Silber and *Sing Out!* praised them profusely, calling Seeger "an outstanding people's artist of the generation" and pointing out that he had sung for more people "in the flesh" than any other singer of folk songs in the history of the United States. "Self-appointed vigilantes of our time began to attack the Weavers," Irwin commented innocently, excluding himself. These tributes were no doubt welcome; but they were also a reminder that radicals sometimes embrace failure more easily than success, that losing for the right cause can seem superior to winning.

AT LAST SUMMER CAME. Schools were on vacation, and Seeger spent more time at home, where visitors were already encamped and erecting a barn/office where he could plunk away in peace. In the first week of August 1955, Seeger and his helpers prepared to raise the barn's walls. He was so engrossed in his work that at first he didn't notice the shiny black car that bounced up his driveway and stopped. A man in a suit got out.

"Are you Pete Seeger?" the man asked. Seeger said he was.

"I've got something for you," he said, handing him an envelope and turning on his heel. Pete's eye caught the seal of the U.S. House of Representatives: It was a subpoena from the House Un-American Activities Committee to testify in two weeks.

Seeger stood motionless at the top of the driveway. He heard the activity all around him: hammering, teenagers laughing as they hauled water up from the brook. For five years he'd been expecting this, his turn before the congressional committee that specialized in harassing left-wing artists and professionals. Many who were called to testify lost their jobs or ended up with jail terms and fines for refusing to cooperate; the resulting chaos broke up families, even caused suicides. He turned back toward the house and braced himself for the next weeks.

It wasn't so long since he'd talked with Oscar Brand about testifying. When Josh White, a close friend from the Almanac days, had testified, it had cut Seeger to the quick.

"I wanted to write Josh and let him know what I felt. . . . He'd hated [HUAC's John] Rankin so much! The Josh White I know would literally rather have died than go and crawl before that committee. I found out he had called Robeson the night before and said, 'Paul, I just have to let you know that tomorrow I have to go and make a heel of myself.'

"'Well, why do you have to?' Robeson said.

"'I can't tell you why, but I just have to, I don't have any choice.'" Seeger shuddered at the memory. He never mailed the letter he'd written Josh. He still had it in his desk: a picture of a guitar, broken in two.

Now it was his turn to testify—just when he was back on his feet financially. If only HUAC had subpoenaed him following Matusow's testimony; at least he wouldn't have had to go through all this yet again. Now, if liberal schools and camps continued hiring him, they might face a subpoena of their own and possible bankruptcy from legal expenses. Counting the blacklists of the Almanacs and the Weavers, this made a third round of right-wing attacks.

They chose a lawyer—Paul Ross of the Madison Avenue firm of Wolf, Popper, Wolf, Ross & Jones—and arranged to meet with previously subpoenaed friends to find out what to expect. The situation didn't look good, Ross told them. Apparently if a witness didn't plan to cooperate—which Seeger didn't—the most common choice was to invoke the Fifth Amendment (and refuse to testify against yourself) or the "modified Fifth," the position Lillian Hellman described in *Scoundrel Time*: testifying about one's own life, but not about one's friends. The third alternative was the First Amendment. Challenging HUAC on First Amendment grounds, however, meant years of court battles, with no assurance of avoiding jail at the end. The Hollywood Ten had tried this and received a year in prison. Think it over carefully, the lawyer advised.

None of these options appealed to Seeger. The "unfriendly" witness always had a hard time, as Frank Donner wrote in *The Un-Americans*: "He knows that the Committee demands his physical presence in the hearing room for no reason other than to make him a target of its hostility, to have him photographed, exhibited and branded. . . . He knows that the vandalism, ostracism, insults, crank calls and hate letters that he and his family have already suffered are but the opening stages of a continuing ordeal . . . that his family faces a kind of community outlawry." Most of all—and here the tension arose between Seeger's moral rigor and the laws that confronted him—"he is tormented by the awareness that he is being punished without valid cause, and deprived, by manipulated prejudice, of his fundamental rights as an American."

From HUAC Seeger could expect none of the privileges guaranteed citizens in a court of law. He had no right to be informed in advance of the charges against him; no right to cross-examine accusing witnesses or present his own evidence; and no right to be represented by counsel, except in an advisory role.

Pete Seeger had expected a subpoena in the late '40s and had talked over his situation with his father.

"Father," he said, "I sometimes wonder if it wouldn't be more sensible just to give up and go to prison. It'd be one or two years. Friend of mine is there now and I went to visit him—it's not so bad."

"I begged him not to do it," Charles remembered, bringing up parental concerns: He was not a boy now, he had a family to support; he could do more good outside prison than by rotting away inside.

Pete's father also had his own reasons for wanting him to stay out of trouble. Charles was himself under surveillance by the FBI. He had just two years to go before a full pension (barely enough to support his four children: Mike, Peggy, Barbara, and Penny Seeger). Each year the red-hunters' nets had drawn tighter around him, and his son's notoriety wasn't helping. As one of the founders of the International Folk Music Council, Charles had enjoyed a diplomatic passport in 1950. In 1951, he was downgraded to a regular passport, without explanation. In 1952 his passport was suddenly limited to official travel. Then in 1953, it was revoked; no one would say why. On top of his other troubles, Ruth had fallen ill. He went to the head of the passport division and volunteered to quit his job at the Pan American Union, where he'd worked since 1940, to "keep things down."

His sacrifice didn't help. In 1952, the FBI visited Charles in his home—arriving almost the same day doctors discovered Ruth had incurable cancer. "They really grilled me. I confessed to being a member of the Composers Collective." The Bureau brought up his days in Berkeley and his refusal to buy war bonds; everything was in the files. The next day he resigned from his job. Charles Seeger eventually got his passport back, but the price meant humiliation by the FBI. Soon afterwards, Ruth died of cancer.

The year Seeger received his subpoena, Charles left DC, moving the family to Cambridge, where his eldest daughter, Peggy, was attending Radcliffe. Charles didn't tell the children how he'd been forced from his job.

Constance, now in her sixties, was more upset by Peter's subpoena. In her retirement in Florida she had grown more conservative. She didn't know what to make of her youngest boy. Not only was he moving further from the virtuoso she had hoped for, but he was in trouble with the law. Seeger remembered her acting "pretty brave, all considered," comforting herself by thinking, "I'm not responsible for what my son does." If Peter landed himself in jail for contempt of Congress, it would be that stubborn streak of his that got him there.

AUNT ELSIE, who'd taught him drawing at Patterson and whose *Pageant of Russian History* was recently published, was more supportive. Seeger had written to warn her of impending headlines.

"No, I am not troubled or embarrassed," she wrote back, "I am disgusted at the demand that people inform on their former associates and hope that both you and Arthur Miller [scheduled to testify later] will refuse."

—

DISCUSSIONS ABOUT LEGAL ALTERNATIVES continued nonstop. Whatever he and Toshi decided, lawyers and friends warned, the decision would haunt them. He already knew he wouldn't cooperate with HUAC. Once he'd decided not to cooperate, however, the next choice was neither obvious nor easy: taking either the First or the Fifth Amendment.

One of the most infuriating parts of Seeger's situation was the shadiness of HUAC's legal authority. The U.S. Constitution has no provision for government by exposure; Congress may only enact laws. From this beginning, Congress assumed the power to hold investigative hearings to inform their lawmaking—but HUAC's showy interrogations did not produce legislation. By 1955 the Committee was seventeen years old; having exhausted or jailed its most headline-worthy witnesses, the Committee now played reruns and the also-featureds. HUAC's goal was not gathering information so much as impugning the reputations of witnesses unwilling to provide names it already knew. Seeger was not alone in opposing this character assassination. The year of his subpoena, HUAC called 529 witnesses—its best box office came from its Hollywood stint, of course—and an incredible 464 (88 percent) remained silent.

Seeger had to decide which draft to swallow: a short, bitter drink of gall, as he took the Fifth; or the nettle cup of litigating his First Amendment right to free speech—in his case, free song. Though sweeter, this second drink cost far more time and money and was not without unpleasant aftereffects.

"The expected move would have been to take the Fifth. That was the easiest thing, and the case would have been dismissed. On the other hand, everywhere I went, I would have had to face 'Oh, you're one of those Fifth Amendment Communists. . . .' I didn't want to run down my friends who did use the Fifth Amendment, but I didn't choose to use it." The presumption of guilt was more than he could stomach.

Seeger also felt a duty to defy HUAC because "I was peculiarly able to do it—after all, there was no job I could be fired from." In 1953 I. F. Stone had written, "Great faiths can only be preserved by men willing to live by them. . . . [HUAC's violation of the First Amendment] cannot be tested until someone dares invite prosecution for contempt." Seeger was just the man to take up such a dare.

Scheduled to testify at the same session, Lee Hays had already made up his mind: "I wanted to take the Fifth and be done with the whole thing. I never did think much of the 'Hurrah!' side of the First Amendment." According to Lee, Harold Leventhal, now Seeger's manager, also urged him to take the simple route. How, Seeger was asked, did he intend to pay for a First Amendment battle? He had to admit he had no idea.

As the days ticked by, he looked out at the cement blocks piled up for the barn. In the last stormy days, all work had stopped; his tools and siding sat forlornly by the side of the cabin. Seeger hiked off by himself with a notebook, jotting down answers to as many of HUAC's probes as he could anticipate: "That question's like 'When did you stop beating you wife?'" He couldn't help his outrage: Men he considered a national disgrace would question *his* patriotism, and his right to sing where and when he pleased.

"Not only have I not done anything criminal or subversive," Seeger planned to state, "but no one I know has, or would. Immoral or sinful, perhaps, but not criminal or subversive—why I'm often accused by family and friends of being an old New England Puritan." In his notebook, Seeger's anger finally led him to immodesty. "(Are you a radical?) Why, yes, you know, like Jesus Christ was. And a number of my ancestors were."

These jottings were Seeger's rehearsals for inquisition. He tried to clear his mind of pressure, but for this he needed more than a notebook.

Chapter 8

WHERE HAVE ALL THE FLOWERS GONE?

—

A FEW DAYS BEFORE HIS HUAC TESTIMONY, IN MID-AUGUST 1955, Pete Seeger was strumming banjo at Camp Woodland, nestled in the green Catskill Mountains of New York. Singing was his private remedy for law books, and he indulged himself.

His stage was a wooded amphitheater cut into a hillside, with gray shale covering the brown, loamy soil. The sun dried the dew from the moss, which gave off the smell of warm woods and shadow. Kids crowded in to hear the man adults whispered about: "What's so dangerous about him?" an eight-year-old asked disappointedly. To the children, his banjo seemed as long as a canoe. The metal pegs shone and the strings glinted like taut metal hairs. He swiped the strings gently, barely touching them with his nails. The children absorbed his music; a few words passed them by, but others caught in their memory, where the songs lay like broken pottery until patched together at the next singing.

The children knew little of Seeger's legal trouble, and he didn't force it on them. He wanted a morning of good singing, an excuse to be outside in the woods, playing banjo instead of writing out statements. Once HUAC finished with him, there was no telling when he'd get another chance. He sang "Die Gedanken Sind Frei" ("Thoughts Are Free") that morning, and his voice nearly cracked. Then he sang his Bantu story-song, "Abiyoyo," about a wicked giant in the days before congressional investigations.

Once upon a time there was a little boy, who played a ukulele. He'd go around town: Clink, clunk, CLONK! Of course, the grownups would be busy, and they'd say: "Take that thing out of here. Git!" And they'd kick him out of the house. Not only that. The boy's father would get in trouble, too. His father was a magician. He had a magic wand. He could go Zoop! with it, and make things disappear. . . .

People got tired of all this. They said to the father: "You get out of here too. Take your magic wand and your practical jokes and you and your son, just git!" They ostracized them. That means, they made 'em live on the outskirts of town.

Now in this town they used to tell stories about Abiyoyo. They said he was as tall as a house, and could eat people up.

One day, one day, the sun rose blood red over the hill. And the first people that got up saw a great big shadow in front of the sun. They could feel the whole ground shake (stomp, stomp). Women screamed. Strong men fainted. They said, "Run for your lives! Abiyoyo is coming."

Just then the boy and his father woke up. . . . "Oh son," the father said, "if only I could get him to lie down, I could get him to disappear." The boy said, "Come with me, Father." Over the fields they went, right up to where Abiyoyo was. People screamed, "Don't go near him! He'll eat you alive!"

There was Abiyoyo. He had long fingernails, 'cause he never cut 'em. He had slobbery teeth, 'cause he never brushed them. Matted hair, 'cause he never combed it. Stinking feet, 'cause he never washed them. He was just about to come down with his claws, when the boy whipped out his ukulele and sang "Abiyoyo, Abiyoyo." Well the monster had never heard a song about himself before, and a foolish grin spread across his face. And he started to dance.

The giant got out of breath. He staggered. He fell down on the ground.

Zoop, zoop! went the father with his magic wand, and Abiyoyo disappeared.

People said: "Come back to town. Bring your damn ukulele; we don't care." And they all sang (the banjo pointed into the crowd and eighty squeaky voices sang at the top of their lungs), "Abiyoyo, Abiyoyo."

At the end of the song Seeger, still huffing, stopped and spoke: "Some good stories have a moral: here, one good song beat a giant. Next week, I'll be questioned by some men who want me to stop singing," one child remembers hearing. "Maybe they've talked to your parents." A few of the older children looked around knowingly. Seeger quietly kept strumming the chords to "Abiyoyo," captivating an audience that would stick by him for decades, through Bo Diddley and the Beatles.

"Even though the townspeople scoffed at the boy's music," he continued, "it helped solve their troubles. A good song reminds us what we're fighting for. Help me with this one":

We'll sing out danger
We'll sing out warning
We'll sing out love between
My brothers and my sisters
All over this land.

Anti-Communists still didn't bother about Seeger's singing for kids. This long march through the summer camps and schools was an unexpected by-product of the blacklist. It started from necessity, but like many of Seeger's enthusiasms, he soon made it a creed. In *Sing Out!* he praised "the thousands of boys and girls who today are using their guitars and their songs to plant the seeds of a better tomorrow." Seeger became a gardener of song, fertilizing and breaking ground at every stop. But if Ted Kirkpatrick, editor of *Counterattack*, rejoiced that the former nightclub star earned only twenty dollars a show in summer camps, he underestimated Seeger's determination to be heard.

Before he headed home, he stopped at Woodland's mess hall to eat dinner. The good food could not dull the metallic taste of apprehension. "You could tell Pete was upset by the way he'd talk about it," Bess Lomax remembered. "He was very serious about the hearing; this was no joke." Seeger's choice between the First and Fifth Amendments might today seem academic, but this same decision had brought bitter fights and recriminations to a generation of radicals. If he acted according to his material circumstances, the Fifth would be the logical choice; then he could have walked out the hearing room doors a free man with a smallish blot on his moral armor. If he chose by character, he would storm HUAC head-on, proclaiming for free speech.

Seeger's discussions about HUAC with Paul Ross sometimes degenerated into arguments decidedly not Ross's fault. The attorney, formerly Mayor Fiorello La Guardia's right-hand man, had more patience than his client. One afternoon, stretched out in Paul's comfortable Madison Avenue office, Seeger told Ross of his plans to get on the witness stand and tell the committee off.

"No, if I'm going to represent you, Pete, you have to take my advice. Don't argue with them. Be polite, and politely decline to answer."

"I want to get up there," Seeger insisted, "and attack these guys for what they are, the Worst of America, the witch hunters."

"Don't try and be a smartass," Paul repeated. "Don't be clever. If you're not going to answer it, say why. Don't try and make speeches." Each time the committee found him in contempt, Paul soberly reminded him, he was liable to a year in jail. Pete agreed to do his best, but he couldn't promise. "It all took a lot of time. I wanted to be more brash, like Paul Robeson, and say 'You are the un-Americans.'"

FORMER RADICALS CONTINUED to fill Seeger's concerts, even as many tried to bury their political pasts. His performances provided an excuse for old friends to mingle and to pass on left-wing culture to their kids. In this way, Seeger helped preserve a community under siege. Children thought him a martyr and an adult who wasn't afraid of looking silly. He would squeal like a barn hinge at the top of his voice and croak like a frog. Such qualities made Seeger a new generation of fans in the 1950s, including the "red-diaper" babies, who later sat in and marched their way through the 1960s. If a novelist is studied through the characters he devises, and the politician by the key votes and the sudden reverses, the test of an entertainer such as Seeger is his audience.

As he vanished from general public view, Pete Seeger became the flagpole of the Left, among the tallest of those who could be seen above the madding crowd of anti-Communists, who dominated public discourse. He fit an American mold: the underdog seeking justice, a patriot whose peculiar heroism lay in acts of conscience. Including progressive social clubs, summer communities, and unions, perhaps a hundred thousand young people grew up listening to Pete Seeger—not a large number in a country of 160 million. Pop stars like Little Richard and Fats Domino probably had twenty times as many fans. But Seeger's followers were more than record buyers, and he was more than an entertainer. He had become, in the broad sense of the term, a music educator.

A growing number of nonradical young people also listened to Seeger's children's records and traditional folk songs. In person, his musical imagination was inspiring. One teenager who took banjo lessons from Seeger in 1954 remembered sitting with him on a bus one rainy afternoon. Seeger stared off into space as they rode, then turned to the boy and said, "You know, we could do something to the rhythm of those wipers." "Pete's Eager," two

Glasgow girls called him later, and earnestness wins the hearts of youth.

"Pete kept joking that all these kids would be adults someday," Moe Asch said. "*Then* he'd be popular—and that's just what happened. Seeger's vast audience in the 1960s would come from those same kids—who now ran the campus folk music club. They would bear any kind of controversy to get Seeger there."

ON THE EVENING of August 14, 1955, the House Un-American Activities Committee arrived in New York for hearings on Communist infiltration of the entertainment industry. Three members of the committee, Gordon Scherer (D-Ohio), Edwin Willis (D-Louisiana), and Chairman Francis Walter (D-Pennsylvania), conducted the four-day hearings. They were welcomed to New York by anti-Communist notables Victor Lasky and Vince Hartnett (who allegedly supplied HUAC with the documents to identify Seeger). Someone joked that the committee was hunting musicians overthrowing the government by "force and violins." Actually, the congressmen had not chosen Seeger or any of the twenty-two other witnesses testifying before them. The selection had been made months in advance under the previous chairman, Harold Velde, a man famous for the number (rather than quality) of his public hearings. Velde had even subpoenaed Harry Truman after the ex-president called HUAC "more un-American than the activities it is investigating."

By 1955, the old McCarthy hoot was getting old. The Korean War had ended; McCarthy had been censured a year earlier. The only A-bombs falling on American soil were our own, tested in the Nevada desert. Seeger and his kin were only chum HUAC was tossing out to reporters.

The first day of the hearings, August 15, brought few surprises. Most of the witnesses were excused after taking the Fifth. That night Chairman Walter was the guest of honor at an anti-Communist rally where he claimed that 99 percent of his witnesses had been reds. In Washington, I. F. Stone published a report on soldiers decommissioned because their families had left-liberal leanings; one soldier was accused of being "closely associated with your mother . . . a reported CP member, whom you continue to correspond with."

On the second day, Lee Hays testified. The actor Eliot Sullivan preceded him in the morning sessions, accompanied by his attorney, Bella Abzug. Sullivan refused to cite any amendment and attacked the committee. This put Chairman Walter in a dour mood; he told his fellow congressmen that "it doesn't seem to matter" to the witness that he would be charged with contempt of Congress.

"Of course it makes a difference to me!" Sullivan replied heatedly. "I have a wife and two children and I am anxious to work." Committee members promised he would pay for his speeches in jail. After lunch, Lee came to the stand; the *New York Times* dismissed him as "a burly sandy-haired folksinger." The first order of business was straightening out Hays's identity; it turned out another Lee Hays, a television actor greatly preoccupied about his reputation, had been subpoenaed by mistake. Asked about People's Songs, Lee invoked the Fifth Amendment; after another half-dozen questions brought the same response, Hays was excused. The audience saw how effortless testifying could be—if the witness took the Fifth.

The morning of Seeger's hearing, over breakfast, he read the *New York Times*' praise of Chairman Walter for running HUAC's hearings with "decorum." "It is a duly constituted committee of Congress," the editorial commented, "and, as such, witnesses who fail to give it their cooperation must bear the onus of public suspicion that they have something to conceal."

A couple of hours later, Pete Seeger entered the hearing room in the imposing U.S. Court House on Foley Square, site of the Smith Act trials six years earlier. He might have been the only person ever carrying a banjo to a congressional hearing. He quietly listened to Tony Kraber, a friend from People's Songs, cite both the First and Fifth Amendments in his defense. Then he watched Congressman Scherer needle the witness like a picador, until Kraber lost his temper.

Finally, Seeger's name was called, and he stepped forward, "amid the popping of flash bulbs . . . the clicking of still cameras, and the bustle of the press table." The high ceilings made the room echo, reducing all sounds to a dull clatter, over which the chairman's gavel was barely heard. Facing Seeger and his "silent" counsel—lawyers could not officially address the hearing—sat the three members of the committee and its chief counsel, Frank Tavenner, who did most of the questioning.

Of those interrogating Seeger, Francis Walter was the most imposing. His thick, black-framed glasses and his thin gray hair, combed straight back, made him look perpetually sour, the sort who sues at a small dent in his car. He was red-faced, as if he drank too much. Walter also headed two other committees, as a colleague pointed out: "One is the House Patronage Committee; if you cross him, you can't get an appointment through. The other is the House Immigration Committee; if you cross him there, you have no chance of getting some poor fellow into the U.S. through a private immigration bill." Spite and anger ruled Walter's emotions to the extent that the *Washington Post* once termed him "unfit" for public office; he continually conjured up a "Terroristic Marxist Criminal Conspiracy."

Gordon Scherer was HUAC's "ideological sergeant-at-arms" and a sponsor of the John Birch Society. Fond of phrases like "It is significant that . . ." he specialized in carving innuendo out of coincidence and glaring at witnesses to unsettle them. Scherer always made sure, in the heat of exchanges with witnesses, that the hearing record had everything necessary for quick and efficient contempt citations.

Representative Willis wasn't as vocal as his two colleagues. A newcomer to the committee, he was best known for his comment, "If you can't trust the FBI, whom are you going to trust?"

The first questions concerned Seeger's residence and occupation—with these, local vigilantes could take matters into their own hands. Seeger answered willingly: "I make my living as a banjo picker—sort of damning in some people's opinion." The committee ignored this veiled attempt at a joke. Seeger had told Paul Ross he'd behave himself, but it wouldn't be easy.

Though music hadn't been his intended profession, Seeger declared, "I continued singing and I guess I always will." Seeger kept his anger in check. On their side, the investigators had already chosen parts: Walters lorded his authority, Scherer scowled, and Willis watched silently.

Trouble began with the first substantive question. Tavenner asked Seeger about singing for the Communist Party, quoting an ad from the *Daily Worker.* The musician answered, "I refuse to answer that question whether it was a quote from the *New York Times* or the *Vegetarian Journal.*" The investigators now knew—if they hadn't guessed—that Seeger wasn't "friendly."

As an "unfriendly" witness, Seeger would be forbidden to sell liquor, collect unemployment, tend bar, or perform as a wrestler if he was cited for contempt. Each state had different restrictions; in Washington, DC, he couldn't legally tune a piano. To HUAC, he was just another unrepentant subversive, and they gave him no quarter:

> MR. SCHERER: He hasn't answered the question, and he merely said he wouldn't answer whether the article appeared in the *New York Times* or some other magazine. I ask you to direct the witness to answer the question.
>
> CHAIRMAN WALTER: I direct you to answer.
>
> MR. SEEGER: Sir, the whole line of questioning—

CHAIRMAN WALTER: You have only been asked one question, so far.

MR. SEEGER: I am not going to answer any questions as to my association, my philosophical or religious beliefs or my political beliefs, or how I voted in any election or any of these private affairs. I think these are very improper questions for any American to be asked, especially under such compulsion as this.

The first round went to Seeger, for confounding his questioners. Instead of citing an amendment to justify not answering, he dismissed their questions as improper. He sat before them, staring into the future. Seeger no longer spoke to anyone in the room; they had vanished, and he addressed history.

Yet if Seeger thought, as he sat there in his plaid shirt, checked suit jacket, and garish yellow tie, that the committee would simply accept his statement and be done with him, he was mistaken.

Tavenner pulled out a clipping advertising Pete Seeger at a May Day rally in 1948. Had Mr. Seeger sung on that occasion? Seeger consulted with Paul Ross before answering:

MR. SEEGER: I feel that in my whole life I have never done anything of any conspiratorial nature and I resent very much and very deeply the implication of being called before this Committee that in some way because my opinions may be different from yours, or yours, Mr. Willis, or yours, Mr. Scherer, that I am any less of an American than anybody else. I love my country very deeply, sir.

CHAIRMAN WALTER: Why don't you make a little contribution toward preserving its institutions?

MR. SEEGER: I feel that my whole life is a contribution. That is why I would like to tell you about it.

CHAIRMAN WALTER: I don't want to hear about it. . . .

MR. SCHERER: Let me understand. You are not relying on the Fifth Amendment, are you?
MR. SEEGER: No, sir, although I do not want to in any way discredit or deprecate the witnesses that have used the Fifth Amendment.

As Seeger waived his Fifth Amendment protection, his responses shrank to one-liners, such as "I have given you my answer." He knew what he was doing; he needed no reminders of the legal battles to come, where court costs would amount to more than he earned in a year. He was mildly awed at his courage: "I realized that I was fitting into a necessary role. . . . This particular time, there was a job that had to be done, I was there to do it. A soldier goes into training. You find yourself in battle and you know the role you're supposed to fulfill. And similarly a musician trains to find himself on the stage." Seeger knew the stage and his duty and the consequences.

In the hot, airless courtroom, Seeger and the committee implicitly battled over patriotism: Who passed the loyalty oath—those who took it or those who refused? Who was more American: Francis Walter, goading witnesses to testify, or Pete Seeger, claiming no one should be questioned on his beliefs? After questions on "Wasn't That a Time," a song they thought subversive but that he considered deeply patriotic, Seeger offered to perform the song for the committee.

The congressmen didn't know what to think. The request sounded like a joke; but he wasn't kidding. Seeger had a physical need to make his voice heard, to demonstrate what he did. Lead Belly had his chance to sing his way out of trouble and succeeded. Perhaps Seeger hoped his song too might slay a giant.

Walter would hear none of it. The committee made people pay in full for disobedience, sending them to jail, ruining lives and reputations. The fact that Seeger did not seem to care about HUAC's power probably disturbed the congressmen more than where or what he sang. When defied politely—and Seeger kept using "Sir" in his answers, to his lawyer's delight—the committee became powerless. Their threats of contempt were real, as Seeger would discover, but if a witness would not play victim and soil himself, the committee became a Wizard of Oz confronted by a determined twelve-year-old.

Tavenner kept pulling out more folders with clippings from the *Daily Worker*, and Seeger kept declaring his belief in the power of song: "My songs seem to cut across and find perhaps a unifying thing, basic humanity, and that is why I would love to be able to tell you about these songs, because I feel that you would agree with me more, sir."

Either Seeger was satirizing the committee (unlikely) or, like an early Christian, he genuinely believed in the power of a song to turn away wrath. Finally the committee moved toward the Big Question: Was he paid by the Communist Party?

> MR. SEEGER: The answer is the same, and I take it that you are not interested in *all* of the different places that I have sung. Why don't you ask me about the churches and schools and other places?
>
> MR. TAVENNER: That is very laudable, indeed. . . . If you were acting for the Communist Party at these functions, we want to know it.

Seeger was tempted to open up his involvement with the Party. But if he, like Lillian Hellman, had been willing to testify on his own membership, the second question put to him would be "Who else?" If he refused to answer this, he would be as much in contempt as if he had refused to answer at all. If he answered the second question, he would be confronted with others: "Who are your relatives? Your friends? Your business associates? Your acquaintances?" If he complied with these questions, wrote Dalton Trumbo of the Hollywood

Ten, "he is involved in such a nauseous quagmire of betrayal that no man, however sympathetic to his predicament, can view him without loathing."

> MR. TAVENNER: I hand you a photograph which was taken of the May Day parade in New York City in 1952, which shows the front rank of a group of individuals, and one is in a uniform with military cap and insignia, and carrying a placard entitled CENSORED. Will you examine it please and state whether or not that is a photograph of you?
> *(A document was handed to the witness.)*
> MR. SEEGER: It is like Jesus Christ when asked by Pontius Pilate, "Are you king of the Jews?"
> CHAIRMAN WALTER: Stop that.
> MR. SEEGER: Let someone else identify that picture.

Seeger was diffident, and Scherer leaped in to press the advantage home.

> MR. SCHERER: Again, I understand that you are not invoking the Fifth Amendment?
> MR. SEEGER: That is correct.
> MR. SCHERER: We are not accepting the answers or the reasons you gave.
> MR. SEEGER: That is your prerogative, sir.

Except for calling one of Pete's summer camps "slimy," Willis remained silent. The others kept pushing Seeger: Did he understand he was in contempt? Didn't he want to save himself and name names?

> MR. SEEGER: I am saying voluntarily that I have sung for almost every religious group in the country, from Jewish and Catholic, and Presbyterian and Holy Rollers and

> Revival Churches. . . . I love my country very dearly, and I greatly resent this implication that some of the places that I have sung and some of the people that I have known, and some of my opinions, whether they are religious or philosophical, or I might be a vegetarian, make me any less of an American.

After nearly an hour under the lights, Seeger walked slowly from the courtroom. The next day the committee adjourned the hearings, claiming they had succeeded "in alerting people to the situation in theater." The committee returned to prepare its contempt citations—back to Washington, "a city of whispers, of tapped phones and cautious meetings," as Dalton Trumbo called it, "a city whose very air is polluted with the smell of the secret police."

AFTER THE SCORCHING DAY in New York, the return home to Beacon must have been soothing. A creek ran behind the Seeger property, the perfect place to sit and dangle his feet in the water or look up into the canopy of blue sky and trees, thick with summer leaves. Toshi was digging in the garden. The view along the Hudson was as restful as ever.

Here he passed the next few weeks, as he slowly faced the seriousness of his situation. Others had received a year in jail for refusing to answer one question; he'd brushed off nearly two dozen. Having hobbled the giant, he must now pay. Seeger busied himself with simple tasks and for a while felt protected in his family and home, far from legal harassment and commotion.

Contempt of Congress citations proceeded routinely, and Seeger knew what lay ahead. First, the House would vote to cite; then a federal grand jury would hand down an indictment. He would appear in court for trial. Since the government won most of these trials, Seeger could look forward to an expensive appeal in Circuit Court and, if that was unsuccessful, to the U.S. Supreme Court. Then came a fine and jail, perhaps for as much as ten years.

By then the forest would all have changed; his children would be teenagers.

"He never allowed himself to speak out," Bess Lomax recalled, "and he resisted a lot of cheap shots he could have gotten off at people who didn't behave so well." Yet he had worries enough to cause a breakdown; all he owned was his cabin and his land, and bankruptcy from court costs could take these away.

From this point on, Seeger's life was punctuated by a succession of court dates which only people who have had serious legal problems can appreciate. He could count on Toshi, Moe Asch, Harold Leventhal, and his friends to help him through the next years, but his prospects were poor. His life had fallen into a pattern: initial success, attacks, and censorship. This had happened when the Almanacs rode the patriotic, beat-Hitler sentiment, then lost their jobs and reputation to the blacklist. Then there had been the Weavers' sudden rise and painful fall. Now, beginning anew, he had been slugged again—just in time to lose a round of bookings as the school year began. Any professor or administrator who hired Pete Seeger after that testimony had to be willing to pay with his job for the privilege.

Not long after this, Seeger began quoting a fragment of Walt Whitman's poetry in his performances:

> Have you heard that it was good to gain the day?
> I also say it is good to fail.
> Battles are lost in the same spirit they are won.

The end of this cycle of Seeger's was a burst of musical creativity that followed personal trials. In 1949, after People's Songs had fallen into shambles, he had turned inward for his most lasting tunes; his music was his hope and solace, and it did not desert him. Locked out of the clubs, he went into the recording studio, turning out discs at the astonishing rate of six per year from 1954 to 1958. (This level of production was due to Folkways' complete disregard for normal recording procedures. Moe Asch never even kept a list of Seeger's sessions.)

Many of the records were for children, and they introduced songs Americans now take for granted: "Frog Went A-Courtin'," "This Old Man." Probably a few hundred thousand children first heard American folk music through these recordings.

In 1956 Folkways released *American Industrial Ballads*, one of the most comprehensive collections of American labor songs recorded. By playing fast, brief versions, Seeger managed to squeeze twenty-four cuts on a single album, rescuing songs from obscure volumes. It wasn't only Seeger's musicianship that distinguished him from those beginning to throng Washington Square Park, it was the fresh repertoire he'd unearthed.

Perhaps because of pressures he kept inside, Seeger sang and played with a fervor he rarely matched before or after. Records had become his outlet. He performed where he could, but since few heard him live, he visited Moe Asch's studio—where he was always welcome—to record for posterity.

While he shuttled between Beacon and New York City to make records, most of the stay-at-home business fell to Toshi. In the fifties, Beacon remained a bustling upstate town of thirteen thousand or so, with a ski slope, a hospital for the criminally insane, and a textile factory. The people were of conservative Dutch, Italian, Irish, or other European stock; passersby on Main Street sometimes stared at Pete and Toshi—imagine that, an interracial couple!

Following the headlines about HUAC, "the family was scared, to say the least," Seeger said. By this time Danny was eight and Mika six; they had a new sister: a blond, Asian-American baby, Tinya. "I had been singing with the PTA, and they asked that we discontinue the group. They couldn't stand the controversy." But the local principal called in his teachers and said, "I want you to let me know if anyone makes it hard on the Seeger children." The Klansmen who had stoned the Seegers at Peekskill continued to live in the area, and when HUAC singled Seeger out, their suspicions grew.

Toshi put aside her pottery to manage her husband's defense campaign. Previously, she had launched the Weavers, kept track of Pete's bookings, and managed the family. Now, in addition to finishing a house lacking plumbing and privacy, where loads of itinerant folk singers trooped in at all hours, she coordinated meetings with lawyers and fellow defendants.

While Toshi ran the house, he kept to the top of his hill. Mornings, he'd drive down, pick up his mail and the groceries, and come home. Once a gray-haired hardware merchant looked him right in the eye and said, "I don't know what your politics are, young fellow, but this is America, you got a right to your opinion."

Clearly, everybody wasn't in agreement. One time Seeger stopped on his way home for a beer in nearby Cold Spring. A fellow walked up to him and loudly stated, "You know what we ought to do with these Commies? We should stand them up against the wall."

About this time a man came around to "inspect their water." Since the Seegers had only recently hooked up, they thought this odd. Then, small fires began to break out on their hillside. They called the police when they saw smoke rising from nearby woods. "They caught him," Seeger said. "We felt a little safer."

As if their troubles in Beacon weren't enough, more arrived by mail. Two weeks after the hearings, a letter came from a family in Pittsburgh: "Because of the recent adverse publicity, my family and security responsibilities force elimination of your plans to stop over with us on September 8. Though our acquaintanceship with you has never had any political under or overtones, I'm afraid the times and temper will not understand." The letter sounded like its author had sent a carbon to the FBI. "Save to show to his grandchildren," Seeger penciled sadly in the margin. Somehow Seeger knew exactly what this note would mean fifty years later; he knew the world would change.

If the FBI didn't see that letter, they certainly read a lot of other mail on Seeger and his circle. A month before Seeger's testimony, the Bureau had begun a procedure to classify People's Artists as subversive under the Internal Security Act. In October 1955, informants removed and duplicated the group's correspondence. The FBI monitored the group's mail—even its trash. J. Edgar Hoover wrote Assistant Attorney General William F. Tompkins discussing "technical installations" for gathering "data." Then, just as the FBI completed their investigation, the group dissolved for lack of funds.

The FBI's interest in "folk music" did not stop here. Throughout the fifties the Bureau actively recruited informants, including some who went on to small and large careers as folk singers. The Bureau would approach a singer known to be on the outs with *Sing Out!*, someone who wouldn't do benefits, or who mistook political criticism for censorship. The agent would appeal to the individual's patriotism, to his "good reputation," and occasionally to private information at their disposal. The FBI filed everything: the date the subject's father Americanized his name, the informer's fear that his name would be made public. Even more common was placing "volunteers" in People's Songs or People's Artists. If they played the guitar, so much the better. Once the Bureau sent a phony typewriter repairman up to the PA office; he managed to spend the entire morning tinkering with the keyboard while eavesdropping on the organizers of a benefit.

While FBI agents stole into People's Artists, Seeger experienced a vaster theft—of his audience. The Folkways recordings kept him singing, but Seeger was no studio musician; without an audience life paled. He thirsted for a singing crowd the way a wilting plant seeks nourishment. He looked for work as far away as California. To cover his travel and lodging, he was forced to perform four times a day there; twenty-five dollars was the maximum he could get. "So I sang at a school in the morning, another school in the afternoon, and a little playground later in the afternoon. In the evening, I did a party." At the end of a grinding day like this—four bookings, with transportation required from one place to another—Seeger slept soundly.

Later, he would insist that his blacklisting didn't exhaust him: "I thrived on it." His music was being taken seriously. Like his father before World War I, he'd stood his ground. Yet Seeger was demoralized when his union, Local 802 of the American Federation of Musicians, almost expelled him following his HUAC appearance. Getting kicked out of the union would have further barred Seeger from stages in New York, where union membership is often required by contract. The union actually held a preliminary hearing on Seeger, but Paul Ross reminded the executive board that the singer wasn't even accused of a crime—and it would take a pretty poor union to oust a member on hearsay. The board stopped short of lodging charges, but the irony of the situation was not lost on Seeger: The man who had done the most to spread labor songs in the United States was asked by his own union if he was loyal enough to be a musician.

"That was hard," Seeger reflected in 2006. "But the funny thing is I don't remember being troubled. It's a crisis, and you have to figure out how to get through it."

If the world praised the inflated or the shrill, he had his own standards, and no amount of neglect (or attention) from the world threw him off course. Right-wing attacks were only a perverse tribute to his effectiveness. The HUAC ordeal was the making of Seeger, it turned out, rather than his undoing. Until challenged, his puritan habits had a Boy Scout leader's blandness, and his music was too wholesome and rural for mass audiences. Under HUAC's attack he became a warrior of song.

Nonetheless, organizations he had counted on for support began to hedge, and Seeger's native optimism could turn to sarcasm. The head of California's Idylwild Folk Music Workshop, Max Krone, asked him for a "forthright statement about present membership in any party advocating force or violence." "Come to think of it," Seeger replied, "I am a registered Democrat. I rather think some of the Southern members of this group do believe in force and violence. . . . If your board will overlook this, I will be glad to."

"Dear Mr. Seeger: We regret that we have to cancel your concert," began a January 1957 letter from the New-York Historical Society. "We did not know until the last minute that there was any political unpleasantness . . . we have to be careful to avoid criticism and unpleasant publicity." Seeger has files crammed full of correspondence with trustees who deeply regretted, sincerely apologized, and under-the-circumstances-sought-to-avoid having Seeger play in their communities.

Underlying these battles (and hundreds more that followed) was one critical factor his defenders rarely knew: that Seeger *had* been a member of the Party. Though his participation was insignificant—over the years he had attended a few dozen meetings—at the point when his membership became a public issue he did not step forward.

Suppose Seeger had been blacklisted for actually belonging to the Communist Party, rather than for helping or associating with Communists—would there've been a feeling of "Well, he got what he deserved?"

"This would have meant I'd have had to argue politics ninety percent of my time," Seeger later said. "Let the songs carry it. It's misleading to get into all those arguments about words. I didn't want to do that. I wanted to sing songs." Seeger often preferred the complications of politics to vanish, leaving issues as sharply defined as a ship's mast against a clear sky, as uncompromised as a woodsman's lair.

In the midfifties, public debate on Seeger centered on issues of free speech. Instead of asserting that he (and his music) was revolutionary, his partisans battled over his right of dissent, a battle liberals wage more comfortably. The public heard "Pete Seeger has a right to sing," not "Revolutionaries have a right to organize" or

"Communists, too, have a right to free speech." Midway through his career, attention shifted from Seeger's musicianship to his symbolic role as a censored voice of his time.

Though he ultimately benefited from this shift, Seeger, preoccupied with truth, had urges to make public his CP ties. This tension had surfaced as early as 1950, when the Weavers first made their way out of Greenwich Village and into the fancy nightclubs. He had a dream then of stripping off his clothes in public and proclaiming himself "a nudist at heart." Lee Hays's interpretation revealed his deep understanding of his friend: "Your great urge to unveil yourself for what you are is constantly thwarted, and you are in a turmoil of frustration and suspense."

Seeger's discontent would have been far easier to bear if not for critical changes in the Communist Party U.S.A., which worsened his situation as an ex-member: Khrushchev's denunciation of Stalin and the invasion of Hungary by Soviet troops in 1956. Separately, each was momentous; together and in quick succession, they marked that phase of an organization when its core shatters. The fallout affected even fellow travelers and lapsed members like Seeger.

In the spring of 1956, following release of its leaders, such as Gene Dennis, jailed under the Smith Act, the Communist Party finally reached the conclusion Seeger had after Peekskill: The Left had been speaking too narrowly and not democratically. But before the Party could consider any changes, Nikita Khrushchev gave his famous speech denouncing Stalin's crimes at the Party's Twentieth Congress. This came as a bombshell to members who had defended Stalin's excesses for decades—including Seeger, who had considered Stalin was only "a hard driver." His friend Howard Fast thought the revelations "a terrifying list of informers, murders, tortures, and betrayals."

Khrushchev's speech drove thousands from the already shrunken organization. Then, before the disbelief had waned, in November Hungary was invaded by Soviet troops for the second time. The *Daily Worker* dispatched a senior correspondent, but when he sent in reports sympathetic to the Hungarian rebels, the paper killed his stories. His conclusion could serve as an epitaph for the Party, now moribund.

"We were still the victims of our own eagerness to see arising the bright new society that we so desperately wanted to see in our lifetime; and that our propaganda told us was being built."

If some Party members felt, with Peter Fryer, "betrayed and wondering . . . if their political lives had been built on self-delusion," others did not. Gene Dennis's wife, Peggy, talked a delirious optimism: "The niceties of correction are expressions of the stability of the Soviet Union."

In retrospect, Seeger regrets this temporizing: "People *should have* criticized the Party. People who wanted the Soviet Union to succeed should have found ways to speak out."

Seeger was caught somewhere between longing and regret. This was a time when people who'd devoted their lives to the Left not only saw no way to move forward, but were deadly scared of admitting where they'd been. They had jobs they couldn't lose; they were worried about loyalty oaths even though they didn't believe in them.

Soon after these shifts, Seeger was singing in Canada when an ex-Party member remarked how his world had changed. "Well, I don't think much has changed," Seeger said, leaving the other open-jawed at his naïveté. Refusing to take the Fifth Amendment was only the most recent evidence of Seeger's individualism; the Party favored taking the Fifth to give comrades more time to work on the outside. Seeger had been warned before. Earlier he had visited San Francisco and received a caution not to visit a Berkeley friend, Barbara Dane. "Why not?" Seeger had asked. "Simply because she *associates* with Trotskyists?"

He did not criticize the Party publicly, however. Criticizing automatically made one a renegade, for the organization refused to distinguish the ex- from the anti-Communist. Members either followed Party discipline or they were out in the cold, isolated from friends, and suspect. Newspapers promoted only the god-that-failed ex-Communist, but people actually took different routes on leaving the Party. The Paul Robesons and Pete Seegers did not find fault publicly; to do so would have challenged not merely their pasts, but their dreams. Seeger wouldn't publicly criticized Stalinism for a half century.

As usual, the *Bosses Songbook* had a few sharp choruses to needle him, this time a revision of his "Talking Union":

. . . So he joined the Party, he was doing fine
Parroting out that old Party Line.
He'd carry an umbrella if the weather was fair
'Cause if it rained in Moscow that's all he'd care
He was loyal, True blue,
Just like His Master's Voice.

The Hungarian invasion and the denunciation of Stalin came at a particularly awkward time for Seeger. To risk jail for refusing to discuss his CP membership was bad enough; to go through this while doubting the Party was worse. Al Richmond, editor of *People's World*, called the situation "absolutely tragic."

Fortunately Seeger's business affairs were taking a turn for the better. Harold Leventhal (and occasionally Manny Greenhill) had taken them over from Paul Endicott, a disorganized, Detroit-based manager only mildly helpful since the Weavers disbanded. Harold decided to orchestrate a Weavers reunion concert at the end of 1955, bypassing the usual ifs-and-buts of a decision by renting Carnegie Hall and *then* telling the singers.

"I just went to everybody and said I had the hall, and that if I canceled, I'd lose a lot of money. An old trick."

Leventhal, the same age as Seeger, had kept in touch. In the two-and-a-half-year lull, Ronnie Gilbert had married and had a child. Fred Hellerman had become a producer-arranger, and Lee Hays was writing mystery stories for *Ellery Queen's Magazine*. After a few rehearsals, the old harmonies fell into place. The concert was sold out months in advance. Seeger had his old group to perform with—as long as he could stay out of jail.

AT A FOLK FESTIVAL in Louisiana a few months before the Weavers' reunion, Seeger had an amusing shock. After a performance, he accepted an invitation to learn Cajun songs at a house outside of town: "They met me at the door, saying, 'Mr. Seeger, meet Congressman Willis.'

"You could have knocked me over with a feather. Willis [one of his interrogators from HUAC] didn't bat an eyelash, but there I was sitting in his house; we were singing songs, having a good time, and I could see him growing more and more uncomfortable, watching me sip his liquor.

"'Mr. Seeger, small world, isn't it? How did you get here?' he said to me in the kitchen.

"'I was invited.'

"'Well, you're not welcome.'" Seeger relished his opportunity; the congressman's wife had been singing along gaily.

"The local people tried their best for me to stay. I was due to sing in the public school and so on, but Willis said he'd raise a holy fuss. Well, they didn't want to embarrass him, and I didn't want to embarrass him—it wasn't his fault I got invited—so I said goodbye to my friends and went off to Houston." The incident showed that Seeger's testimony had been accurate: his songs did "cut across and find a unifying thing, basic humanity." (Of what the congressman said to his wife afterward, there's no record.)

Soon after this, on July 26, 1956, the House of Representatives voted 373 to 9 to cite Pete Seeger and seven others (including playwright Arthur Miller) for contempt.

After the citation would come an indictment (1957), and then a trial (1961). Seeger carried on, singing for young people at liberal colleges like Oberlin and Reed. En route to one of these concerts, Seeger had the inspiration for "Where Have All the Flowers Gone?"

On the plane, he pulled out his pocket-size song notebook: "Leafing through it, I came across three lines I'd written down, oh, at least a year or two before: 'Where are the flowers, the girls have plucked them. Where are the girls, they've all taken husbands. Where are the men, they're all in the army.'"

He'd read this in a novel by Mikhail Sholokhov, *And Quiet Flows the Don*; the three lines came from a Ukrainian folk song. For a year he had searched around for the original song, then given up, jotting down this fragment in hopes of using it some day. This time he glanced at the words, and "things just slipped into place."

For four or five years, Seeger had carried a musical phrase in his head, like an man saving string: "long time passing." He had been struck by its melodic beauty: the four vowel sounds are sequential, opening up the mouth as they are sung.

"All I knew was that those were three words I wanted to use in a song; I wasn't quite sure how, where, or when. Suddenly it fit with this 'Where have all the flowers gone—long time passing.' And, five minutes later, I had 'Long time ago.' Then without realizing it, I took an Irish American tune, a lumberjack song."

Where have all the flowers gone?
Long time passing.
Where have all the flowers gone?
Long time ago.
Where have all the flowers gone?
The girls have picked them, ev'ry one.
Oh, when will you ever learn?
Oh, when will you ever learn?

Where have all the young girls gone?
Long time passing.
Where have all the young girls gone?
Long time ago.
Where have all the young girls gone?
They've taken husbands, everyone.
Oh, when will you ever learn?
Oh, when will you ever learn?

Where have all the young men gone?
Long time passing.
Where have all the young men gone?
Long time ago.
Where have all the young men gone?
They're all in uniform.
Oh, when will we ever learn?
Oh, when will we ever learn?

At first, the song seemed too short to be serviceable, only three verses. Seeger sang it once in a medley of short tunes (on a fine but obscure disc, *Rainbow Quest*) and forgot about it.

But a song is like a child; once it gets out into the world, it often surprises the parent. In 1958, Harold Leventhal asked Seeger if he'd written "Where Have All the Flowers Gone?" The Kingston Trio had recorded and claimed the song as theirs. Seeger called them. "We didn't know you recorded it," Dave Guard said. "We'll take our name off."

The song traveled the world. In Germany, Marlene Dietrich's daughter insisted she record it; both Peggy Seeger and Dominic Behan, the Irish writer and singer, told Seeger that it was his best song.

"When I came out to Camp Woodland the next time," Seeger continued, "I found a young counselor, Joe Hickerson, singing the song with his kids. Group singing gave it more rhythm." Hickerson repeated the first verse at the end, giving it a cyclical feel, and added two verses. His kids at camp taught it in 1959 to Peter, Paul and Mary, whose recording reached the Hit Parade.

A dark period again had produced a universal song, later recorded by hundreds. The musician who thrives despite poverty and despair is a cliché; yet in Seeger's case, when everything tipped against him, when his liberty, profession, and safety were in jeopardy, a spark ignited into song.

PETE SEEGER, Lomax suggested, planned his life in five-year blocks. In the midfifties, this meant not only a folk song revival but a youth rebellion, both arriving in the 1960s. "I am glad to report partial success in my campaign to lead the younger generation astray," Seeger wrote in *Sing Out!*, "by persuading them to spend their college vacations hitch-hiking around the country, learning about people and regions." These are the years when *Life* photographed college students swallowing goldfish and crowding into phone booths. He regularly tossed in songs like "Poisoning the Students' Minds."

"There's a big folk-singing revival going on," he told *Labor's Daily.* "I'm trying to do my part. I sure wish more unions would get interested."

In *Sing Out!*, Seeger introduced songs he hoped would catch on, including one from the Georgia Sea Islands, "Michael Row Your Boat Ashore," and "Guantanamera." In his column, he suggested people set up singing groups. Hold potlucks and sing! If Seeger had run the land, these singing clubs might have been a unit of government. (Would they have been mandatory?)

One such club was at his father's house, where Peggy and Mike Seeger lived. The singing Seegers even recorded a little-known family album for Folkways, with Barbara and Penny, Peggy's sisters.

Mike, twelve years younger than Pete, was a shy, rangy fellow in blue jeans. He'd studiously avoided music. "My parents would offer him these tests," Peggy remembered. "Empty the garbage or play a musical instrument. Mike preferred to take out the garbage." Thus the story of Mike Seeger learning to play the banjo, in the shadow and (in Charlie's case) baleful eye of his family, has itself become folklore.

Around the age of eighteen (some say earlier), Mike came down with shingles in his eyes. He had to lie in darkness for six weeks. Pete had just sent Peggy and Mike a copy of his banjo manual, and Mike hooted, "You can't teach the banjo by a book!"

"Prove it," his mother Ruth said cagily. "You try it and see if you can."

"So there was Mike on his back," his sister Peggy recalled. "This banjo appeared. I'd sit up there and read the passage, 'You've got to go plunk—di-de, plunk—di-de,' and Mike practiced in the dark. That's how he started playing banjo, and he never looked back after that. Once he discovered he could do 'plunk—di-de,' he went on to 'bump—ditty, bump—ditty.'

"Then, *I* wanted to try it," Peggy said, but Mike said, "'The banjo's a boy's instrument.' So of course me, wearing jeans and climbing trees and playing football, I thought, 'If it's a boy's instrument, that's for me!'"

Mike was a natural instrumentalist, exceeding Pete on mandolin, with a different approach to the banjo: old-time stringband music. With two friends, Tom Paley and John Cohen, they formed the most influential old-timey band of the revival, the New Lost City Ramblers, in 1958. Peggy dropped out of Radcliffe to see the world. She became an enormously talented balladeer, banjoist, and feminist songwriter, whose "I Want to Be an Engineer" Pete often sang. At the Seegers', the folk music revival was a family affair.

Seeger had caught the tail end of the revival of the 1930s at the Archive, but the era of "Talking Union" had passed, and along with it, songs asserting the Left had a hammer. Now the question was, What did all those sacrifices mean? Where *had* all the flowers gone? Seeger's music had moved from activism to new functions: sustaining hope, reminding radicals of a better world to come.

Seeger liked to tell one of Woody's stories about two rabbits chased by hounds. They ran until they couldn't stand it anymore; finally they holed up in a hollow log. The hounds bayed, but the little rabbits nestled inside, out of reach. The boy rabbit turned to the girl rabbit: "What do we do now?"

"Stay here till we outnumber them," she answered. In the fifties that log—where the old Left snuggled with itself—included just enough room for a skinny banjo picker.

In this time, Seeger faced the dilemma pointed out by poet Stephen Spender: Those writing revolutionary songs or poetry must confront the antimaterialist form of their own art. Songs of injustice become something beautiful, when they're beautifully sung. The most moving political songs actually distract listeners from social reality, as the music and the performance spellbind their audience.

"Music is the most powerful of all the idealist drugs except religion," Spender wrote. In this way, Seeger's best political songs evoke not the bitterness of repression but the glory of its solution and the potential beauty of a world remade. His music couldn't overthrow a corrupt government, he had come to realize, but the children he sang for might make the earth a better place. He wasn't inspiring direct political action, he was inspiring people.

NEWSPAPERS CALLED HIM a modern Pied Piper. Seeger charts the folksong revival in the fifties by his Oberlin appearances: "In '53 I sang for two hundred. In '54, six hundred came. In '55, a thousand." The blacklist only made Seeger heroic: "I felt wildly successful."

From where he stood, looking back on decades of isolated work by the Lomaxes and the Seegers, the seedlings of a folk song revival were sprouting, and with it, youth rebellion. The music was no longer left-wing. Other folk song performers followed the college trail the Seegers had blazed: Jean Ritchie, the exquisite Appalachian dulcimer player; Jack Elliot, Woody's protégé; and many others. Guitar sales hit the half-million mark in 1956; his banjo manual had entered its second edition; and royalties from Folkways increased steadily.

The best part of this was honoring old friends. Also in 1956, Seeger performed in *California to New York Island*, a stage adaptation of Guthrie's autobiography. Guthrie sat in the balcony, smiling. Huntington's disease had tied Woody to his hospital bed, but he came out for occasions like this. Seventeen years had passed since Woody and Pete had first sung together. Tears rolled down the faces of old-timers as a thousand voices, mostly Seeger's teenage audience, earnestly sang "This Land Is Your Land."

Seeger hadn't seen much of his old friend in the 1950s, after turning down Woody's invitation to restart the Almanacs. They hadn't performed together since after a party in Topanga Canyon at Will Geer's place in 1952.

Before Guthrie's diagnosis, "We had thought he was drinking too much, because he was having attacks of Huntington," Seeger reflected. "He was no longer the reliable singer we'd known and he wasn't writing as many good songs. He wrote some.

"He was quite critical of us too. After the Wallace campaign, he wrote a serious letter to People's Songs, said we didn't have any real songs. Money was being spent on the cold war and people were hungry. He wanted a song that really slapped that tragedy in the face.

"Then he went back to California and came back with his third wife, Anneke. He'd go off hitchhiking and get picked up by the police for acting irrationally." By the end of 1952, he'd checked into a state hospital, "Gravestone Park," he wryly called it.

"They treat me fine; the food's fine," he'd say. "Besides, this is the freest place in America. Here I can jump on the table and shout, 'I'm a Communist,' and they say 'Oh, he's crazy.' Try *that* where you live."

—

ON MARCH 26, 1957, just as the Weavers' reunion concert was at #3 in *Variety*'s charts, Seeger moved a step closer to jail. A federal grand jury indicted him on ten counts of contempt of Congress. On March 29, he pleaded Not Guilty and was released on one thousand dollars bail, having no prior offenses. Seeger expected the trial within three to eight months, telling his friends, "I still feel I committed no wrong, and that my children will not feel ashamed of me in future years. If only we could look down like the Gods upon the scene, it might even appear funny, if it were not also tragic."

The indictment checked his travels. The judge forbade Seeger to leave the Southern District of New York without permission.

He couldn't take the subway to Brooklyn without the court's consent, much less cross the Hudson to New Jersey to see Woody. Eventually Paul Ross negotiated this to notification. Every time Seeger traveled—practically daily—he had to send the District Attorney a telegram stating where he was going, when, and by what transportation. This left him in a paradox: He had to travel farther to find jobs, but the court was limiting his travel. Out on the road for long stretches, Seeger made a lone figure carrying his banjo and his duffel along bus station corridors. When he arrived at a hotel, he checked the closets for a frame-up. His family life deteriorated as he was away performing more to pay legal costs. Harold would come up with dates, and Seeger would perform both solo and with the Weavers. Between 1956 and 1958, he performed in nearly every state and Canada.

"This [Canada] trip is the hardest one I ever took, from the standpoint of being away from the family," he wrote Moe Asch. "I hope never to be away so long for any reason whatsoever."

AS FOLK MUSIC increased in popularity, Seeger became the odd celebrity. Bobby-soxers did not wail for him. Professionals disregarded his music. Only a fraction of the population knew his name.

And few scholars took him seriously. When folklorist John Greenway published *American Folksongs of Protest* in 1954, he accorded Seeger two footnotes.

An interesting comparison is with Burl Ives, who had advantages Seeger didn't: skills at acting, popular acclaim, wealth. In reviewing Ives's book for *Sing Out!*, Seeger made sure readers understood the different paths he and Burl had taken.

He hadn't forgiven Burl's "fingering, like any common stool pigeon, some of his radical associates" before HUAC. Ives had done this, according to Seeger, "because he felt it was the only way to preserve his lucrative contracts; and that makes his action all the more despicable." Seeger compared him to Falstaff, "gross, gargantuan, talented, and clever; he was also not quite intelligent enough to be honorable." It was a surprisingly cruel critique his Puritan forerunners would have found in *Pilgrim's Progress*: "Come hither, you that walk along the way/see how Pilgrims fare that go astray."

"When he comes up before the bar of judgment," Seeger ended, "let us be generous enough to allow him to present his positive contributions, which have been many." These are lines Seeger later regretted. "Who did Seeger think he was—Saint Peter?" one reader thundered.

By this time, Seeger knew who he was: "a master musician with music in his bones, nerves, and fingers," as his former hero Mike Gold called him in 1958. In "A Paean to Pete Seeger and American Music," the writer who had chided Seeger's father in the *Worker* for ignoring folk music now lauded the son for popularizing it.

In July 1958, a U.S. Circuit Court judge faced a challenging decision on Seeger's music, one that effectively sums up his situation. The case began when the Detroit Labor Forum wanted to present Pete Seeger at the Institute of Arts auditorium. The Detroit Arts Commission banned him on the grounds that the auditorium "may not be rented for programs of a political or controversial nature." The Labor Forum took this ruling to court, insisting, "Mr. Seeger was being presented not as a political figure but as a singer."

The case was heard by Wade McCree (later U.S. solicitor general) and Thomas J. Murphy, ruling on an issue that would puzzle even a professional critic. Was what Seeger did with an audience musical or political? According to the Art Institute, singing was allowed in the auditorium; politics were not.

Judge Murphy adopted the easy way out in his decision. Seeger would be singing; ergo, he was a singer; and the concert could proceed. "Judge Murphy's position was that singing songs isn't likely to start a riot," the *Detroit Free Press* wrote. Underlying this legal attack were fundamental questions: Was Seeger (or any musician) primarily a politician? Do governments have the right to suppress a singer (or any artist)?

In Seeger's case, answers were elusive. Yet during the next decade, the naked-hearted singer would (with Paul Robeson) become the most picketed, blacklisted entertainer in American history.

Chapter 9

JOHN HENRY

—

SEEGER'S LEGAL TROUBLES SHADOWED HIM. THE JUSTICE Department agreed to hearings, then postponed them, searching for the best moment for a conviction. Instead of the three to eight months Seeger had expected, the proceedings stretched out for years. No one knew what would emerge at his trial. Seeger was set to challenge HUAC publicly; the committee had Seeger's FBI files, including damaging information about his Party membership. "Don't be in a hurry," Paul Ross told his client. "A trial next year will be better than one this year."

The Seegers tried to enjoy what tranquillity they had. In 1958, for the first time in twenty years of singing, Seeger turned down work to drive Toshi and the kids across the country. For one brief vacation the Seegers toured Yellowstone and the Grand Tetons like any other American family. They met no pickets, no police moving them on. He threaded through the enormous plains and miles of wheat and corn that Woody had first shown him back in 1940. The family camped out and Pete chopped stacks of wood for campfires. At dusk he played quiet tunes on his recorder, and the notes floated out across the forest. Driving the western highways, he was moved by the American landscape. At the end of one long afternoon behind the wheel, he pulled over to watch the mountains color at sunset. He actually burst out with "America the Beautiful."

Seeger wanted more time. He was drifting away from the

Weavers. He no longer needed a performing group—he found a new one at every stop. And because of the blacklist, the Weavers never regained their earlier audience. When they finally had a chance to return to the airwaves, it was a mixed blessing: a commercial for Lucky Strike cigarettes. This wasn't the first commercial scheme; earlier, they'd recorded "Take This Letter," a dubious novelty version of "Take This Hammer," which Seeger had once collected in a Texas prison.

This was worse. The quartet argued about the commercial. They were to sing a jingle, backed by a big band. Though all but Seeger were smokers, nobody was really enthusiastic, but they weren't getting many jobs. A commercial might open access to radio and TV. The Weavers voted, and Seeger was in the minority. He really *didn't* want to do an ad for cigarettes; with his mother-in-law suffering from lung cancer, he thought the job "shameful" and "the most commercial thing I'd ever been asked to do."

"We need the money, Pete. Maybe you can live on beans, but we have rent to pay," one of the Weavers said.

"Why couldn't it be for yogurt?" Seeger reportedly muttered. "At least I like yogurt!"

"That's easy for you to say," Fred said. "You have a solo career. We need this." Seeger was outvoted.

He asked his father for advice. He couldn't refuse the group's wishes, but he couldn't stomach making the commercial.

"Peter," Charles answered, "you ought not to try and sing with the Weavers forever." Seeger went back to the group and did the commercial. That night he invited them to Harold's apartment. He was leaving the group for good, he said, "and would have nothing more to say about the subject, ever." He suggested the Weavers hire Erik Darling, his former banjo student.

The Weavers felt they'd been left hanging. "It came out in the guise of going ahead to do something pure and noble," Lee Hays said later, "which had the effect of making the rest of us feel guilty as hell. . . . He just walked out on us and it was a terrible blow."

The group hadn't expected the golden goose to flee the barn: "When Pete left, he took away much of our stock in trade, as was his right to do. There was extreme bitterness all the way around, which could be said to be a result of seeing our meal ticket vanish or possibly realizing that from now on we'd have to work ten times as hard."

"In dreams begin responsibilities," wrote poet Delmore Schwartz; and Seeger's dreams made him severe. If he had been born in his father's time, Seeger might have become a Kodaly, a Grieg, or a Bartok: a symphonic composer who wrote nationalistic music based on folk tunes. Instead, as a child of the Popular Front, Seeger had fused America's folk and popular musics. A vision of Americans playing their own music—instead of hearing professionals perform it on radio or discs—captured Seeger as few other goals did. To him, folk songs had always had a patriotic undercurrent; the music had been carved from the rhythm of daily lives, the curves of the American land, the outline of its architecture, and its climate. For generations, the stream of folk music had flowed underground, beneath America's pop and high culture: Indian dance tunes, Irish airs, Afro-American shouts and blues. Seeger wanted to bring these traditions close to the musical surface, so Americans could reclaim their riches. He had endured and kept his hands cupped around the flame till others were ready to receive it.

In the fall of 1958 the Kingston Trio's recording "Tom Dooley" publicized folk music as dramatically as the Weavers had earlier; the record sold 2.6 million copies. The song echoed from radio to radio, saturating an urban nation with nostalgia for country roots. Record companies signed up groups like the Chad Mitchell Trio, the Brothers Four, the Tarriers, and the Limelighters.

But it wasn't just commercial recordings that were selling, as Seeger's correspondence reveals. As of December 31, 1957 Seeger earned $1,826 from Folkways' royalties, a 50 percent increase over the year before. As Seeger was breaking up with the Weavers,

America's Favorite Ballads (which were neither exclusively American, nor ballads) was on the best-seller list for twenty weeks, according to *Variety*.

Charles Seeger had predicted this revival back in 1939, anticipating his children's musical careers in that essay "Grassroots for American Music." Pete Seeger associated folk music with a down-home lifestyle uncomplicated by materialism, and he convinced many of this association. Folk songs came to represent campfire sing-alongs instead of TV bandstands, hiking boots and flannel shirts instead of penny loafers and button-down collars.

An industry was emerging from Seeger's enthusiasms, and he was in the position of a master painter whose work is discovered. He not only had a warehouse full of product, but he'd taught most of America's young folk performers. At a single 1954 concert in Palo Alto, for instance, Seeger had inspired the careers of both Joan Baez and Dave Guard (of the Kingston Trio). All this would have mattered little, however, if not for the work of Moe Asch and Harold Leventhal, who formed a phalanx to promote Seeger and folk music.

Leventhal had come a long way since he'd introduced himself to the Weavers at the Vanguard. Leaving behind his garment business, Harold had prospered. He had put on weight and taken to wearing suits, but he still cut a boyish figure compared to his peers in the music industry, who talked only gross and net. Harold often entered his office with a smile on his round face, as if humming a lovely tune he couldn't quite remember. At times his soft-spokenness led performers to wonder if he represented them forcefully. He did. Seeger was his Number One, though; Harold saw a long career for him.

One of the factors cementing their relationship was a shared political philosophy; Leventhal was, according to Joe Klein, the author of *Woody Guthrie*, "a Communist, which meant he could be trusted." He was an informal confidant for progressive musicians, becoming one of the only managers to handle both the mercantile and the philosophical problems of a politically oriented musician. Leventhal understood why Seeger enjoyed benefits, and Seeger turned to him as a sounding board for his eccentric ideas. If he suddenly decided to write a dance based on a Chopin étude (which he once did), Harold would have a say (but not the final word) on whether to publish it. Harold kept track of Seeger's pet concerns—and learned to call Toshi if he needed anything signed.

After years of practice, Toshi had become the organizer Seeger had hoped to be. While her husband wrote songs in the barn, Toshi would take a notebook and fill in his schedule, and "God help Pete Seeger if he lost that book," family friend Jimmy Collier laughed. When he left the house on a booking, Toshi stuck a few dollars in his pocket. "When she forgot—and it didn't happen often—Seeger ended up bumming money for his tea."

Despite the sudden, widespread interest in folk music, Seeger fared no better with his old enemies: *Counterattack*, HUAC, and the American Legion. As the red hunt subsided in America and the "Impeach Earl Warren" billboards yellowed, anti-Communists increased their fire on "Khrushchev's Songbird," as Seeger's hunters fondly called him. If these groups weren't up to many new targets, at least they weren't letting the old ones slide.

By now the Seegers took the harassment for granted. On a 1959 tour of England, he found to his surprise that his approaching trial had created a stir there. He had to convince people that he was not fleeing America to avoid jail: "It never even occurred to me." Given the seriousness of the charges against him, the expectation wasn't unreasonable. The attacks worsened in the year following his return. In December 1959, an appearance in Great Neck, Long Island, had the community in an uproar. A few months later, the San Diego Board of Education demanded Seeger sign a loyalty oath before singing in a high school auditorium. He refused. The usual drama unfolded. The local American Legion insisted Seeger was criminally subversive; he was, after all, under indictment.

Liberal sponsors of the concert called for freedom of speech. One school board member actually listened to Seeger's music before passing judgment; William Elser checked out "Cindy," "Frog Went A-Courtin'," and other tunes from the school library. "I couldn't see anything wrong with them," Elser said. "There's nothing communistic about these songs."

Seeger's critics failed to realize that these challenges only brought more listeners. When he finally sang in San Diego, the pickets carried signs reading "Ban the Bum." Seeger had the last laugh. Halfway through the concert, as he was building up steam, he peeled off his sweater, showing the audience a bright scarlet shirt. Laughs. He smiled sweetly and slowly bent over to expose matching red socks.

Near Beacon, the American Legion tried to cancel a Seeger performance in nearby Nyack. They held a press conference with one of HUAC's staff, who traveled three hundred miles for the occasion. Rockland County papers praised the local citizens who opposed the "beards, berets, and beat-up attire" of visitors from New York City. A local official discovered the theater had an out-of-date license and ordered the place shut before Seeger could sing a second night. If the theater was to stay open, a special licensing fee had to be paid immediately; with a creative skulduggery, municipal offices yanked down their shades, and the town clerk and mayor arranged to be out of town for the day.

"That theater was right across the street from where my mother had lived, a hundred yards away," Seeger reflected. "It's where I saw Rudolph Valentino when I was six."

Seeger could barely hold on to his past, much less the present; a right-wing group, Texans for America, managed to convince textbook publishers to delete all references to Seeger's singing. He tended to underestimate his attackers: "I have a Pollyanna streak," he said. "I assume everything will turn out right." But a letter-writing campaign could still frighten a network; having Pete Seeger sing at a barbecue could bring a HUAC subpoena, as it did to one woman in Ohio. No matter how popular Seeger became, a few would only hear a Communist plot in his songs.

Just as Seeger performed "Nobody Knows the Troubles I've Seen" and "Worried Man Blues" at the time of his HUAC appearance, he now sang "John Henry." All his life, he'd found inspiration in the story:

The captain said to John Henry
"I'm gonna bring that steam drill around,
I'm gonna bring that steel drill out on the job,
I'm gonna whup that steel on down."

Now the man that invented the steam drill,
He thought he was mighty fine;
But John Henry drove fifteen feet,
The steam drill only made nine.

John Henry hammered in the mountains,
His hammer was striking fire,
But he worked so hard, it broke his poor heart,
And he laid down his hammer and he died.

John Henry had a little baby,
You could hold him in the palm of your hand;
And the last words I heard that poor boy say,
"My daddy was a steel driving man."

"It's a good example of how a folk song means almost as many things as you want it to mean," said Seeger. "When I was fourteen, it was simply a Paul Bunyan–type extravaganza, a tall tale like 'Jack and the Beanstalk,' with a strong man exaggerated beyond belief. Then Alan Lomax told me of the bawdy significance: a man sitting holding the drill between his legs and coming down with a big hammer on top of it. . . . Later on, I think I understood more of the tragedy of the song, and at the age of sixty, the verse I would never leave out is 'John Henry had a little baby.' "

Seeger believed the John Henry myth: that a person of good intentions who gave his all could defeat any opponent. As a symbol, John Henry aroused his class sympathy: an African American working man, relying on strength and tools to resist dehumanizing progress and profits. Seeger's own struggles pitted him against an equally impersonal machine: television.

One afternoon in December 1960, Seeger sat in his drafty office in the barn. Huddled by the old-fashioned space heater, he typed unevenly, with more determination than accuracy. In the pale winter light he looked frail and bony, though his arms showed a wiry strength from chopping wood. His face had the first lines of middle age, and his nose a reddish hue. His trial had finally been set for March, three months hence; Harold had begun organizing a legal defense fund, but it was not on this that Seeger typed. He had a new hope: televising folk music. Over the past five years he'd concluded that television would shape cultural movements of the future. Seeger was ready to approach (and eventually assault) the medium. That he had been kept off network TV for a decade only increased his estimation of its power.

Television could be a new beginning for him. Singers had begun telling audiences, "Here's a song I learned off an old Pete Seeger record." Seeger was only forty-one, but thanks to the blacklist, he might have been dead and buried. He wanted America to hear its folk songs—and he wouldn't mind being the guy who sang them on TV.

Throughout December 1960, Seeger labored over drafts of *Pete Seeger, Banjo Traveler*, for the Canadian Broadcasting Corporation. The scope was enormous: twenty-six half-hour documentaries, with locations in French Canada, the Caribbean, and throughout the United States—an ambitious project for a man who might be in jail before the first filming began.

With the first snows, the Seegers' driveway grew icy slick, and visitors departed. Unfortunately, the mail increased proportionately, until the only time for music was early in the morning and late at night, when he was too drowsy to answer letters. The mail had become a major ritual: Toshi would pick it up and screen it. Then he would write answers while Toshi pulled the paper out from under his pen and addressed them. They could get through seventy-five letters a day this way, each brief but handwritten, with a banjo sketched beneath his signature. Seeger was in a bind; he disliked dictated letters for their impersonality, but mail days left him cranky and tired.

As his trial neared, the Seegers held on. If Toshi had wavered, if in protest she had stopped answering phone calls and fending off reporters, who knows what might have happened. Under similar circumstances, other spouses had fought bitterly for a more "reasonable" stance, even using the children as a threat that charity begins at home. Seeger could have reconsidered; he could have told the judge he wanted to make a clean breast of it. No one would have blamed him.

Toshi did not flinch; she was Seeger's full-time partner. At concerts, it was Toshi who examined the crowd: a short, unstylish, intensely quiet woman in her late thirties, leaning against the wall, smoking a cigarette. Her hair was shiny and dark; her eyes flicked around the room, staring through people. She got things done, always the last to leave: "staying after every concert," a young admirer recalled, "in dark auditoriums to pick up papers and trash long after the audience and performers had left." It was no secret to fellow performers that Seeger's reputation was as much hers as his.

Other family members suffered under blacklist pressure from Seeger's trial. His eldest brother, Charles III, had trouble obtaining jobs and government clearances; eventually he moved to Europe for his career. In 1958 Mike quit one of his first jobs, with the Social Security Office in Washington, because of a security check. "The government later sent me a dossier on my father, brother, and sister, asking me to comment on it. . . . They told me that if I didn't answer and tell them yes or no, I would never get another government job again." To test this blacklist, Mike Seeger got himself hired on a radio show sponsored by the Social Security Administration. When it came time for the musicians to get their checks, Mike stepped forward and gave his name. The producer refused to write him a check, making it out instead to Mike's friend, folklorist Ralph Rinzler.

Mike staked out a territory where he could be recognized as more than Pete's kid brother. If Pete Seeger was a popularizer, Mike Seeger became a preservationist, duplicating tunes note for note from the original sources. Radical songs and audience singing did not inspire him; he would rather teach four reverent people country mandolin than get four thousand singing.

Peggy Seeger also had a specialty: traditional Appalachian ballads, many learned from her mother's transcriptions. She also sang folk songs in a feminist vein, frailing and double-thumbing the banjo better than Pete did. In the late fifties, she left Radcliffe for Europe and China; she found herself harassed by customs officials. On returning from England to visit her family, she had a thick dossier labeled "Seeger" slapped in front of her. "In 1957 you said this," they told her, and "Would you say this is a likeness of you?" British immigration officials later peered into a similar file and put Peggy on a ferry back to France. The United States took her passport away—as they had done to her father and her half-brother Charles.

ON MARCH 27, 1961, Pete Seeger went on trial for contempt of Congress in New York City. Judge Thomas Murphy presided. This was, by coincidence, the young former district attorney who'd applauded the Weavers at the Blue Angel and the man who allowed Seeger to sing in Detroit in 1958.

Arriving on the first day, the government's lawyer, Irving Younger, had never seen so many people in a court before—five hundred spectators, mostly of college age, and more lined up at the door. Younger had inherited the case.

"As a lawyer," he said later, "I speak for whoever retains me; I didn't think twice about prosecuting Seeger. I'd never heard of him."

Younger told the jury that the case was one of contempt, not of Seeger's involvement in the Communist Party. Paul Ross's defense was to attack HUAC head-on: "In no instance in this committee's investigation was the matter of national security, espionage, sabotage, or the advocating of the violent overthrow of the government involved."

Seeger watched this spectacle soberly; he had received the depressing news that Canadian television had rejected his television project. If the liberal CBC wasn't interested, no American network would touch it.

For his trial, Seeger had the idea of subpoenaing the subpoenaer—Francis Walter, former HUAC chairman, now a key defense witness—to testify on HUAC's purpose in investigating Seeger. But Judge Murphy didn't intend to have the congressman harassed. Paul Ross had a rough day. Murphy excluded 102 of Ross's questions. During the whole challenge to HUAC's authority, Murphy ordered the jury from the room. "Seeger will be lucky if he gets off with the electric chair at this rate," gibed one reporter.

Murray Kempton of the *New York Post* noted Walter's "expression of dyspepsia" as he left the courtroom. "The menace Seeger," Kempton wrote, "sat through the proceedings slouched and far away over the distant hills," quietly doodling snails with fancy tails.

One of the factors prejudicing Judge Murphy was Seeger's FBI files, which made yet another appearance—this time in closed session, when Irving Younger used them to cross-examine Seeger's character witnesses, inserting into the trial record allegations of three informants on Seeger (among them the professional anti-Communist Louis Budenz).

The best trial coverage came from the *Harvard Crimson*, which did not miss the irony of Irving Younger (class of '53) prosecuting Seeger (whom they flatteringly called class of '40). A reporter from the *New York Times* attended the trial each day, an indication of the importance Seeger now had in the music industry.

Harold Leventhal also appeared at every session, despite the fact that he was now the best-known manager in folk music. He'd sit and chew on an unlit cigar. "For Pete's Sake," the newsletter of the Friends of Pete Seeger, was his idea.

On the final day of the trial, Seeger's lawyer urged the jury to find him not guilty: His answers had been in good faith, even if they didn't satisfy the committee. But he was guilty of refusing to cooperate, Younger insisted. When the judge gave the jury its charge, Ross and Seeger knew he was in trouble. Murphy "determined as a matter of law" that HUAC's questions were pertinent to the committee's legitimate investigations. Seeger's case wilted.

The jury began its deliberations at 3:30 p.m. One hour and twenty minutes later, they returned the verdict: guilty. Jail was no longer an abstraction; he would be sentenced in six days. Toshi, Mika, and Danny sat in the courtroom with him. He gathered up his family and drove home.

DANGEROUS MINSTREL NABBED HERE wrote the *New York Post* on March 31, 1961: "Amid our larger tribulations, the Justice Department has moved fearlessly and decisively against ballad singer Pete Seeger. . . . That the combined powers of the House committee and the Justice Department should be rallied to imprison him is a bitter burlesque. Some jail will be a more joyous place if he lands there, and things will be bleaker on the outside."

Seeger's public reaction was steely cold. He was only doing his duty; in 1955, that had meant speaking one's mind.

Seeger's anger came out in other ways. He fumed when Canadian immigration authorities wouldn't admit him on a concert tour without guarantees that he would return to the United States for imprisonment; they didn't want the minstrel loose in *their* country. He watched grimly as "John Henry" was turned into hoked-up parodies by crew-cut singers and their packager-producer-arrangers: John Henry the street cleaner, John Henry the idiot or math whiz. Worse, in Seeger's view, songs not destroyed were often appropriated; attaching the words "adapted and arranged by" gave two cents extra royalties per disc to the person claiming the song.

Commercialism in folk music wasn't new, but the contradictions of copyright had sharpened as "Tom Dooley" made thirty thousand dollars a week for the Kingston Trio, while Frank Warner, the song's collector, and Frank Profitt, the singer, barely earned gas money. A particularly painful copyright problem had emerged in the early fifties, when Alan Lomax had asked Seeger to acknowledge him as the owner of folk songs Alan and his father collected—many unearthed in an effort underwritten by the federal government. Seeger had been upset. How could Alan, who ought to know better, claim royalties from songs that belonged to the public domain? "Everybody was being so fucking opportunistic," Irwin Silber fumed. "I didn't see how Lomax's position could be justified, since the collecting was financed by the Library of Congress."

The folksong revival magazine, *Little Sandy Review*, also weighed in: Folkies were irked at seeing "collected and arranged by Alan Lomax." "'Why can't he keep his damn thumb out of the soup and just give us documentation,' they cry. . . . They will find that 'Shady Grove' has the tune collected from a Kentucky singer but the text lifted from the *Journal of American Folklore*." To better his copyright claim, Lomax was creating composite versions, a "put up job that probably never existed until Lomax invented it." Charles Seeger was so mad he broke with Alan.

The copyright topic sickened Seeger, but he didn't want to dampen the huge audiences of commercialized folk music. A few months before his trial, Columbia Records had asked him to sign with them. (Moe Asch had agreed, provided Folkways could continue releasing its previous recordings.) Before producer John Hammond could get final permission, though, he had to consult senior CBS executives. Hammond met with Columbia Records' president, Goddard Lieberson, in his plushly appointed office; Lieberson called in Richard Salant, a corporate VP.

"I've got a question in a delicate area. It's Pete Seeger. Can we use him?"

"We don't need him, and he's not welcome on CBS television," Salant said flatly.

"We want to sign him to Columbia Records."

Salant asked if he thought Seeger would sell.

"I wouldn't be calling you if I didn't," Goddard replied.

"Well, you're big boys now," Salant decided. "Do what you want." They signed Seeger, but they didn't completely trust him; Seeger didn't hear about this conversation until fifteen years later.

Columbia promised to put his records in stores across the country. Malvina Reynolds, who also signed with Columbia, understood Seeger's decision: "The only reason Pete and I are interested in whether records sell is that people get to hear our voices. . . . It's not as simple as commercial or noncommercial. You become surrounded by this complex of grabbing people and wonder, as you become a big commercial property, if you'll be cut off from the very thing that made you special."

THREE DAYS AFTER his conviction, the Seegers walked in the annual New York Easter peace march, sponsored by the Committee for a Sane Nuclear Policy. The weather blew cold and rainy, but the marchers kept their spirits up by marveling how their numbers had grown. In the fifties, hundreds had turned out; now, with papers discussing the Ban the Bomb movement, 3,500 marched. The Seegers trudged along, keeping out of the public eye. Pete's shyness made him appear remote; a hardness in his face kept people from asking his feelings.

Twelve blocks long and the width of Broadway, the march crossed midtown Manhattan to the United Nations with petitions for nuclear disarmament. The East River stretched icy gray and silent on the sidelines. Easter paraders watched their lacy hats flopping in the wind. Families pushed baby carriages with picnic baskets tucked inside. "Peace in the world or the world in pieces" read a six-year-old's sign.

From summer camps to peace marches, the baby-boomer children that Seeger sang for had reached adolescence. To them, Seeger remained a John Henry–like figure, the man who fought the machinery of blacklisting.

As the rally at UN Plaza ended, a speaker noticed Seeger in the throng. "The demonstrators throbbed the chant 'We Want Seeger,'" according to the *Journal-American*. The sound must have rung in Seeger's ears like a fire alarm to a man with a hangover.

"Pete Seeger" (applause). "Let's bring him up here, what do you say?" (The applause swelled to an ovation.) "Pete's been through hard times recently. For fighting HUAC, the government wants to lock him away! Let's give him our support." Seeger reluctantly climbed atop the platform, but instead of speaking, he nodded to the crowd like an old friend. He sang a peace song, asked everyone to work hard for disarmament, and began to climb down. "What about your case?" someone called.

He looked around in protest. He rarely talked about himself in public, but his feelings swelled almost out of control. Seeger hesitated, caught between embarrassment that people thought him a hero, and frustration at his unjust conviction. In the end, he shook his head and stepped down, unable to shed his optimist's garb: "I don't think I did much talking that day. One of the hardest things I learned to do was to smile and acknowledge the applause."

Later he discovered that when the crowd had called out his name, the sponsors of the march were more distressed than he was. A disagreement had taken place backstage: Was a convicted felon to address their crowd? The liberals of SANE later wrote Seeger: "Unless we ask you to be on the platform, please don't." Fear of controversy knows no Left or Right.

TUESDAY, APRIL 3, 1961, arrived, and Seeger drove to New York for sentencing. He walked into the courtroom wearing a suit with his banjo slung over one shoulder. Photographs show him looking chipper, more like a man headed for vacation than jail. Before passing sentence, Judge Murphy asked Seeger if he had anything to tell the court.

"Thank you, your honor. After hearing myself talked about, pro and con, for three days, I am grateful to say a few unrestricted words." Seeger thanked his lawyer and again declared he hadn't "sung anything in any way subversive to my country." Just as in his testimony, he addressed an audience beyond the courtroom.

"Some of my ancestors were religious dissenters who came to America over three hundred years ago. Others were abolitionists in New England in the eighteen forties and fifties. I believe that in choosing my present course I do no dishonor to them, or to those who may come after me."

("Don't forget, Peter—you come from good stock!" Grandmother had said.)

"I am forty-two years old, and count myself a very lucky man. I have a wife and three healthy children, and we live in a house we built with our own hands, on the banks of the beautiful Hudson River. For twenty years I have been singing the folk songs of America and other lands to people everywhere. . . . The specific song whose title was mentioned in this trial, 'Wasn't That a Time,' is one of my favorites. The song is apropos to this case. I wonder if I might have your permission to sing it here before I close?"

"You may not," Judge Murphy said firmly.

"Perhaps you will hear it some other time. . . . Do I have a right to sing these songs? Do I have the right to sing them anywhere?"

The judge brushed aside Seeger's concerns and sentenced him to a year in jail for every count: ten years. The sentences could be served concurrently, however, leaving him a year and a day in federal prison. To this, the judge gruffly added the costs of prosecution; Seeger had to pay for the government's expenses in trying him, even Francis Walter's lunch.

Seeger was still standing, facing the judge, when Paul Ross stood up and said, "Your honor, I want to see about bail."

"There is no bail. Bailiff, take him away."

There was a gasp in the courtroom. Seeger didn't have time to turn around before the bailiff clamped handcuffs on. Toshi walked up from behind and lifted his banjo from his arms.

He was led through a door and down a flight of stairs to the basement of the courthouse; there they locked him in a cell with three or four men awaiting trial.

Upstairs, Seeger's lawyer ran over to the Court of Appeals. The Circuit Court could set bail; if they didn't, Seeger might stay inside for quite a while. Harold had to find cash in a hurry; he hopped in a cab and started visiting friends who worked near banks.

A hundred demonstrators had assembled outside the courtroom, chanting that Seeger be set free. He could barely make out what they were saying. Outside the cell a visitor looked out and said, "Hey, there's a big crowd outside for somebody. Some Commie." He came over and peered in at Seeger. "Oh, you're the guy," he said, disappointed.

"We'd been talking before," Seeger said, "and now I was just sitting there. The guy was so surprised; I was mildly eating a sandwich, and he was expecting to see some real revolutionary-type person."

Somewhere, he knew, Toshi and his friends were doing their best to get him out. But being in jail for the right reasons wasn't so terrible. He felt "momentarily speechless," but he had a warm glow. He would go down fighting like John Henry, or Uncle Alan, who'd have been proud, he who charged gallantly to his death in the Foreign Legion. It would be worth the fifteen thousand dollars the trial cost.

"It's a hard thing to explain," Seeger later said, stumbling for words to describe the sensation of righteousness. "But when you're following what you think is the right course, it may not be fun, but you feel a certain satisfaction in doing it."

Paul Ross got the petition for appeal approved, though it took hours. He rushed back to the courtroom to find Harold: Seeger's freedom could be had for two thousand dollars cash. Toshi and Harold and Paul together counted out the bills to the clerk.

Downstairs, a black man next to Seeger was singing: "If that judge believes what I say, I'll be leaving for home today." The guy next to him said, "Not if he sees your record, you won't." In his few hours behind bars, Pete Seeger learned a folk song.

IN NEW YORK, Seeger's situation sent a tremor through the folk music community. The recently arrived Bob Dylan expressed the feelings of many Greenwich Village folkies: "They're framing him—they just want to shut him up."

His conviction added to an antiestablishment atmosphere in the Village. Six days after his sentencing, a small-scale riot broke out, the Battle of Washington Square. For fifteen years, singers and guitar players had gathered on Sunday afternoons in the park at the foot of Fifth Avenue. Then, in April 1961, Parks Commissioner Newbold Morris made the mistake of trying to ban singing in the park, at the request of the Greenwich Village Chamber of Commerce. Commissioner Morris based his order on an all-but-forgotten law forbidding minstrels in public parks.

On April 9 singers gathered in the Square to test the ruling, led by Izzy Young, influential columnist for *Sing Out!* and owner of the Folklore Center. The police duly instructed them to sing *a cappella*: If they played instruments, they would be arrested for ministry. The singers laughed and displayed signs reading MUSIC

TAMES THE SAVAGE BEAST. This was the kind of symbolic battle Pete (and Charles) Seeger relished; if he had been less weary of publicity, Pete might have attended.

News of the demonstration appeared in *Time* and as far west as the *San Francisco Chronicle*. The Greenwich Village Right to Sing Committee formed. After a month, Parks Commissioner Morris rescinded the order, and freedom of song returned to Greenwich Village. Columnist Walter Winchell wrote of an officer who stopped a stroller near the Square.

"Whatcha doin' here?" the law demanded.

"I'm looking for someone to mug," admitted the man.

"Sorry," the law apologized, "I thought you were a folksinger."

The lyrics to a brand-new "Ballad of Washington Square" were taped to the mike when Seeger visited the Village Gate at his first session for Columbia Records, *Story Songs*, three weeks later. He looked "shy and nervous," according to Peter Bogdanovich's liner notes. The audience included Columbia executives and ex-members of the Almanacs and Weavers. As usual, Seeger wore bright colors (aqua and tangerine); a half-hour into the concert, he asked the audience to join him in a yodel.

Waiters rushed about the room, taking orders and spilling drinks. No one noticed; even the dink of ashtrays and glasses had stopped. The audience hadn't come to yodel, but Seeger demonstrated how with a smile; he knew they'd go along. Sure enough, a few minutes later the room sounded like a convention of drunken alpinists, the high-pitched falsettos bouncing off the rafters.

"It's amazing how Pete does it," his sister Peggy once said. "He's perfected certain motions and things you say to an audience until it seems spontaneous. He'll pick out one person in the crowd and address something to them. This helps the singer look on the audience as an aggregate of individuals, rather than a blurry mass. Sometimes he brings up someone from the audience to play. It's not a ruse, it's a way of putting yourself in the audience's shoes, and putting them in yours.

"I'm letting you in on trade secrets now," Peggy continued: "If you appear night after night, you have to keep yourself fresh. . . . You know what you're going to say for the next song, but you stop, and you have a silence of about three or four seconds. This makes it look as if you're thinking, groping for something new. The audience is waiting; you know what you're going to say; but you can relax your shoulders, take a breath and think 'I don't have to push anything out.' The boxer gets a minute between rounds, you get four seconds."

On stage, Seeger told a story of two cats: Male cat says to the female, "Meeow," and the female answers "Not meeow." The audience laughed; the musician was warming the audience like a fire on a starless night. He led them through a tricky song, then took an intermission.

"Pete Seeger makes it all look easy," fellow singer Mike Cooney pointed out. "Don't believe it. All great art looks simple, but Pete's professional reputation was built on musicianship. His appearance of ease is deliberate. 'Look at me,' he seems to say, 'I don't have a voice as smooth as dewdrops rolling off rose petals—you can sing this too.'"

After the break, he did "John Henry," allowing himself some virtuoso banjo work. By its utter simplicity, the song represented an aesthetic challenge: taking three chords (and a story everyone knew) and dramatizing them. To accomplish this, he leaned on his vocal delivery, calling to John Henry as if he stood in earshot. On the line, "Hear John Henry's hammer ring," he brushed the strings so smartly the steel sang.

"Two more songs, then I have to go home." He started "Bells of Rhymney," where the bells of Welsh coal towns toll on his guitar. In Seeger's setting of a poem by Idris Davies, each phrase was repeated in a fast tempo; they blended into one another with a hint of dissonance. Only on the last phrase did the sound soften; the effect was like walking on a country road when two sets of bells pealed together. The musical tension rose until the last cadence resolved, and an enormous sigh swept the room. After Woody's "So Long," Seeger stepped off the stage with material for two albums. He bowed and applauded the audience as they applauded him.

Evenings like these raised Seeger's spirits. Jail seemed distant, unbelievable; if he was scared of anything it was his own success. When Moe Asch publicized Seeger as "America's Greatest Folksinger," even his long friendship didn't spare him: "If 'America's Greatest Folksinger' were true," he wrote Moe, "it wouldn't be necessary to say it. The puffier the publicity gets the more embarrassing the collapse later on, no?"—a shrewd and stoic assessment from a man famous for optimism.

Ever since Hays had noted his "arrogant modesty" in the Almanacs, Seeger had downplayed personal triumphs for his larger, social ambitions. This can be traced in part to the Old Left's antipsychological bias, that individual actions didn't matter: "I am always uncomfortable about anything that tends to give the impression of immodesty, egocentrism, individualism," wrote Gus Hall, head of the CP, in words Seeger might echo. But by the 1960s, Seeger was so established that a music critic could complain in the *San Francisco Chronicle* that audiences weren't hearing genuine folksingers: "Seegers take mainly from Lomaxes and the Lomaxes take mainly from God" (parodying a saying about the Cabot and Lowell families).

"An artist like Pete Seeger starts off with twenty, thirty years of experience before he surfaces," Don McLean said. "He's drawn to this, he's drawn to that. He develops his inner self. He refines that line of communication until the feedback starts. Then everything happens. When his experience is put through the recording industry, through the television screen and radio, that's when the enormous return comes from the audience. It's also when all the external, meaningless pressures start to box you in—when people who haven't the slightest clue what you're about try to mold you.

"It's those years you spent in the tunnel with the light on your hat that determine whether you'll stay true to your goals as an artist; or whether you'll sell out for money. Money is the key to it all. Pete prefers the light on his helmet."

Now that Seeger was in great demand, money entered his life in embarrassing quantities; song royalties pushed his income into six figures. But the more money he had, the less he wanted to know about it. In the decades since Seeger had served as the Almanacs' accountant, he had stopped handling money. People sheltered him from his finances. One of his rare fights with Harold occurred when a concert producer mistakenly handed Seeger his check. Looking into the envelope he was horrified to find several thousand dollars. The next day, Seeger demanded that Leventhal lower his concert fee immediately, an anecdote Harold told with relish.

Success seemed less righteous than failure and further from his adolescent hermit's den. He didn't mean to be the first musical revolutionary tycoon. Soon after his tiff with Harold, he wrote a poem about his wealth: "My son and daughters, if I had three million dollars, I would not will them to you, for I would not want you to be hated . . . by the determined poor people of this our world."

"Seeger's puritan lifestyle had a bit of Hawthorne: don't lie, compromise principles, waste time or resources," said Archie Green, folklorist. "He didn't believe in making a reputation or money. Acts should be done for their own intrinsic good."

Yet his predicament would not have bothered many. He might have traded in his battered VW bug or built a swimming pool. Or quickly given away the money. He took out his discomfort with money and fame on the wrong people. When the publishers of his songbook *Goofing Off Suite* advertised PETE SEEGER on the cover, their singer tore off a bitter note: "My name has been blown up like a goddamned star." An offended editor replied that Seeger was in the music business: "Accepting the benefits of commercialism on the one hand, you should not damn it on the other."

—

IN THE FALL of 1961, Seeger obtained court permission to tour England. In the two years since singing there with Jack Elliot, he had developed a large following; four thousand turned out at London's Royal Albert Hall. England had its own "Pete Seeger Committee," with Paul Robeson as president, the great ballad singer Ewan MacColl (now Peggy's husband) as chairman, and Benjamin Britten, Doris Lessing, and Sean O'Casey as sponsors. Again, blacklisting brought him prominence.

The five weeks in Britain were precious, tender times, a vacation Pete and Toshi sorely needed. No Un-English Committee stalked him; no FBI monitored his singing. In a rented car, the couple and their six-year-old girl, Tinya, visited the cozy inns that dot the English countryside. They would stop at a country bed-and-breakfast. In the morning they'd awake to the smell of home-cured ham and broiled tomatoes, he wrote in his journal.

The damp English winter had not yet begun. They motored through the heath country of Yorkshire. Some days the clouds would break and the country lanes would flood with sunshine. The enormous golden fields and ancient stone fences appealed to the folklorist in Seeger. Here, on the fog-covered moors of the Scottish border, crimes and wars had launched a hundred ballads. Driving the deserted country roads, Seeger could almost hear the songs of false knights and castles. Sometimes, through a tip at a local pub, they visited a traditional singer and heard songs as they were sung centuries ago.

The political songwriting of Great Britain revitalized Seeger, and he returned and talked with Sis Cunningham (of the Almanacs) about starting a magazine of topical songs, *Broadside.* The songs of Bob Dylan, Phil Ochs, Tom Paxton, Eric Andersen, and others soon filled its pages.

ON MAY 18, 1962, the Court of Appeals ruled that Seeger's indictment was faulty and dismissed his case. It was over.

The judges disappointed him by sidestepping questions of his freedom to sing when and where he pleased. Instead, the court found that HUAC's authority hadn't been clearly explained. Seeger thought this absurd; he'd hoped to attack the whole edifice of un-Americanism, but all he won was an instruction for the government to draft better documents.

In closing, the court couldn't resist a subtle insult: "We are not inclined to dismiss lightly claims of Constitutional stature because they are asserted by one who may appear unworthy of sympathy." Seeger laughed. He did not receive his vindication, but an acquittal is an acquittal, and he was now free—unless the government appealed or retried him. Not too likely, with the *New York Post* calling the decision a "return to reason" and "a big day for Miss Liberty."

"Hooray for us all and for Tom Jefferson," Seeger told *Sing Out!*

The week of his acquittal, in one of those happy coincidences fate periodically offers, "Where Have All the Flowers Gone?" hit the top-forty charts. The Kingston Trio had recorded the song two months earlier, and now Peter, Paul and Mary (Travers, his former student) had a success with it. Folk music was reaching a nation accustomed to Harry Mancini and Burt Bacharach, to "Runaround Sue" and "Please Mr. Postman."

With Lead Belly gone and Woody in the hospital, Seeger saw himself as a link in a chain tying these two to new audiences. Guthrie could no longer play or sing, but he did recognize visitors, and Pete and Toshi occasionally stopped by. After Woody was transferred to Brooklyn State Hospital, Pete and Arlo visited to sing one of his favorite songs, "Hobo's Lullaby," and the hospital odor and bare walls dropped away. Woody no longer had the muscular control to speak or applaud, but he heard. A light shone from his eyes, and he blinked tears.

All that was left of Huddie Ledbetter was a rough film clip, and Seeger spent the next summer at an editing table, synchronizing his image and voice. It would be understandable if Seeger's mind wandered to the world outside. Having survived his seven-year legal battle, new possibilities shimmered before him in the silvery light of the editing machine. Next he would introduce America to folk music via television, and as he peered into the tiny screen where Lead Belly capered and sang about the invincible "Gray Goose," Seeger believed in its power.

The fork couldn't stick him.
And the knife wouldn't cut him.
They throwed him in the hog pen,
And the hogs couldn't eat him,
And he broke the hogs' teeth out.
They put him in the saw mill,
And the saw couldn't cut him,
And he broke all the teeth out. . . .

The goose and John Henry had a lot in common with Seeger; he, too, had broken the saw's teeth.

Bleary-eyed from editing, he imagined his own television show. By August, the idea had taken shape: a musical fantasy, *The Magic Thinner.* A girl invents a solution that makes everything paper thin. To restore the objects, she plays a tune on an accordion, and *pop!*, everything returns to normal. Here was a parable after Seeger's heart: Song was the amulet, the magic restorer of balance. Ideas like this one inhabited the imagination of the man who brought a banjo to his trial. If someone spilled magic thinner on the judges and prosecutors, Pete Seeger would have the songs to restore them—if he chose.

Typical of his high spirits that summer was one of his finest recording sessions, which Columbia released as *The Bitter and the Sweet.* The album included "Where Have All the Flowers Gone?" and a superb performance of "Lady Isabel" (misidentified on the record), where Seeger's banjo brought a new tension to the ballad, subtly punctuating it with strums and arpeggios.

Then in July 1962, Seeger stumbled on a terrific new song: "Guantanamera." At Camp Woodland, where he'd performed before his HUAC appearance, Counselor Hector Angulo sang him a poem of José Martí set to a Cuban folk tune. Seeger arranged the song, giving the counselor credit. Eventually, the song traveled across Europe, Japan, and South America.

With "If I Had a Hammer" and "Where Have All the Flowers Gone?" Seeger realized that his own compositions had entered the American repertoire, perhaps to reemerge as folk songs.

"My essential purpose in singing is to help the listener understand reality," Seeger wrote in a telling letter to friend and music critic Henrietta Yurchenko. "And the path to understanding the reality of any age lies through the 'here and now' and thence to the 'faraway and beyond.'" Others sought this distant, harmonious land through religion or drugs or mysticism; Seeger reached out for it in music.

CAPACITY AUDIENCES NOW turned out wherever he went. Anti-Seeger pickets at campuses like Chapel Hill were outnumbered a hundred to one by students eager to hear him. Folkways calculated that they had sold a million of Seeger's records since World War II. Slick magazines ran flattering profiles. Seeger was making a thousand dollars doing what paid him twenty-five dollars in the fifties. Yet if history had been his guide, Seeger might have suspected his good fortune; as the Grateful Dead would later sing, "When life looks like easy street, there is danger at your door."

The boom in folk music was now so prominent that *Time* placed photogenic Joan Baez on their 1962 Thanksgiving cover: "Guitars and banjo akimbo, folk singers inhabit smoky metropolitan crawl space; they sprawl on the floors of college rooms; near the foot of ski trails, they keep time to the wheeze and sputter of burning logs." Seeger had hoped folk music could avoid this sort of attention; his pain at reading Lead Belly described as "a whooping primitive" can only be imagined.

Nor did *Time* forget to insult the man they called the "current patriarch of folk singing": "Seeger commands so much respect among folk singers that the only criticism leveled against him is that he can't carry a tune. But that gives him the seal of authenticity. His voice sounds as if a cornhusk were stuck in his throat."

Seeger's audience of five hundred at New York's P.S. 84 disagreed. Reaching these squirmy kids was a challenge; their music teacher had barely managed to finish "America the Beautiful" without being booed off stage.

"Seeger walked down the aisle," journalist Peter Lyon wrote, "wearing a fuzzy sweater, a shirt of firehouse red, rough worsted trousers and heavy thick-soled shoes." Until he started playing, he looked like a gaudy scarecrow: "But when he unlimbered his banjo and gave the children a warm, inclusive smile, something magical happened in the room. He sang:

Lou, Lou, skip to my Lou . . .

"At the second line, fifty voices were singing with him. At the third, a hundred had joined in, and scandalized teachers were shushing all over the hall. To no avail: Seeger and the children understood each other perfectly. . . . This routine miracle achieved, Seeger walked back up the aisle, submitted to an interview by three small shrewd reporters for the school paper, signed several autographs, rescued his instrument from a group of eager experimenters and made his way to the street.

"'Can I,' he asked his wife Toshi, 'have some breakfast now?'"

THE KIDS WOULD SING, but adults wouldn't always let them. It was a time of two steps forward, one step back. He won "Best Children's Record" from the National Academy of Recording Arts, but twice in one week in April 1962, he was canceled from singing with students: At Queens College, the president denied he'd ever been invited to sing there; at a Pittsburgh TV station, he was canceled before he could tune up. Then in January 1963 Seeger finally had his break: CBS-TV called Harold Leventhal about having Pete and the Weavers perform on *Dinner with the President*, sponsored by the Anti-Defamation League of the B'nai Brith. With his old classmate, John F. Kennedy, he would break bread and the blacklist.

His chance might never have come but for Leventhal, who had fought Seeger's censorship as if it were his own. The manager seemed to be everywhere at once; from his midtown office high above Seventh Avenue, he could book (and fill) virtually any auditorium in the country with Judy Collins, the Weavers, Odetta, and Theodore Bikel, among others.

One afternoon, soon after Harold had received the offer from CBS, his phone rang. A spokesman for the Anti-Defamation League had the unpleasant job of telling Harold a mistake had been made. The caller referred obliquely to a blacklist: Did Harold know some people wouldn't televise Seeger? According to Nat Hentoff, the man "had the chutzpah to ask Leventhal if he would try to get Joan Baez for the program. To his credit, Leventhal explosively refused."

What was CBS afraid of? What could Seeger have sung that made him dangerous enough to censor? Perhaps the networks didn't care what he sang, the "Internationale" or "Jingle Bells"; Seeger's reputation was more dangerous than his songs. "I'm not afraid of him," Seeger imagined network executives saying, "but I'll be damned if I want to put him on my program. Let somebody else hire Seeger. Let them stick their neck out."

He might have been more upset had he not heard that ABC-TV was planning a new weekly folk music series, *Hootenanny*, and that he would be included. Since nobody at ABC knew much about folk music, they relied heavily on talent consultants, all of whom grew up on Pete Seeger. It's an old story: Stay in one place long enough, and a city grows up around you.

Some thought the show's title a bad omen; since folk music had become popular, the word "hootenanny" had been tarnished. The editors of *Webster's Third New International Dictionary* included *hootenanny*: "a gathering at which folk singers entertain." The word Seeger and Guthrie had brought back from Seattle now adorned pot holders and pencil cups. *Look* printed a column on what to wear to a hoot: "Bulky knits and . . . a vaguely beat but neat look. Fashion is stylishly singing along."

Afterward, the show's chief adviser, Fred Weintraub, called Seeger to encourage him: "Pete, I'll try to get you on. First, we have to get the show on a firm basis commercially, so we're in a strong position."

Then Columbia Records seemed to lose interest. Seeger had signed on in hopes of a broader audience, but his records didn't turn up in the shops. There was nothing Seeger could put his finger on. Hammond was an old friend, loyal and pleasant to work with, though Seeger felt folk music never captured his attention the way jazz did. It dawned on Seeger that Columbia wanted his name more than his music: "If somebody accused Columbia of not recording folk music, they could say, 'Look, we have Pete Seeger.'" He had left Folkways willingly and helped Columbia attract Bob Dylan and others, but he felt used.

Toward the end of February 1963, Seeger wondered why he hadn't heard from *Hootenanny*, which had already filmed its first shows. He had Harold check matters out. From the first show on, there was something bogus about *Hootenanny*, like a half-dollar without enough silver.

Weintraub called back to reassure him. Everything was fine, he said: "We're going to get you on this show somehow. Can't do it in the first shows, but I'm going to get you on somehow."

On March 6 attorney William Kunstler received a letter from a young Seeger fan at Brown University, where two of the ten *Hootenanny* shows were being taped. When the camera crew arrived, this junior detective grew chummy with an associate producer and asked about Seeger and the Weavers. No, the answer came, they wouldn't be on because of "pressure from advertising agencies, sponsors, and stations." Kunstler passed the note along to Harold, asking if he wanted to do anything about it. Harold told Seeger and Nat Hentoff, columnist for the *Village Voice* (and a veteran campaigner for freedom of speech).

Hentoff tracked down the rumor. To his dismay, he confirmed it: Seeger wasn't scheduled. A little publicity, however, might change the producers' minds. Hentoff broke the story on March 14, in an article prickly with indignation: "That Ole McCarthy Hoot!" Keeping Pete Seeger off *Hootenanny*, a word he had brought to national circulation, was like barring Charlie Parker from Birdland. "At least we'll be getting folk music to a lot more people," Weintraub told Hentoff apologetically. "It's tough on Pete, but after all, he's been turned down on all three networks. Why pick on us?" Hentoff challenged performers to follow Joan Baez, who had refused to appear where Seeger was unwelcome: "What are you exposing when you go out there and leave Mr. Seeger behind?"

Hootenanny also turned down the Tarriers, an interracial folk group, but under pressure, the show's producers gave them a spot, making them one of the first integrated ensembles on network TV. There was one problem: The Tarriers had to perform at a Village café on the night scheduled. Who could they ask, on short notice, to stand in so they could appear on *Hootenanny*? Pete Seeger, of course. When he heard their situation he agreed, chuckling to himself at the irony.

The folk community chose up sides. "I can't blame Mother Maybelle Carter for going on *Hootenanny*," Joan Baez said. "But it's disgusting that there are city folksingers—including some who don't need the bread or the exposure—who perform on those programs. They should know what it's about." Fifty performers formed a *Hootenanny* boycott committee of artists against the blacklist, among them Barbara Dane, Mary Travers, and Bob Dylan. Rumors circulated of Peter, Paul, and Mary turning down twenty-five thousand dollars for one *Hootenanny* show. A *Hootenanny* appearance became a dividing line: Which side were you on? Joan Baez refused, Judy Collins accepted; Tommy Makem boycotted, but the Clancy Brothers appeared; Dave Van Ronk wasn't interested, but Theo Bikel appeared, self-servingly telling *Billboard* if everyone acted like "sane responsible people" and avoided "ineffectual public protest," the situation would resolve itself.

The Weavers, in their last year (and second Seeger replacement banjoist) joined the boycott. Lee Hays was growing extremely bitter about the group's decline: "Some of us were too busy with other matters," he wrote Leventhal, overlooking that he was the group's most unreliable member, regularly canceling rehearsals. The one thing they all agreed on: no *Hootenanny* appearance.

Seeger had become—for the umpteenth time—a test case. He bided his time. Controversy-fearing advertisers might still arrange an appearance. On April 14, in the *San Francisco Chronicle*, Ralph Gleason reported a *Hootenanny* producer saying Seeger was "too slow and thoughtful" for the show.

"I'm outraged," Seeger told Ralph Gleason. "I actually get hot and flushed just thinking about it. We have all this richness and variety in our country but a bunch of schmoes, out to sell soap, keep the whole country seeing the same dreary things night after night."

Fifty angry pickets carrying END THE BLACKLIST signs paced the street outside ABC-TV's Manhattan studios. Late on a Saturday afternoon, the place looked deserted. The network had decided its position on Seeger: If asked, the show's producers could claim that they wanted Seeger, but the sponsor (Procter & Gamble) wouldn't agree. The sponsor was to say that they wanted Seeger, but the public didn't.

When no one came out to meet the pickets, they grew angrier. Who did ABC think it was, keeping Seeger off TV? Nobody was throwing bricks, but the crowd was irate. Folksinger Hedy West (daughter of Appalachian poet and Highlander leader Don West) played the banjo and led Seeger's supporters in improvised lyrics insulting ABC. Strange, this picket *for* Seeger, after the hundreds of right-wing picket lines he'd braved to perform.

Hootenanny offered unparalleled audiences, fees, and exposure. Seeger couldn't bring himself to attack the show; it would seem self-serving. In fact, when he met with the boycott committee, he told fellow performers, "You can't *not* go on the show. The fact they've blacklisted me attracts more attention to the folk-song movement. I told my brother Mike to go on."

"Call it 'Pete Seeger's logic,'" explained Howie Richmond, Seeger's supportive music publisher. "Pete only sees the life of the songs."

"Harold and Pete both encouraged me to do the show," Judy Collins said. According to Robert Shelton of the *New York Times* she appeared three times and quickly discovered that "their taste was, shall I say, not impeccable." Midway through her rendition of "John Riley," the producers cut two verses to "speed things up."

In May 1963 executive producer Richard Lewine held a press conference. There was no blacklist on *Hootenanny*, he explained. With limited space on the show, he couldn't hire everyone. After considering Pete, listening to his records and all, it boiled down to one thing: "Pete Seeger just can't hold an audience."

"ABC made its position even worse by saying it was not blacklisting Pete, but had simply decided he was not up to their artistic standards," Dave Van Ronk reflected later in a memoir. "At that the entire entertainment business, left, right and center, broke into howls of laughter—I mean, you should have heard the crap they had on that show!"

"Pete himself was kind of embarrassed by the whole business.

He had always felt that the music was the important thing—the man is nothing; the work is everything," Van Ronk wrote.

"Our position was 'Sorry Pete, old man, but you're a symbol.'"

"What a mistake I made in not trademarking the term 'hootenanny,'" Seeger later reflected. "To think that a nice word which Woody and I had found out in Seattle was being used for a cheap TV show. If there was anytime I was bitter, I guess that would be it."

After it became clear *Hootenanny* would not have him, Seeger let loose: "This story needs to be told now, not next year, or even next month," he wrote in *Sing Out!* "The ABC network, the talent agency (Ashley), the sponsor (Procter & Gamble) are all charging ahead with the idea of making a fast-paced show, 26 minutes of screaming kids in the studio audience." Seeger pointed out how Alan Lomax and others—he didn't mention himself—had long proposed a TV series on folk music, to no avail.

"When will the TV producers learn that some of the best music in our country is made by unlettered farmers, miners, housewives?" Seeger asked sadly. Readers could write and let ABC know their feelings: "These hucksters have no minds of their own, you know."

That was as much bitterness as he allowed himself in print. He had been taken for a ride, but his rage turned inward, to sadness and futility. The Seegers had been planning to leave the country for a year. Now it was time. They told the press they wanted to travel as a family before the kids grew too old. Interestingly, the bulk of their baggage was movie equipment. They were determined to film folk music in authentic settings, not in front of screaming college kids. Just before he left, *Hootenanny* offered him a spot—if he would sign a loyalty oath. "Dear ABC," he replied brusquely, "I just finished a seven-year court battle to prove the principle that such oaths are unconstitutional, and I was acquitted and vindicated." Next to this he noted: "Release after departure" and "Leave country without a stir."

He'd let his hopes carry him away. *Variety* and *Time* recognized him as the leader of the folk music movement, and the courts had cleared him of wrongdoing. Then came *Hootenanny*, grinding in his vulnerability. If Seeger had been made of soft wood instead of oak, he might have cracked and split.

Chapter 10

WE SHALL OVERCOME

—

THE SEEGERS' DEPARTURE WAS SET FOR AUGUST 18, 1963, three months hence. Plans for the trip grew more and more elaborate, until they were to visit thirty countries. Before leaving, however, Seeger's attention turned to a fast-growing interest: civil rights.

During the past year, he had heard about freedom rides, sit-ins, and the music blacks sang as they were dragged off to jail. When Seeger finally had an invitation to sing in the South, he'd agreed enthusiastically, and in October 1962 he found himself bumping along the back roads of rural Georgia to sing at a black church. He was headed into the thick of the street fighting sweeping this once-quiet corner of the Black Belt.

FOR MONTHS ALBANY, GEORGIA, had been on the brink of a race riot. A thousand black demonstrators had already been jailed, and white vigilante gangs burned crosses on hot summer nights. A pray-in at the city hall had brought a young preacher down from Montgomery, Alabama, Martin Luther King Jr., who was arrested along with seventy-five other clergy. The nearby Mount Olive Church was burned to the ground after a sheriff discovered a civil rights meeting there. Another organizer had been shot and paralyzed when a bullet tore through the wall of a home she was visiting.

These were minor skirmishes in a war for racial equality that had been spreading since the midfifties, when Rosa Parks's refusal to sit in the back of a bus sparked the now-famous bus boycott in Montgomery and made public a steadily growing movement. Sit-ins, jail-ins, even swim-ins broke out in dozens of southern cities. On the evening Seeger drove into Albany, a convoy of two hundred National Guard trucks and jeeps guarded James Meredith as he registered to be the first black student at the University of Mississippi.

Seeger's car jolted over the hard-packed earth with an uncertain clatter. This was *not* the place for a breakdown; the local White Citizens' Council had threatened outside agitators who fell into their hands. He crossed a lonely stretch of country with the smell of horses at pasture and freshly plowed dirt, a reminder of how far away he was from home. Years before, Seeger had read W.E.B. DuBois's *The Souls of Black Folk*, with its stories of Georgia sharecroppers and slave violence. The one-room cabins still dotted the horizon, marking the boundaries of the old plantations. It was close to harvest time, and now, as in DuBois's time, the fields of cotton were "like a silver cloud edged with dark green." Pecan trees rattled in the wind, and the unpaved roads rolled over red clay soil.

Albany had a singing movement. The black community used the old hymns for their battles, and they sang so loud and so long, they were ready for any enemy when they finished. They had invited Seeger so they could see what they could learn from a veteran song leader.

WHEN HE PULLED UP at the church, the building was packed. From the back entrance, Seeger could already hear singing:

And before I'll be a slave
I'll be buried in my grave

The Georgia Patrol circled the neighborhood in their sleek sedans, ready for trouble. Off to one side a crowd of whites gathered to jeer at the churchgoers; three or four carried lead pipes. Seeger hurriedly unloaded his instruments and stepped inside.

Few onlookers would have suspected this erect forty-three-year-old in blue jeans was now one of the country's top songwriters. ("If I Had a Hammer" topped the hit parade.) Yet here he stood in Dougherty County, where "nigger lovers" were welcomed with buckshot and beatings.

Inside the church, six fans provided little relief in the soupy heat. The room was overcrowded; if someone had shouted "Fire," people would have been trampled to death. An eighteen-year-old girl, Bertha Gober, led a traditional spiritual with new words, and the congregation sang verse after verse in slow, surging meter.

We been 'buked
And we been scorned

Their singing moved Seeger more than any speech could. The harmonies floated down like the echoes of a summer rain. Between songs, the congregation told of beatings and harassment at the courthouse; anger mixed with amens until another song began to rise. The pastor stood up to introduce Seeger, who hurried to the pulpit.

He was an odd choice to address a mass meeting of African Americans in Georgia. The only Negroes he'd seen at Avon played on a nearby football team. In later years, he had known Paul Robeson and Langston Hughes. In the fifties at Highlander Folk School, where Rosa Parks was trained in civil disobedience, Seeger had met Dr. Martin Luther King, of the Montgomery Improvement Association. Afterward, King wrote him a flowery note, praising his "moral support and Christian generosity." Seeger had promised to return if needed, and now he volunteered his time and paid his own expenses.

In an unusual move, Seeger had decided beforehand what he would sing. He wanted to explain how in the 1930s white labor organizers had also adapted hymns; he wanted to give "a wide picture" of organizing through music and the Old Left. Unfortunately, Seeger's timing was off.

STANDING IN THE MINISTER'S place, Seeger picked up his banjo. It might have been wiser to have left the instrument at home. Among black churchgoers the banjo, an African-based instrument widely played during slavery, was associated with minstrel shows and loose dancing; this was not church music. Unaware, Seeger kept on picking. He did notice that the audience seemed surprisingly restrained as he began "If I Had a Hammer." He discovered later that the audience liked to sing the song with their own lyrics.

When he started the union hymn "Hold On" he found himself singing not only different words, but out of rhythm and out of tune with the audience, who generally sang it in a minor key. People stirred in their seats, asking each other how this guy was supposed to help them sing. Something had gone wrong. Perhaps they were tired. Seeger decided to sing a long ballad and give them a rest.

It was the wrong move. He had half finished an old English tune when someone whispered, "If this is white folks' music, I don't think much of it."

"Shush," Cordell Reagon replied. "If we expect white folks to understand us, we've got to try and understand them."

If he had known that Guy Carawan (from Highlander) had earlier run into the same problems trying to teach labor songs here, Seeger might have avoided all this. Carawan had stayed in the community, however, and eventually won acceptance. Seeger rushed in and attempted his customary miracle in two hours.

"There I was, repeating the same unrhythmic melody over and over with little or no variation. . . . The story was so ancient and so unfamiliar as to have little meaning for the listeners. I sang with a deadpan expression purposely not to detract from the words, and this only made the melody seem more boring to them." The situation drifted from bad to worse. The only song that roused the crowd was "We Shall Overcome."

"If you'd begin back at the Montgomery bus boycott, they were doing things like 'Onward Christian Soldiers,' and they did 'Freedom' based on 'Amen.' They did 'Lift Them Up Higher.' It was a heavy church and an educated one; their songs came out of the hymnbooks, kind of."

Seeger had first heard "We Shall Overcome" in 1947, when Zilphia Horton (one of the founders of Highlander) had taught him a version from striking black tobacco workers in North Carolina. The song was originally an old spiritual by Charles Tindley, "I'll Overcome" or "I'll Be All Right." Zilphia sang it "We Will Overcome." Seeger made a few key alterations: "I changed it to 'We shall.' Toshi kids me that it was my Harvard grammar, but I think I liked a more open sound; 'We will' has alliteration to it, but 'We shall' opens the mouth wider; the 'i' in 'will' is not an easy vowel to sing well."

He also added new verses: "We'll walk hand in hand" and "The whole wide world around." In the fifties Highlander students taught the song to Frank Hamilton, a musician in California, who in turn taught it to Guy Carawan, a lean-looking sociology MA from Los Angeles who ended up at Highlander as a song leader in 1959. Carawan had then reintroduced the song to the community that had started it: black labor and civil rights workers. Since then, without a recording, "We Shall Overcome" has traveled orally across the South, a widely known nonhit.

"'We Shall Overcome' loosened way up with lots of space for improvisations, lots of antiphony and answering and calling, and it stayed that way in terms of the black movement in the South," Bernice Reagon remembered.

"The song was different than in union days," one organizer for the Student Nonviolent Coordinating Committee (SNCC) remembered. "We put more soul in, a sort of rocking quality, to stir one's inner feeling. When you got through singing it, you could walk over a bed of hot coals, and you wouldn't notice."

By the time Seeger performed it in Albany, "We Shall Overcome" had evolved from a song to a ritual, where the audience stood and swayed, crossing hands. Seeger gave up on educating his audience and let them sing. This mollified the crowd, and they thanked him politely as he left the church.

FIFTEEN YEARS LATER, Seeger would look back on the Albany concert and shake his head, calling it one of his great failures. Many professionals would have chalked it up to a bad night and moved on; but Seeger could not. Misreading an audience threatened Seeger's self-confidence. Two summers before, he'd brashly written in *Sing Out!*, "There are plenty of young people who can play rings around me on guitar or banjo. But I'm proud that I hardly ever met an audience I couldn't get singing."

In Albany he'd confronted a new culture, where songs really were at the center of change, when the community itself sang. Civil rights was a genuine mass movement, not one born of left-wingers in New York, and Seeger's radical traditions seemed remote to blacks facing police with cattle prods. Perhaps no one needed a white, middle-aged New England radical in a black church in Georgia.

Since the forties, Seeger had maintained that music would transform society. He, Sis Cunningham, and Gordon Friesen were virtually the last of the Almanacs to work for this end. Alan Lomax had drifted into editing records and then to grant-getting and his study of world song styles, cantometrics. Lee Hays still sang with the Weavers (who had replaced tenor Erik Darling with Frank Hamilton). They performed the new freedom songs, but didn't follow them into towns where they could have their heads blown off. Josh White had medical problems, which made playing painful. Mill Lampell had finally fought his way out from under the blacklist with his first Hollywood film writing credit. In many ways, Seeger stood alone. Duty and good causes beckoned him long after his friends decided to let someone else sing up a storm.

Seeger's failure in Albany made his world tour more urgent, a quest to see how far his music could reach: "to test myself," as he wrote in his journal, "by the toughest means possible that my chosen work has a basic, universal validity." By setting his standards so high, however, he made the trip an ordeal he could not afford to fail.

AS HE CHANGED PLANES in Atlanta the day following his Albany concert, he stopped to sing at a benefit for SNCC, a group of young organizers, mostly black and southern. Afterward, the singers gathered at the house of Dr. King's aide, Andrew Young (later Atlanta's mayor and U.S. ambassador to the UN), where Seeger met a young singer from Albany, Bernice Johnson. A short stocky woman with tightly curled hair, Bernice had a voice like a cannon; when she sang the largest room filled with her rich, resonant tones.

When Seeger had met her in the fall of 1962, nineteen-year-old Bernice already had a reputation as a civil rights singer. The daughter of a minister, Bernice had a deceptively quiet air and large, gentle eyes. Her temper could be peppery, however, and she had been suspended from Albany State College for demonstrating. Seeger encouraged her to start an ensemble of SNCC singers who could spread freedom songs the way the Almanacs had stumped for the CIO. Bernice took Seeger's advice literally. "The day after Pete flew to New York, I quit Spelman College, packed my bags, and left. I went back to Café Lena in New York (where I worked the previous summer) and called Toshi Seeger and asked her if she would help me put together a tour for the Freedom Singers." Bernice became a member of the Seeger family.

The civil rights movement quickly became a major priority in the Seegers' lives. Their work had suddenly doubled, for Harold had overbooked him, assuming that he might soon be in jail and half the dates canceled. By the time his conviction had been overturned, he was already committed. Seeger turned these dates into a musical forum for civil rights, carrying freedom songs like a gardener bringing in flats of vegetables. He stirred up interest, but the marathon schedule nearly flattened him.

The first week in April he performed in Newark; a week later he sang at a sold-out Civic Opera House in Chicago. A few days later it was Winnipeg, Canada, and the day after, New York's Town Hall, standing room only. Six days after that, Joan Baez and he filled the Washington, DC, Coliseum, after which he returned to New York to perform at Carnegie Hall, two nights in a row, for the Weavers' fifteenth anniversary concert. His voice sounds tired on those recordings, and it must have gotten worse the next day in Los Angeles, when he sang at the UCLA Folk Festival, before flying off to Minnesota for a concert.

Judy Collins visited the Newport Festival office in New York and found Seeger asleep on the floor, too tired to drive back to Beacon. Toshi finally told her husband, "Look, you have to ease up—you're going to drop dead if you don't."

He managed all this travel without roadies. Often Seeger marched by himself from one airport café to another, banjo strapped to his shoulder, a traveling music machine.

Of course, Seeger wasn't the only one busy—booking the Freedom Singers had proved a full-time job. At one point Toshi told them, "You better go to the bathroom now, because next month's schedule's so busy, you might not get another chance." Toshi knew what she was doing; that receipt Seeger had sent home from the army had joined thousands of others and file cabinets of correspondence. A fellow organizer called her labor "a perfect meeting of the Old and New Left. No one went off without instructions, follow-up calls, food after the show, and airplane tickets for the next date."

"Toshi is probably the best organizer that I have ever seen. And I've been with some good ones," said Jimmy Collier of Dr. King's organization, the Southern Christian Leadership Committee. "She taught the SNCC people some of the stuff that they were doing, there's no question about that. See, all of that black movement flowed out of the American Friends Service Committee, Fellowship of Reconciliation, Highlander School, and so on. Toshi and them taught the old union organizing techniques. How to write a press release, how to put on a concert, how to do this, how to not offend the local people.

"Getting in touch with groups on the telephone, having meetings at night, knowing who some of the right people are to have there and getting them there, sometimes counseling somebody that's having a real problem, somehow making logistic arrangements for airplane flights . . . Toshi is—not to take anything away from Peter at all—Toshi is magnificent."

The Freedom Singers (originally Bernice, Chuck Neblett, Cordell Reagon, and Rutha Harris) often visited Beacon. Bernice had now married Cordell, but she remained close to the Seegers, even naming her first baby Toshi. One Christmas she spent the holidays at Beacon, gaining a new insight into Seeger.

Winter had piled the autumn leaves into snow-covered banks, and the cold wind off the Hudson resembled nothing Bernice knew from her childhood in Georgia. Christmas at the Seegers' was a busy time, with relatives stopping in, blankets passed around, kids cooking and making their own wrapping paper. Toshi was friendly but occupied and Pete off chopping wood until he was red in the face. On a walk one wintry afternoon, Bernice stooped to pick up a hickory nut. Returning to the Seegers' cabin, she asked her host what it was.

Seeger raised his head. "You know . . ." he began, staring over her shoulder, and launched into a parable until Bernice broke in, astonished.

"I told him, 'Thanks, but I'd just like to know a little something about hickory nuts.' He didn't know how to handle a real, down-to-earth exchange. Before you get his answer to a question, he's removed it so far from himself!"

Bernice is one of those holding Bob Dylan's hand and singing "We Shall Overcome" in one of the most publicized pictures of the era, taken a month before the Seegers' departure at the 1963 Newport Folk Festival, where entertainers planned the bill and everybody, at Seeger's insistence, received the same fee. Forty thousand attended that year for the all-star team at Newport: Peter, Paul and Mary; Dylan and Baez.

Dylan had made a profound impression on Seeger and Sis and Gordon at *Broadside:* "As soon as he got to New York, they were madly in love with him," Dave Van Ronk recalled. Dylan and Seeger had performed together in Greenwood, Mississippi, to support voter registration drives. At Newport, they sang their only recorded duet, "You Playboys and Playgirls, You Ain't Gonna Run My World."

The singing of "We Shall Overcome" at the end of Newport 1963 was "the apogee of the folk movement," Theo Bikel said. "There was no point more suffused with hope for the future." As David Hadju points out, "Seeger was essentially proclaiming [We Shall Overcome] the blacklist, television, the Hit Parade, Tin Pan Alley." And he was right; for a year or two, no other music in America was as popular as folk.

All the time she'd helped organize the Newport Festival and the Freedom Singers, Toshi had kept preparations for their world tour on a back burner. Now their departure neared. Pete was ignoring the *Hootenanny* affair while Harold concentrated on arranging appearances on foreign television and organized a memorable farewell concert at Carnegie Hall. Harold persuaded Columbia Records to make a live recording.

As this concert and their departure drew close, the Seegers confronted the intricacies of transporting a family, baggage, and instruments around the world. The Pete Seeger who as a teenager wouldn't even carry a sleeping bag now had a caravan of equipment. Toshi made sure they had all the equipment for lighting, recording, and shooting movies. The next few weeks passed in securing visas and being injected with a bewildering array of shots.

If Seeger and the Freedom Singers were busy, civil rights workers were equally pressed in that spring of 1963. Veterans of the Albany movement now gathered in Birmingham, Alabama, a die-hard city that preferred to close public parks rather than integrate them. In April, Birmingham's notorious sheriff, Bull Connor, had slapped Dr. King into solitary. In May 969 children, six to sixteen, were arrested in one day, a record for civil disobedience in America. The next day, as crowds of blacks gathered in prayer outside a church, police sealed off the exits and unleashed their dogs.

Like millions of Americans, Seeger watched the dogs attack on TV. A fire hose sprayed into the crowd, and a slender teenage girl jerked along the ground in its blast. As the TV crews panned the scene, they picked up the nonviolent demonstrators singing Seeger's arrangement of "We Shall Overcome." Here was a triumph that dwarfed any stupid television show.

Leaving this battle for a world tour made Seeger self-conscious. To Chuck Neblett, Bob Moses, and Sam Block of SNCC's Mississippi office he wrote, "I promise you I'll sing songs that tell of the great freedom fight you are putting up."

His farewell concert turned out as much of a test as his tour, but of a different sort. Columbia Records was getting impatient; his records weren't selling well. Two talented producers had tried, but no one had captured Seeger in the studio; he was the classic "live" performer, whose electricity came from the crowd. Unless matters changed, Columbia might have to drop him. Seeger determined to "do as good a job as I can" on this record and rehearsed an informal chorus to sit on stage, where the mike would pick up a balance of voices. The concert, released as "We Shall Overcome," took place on June 8, 1963, just as John F. Kennedy was preparing a major civil rights speech.

—

"IF YOU WANT to get out of a pessimistic mood yourself, I've got one sure remedy. Go help those people in Birmingham or Mississippi." The words rolled smoothly through Carnegie Hall's plush triple balconies. College kids in rumpled work shirts cheered as Seeger struck up "Oh, Freedom." They wanted to do their part, a thousand miles north of the fray. By the end of the evening, his audience embraced civil rights the way Seeger had revered Republican Spain twenty-five years before:

Keep your eyes on the prize, hold on
Hold on, hold on . . .

The biblical images of the song had withstood the long transition from hymn to song of action. Seeger sang the news, as his predecessors, the troubadours, had hundreds of years before. For a few short hours the audience had the illusion that by singing they, too, were fighting. Did the music, or the musician, really change them? At least his performance left a deep impression.

On evenings like this Seeger reached for two emotional centers in the audience: One touched off a physical reaction—whistling, hollering, clapping; another lay farther inside, accessible only to art. "Pete aims deep," commented banjoist Mike Cooney. "Most of the time he doesn't want whistles or applause; he reaches for the audience's core." Spain had Hemingway, Malraux, and Orwell; the civil rights movement had its chroniclers, who worked in song: Malvina Reynolds, Phil Ochs, Matt Jones, Len Chandler, and Bob Dylan.

Finally he strummed "We Shall Overcome": "There're all kinds of jobs that need to be done. Takes hands, hearts, and heads to do it—human beings. Then we'll see this song come true."

Seeger's song introductions combined oratory and exhortation. "In other days, Pete Seeger would have been a politician or an evangelist," a reviewer wrote in 1963. "He has some sort of inborn sensitivity to crowd techniques." Seeger worked in the tradition of great American stump speakers, like William Jennings Bryan, the Great Commoner, or Frederick Douglass, assailing slavery.

"We shall live in peace. The whole wide world around." "We Shall Overcome" rose on its own power and crescendoed in layers of harmony. Seeger used his broad range to carry two harmonies at once, catapulting his voice from a rolling bass to his upper tenor. The desire to overcome tightened in chests filled with song. "We are not afraid," Dr. King had sung in Montgomery in 1955; eight years later in Carnegie Hall, the walls seemed to buckle with sound.

By sharing the singing, Seeger convinced people that they, "his great audience," did all the work; they were the stars. Like a concave mirror, he focused his listeners' admiration back out into the balconies, inspiring people with an image of themselves as better (more tolerant, compassionate, international) than they were.

If someone had walked into that hall recruiting kids to fight racism in the South, they'd have filled their quota in minutes. Yet in the finale, as the audience stood and linked arms, friends and strangers singing "We shall overcome someday," the first discords echoed. The young and irreverent got carried away. To carry the song home and out into the streets, a few had begun singing "overcome *today*." A small difference, perhaps, but within three years the militant minority would outnumber the old guard. "We shall overcome today," they sang, "right *Now!*"

If Seeger noticed the substitution, the crowd couldn't tell. Head tilted back, he rocked on his heels and drummed the bass strings of his guitar. The audience closed their eyes and swayed. When Seeger slowed to his finish, a suppressed sigh whooshed through the hall.

"When I got that *We Shall Overcome* album what was most striking was that here was this whole audience that surrendered to this experience," musician John McCutcheon said. "People singing along in a concert is something that taps into what it takes to change the world. It requires courage, and it takes relying on all the people around you. The point of it all is to enter into something unknown and almost dangerous. You don't know what the next song is. You might sing along, you might not. It's a testimony to Seeger's audiences that they go along for the ride."

The concert was a triumph, but not the kind he most sought. His mind continued to dwell on his tour: "What happens on this trip will tell me much, I think, about my work, and about myself. . . . I really do feel like a man headed, with faltering step, straight toward the moment of truth." At forty-four, Seeger had health and wealth, more than he could spend. Yet he wondered what his art had accomplished.

Answers were hard to come by. The change Seeger hoped to inspire was nearly impossible to measure, for the effect of a song is subtle, and often separate in time and space from the original singer. Audience response is not always audience change.

Singing for social change and actually making that change happen have always been different activities. Much as Seeger tried to collapse the distance between singing and organizing, songs were not the same as notes or bullets. But a song is made of unbreakable stuff, words and music that need only breath and spirit to live. Torture might have been easier than neglect for Seeger, for it and crude censorship create partisans rather than vassals. Even in the most socially explosive moments in history, songs must butt against authority to be subversive. Sanctioned or subsidized, they pose little danger.

"Do books pose danger?" Seeger wondered decades later. "The Torah? *Das Kapital*? Do speeches, architecture? Does a boat? A law? The Bill of Rights? Do songs?"

Entering middle age, Seeger realized his talent shone most brightly when TV executives or school administrators blundered into censorship. If he had been *really* successful, perhaps the government would have tried harder to silence him. Seeger resembled

Woody Guthrie at that tryout in the Rainbow Room—that in his success, he had enough freedom to hang himself.

THE FAMILY FINALLY left the country in August 1963. In October, having stopped in Samoa, Australia, and Indonesia, they landed in Japan, where the Seegers (or the Ohtas, as they were called there) had a busy visit. Toshi brought the children to visit her father's birthplace. She filmed playground songs in a Tokyo schoolyard. The footage might not impress a film critic, but the pair seemed to be having a second childhood. From Japanese television Pete received a warm welcome. Yet this was no Cook's tour: "We earned in each country the plane fare to the next," Toshi reflected, "and grew adept at cleaning up other peoples' room-service trays and airline food."

The Seegers looked forward to visiting India. The language and cultural barriers were as severe as in Japan, but there were parallels between the civil rights movement he had left behind and Gandhi's Satyagraha ("holding to the truth"). Both used nonviolence and inspiring songs. Gandhi, like Seeger, fought in symbols, reviving the spinning wheel and living sparsely. He would have felt at home in the Seegers' log cabin.

Seeger's reception in India seemed to be passing his own test. Thirty thousand people, including the U.S. ambassador, turned out to hear him in Calcutta, and the *New Delhi Statesman* reported his singing had "a fervour that is almost evangelical." On All-India Radio, his listening audience was estimated to be as large as the entire population of the United States.

Yet departing for Africa, Seeger was still unsatisfied: "Nowhere on this whole adventure," he wrote, "have I had quite the same feeling . . . the wish—more than a wish or a hope, the ache—to carry out my purpose where the odds against it seem large but the stakes high. . . . I don't delude myself that what I know of the American Negro is going to help me here."

From the moment they landed in Kenya, mistaken schedules

and minor illnesses disturbed the trip. The Seegers were expected either two weeks earlier or a month later. Once the family spent hours setting up their equipment—with Mika, fifteen, taking a light reading, Danny, seventeen, hunched over the tape recorder, and little Tinya squinting into the camera eyepiece—only to discover, after they finished shooting, that a pin had rattled loose from the camera, ruining their film.

From Nairobi, the family drove south in a rented car. They entered a vast, dry plain of thorn trees and peaks ending in clouds. They crossed herds of zebra, hartebeest, and antelope. Seven-year-old Tinya squealed at the giraffes and wild buffalo. They were in the country of the Masai, tall herdsmen with eight-foot spears to fight lions. As Mount Kilimanjaro rose steeply before them, nineteen thousand feet, Seeger had to remind himself this was real, not some dream in Beacon.

Descending into Dar-es-Salaam, Tanganyika, a sun-baked city on the Indian Ocean, they hit a road so bumpy the strings on Seeger's banjo snapped. Driving a Mercedes—all they could find—didn't exactly make them feel at one with the natives. Then jars of peanut butter and jelly opened up all over their food and clothing.

Pictures from that trip show Seeger happier than the others. Danny looks bored; Mika casts her eyes slightly down. Tinya shyly holds her mother's hand, while Toshi, in a sari, looks as if she has a clipboard of details on her mind. There seemed a centrifugal force at work in the family: "As soon as we possibly could," Toshi recalled with a wry smile, "we'd get away from one another to different sides of the plane or hotel room."

A few days before Christmas 1963, Seeger walked on stage in Dar—and discovered there was no microphone: "And all those faces, turned eagerly to me, waiting, with no notion I'm in trouble." He banged out a few loud square dance numbers on his banjo, bringing home a once-familiar instrument. Then he tried freedom songs, hoping his voice would hold out. He sang one that caught their attention, and as he wrote in his journal, "That does it. I can always tell, to the split second, when that marvelous moment comes—the 'click' of singer and listener—when I have really found my audience and it has really found me." The song was "We Shall Overcome."

It wasn't easy to stand up without a mike in a ballroom in Africa and teach black teenagers the meaning of—and how to sing—"We Shall Overcome." Yet he had traveled halfway around the world for this sort of interchange. "Wimoweh" was another hit, particularly among the exiled South Africans who knew the song: "It goes so well, I don't want to stop it. Some of the South Africans start a dancing line. So long as they keep it up, I've got to sing. But now I'm getting hoarse. Finally, breathless, I hold up a hand, take a last bow. Did it! What a feeling!"

He had three days of laryngitis afterward, but felt fulfilled. "One wonders why this image of America is never promoted here," a paper in India had commented after one of his concerts. "There was not even a suggestion of the loud gawkiness one associates with American pop music in his program." He had overcome barriers of language, race, and culture; words were limited, but music universal. Forced to rely on musicianship, he relearned how music can say what words cannot.

Back home, Harold was placing weekly ads in *Variety*: "Seeger in Indonesia," "Seeger in Japan." And Seeger had his first solo hit, "Little Boxes," which Columbia had excerpted from *We Shall Overcome*. For the first time in a dozen years, his voice was on national radio.

As Seeger triumphantly flew from Ghana to Europe on the last leg of his tour, he felt a rising impatience to get home. If he could get Africans harmonizing, he would not fail again in the South.

FATIGUED BY TRAVEL after visiting four continents, the Seegers boarded a flight home to New York on June 2, 1964. "The U.S. seems very big, very rich, the cars huge," Seeger wrote. "The

Hudson Valley still seems one of the most beautiful spots on earth, even if it does stink with sewage."

In the ten months he'd been out of the country, Seeger had missed a great deal. The March on Washington for Jobs and Freedom had brought a quarter of a million people together, with Seeger's friends singing. JFK had been shot in Dallas. Racial violence had escalated. Four young girls had been killed in an explosion at a church in Birmingham, and SNCC workers now called themselves "guerrilla fighters." The 1964 Mississippi Summer Project, sponsored by SNCC and Dr. King's Southern Christian Leadership Conference, seemed like a Huck Finn attempt to redress racial injustice in one intense summer. Many of the most dedicated teenagers Seeger knew were involved. If they could risk their hides in Mississippi, he could at least provide musical support.

One Freedom Summer volunteer, Paul Cowan, described his motivation for going to Mississippi: "The project seemed to be a turning point in America's history. We were an army of love, and if we integrated Mississippi, we would conquer hate's capital." Meanwhile, in the first weeks, three white civil rights workers went missing.

Mississippi welcomed Seeger and these young initiates with rifles and clubs; in those days, SNCC organizers were called Negro, not yet black or African American, and mixed marriages were not merely taboo, but illegal. Before the summer ended, eighty volunteers would be beaten, thirty-five black churches bombed or burned, and dozens of shootings reported. "We've been told over and over about brutality and beatings and murder," a volunteer wrote home. "They say none of us believe it inside. We probably feel we have a lucky charm which will give us a halo of sanctity."

Others cold-bloodedly talked of the volunteers as decoys. "It was high time for the U.S. as a whole, a white-dominated country, to feel the consequences of its own racism," wrote James Forman.

—

ON AUGUST 2, 1964, Seeger visited voter registration projects in Mississippi. African Americans had only 1 percent of the total vote, and the Mississippi Freedom Democratic Party was challenging the credentials of the all-white Democrats, with some success. Though part of a caravan of entertainers, Seeger traveled alone. At the last minute, Toshi's father worriedly asked them not to go; news reports disturbed him. Seeger wouldn't be dissuaded. His mind was made up. After much back-and-forthing, Toshi stayed in Beacon and Pete departed.

Trouble started before he could get out of the airport in Jackson. A man followed him off the plane, a Mississippian who had overheard Seeger talking with a reporter from *Life* on the flight.

"He accosted me with blood in his eye," Seeger wrote his father. "'Are you coming down here to sing for the niggers?'

"'I've been asked down here by some friends to sing,' says I, trying to be at my most gracious. 'I hope that anyone who wants to hear me can come, Negro or white.'

"'Well, you just better watch your step. If we hadn't been on the plane when I heard you talking I would have knocked the shit out of you.'"

As Seeger sped from this welcome, he rode into another tense situation. The white volunteers from the North had brought unexpected problems, such as black-white extramarital sex (welcome as bubonic plague in small southern towns). SNCC's southern black staff felt displaced as the earnest young whites moved in and ran the offices.

"They were a group of people coming out of Howard University: Courtland Cox, Stokely, Lawrence Guyot," Bernice recalled. "Northern blacks were coming into the organization, and that changed leadership positions. It changed the timbre, rhythm, and style of the organization. Up till that point, it had been paced by southern black students.

"At SNCC meetings, those would be the only people talking. And they were more glib, articulate, flowing, had read more, and so you couldn't talk about what happened the night you arrived down the road and got shot at any more, because there was all this higher level of analysis going on. I remember one meeting Stokely got up and said, " 'Well, I is sorry that I graduated from college and learned to talk.' "

ON A DRENCHINGLY HOT August afternoon in 1964, Seeger pulled into Hattiesburg, Mississippi. Walking through town, he met an old friend: Irene Paull, the woman known as Calamity Jane, who'd put him and Woody up in Duluth, back in 1941.

"Pete arrived with his guitar over his shoulder, playing," the white schoolteacher recalled. "He was sweating, and the shirt clung to his back." A black minister guided him to a seat in the shade and sent his daughter for ice water. Soon not only civil rights workers but townspeople wandered over to what sounded, with clapping and amens, like a revival meeting. Paull was amazed—only days before, black and white SNCC workers had been yelling at each other.

"Get off our backs," Seeger's friend had finally told one of her local black critics. "If we weren't for you, we wouldn't be here. Since when are *we* the enemy?"

"Listen," a black organizer had answered. "It would be nice if we could give you all big badges: 'I WAS IN MISSISSIPPI. I'M A GOOD WHITE.' Our people are angry and you may be killed or hurt with the rest. We can't say these are innocent and those are guilty."

Into this situation Seeger brought a truce. Everyone sat down together. The heat, the ever-present threat of violence melted, and, for a moment, volunteers and locals sang together in a cool meadow. No one stirred, for fear of breaking the spell. They sang "We Shall Overcome" and they again had one cause, one enemy. Too soon, the songs ended. Ragged from the heat and from hold-

BELASCO · JUNE 3RD

Friday Afternoon at 4:30

CONSTANCE AND CHARLES

SEEGER

"TRAILING MUSIC"

Violin and Piano Recital

TICKETS, 50c, 75c, $1.00, $1.50 - BOX SEATS, $2.00

Poster, the Seeger family, "Trailing Music," 1922

Pamphlet written by Peter's maternal grandfather

THE STORY OF THE

U. S. GUNBOAT GLOUCESTER

TOLD BY

DR. J. TRACY EDSON

Of the Class of '71, U. S. Naval Academy, late ENSIGN U. S. NAVY, Watch and Division Officer of the Gloucester, at the Battle off Santiago, July 3d, 1898

The Seeger estate at Patterson, New York

SEEGER FAMILY COLLECTION

Constance, Peter, and the baby's grandfather, Dr. John Tracy Edson

SEEGER FAMILY COLLECTION

Charles Seeger and infant son Peter

SEEGER FAMILY COLLECTION

Constance Seeger, young violinist

SEEGER FAMILY COLLECTION

The Seegers on tour, 1922.

SEEGER FAMILY COLLECTION

Five-year-old Pete Seeger, c. 1924

SEEGER FAMILY COLLECTION

Peter, under the influence of Ernest Thompson Seton's Indian lore, 1929

SEEGER FAMILY COLLECTION

Peter and his eldest brother and roommate Charles, on Manhattan rooftop, 1939.

SEEGER FAMILY COLLECTION

Private Seeger performs for sailors and Eleanor Roosevelt, 1942

FARM SECURITY ADMINISTRATION

Charles and Ruth Seeger with their children, Mike and Peggy

AMERICAN FOLKLIFE CENTER COLLECTIONS

The Vagabond Puppeteers, Seeger's first troupe, 1939 SEEGER FAMILY COLLECTION

The Almanac Singers in performance in 1941; from left, Woody Guthrie, Lee Hays, Mill Lampell, Pete Seeger WOODY GUTHRIE ARCHIVE

At the foot of Woody Guthrie, c. 1940 AMERICAN FOLKLIFE CENTER COLLECTIONS

In the army on the island of Saipan, in the Western Pacific, Pete sings to local kids.

SEEGER FAMILY COLLECTION

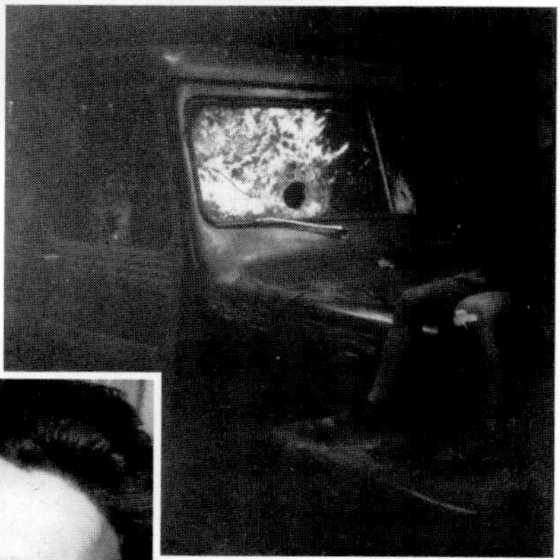

The Seegers' car after the Peekskill attack, 1949.

SEEGER FAMILY COLLECTION

Toshi Ohta and Peter Seeger courting, c. 1940

SEEGER FAMILY COLLECTION

Seeger's banjo, whose legend reads: "This machine surrounds hate and forces it to surrender."

TCDAVIS OF WILMINGTON, DELAWARE

Pete Seeger testifies before the HUAC, August 1955

BETTMANN/CORBIS

Seeger and presidential candidate Henry Wallace, 1948

PEOPLE'S SONGS

Right-wing pamphlet, late 1950s

Early publicity photo: The Weavers, c. 1951

LEVENTHAL ESTATE

The Seeger cabin and barn near Beacon, New York

DAVID DUNAWAY

Peter Seeger, Dr. Martin Luther King, and friends at Highlander Folk School, Tennessee, mid-1950s HIGHLANDER RESEARCH LIBRARY

With Muddy Waters and Memphis Slim; Alan Lomax on guitar, 1959
JOHN COHEN

Peace march, late 1950s

SEEGER FAMILY COLLECTION

Seeger with guitar, late 1980s

DAVID DUNAWAY

Pete Seeger at student folk festival ROBERT KRONES

Pete Seeger and Jimmy Collier, 1977 PAT GOUDVIS

Pete Seeger studies Mike Seeger's guitar work, 1959 JOHN COHEN

First crew of Clearwater, *including Lou Killen and Don McLean (left); Reverend Fredrick Douglass Kilpatrick, Jimmy Collier, Len Chandler, and Fred Starner (to Seeger's right); and Rambling Jack Elliot (extreme right), 1969*
HUDSON RIVER SLOOP CLEARWATER

Bob Dylan, Freedom Singers, Peter, Paul, and Mary, Theodore Bikel, Pete Seeger at Newport, 1963
JOHN BYRNE COOKE

The sloop Clearwater *before Statue of Liberty*

HUDSON RIVER SLOOP CLEARWATER

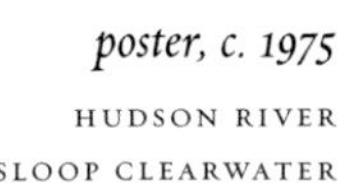

Broadside concert poster, c. 1975

HUDSON RIVER SLOOP CLEARWATER

Seeger moving the crowd to sing DAVID GAHR

Mike, Peggy, and Pete Seeger in performance, 2005 PHILIP RYALL

ing within him the group's tensions, the singer dragged himself to the next town.

On August 3, Pete Seeger performed in Meridian, Mississippi. "We sang a lot of freedom songs," remembered one volunteer, "and every time a verse like 'No more lynchings' was sung, or 'Before I'd be a slave I'd be buried in my grave,' I wanted to stand up and shout: Think about what you are singing—people really *have* died to keep us all from being slaves."

In the middle of the concert, someone handed Seeger a note: SNCC workers Andrew Goodman, Michael Schwerner, and James Chaney had been found nearby, buried in an earthen dam.

Amid the crying and shock, Seeger closed by saying, "We must sing 'We Shall Overcome' now. The three boys would not have wanted us to weep, but to sing and understand this song." He didn't rage, or stir up an assault on the Klan. His comment was like the inscription on his banjo: "This machine surrounds hate and forces it to surrender."

"What am I accomplishing, some may ask," Seeger wrote friends. "Well, I know I'm just one more gram of sand in this world, but I'd rather throw my weight, however small, on the side of what I think is right, than selfishly look after my own fortunes and have to live with a bad conscience."

IF PETE SEEGER salved his conscience in Mississippi, the prescription soon lost effect. Freedom Summer was a peak in the brief alliance between white and black liberals. On the journey down to earth, as the racial gradualists fell behind and those for justice "today" took command, fellow travelers like Seeger would be left behind; but not quite yet.

The musician returned with a lightness to his step and a notebook full of songs. He had used his talents as the movement asked, not taking sides, floating above factionalism to a high harmony. And he'd learned something.

"In this movement, he was being led," civil rights activist Jimmy Collier reflected. "He didn't have to take a bunch of white people who were shy about singing and no rhythm or anything like that. He was watching. He was being taught."

His bookings rose faster than he could follow. Countries he had visited now requested return engagements; he could have taken another world tour. "I'm studying Russian for the next trip, editing films from the trip, and sailing! Our whole family has quite fallen in love with sailing and rented a boat for a few weeks last summer," Seeger wrote to artist Rockwell Kent.

Life published a feature story on him after that Mississippi interview. This fame touched off a peculiar need to deprecate his achievements. He wrote a fascinating self-criticism in *Sing Out!* (which he signed with Toshi's name). He called his sixty or seventy records "one of the most uneven bodies of recorded music that any performer could boast of, or perhaps be ashamed of. . . . If one could dub onto a tape a few songs from here and there on his many LPs, one might have quite a good one-hour tape of Pete Seeger. The trouble is, no two people would make the same selections. Therein lies his defense."

Characteristically impractical, he urged his fans *not* to buy his records. He wanted to make songs available, but preferred people to sing them rather than play the records. (This must have struck his record companies as a novel, if unsatisfactory idea.) This awkward self-criticism troubled fans, suggesting either a tension between the Seegers or some deep self-dissatisfaction.

Also making him uneasy was his public association with the civil rights movement. He hadn't spent that much time in the South. Once, when Seeger was performing at Martha's Vineyard, Lillian Hellman invited him to a reception at her house. No sooner had he sat down than she complained to him about "We Shall Overcome."

"You call that a revolutionary song? What kind of namby-pamby, wishy-washy song is that?" Hellman browbeat him.

"Mooning, always 'Some day, So-o-me-day!' That's been said for two thousand years." Her remarks disturbed him enough that he wrote them to Bernice Reagon, who pointed out, "Well, if we said we were going to overcome next week, it would be a little unrealistic. What would we sing the week after next?"

ON MARCH 24, 1965, the Seegers joined a march from Selma to Montgomery, Alabama, at the personal invitation of Dr. King. Marveling at the line of demonstrators trudging under the hot Alabama sun, they had no idea of the danger of the next few days, or that this would be their last march for SNCC.

"It was Pete Seeger's thing come true," a fellow marcher remembered. "He went nuts trying to take down all the songs." Seeger had walked into a song agitator's dream: poor people singing together, black and white, well organized and in high spirits.

The march had its origins in demonstrations led by Dr. King in February, when Selma's sheriff, Jim Clark, had locked up 1,150 people marching toward the Edmund Pettis Bridge. A young voter-registration worker, Jimmie Lee Jackson, died after being shot in the stomach by police. King and his staff called for a massive march to Alabama's capital, which SNCC, fearing bloodshed, joined reluctantly. On March 7, two thousand people started for Montgomery, but Jim Clark's posse turned them back with cattle prods and clubs. Then the call went out to Seeger and other celebrities.

The events in Selma echoed across the country. In Washington, a week after the first march, Lyndon Johnson addressed Congress in support of the Voting Rights Act of 1965. "We have already waited a hundred years and more, and the time for waiting is gone. . . . We shall overcome!"

On March 21, the march began again. Clergymen and nuns were at the head of the line, and the contingent grew by the hour as chartered planes landed from all over. When the Seegers arrived on the fourth day, they found twenty-five thousand sweating and determined people. To protect the marchers from attacks, President Johnson posted two thousand armed national guardsmen along Route 80.

"It was very well organized. They had huge tents for people to sleep in, overnight on the way, and there were areas where we stopped every night," a marcher remembered. "It was like a little city. The Klan was around and people didn't know whether they'd be shot."

The crowd stretched six abreast for over a mile. The sun beat down, but the line flowed like an army on the move, with food and latrine trucks bringing up the rear. As the march twisted between cotton fields and dirt farms, Seeger heard three or four freedom songs drifting up from different places along the line: "They were creating one great song after another—before our very eyes! . . . Imagine they were changing "You Can't Make Me Doubt Him" into 'I Love Everybody.' "

But the Ku Klux Klan didn't love the marchers. The organization had promised someone would pay for inviting these agitators to make trouble for "their nigras." The threats were so public, late-night TV host Johnny Carson joked, "Some troops were shipped out and they didn't know where they were going. When they got to Vietnam, they were so relieved—they thought they were headed for Selma!"

The sky was hot and clear. Asphalt oozed onto the marchers' shoes, but no one cared. The Alabama State Troopers—the Dixie Dandies—flashed by in air-conditioned cars on the lanes open for traffic. Behind them passed cars with signs reading "White Citizens' Council—HELP MAINTAIN SEGREGATION." Sheriff Jim Clark sported a new hat, dark glasses, and a button that read NEVER.

The tension did nothing to dim Seeger's enthusiasm. Topical songs, the folk song revival, integration—everything came together at once. Blacks and whites were clapping, eating, singing together, improvising words to rock 'n' roll tunes:

Well, I read in the papers (dadat dadat dat)
Just the other day,

That the Freedom Fighters
Are on their way.
Oh, Wallace
You never can jail us all
Oh, Wallace,
Segregation's bound to fall.

Seeger picked up the next verse:

I don't want no mess
Don't want no jive
And I want my freedom
In sixty-five.

The scion of a family that crossed on the *Mayflower* raised his head back and hollered out "Don't want no jive," his tight Yankee tenor left at home. The uncomfortable diction reflected the continuing dilemma of his always singing for (other people's) justice.

A flash shower turned into a downpour, and soon the road was caked with mud. The rain cooled the air and somehow lifted spirits. Teenagers poured out of school to join the march, adding a carnival air. Feet were a major topic of conversation; the blacktop had heated people's shoes until they felt like twin ovens. When the march turned into camp for the night, Dick Gregory mused, "I'm sure Dr. Scholl's underwrote this march."

After receiving armbands, everyone learned security precautions. Seeger wandered from campfire to campfire, picking up songs. He'd appear at the edge of the light, jotting down lyrics like an anthropologist.

"There was no time for celebrity adulation," said a march organizer. "You have to understand: People didn't know whether the Alabama National Guard would suddenly start dropping bombs from the helicopters which kept circling the camp. This was for real, and we had total security in the camps at night. Guards on all-night shifts. Lighting systems. Evacuation plans. All in all, the place was like a huge caravan with giant tents, everyone huddled together."

Fears of attack made the darkness eerie. "People were scared, really scared," the organizer continued. "But they carried on. People sang like they might never get another chance." Old-time hymns, new songs—the marchers sang to keep back the night. Toshi felt "renewed" by the music.

NEXT MORNING, March 25, 1965, the demonstrators started toward downtown Montgomery. The last day of the march was the hottest yet. Many marchers had faces white with sunburn ointment. The line paused near the Montgomery airport, where thousands joined the demonstration for the final stretch to Alabama's state capitol. The Seegers shared lunch with two black friends, talented songwriters Len Chandler and Jimmy Collier.

Seeger had met Jimmy as a teenager a few years before at the University of Chicago folk festival. Now Collier worked as a song leader and organizer with Dr. King. He stood five feet eleven inches, stocky, with an infectious grin. He walked up and down the line with his guitar, picking behind people as they sang, tossing in words. Jimmy always seemed to be moving, like a child with new sneakers. Seeger admired his ease. Jimmy, about the same age as Seeger's eldest, Danny, became family.

In his little notebook, Seeger was writing down lyrics. "Excuse me, ma'am," he said to one woman, "could you tell me the words to 'Oh, Wallace?'"

"The words? Why, there are no words!"

Seeger tried again. "Well, do you know any of the verses?"

"Why sure. You just make 'em up. Here's a few . . ." She smiled as he earnestly wrote them down. "Don't you know you can't write down freedom songs?"

Right on schedule, the celebrities walked out of the Montgomery airport to join the march: Tony Bennett, Anthony Perkins. The TV cameras began to roll. In its final hours the march numbered thirty thousand. The long night was over and the day looked clear and unthreatening. Seeger kept hopping from group to group like a nervous journalist. Toshi walked alongside, photographing the marchers.

"There were people getting shot and beat up and those three civil rights workers had gotten killed; so there was a lot of violence going on and that's what people felt," Collier recalled. "You know what happens when people are really scareder than shit? They sing like they're not going to ever be able to sing again. And they eat, and it was that kind of atmosphere. People were really scared but they felt that they had to carry on. So the music was very important to making people feel good. Many of the songs were old Union songs, you know, right out of the thirties and so on, just different words. So I'm sure for Peter it was just a dream come true."

He probed for the source of the singers' vitality, as if he could bottle it and bring it north. Back in 1955, during the Montgomery bus boycotts, Dr. King's group had sung African American spirituals in traditional versions, but everyone understood their new urgency:

We are soldiers in the army
We have to fight, although we have to die
We got to hold up the (freedom) banner
We got to hold it up until we die.

In 1960 and 1961, through song organizers like Guy Carawan, the civil rights movement readapted union songs, such as "We Shall Not Be Moved." Then, to Seeger's joy, the demonstrators themselves made the adaptations. Long nights in jail had given activists plenty of opportunity to break in the new songs.

—

ENTERING MONTGOMERY, the marchers turned up Dexter Avenue toward the state capitol. The Seegers had to leave and catch a plane home. As the day was turning dark, a woman volunteered to drive them back along to the airport. They were surprised to find no protection for the returning marchers. A few hours earlier, the road had been filled with demonstrators; now it was deserted.

Bernice Reagon understood why the Seegers traveled without protection: "If you walk from Selma to Montgomery, you may think you can walk or hitch all the way back. You get real loose. . . . You think you can do anything you want with that space—including being blown away."

Later, Len Chandler was driving along the Selma road when he saw a car smashed through a barbed wire fence. "There were about thirty or forty troopers with lights turning. I thought it was an accident. We'd marched right past the spot."

The car had been driven by a middle-aged woman from Detroit, Viola Liuzzo. In the dark stretch of Alabama highway, a car came up behind her carrying three Klansmen, one of them an FBI informant. Someone had a gun. Two shots traveled through her brain, and the driverless car screeched across the road, out of control.

The Seegers were a few hours ahead of her on the same road. The Montgomery airport loomed ahead. Unlike Liuzzo, they arrived in safety, but as soon as they got out of the car, they felt the hostile stares. Toshi told her husband to be careful. "I was stupid, unconscious of danger. . . . I could have been beaten up in the men's room and not survived."

Their plane had not yet arrived, police protection was gone, and the couple began to get nervous. "We had obviously slept with the marchers the night before," Toshi remembered. "We were covered with mud. Finally we found some bathrooms and scrubbed off what we could. Anything could have happened to us that night."

Seeger returned from the Selma march glad to have gone. For two glorious days, he had found the singing movement he'd hoped for since he was twenty. He seemed as excited about the singing as at the movement's more concrete achievements.

But no sooner had he found his place in this movement than it began to slip away from him. The Selma march was more of a turning point than the participants could have imagined. A highway through the Alabama Black Belt might be far from Eden, but a year later, amid cries of "Black Power" and separatism, the march seemed innocent, even blissful.

Perhaps Seeger felt the change coming. In the next few months, he sang increasingly for the new, anti–Vietnam War groups. He helped plan the 1965 Newport Folk Festival, never dreaming of the havoc Bob Dylan would leave behind. The Freedom Singers had separated, though he and Bernice continued to perform together. Yet all this paled before Seeger's memories of the integration at the Selma march.

Separated from the day-to-day workings of SNCC, Seeger knew little of its painful evolution. At the end of 1965, a purge of white "northern middleclass elements" began as chairman John Lewis called for a "Black-led, Black-dominated" organization. SNCC canceled plans to extend a Freedom Summer–type program throughout the Deep South; instead, whites were told to organize in their *own* communities. "If we are to proceed toward liberation," a SNCC position paper read, "we must cut ourselves off from the white people."

The eruption did not occur at once. That summer Seeger was still discussing the best way to build a local integrated base with Myles Horton of Highlander and black SNCC activist Stokely Carmichael. Stokely had by this time been jailed twenty-five times; born in Trinidad and raised in Harlem, he had a street-tough manner that belied his high school days in Greenwich Village and at the Bronx High School of Science.

One afternoon Stokely and Jim Forman paid Harold Leventhal a visit in his office. In the past few years, Leventhal had gone out of his way to help set up civil rights benefits; he had a nodding acquaintance with SNCC's leadership. Stokely arrived in Leventhal's office fresh from backwoods organizing, however, and he was anything but cordial. He began calmly enough, pointing out how much publicity Leventhal's performers had received for their brief time in the South. A lot of work went into setting up those concerts, Harold answered. They raised a lot of money—was he saying he didn't want any more benefits? Carmichael turned on him with a snarl, and "anti-Semitic, anti-white charges crackled in the room. It was a terrible time, and we were wrongly the victims," Leventhal recalled painfully.

An unsettling mood hung in the air, and sensing it, Seeger held tightly to his friendships with Jimmy Collier and Bernice Reagon, who came up for the holidays and helped out. Collier recalled, "Bernice and I represented idealistic kids. I know Theodore Bikel—and a lot of others—felt hurt and angry at what was happening to SNCC. Pete didn't. Maybe he wasn't as sensitive. Maybe he wouldn't know if someone was insulting him. Maybe he just understood.

"The tone of the movement was changing. It was obvious that once voting rights were won, then everything was going to become an economic question. That would necessitate trying to deal with the ghetto. So we focused more and more of our attention to the North.

"There was this 'Go back to Africa' consciousness, and this separatist, 'We don't have to deal with white people' attitude was starting to manifest itself. As they began to change and as the fund-raising began to change, everybody's relationship began to change. Nobody needed white liberals.

"I think Seeger was definitely affected by it; everyone was. The feeling that goodness and truth and light would somehow win over was starting not to be believed by a lot of people. Guys in the ghettos that we tried to get to go do marches would go tear up buildings and shit. . . . It was a very pessimistic and depressing period."

To Seeger's frustration, civil rights singing had also begun to disappear. As in People's Songs, the music faded once its morale-building and media-gathering functions diminished. Len Chandler stopped singing "Black, White, Christian, Jew. We must keep marching through." In its place he performed:

Move on over or we'll move on over you
And the movement's moving on.

Yet, as some American blacks gave up "We Shall Overcome," South Africans picked it up. On April 1, the song was sung on the gallows of the Pretoria Central Prison by one John Harris, just before the freedom fighter was hanged for having planted a bomb in Johannesburg. Agents of the South African security police searched record stores in Johannesburg, according to the *New York Times*: "They were especially interested in one version of 'We Shall Overcome' recorded by the American folk singer Pete Seeger."

Less than a year after Selma, one of Seeger's friends, black songwriter Julius Lester, wrote *Sing Out!* (where he'd worked) a biting letter that could have been aimed straight at Seeger's heart:

> Those northern protest rallies where Freedom Songs were sung . . . began to look more and more like moral exercises: "See, my hands are clean." Now it is over: the days of singing freedom songs and the days of combating bullets and billy clubs with love. "We Shall Overcome" (and we have overcome our blindness) sounds old, outdated, and can enter the pantheon of the greats along with IWW songs and the union songs.

As one SNCC worker put it after the Mississippi March, "Man, the workers are too busy getting ready to fight to bother with singing anymore." They used to sing "I Love Everybody" as they ducked bricks and bottles. Now they sing:

Too much love, Too much love,
Nothing kills a nigger like Too much love.

Here was a protest song Pete Seeger was unlikely to perform.

He had faced abrupt changes in his repertoire before. But as he traveled into the antiwar movement, he left a piece of himself behind. An integrated society seemed more distant than ever. Though outwardly confident, there were undertones of frenzy in Pete Seeger, at first faint, but growing louder, as the civil rights movement and his folkie godchildren moved off.

Chapter 11

WAIST DEEP IN THE BIG MUDDY

—

FOUR MONTHS TO THE DAY AFTER PETE SEEGER RETURNED FROM the Selma march, he opened the 1965 Newport Folk Festival. To tens of thousands he played a tape recording of the cries of a newborn, his niece Sonya Cohen: "Tonight let's sing for this child. What are we going to sing her about the world she's joined?" he asked.

Down South, purges of white civil rights activists had begun, but at Newport, Seeger assumed he was among friends. The festival was his home away from home, a refuge from commercialism and rock 'n' roll. Here, folk music devotees could savor the quiet fire of mountain singers like Roscoe Holcomb and Jean Ritchie. It was a break from *Hootenanny* fakelore and electrified, imitation-folk hits. Though long used by blues artists, electrification had lately come to symbolize demon pop music. It led to the harder stuff, like rock 'n' roll. Seeger enjoyed telling a story about a fellow who walked into a Dublin folk club and plugged in an electric guitar.

"What in the name of God is that?" the café owner asked.

"It's an electric guitar," said the musician.

"And whose electricity are you using?"

"I'm just plugging it into the wall."

"If you can't play it yourself, you're not going to play it with my electricity," the club owner said firmly.

"And out he went," Seeger finished, with a trace of smugness.

At Newport—on whose board Toshi and Pete had both worked—people parked ungrumblingly in vast lots and carried in instruments and picnic coolers. Campgrounds filled with singing teenagers and sleeping bags. When a downpour threatened an outdoor concert, performers and audience only laughed and sang rain songs. This was more than a concert; it was a gathering, Woodstock before drugs and electric guitars.

Seeger was the emcee for the Sunday night concert: Bob Dylan, Peter, Paul and Mary, and Fannie Lou Hamer—fresh from civil rights work in Mississippi. Dylan, at twenty-four, was an accomplished guitarist; his songs were on everyone's lips. Seeger had introduced him at Newport two years before; Joan Baez had brought him out of the wings at her concerts. So by 1965, he needed no introductions. Yet folkies were confused by his latest album with electric backup, *Bringing It All Back Home*, with its high-pitched "Subterranean Homesick Blues," and by AM radio playing his newest single, "Like a Rolling Stone." Newport audiences were an idealistic if self-righteous, flannel-shirt-and-denim crowd. Some were appalled by Dylan's new direction; "a sellout," people muttered in Washington Square. (Many forgot that three years earlier, Dylan had recorded a country-rock single, "Mixed Up Confusion.") Thanks to Albert Grossman, his aggressive manager, Dylan was becoming a pop star.

But teeny-boppers weren't *supposed* to like folk music, and Dylan should no more succeed on AM radio than Pete Seeger should replace Johnny Carson on late-night television. The press at Newport anticipated a confrontation between Dylan's new style and the traditionalists. They got what they were waiting for: A Dylan biographer called it "the most written-about performance in the history of rock'n'roll." Yet one commentator wrote, "The myth of Dylan's 1965 Newport performance has never borne scrutiny well."

LATE SUNDAY EVENING, the stage darkened and the stagehands prepared for Bob Dylan's set. Seeger sat backstage; he didn't notice the long setup time as desk-size electric amplifiers were carried out. Before the Butterfield Band played, the Newport Board had met to debate amplified instruments. Seeger and Alan Lomax opposed them, making them "folk music's stodgy right wing." Seeger, whom Lomax called "folk music's holy man," was outvoted.

A new, stylish Dylan darted on stage. Black leather jacket and black slacks set off his yellow dress shirt and pointed motorcycle boots. He walked out in square night-black shades—carrying a shiny electric Fender guitar. Members of the electrically amplified Paul Butterfield Blues Band positioned themselves around him like bodyguards. The little red lights on top of the speaker-amplifiers glowed eerily behind Dylan.

"Louder," Bob called to the sound man as he tuned up. "More guitar."

No one can say for certain what happened in the next forty-five minutes. Al Kooper, who was playing organ, told one story and Bernice Reagon, near the stage, remembered it completely differently.

Seeger and *Broadside* magazine had boosted Dylan for years, telling a reporter in 1963, "I never saw anything like it: the kid's a genius." Seeger was "hovering over some young songwriters (like Bob Dylan) like a father," said writer Jon Pankake. In Seeger's presence, Bobby had been engagingly humble: "My songs were there before I came along. . . . I just sort of took 'em down with a pencil." Now, intent on broadening his sales beyond folk music fans, Dylan understood that at Newport, playing the electric guitar with a blues band meant a media confrontation, his forte. Fans would complain: "I think he's prostituting himself; this I can't stick." Or, "I came to see Bob Dylan, not a pop group."

After the first "Let's go" to the band, Dylan's "Maggie's Farm" staggered and crashed over an astonished audience. The back-up band, or the mix, made the music too loud to be heard.

Was this deliberate? Dylan thought so: "They didn't like what

I was going to play and they twisted the sound on me before I began." (John Boyd, who was at the sound check, insists that levels were clearly marked.) Even pianissimo, some listeners decided they'd heard too much. Halfway through the first song, the crowd started yelling: "Play folk music! You stink." Dylan played over them, letting the band set up the rhythm while he concentrated on singing, pounding out the words to "Like a Rolling Stone" in his best make-a-point diction.

"It was one of the rare occasions that Pete 'flipped out,'" said Leventhal. Seeger ran stage left.

"Fix up the sound," Seeger shouted at the sound man, "Turn it down!"

"No, this is the way they want it."

"You can't hear the words. Damn it, if I had an ax I'd cut the cable," Seeger said frantically.

"Pete Seeger towered over us [soundmen] by a foot, easily, just screaming and threatening," Paul Rothchild in the soundbooth recalled.

"Lomax [who'd just punched Grossman over his introduction to the band] charged the soundbooth with Pete Seeger nipping at his heels. . . . Pete tried several times to yank Rothchild's hands off the board, until Peter Yarrow declared, 'Pete, if you touch him again, I'll press charges for battery.' It was the loudest sound ever heard at Newport."

"We were sitting in the press section, maybe thirty yards back," guitarist Eric von Schmidt remembered, "and yelling, 'Can't hear ya!' and 'Cut the band down!' In the beginning, only about four or five people were hollering. Then they went into the next song and no one had changed any dials. It was the same thing, no voice coming through at all, just the band doing a solo. After that more people began shouting, 'We want Bobby.'"

In the middle of the third song, someone shouted, "Go back to the Ed Sullivan Show!" The audience laughed. Dylan finished and yelled over his shoulder at the band, "Let's go now, that's all." Bob may have made the right music at the right time, but only he could have made it in such a wrong place.

Dylan plunged backstage as Peter Yarrow of Peter, Paul and Mary took the mike. Dylan pushed right past Seeger.

"Was it to be marshmallows and cotton candy or meat and potatoes?" wrote *Sing Out!*'s Paul Nelson about Seeger and Dylan. "Rose-colored glasses or a magnifying glass? A nice guy who has subjugated and weakened his art through constant insistence on a world that never was and never can be; or an angry, passionate poet who demands his art to be all, who demands not to be owned, not to be restricted or predicted?"

Dylan returned to perform "It's All Over Now, Baby Blue" with his old guitar and harmonica. The audience gave him a standing ovation. While Dylan played his acoustic set, Seeger went from musician to musician, gathering people for a unifying finale.

"Does anyone have an E harmonica? Anyone? Just toss them up here," Dylan continued, charming a half-dozen onto the stage. His acoustic version of "Mr. Tambourine Man" quelled the storm, but Dylan ran offstage faster than he'd entered. He left Newport's stage forever, taking with him most of the folk revival's audience.

Afterward, on the exchange between Dylan and his audience, witnesses disagree. One record producer thought the PA system unable to handle the volume, turning it into a blank wall of noise for the audience. Blues guitarist Geoff Muldaur thought the music good, but its presentation poor and unrehearsed: "Dylan had no idea how to play the electric guitar." Even Pete Seeger couldn't control things, Barbara Dane told folklorist Richard Reuss.

Dylan had his own fanciful explorations: "Whole families had driven down from Vermont, lots of nurses and their patients just came to hear some relaxing hoedowns, you know, maybe an Indian Polka or two. And just when everything's going all right, here I come in, and the whole place turns into a beer factory . . . there were a lot of people there who were very pleased I got booed."

"'Why were you booing Bob?'" Seeger reflected in 2006.

"That's what I should have said at intermission. 'You didn't boo Muddy Waters—he was using electric instruments!'"

But at the time Seeger dictated a "memo to myself," which differs significantly from his account above: "Last week in Newport I ran to hide my eyes and ears because I could not bear either the screaming of the crowd nor some of the most destructive music this side of Hell."

Seeger privately wondered if he was at fault, for all his praise of Dylan: "Who knows, but I am one of the fangs that sucked Bob dry? It is in the hope that I can learn that I write these words: asking questions I need help to answer; using language I never intended; hoping perhaps I'm wrong. But if I'm right, hoping that it won't happen again." He immediately wrote his father that he was reevaluating everything.

The story would be de-emotionalized in Seeger's autobiography: "When Bob Dylan switched to an electric guitar at Newport I was not upset with him," Seeger wrote, his "little eraser" twanging. "I was furious at the sound system . . . you couldn't understand a word because of the distortion."

Dylan's departure from the folk music community might have affected Seeger less had it not opened a floodgate of recriminations. A *Sing Out!* forum on topical song produced unexpectedly bitter responses: Pete's brother-in-law Ewan MacColl (Peggy Seeger's husband) wrote, "The folk magazines seem to compete with each other in the hunt for superlatives with which to describe Bobby [Dylan] and Phil [Ochs] and Tom [Paxton] and Peter [Seeger] and all the rest of the mostest, bestest, youngest and newest." (These were strong words, from a member of the family.) Then, a community organizer and poet, Don West, called Seeger a publicity-seeking hero.

The brickbats continued. Jon Pankake, a writer who grew up listening to Seeger, attacked his "eager-beaver naiveté." A new generation of folk song enthusiasts preferred the less citified picking of Mike Seeger to his brother's smooth, spellbinding concerts.

Richard Fariña, no stranger to Newport and Dylan's friend, also distanced himself from folk songs:

"Folk music, through no fault of its own, fooled us into certain sympathies and nostalgic alliances with the so-called traditional past. The '30s, the highways and open roads, the Big West, the southern mountains, the blues, labor unions, childe ballads—all . . . made their mark, almost as if Chuck Berry and Batman had really nothing to do with who we were. . . . How long would people with contemporary poetic sensibilities be content to sing archaic material? Some of us had been listening to AM radio for a number of years."

The cracks were visible in the stained glass of the revival. Jazz critic Robert Reisner pushed this tide of criticism to ridicule: "Folk music is the shortcut to becoming an 'entertainer' these days. Express yourselves! Make girls! Get a record contract. You buy a guitar, learn three chords, and you are set. The [folk music] society is the easiest in the world to make. There are no standards of wit or intelligence or financial income. All you need are some dirty clothes."

The incident in Newport shook Seeger profoundly. Yet if not for the implied rejection, he might have seen himself in Dylan's rebelliousness. After all, Seeger's decision to experiment with pop music and bring the Weavers into nightclubs had met similar criticisms—especially from Irwin Silber, who had the Jeremiah-like distinction of denouncing both.

SEEGER WITHDREW, AS he had following the bankruptcy of People's Songs. He told Bernice that he felt Dylan was going in the wrong direction: "He said he was just in a lot of pain around some changes Dylan was making, and he felt it had to do with commercialization, and he was finding it very hard to deal with." Disappointment with Bob Dylan was only part of it; in a few months' span, he'd watched the decline of the freedom and topical song movements he had hoped for all his adult life. He wrote friends that he was giving up the Woody Guthrie Trust Fund, even his column in *Sing Out!*, the last tie to his boyhood journalistic dreams. "I am resigning as many things as I can," he wrote Don West.

Seeger left the country for Russia that fall, taking care that what he said and sang would not be misconstrued at home. The concerts went well until one momentous noon concert, when he sang to Moscow students. Afterward, they asked him about the mood on American campuses. Seeger tried out a new song, "King Henry," whose last verse contained these lines:

The year it is now nineteen sixty-five
It's easier far to stay half alive
Just keep your mouth shut while
the planes zoom and dive
Ten thousand miles over the ocean.

The concert was private, but a correspondent from the *New York Times* had asked to come along. "Sure," Seeger said, "you can carry my guitar." Now the reporter recognized what Seeger had in mind: the conflict—few Americans yet called it a war—in the distant country of Vietnam, where American "military advisers" were dying. The reporter dashed off an uncomplimentary story printed by the *International Herald Tribune* and then the *Times* the following day. A headline writer captioned it: SEEGER SONG IN MOSCOW IS ANTI-U.S. Subsequent editions appeared with a toned-down heading, but Seeger was utterly furious. A *New York Times* editor eventually apologized for the headline. ("Not publicly and not to us," Toshi later wrote.) It was too late—the damage had been done. People had begun walking Main Street in Beacon, circulating petitions to keep Seeger from singing in his hometown.

GRADUALLY DURING the next years, Seeger picked up the pieces of his life. Learning from those criticisms from black organizers still willing to work with whites, Seeger began to turn to a movement closer to home, one he'd understood instinctively as a child: environmentalism. He poured his heart into a fine new album of conservationist songs, lyrics to resist the asphaltization of America. The title song, "God Bless the Grass" by Berkeley songwriter Malvina Reynolds, could refer to Seeger; it tells of a hardy grass that grows up through the cracks in the cement: "The concrete gets tired of what it has to do; it breaks and it buckles and the grass grows through."

Out sailing and working on *God Bless the Grass*, he began to glimpse a connection. But in the beginning, sailing remained only a way to lose his cares in the wind.

It was television that enticed him. Seeger still hoped to put his *Banjo Traveler* series on American television. Through Moe and a producer, Sholom Rubinstein, *Rainbow Quest* was born. Initially broadcast on a UHF channel in the New York area, the show seemed like a success. *New York Times* critic Jack Gould called the series "Channel 47's first certain Emmy award." The format was folksy in the extreme. An early show had Tommy Makem, the Clancy Brothers, and Tom Paxton strumming and chatting around a picnic table. Initially only seven stations aired the series, however. The budget limitations frustrated him, particularly since a national audience didn't materialize in the two years he worked on it.

"If we'd had 20 stations, at $100/week we could have kept it going. But in the end only 13 stations carried it, and we lost all the money. We put in every cent of savings that Toshi and I had."

Despite this, Seeger remained determined to chip his way into the Great Hall of network broadcasting. But when Richard Salant had told his colleagues at CBS that the network did not want Seeger on TV, he wasn't kidding.

To gain access to prime-time air, Seeger had three options. The first was to sing what he was told; but he had never learned to tailor his ideals to convenience. His second was to take out ads and sponsor the series himself. His third choice was to set up a grand confrontation and beat his breast in public, a temptation he'd narrowly resisted with *Hootenanny.* Seeger was at heart a confrontationist, shy though he was one-on-one.

To succeed, he needed a strategy every bit as elaborate as his HUAC defense. He'd begun with a UHF series and appearances on a few local programs; then he might get occasional spots on nonnetwork syndicated shows. His first network appearance would be on the one spot not vulnerable to pressure from sponsors: the religious talk shows on TV, the Sunday Morning Ghetto, as it was called. At this point, surely, the stars of a Big Show would throw their weight behind Seeger.

But for a man who hated to argue, what a personal torment—lobbying an industry addicted to mirrors. Even playing the songs of the Hit Parade, first to last, might have been easier.

And to what end was all this struggle? He didn't need the money. He had no use for the publicity. Seeger revealed his motivation in a one-time broadcast on Canadian television: "Folk music's the kind you can make yourself. It doesn't have to come out of a loudspeaker. What a tyrant that little box can be [outlines TV frame with his fingers]. . . . How sad to think, in millions of homes, of a husband and wife sitting back woodenly on the sofa staring at the screen while an expert lover pretends to make love to another expert lover." Seeger ultimately wanted to use television to dissuade people from watching it; no wonder the networks were unenthusiastic.

ONE OF THE THINGS that got Seeger through the initial stages of his television campaign was a new song, "Waist Deep in the Big Muddy"; he called it a love song.

The story is a simple one: Back in 1942, a platoon of soldiers is ordered to ford a river. The sergeant and soldiers tell the captain the river is too deep, but he pushes them on, leading them into the water: waist deep, neck deep . . . until the captain drowns. The last verse, the one that later gave Seeger so much trouble, went:

Now I'm not gonna point any moral
I'll leave that for yourself
Maybe you're still walking, and
you're still talking
You'd like to keep your health.
But every time I read the papers
That old feeling comes on
We're waist deep in the Big Muddy
And the big fool says to push on.

"I was thinking of Vietnam. On the other hand, I purposely decided I would just let it be an allegory on its own, like the political nursery rhymes. As the years go by, the song may make another appearance and be sung in another context." How prophetic: Forty years later Bruce Springsteen would revive both "Waist Deep" and "Bring 'Em Home" against the war in Iraq.

Seeger began writing the song in the spring of 1966, tentatively naming it "General Fathead," starting with only the last line: "Waist deep in the Big Muddy, and the damn fool wants to push on." The words and a short tune arrived together, and he wrote it down in his pocket notebook. He kept pulling it out and telling himself, "Well, I really should finish that, it's a good idea for a song." He worked on it intensively for three or four weeks until he got it. "I sang it in Wisconsin one time, where I was staying at a professor's house. I had lunch with him the next day, and he said: 'Guess what! This morning in my class, I opened up the textbook and said, "Well, let's get cracking on page 183." And from the back of the lecture hall, two hundred people, there comes, "The Big Fool says to push on." The whole place just cracked up. I had to laugh too.'"

Meanwhile, Seeger's TV strategy was beginning to work. In December 1965 CBS TV's unsponsored *Camera Three* televised a Guthrie tribute from the 1950s, *California to New York Island*, with Seeger in the cast. In the summer of 1966, he had his first network

TV appearance on the nondenominational *Lamp Unto My Feet*. A producer, a gentle, middle-aged Englishwoman, had approached him. She had heard about the blacklist, she told him sweetly, but she wanted to have him on anyway. Seeger came in, and after a few quick run-throughs two shows were taped. It was a beginning, but the experience didn't satisfy him; the show was unsponsored, and "I didn't really think of it as prime-time network TV." On October 2 he appeared on *The David Suskind Show*, a popular (nonnetwork) talk show, alongside Robert Kennedy. "Step by step, the longest march can be won," he used to sing.

That fall Seeger visited Columbia to record *Waist Deep in the Big Muddy*. In the studio, he pulled up the mike as far as it would go on its stand and adjusted another for his banjo. Headphones covered his ears and his army-short hair. His Adam's apple danced as he sang, and his tall, bony frame made him look like Ichabod Crane, wired for sound.

On three songs Seeger had an electric bass, drums, and a second guitar backing him up, the first time he'd recorded with electric accompaniment. Following Dylan's lead, Joan Baez, Arlo Guthrie, and Judy Collins had all experimented with folk-rock. Now John Hammond decided it was Seeger's turn. The attempt was a disappointment. The ensemble, the Blues Project led by Danny Kalb, sounded as if they were playing along with a Pete Seeger record. "Pete didn't take the session in hand; Hammond and his engineer were pulling the strings," Kalb said. "The whole session was so un-joyous." Seeger's voice had an odd, straining sound, as if trying not to sound like the singer his fans knew.

"AMERICAN MINSTREL'S Song of Success," read the *New York Times* headline on January 23, 1966, and it seemed true. In the past year he'd begun to appear on TV. *Who's Who* listed him, though confusing him with his brother Mike. On July 7, 1966, the New York Court of Appeals ruled unconstitutional the cancellation of his concert in East Meadow, Long Island, where the school board had prevented him from singing. The decision set a major legal precedent: Neither he—nor anyone else—could be denied use of a school auditorium because of "controversy." When he finally sang in East Meadow, two thousand attended. Six hundred pickets stood outside, the largest number showing up since Peekskill.

Internally, something had gone awry in Seeger. A disaffection began in the midsixties and grew in direct proportion to the number of American troops in Vietnam. The rivers of enthusiasm that had carried him through so many movements dried up. The imperturbable singer, the optimist who inspired the crowds, showed fissures in his personality. As America became deeply involved in the faraway and sordid conflict in Vietnam, Seeger's insides soured. And the folk song revival—what was left of it—had taken off in a direction he hadn't intended. As he told the *New York Times*, using a characteristic metaphor:

> When I feel pessimistic, as I sometimes do, I feel like the man who loved to go out in the woods and track animals. He wanted other people to know what it was like, so he wrote a book about nature.
>
> It was a simple book, but it became a best seller . . . and then there were organized tours . . . and LPs of bird calls, and all the rest. And the man said, "But that isn't what I was talking about at all."

It was the post-Newport, post-Selma blues. On tour with Bernice Reagon, a friend handled the promotion. She worried—after calls from the Seegers—that her basic poster wasn't good enough. So she prepared one with Seeger's name in banner headlines and sent it off.

"When Pete got to town and he saw that [second] poster," Bernice remembered, "he ripped it off the wall. He said, 'Who did this!' She said, 'Well, I did.' 'You!' Pete said and went into a rage, crumpled it up, and threw it on the floor." Bernice calmed him by showing the first poster, which he liked. Seeger pulled himself together and apologized.

"He had this thing about not being a star, and somehow, he went off at that point," Bernice said. Seeger grew steadily less patient, particularly toward groupies. Though a crowd pleaser, he'd rarely attracted sexual propositions; his persona was more grandfatherly than rakish. Nevertheless, he had his opportunities, such as the time he sang at a wealthy psychiatric hospital, a very informal place: "After I finished singing, a woman says, 'Where are you going?' and I said 'I'm due over at somebody's house for supper tonight.' She says 'Come on up and have a drink.' Well, I went up to her room and had a beer, and I suddenly realized she was hoping we'd have a good time together. As soon as I realized that, I eased myself out of the room. It's an old joke in the family: I'm the New England puritan. Matter of fact, I was singing in Dublin once and somebody said, 'Do you want to go hear Seeger?' His friend said, 'Oh, no, who wants to hear that old clergyman.'"

Another time, a singer kept coming up and letting him know she was available. He edged off, politely, but finally he got furious; instead of rejecting the woman, he tore apart her singing. "It's a Jesus mentality." Bernice smiled. "Like the sage of the community, who has to maintain a certain kind of position."

"That isn't what I meant at all," Seeger said to a world that lionized him. The more people praised him, the more he tried to set the record straight, at least in his journal: "The man is a singer, but he obviously hasn't much voice . . . he tries to talk simply, but obviously has a good education and reads widely. He sings about poor people, though I doubt he is poor himself." In his pocket notebooks, eerie interior monologues appear: "I have no employer to fire me, so I will speak my mind. If the day—or night—should come when I am assassinated or put behind bars, you will know that you cannot trust the land of Lincoln any more, and the claws will come unsheathed." Seeger felt the conscience of his country dying around him. He quoted one of his favorite playwrights, G. B. Shaw: "Assassination is the extreme form of censorship."

One stark clipping in his notebook lay bare Seeger's mood: a *New York Times* article about a U.S. Air Force cluster bomb that accidentally crushed a school in Tanuyen, South Vietnam. In apology, Air Force lawyers paid families $33 in crisp new bills for each child killed.

"How do you kill a savage beast?" he went on, profoundly upset. "Poison its water holes," he scrawled. Violence outside, violence within. "Within me are two opposing forces," he wrote to himself:

One says kill
The other says create.
Which will win?
Which will win?
Which will win?

If the one, then my neighbors had best beware.
If the other, then we can learn to share.

That the artist in Seeger didn't wince at reading such doggerel—much less singing it—suggests how far the dire political situation had overtaken his aesthetics. Amid his daily rounds of concerts and fund-raisers, these hot feelings slowly pushed up inside him, like a lava crown.

IN DECEMBER, PETE SEEGER finally resumed his *Sing Out!* column. The photo at the top of the page had changed; Seeger wasn't smiling anymore. He gave his readers a stern and unusually candid picture of the new strains in his life.

> Sitting at a desk while the sun is shining bright outside is bad enough. Standing at a set of rewinds, editing film in a dark room, is worse. OK; somebody has to do it. But I'm getting too old for it.
>
> I was grumbling thus to my wife while we drove into the city, through Bear Mountain State Park. We passed three or four park service employees raking near the highway.
>
> "Now there's a good job. Lots of fresh air," says I.
>
> "I can give you that any time you like," answers my wife. "You can start in on our lawn as soon as we get home." . . .
>
> "No, that isn't the same. The men there looked so carefree. But I can't get my mind off Vietnam."

These lines contained a broad hint of family tensions. Like many couples in the 1970s, Pete and Toshi were arguing over feminism and its political implications. Their friend Don McLean remarked a "tremendous frustration" in Toshi. "She's paid a heavier price than anyone for all this cultural history that Pete has lived through." One year, he'd been away for three-quarters of the year. Toshi began to hector him, insisting he do more cleaning and cooking. "To be able to be Pete Seeger, you've got to have Toshi," Judy Collins said wistfully; women in the arts or professions rarely receive such tireless and effective support.

NEW YORK'S RADICAL folk music community was not as free of sex-role stereotyping as its rhetoric might suggest. In the Weavers, Ronnie Gilbert had struggled mightily to make herself heard over her three male colleagues, particularly Lee and the man they called (among themselves) "The Saint." She had to raise the roof more than once to get them to take her seriously. Sis Cunningham had had similar problems back at Almanac House; she and Bess Lomax had done much of the cleaning around those most-bohemian quarters.

Toshi, who'd never set out to be a performer or a producer, had a different experience from these two; nevertheless, by the end of the 1960s, Pete Seeger had stopped joking that Toshi had earned her managerial 10 percent when she suggested a song to sing or a benefit to avoid: "She felt that she has spent all of her life working on somebody else's career, when she would have liked to have done pottery or a number of things herself," Seeger reflected. "Like many women, she found it easier to put it off. They say, 'No, I can't do it now, I've got to help the children.' Then, too late, they realize they shouldn't have done it, they should have disciplined themselves and said, 'No, I will do this in spite of them.'"

A strange comment: He seemed to be chiding Toshi for carrying out his bidding. But times, and his attitudes, had changed: "Pete bitterly blames himself for what happened," a folksinger reflected. "It's one of the things he sees as a real contradiction and a failure." In the next years, Toshi would vacillate between chiding her husband for his dependency and supporting as much of his work as she could.

If Toshi had her scores to settle, the children had theirs as well. "I don't guess it was much fun having Pete Seeger for a father," said Jimmy Collier, who often stayed over at the house. When Seeger was home—which wasn't often—he could be loyal and occasionally tender, but he had a way of disappearing into himself, even in the same room with his family. With Jimmy Collier, Seeger had a special intimacy both treasured: "He was not distant from me, not off on a mission. I felt comfortable enough to tell him 'Hey Peter, let's get a beer. Stop being so serious.' . . . I was black too, at a time when he didn't have that much real contact with blacks."

AT THE BEGINNING of 1967, Seeger set off on another series of overseas concerts. He performed in Germany for the first time. Harold Leventhal had avoided the country for fear of seeing people his age and wondering what they had done in World War II.

"This was silly," Seeger now decided. "In future years an American will receive the same glances—what was he doing in 1967." Seeger sang "We Shall Overcome" in East Berlin, creating a headache for leaders who assumed protest songs applied only to capitalist countries. For years afterward, young East Germans sang the song.

In late spring he visited first Lebanon, then Israel. Visiting the Lebanese refugee camps further darkened his mood. Meeting Harold in Israel afterward, Leventhal remembered him bursting into tears as he described the camps. He refused to enter the Israeli section of Jerusalem. He wasn't anti-Israel; he just felt each group shared in the problem. He tried bringing the two sides into harmony—literally—by helping organize an impromptu concert at the Tel Aviv Hilton, busing in refugees and kibbutzniks to sing together; he dedicated a verse of "Guantanamera" "to exiles of two thousand years and exiles of nineteen years." Seeger was out of his depth. The tension in the hall so unnerved him he stopped in the middle of his singing, close to tears, and sat in the back. He left Israel the day the Six Day War broke out.

Seeger arrived home just as *Waist Deep in the Big Muddy and Other Love Songs* left Columbia's factories. "Oh, don't I wish it would sell a million," he wrote in *Sing Out!*, wondering when American TV networks would allow songs like his on the air.

Opinion had been changing about the war in Vietnam, particularly as the carnage entered living rooms via TV. Few Americans understood why the United States fought in this distant country. When the draft threatened college-age sons of the middle class, the country split along age lines. "Hell no! We won't go!" was heard on campuses from California to New York. Paying taxes to support the war made him wince. He did even more benefits; what he didn't earn, the government couldn't take away. The government stopped calling the soldiers in Vietnam "advisers"; suddenly, flunking chemistry meant the loss of a student deferment and a trip to fight "Cong."

Seeger sensed this growing opposition. He would choose a judicious moment to sing "Big Muddy," deliberately letting pro-war hecklers interrupt him: "Our boys are dying in Vietnam, and that guy is singing a song like that. I'm not going to let him get away with it. Boo. Boooo," he remembered. What Seeger knew (and his hecklers didn't) was that after the song ended, there would be thunderous applause. The booers found themselves outnumbered.

He could have dusted off the antiwar ballads he and the Almanacs had written twenty-five years before, like "Get Out and Stay Out of War." It was a tribute to his musical powers that the older songs were still singable and that his newer songs, like "If You Love Your Uncle Sam, Bring 'Em Home," were more fully developed. With twelve thousand people at Newport '66, he sang:

There's one thing I must confess
Bring 'em home.
Even if they brought their planes to bomb
Bring 'em home, home, home
Thou' they brought helicopter and napalm

"Bring 'Em Home" left audiences wondering about his rejection of pacifism—as he intended. Here, Seeger had actually aligned himself with the enemy; in his song, the United States became the invader and the Vietnamese the patriots.

Ever since the days of the Popular Front, Seeger had been proud to be an American. His songs, stories, clothes, even his log cabin fostered this native son image. For three decades, he'd harked back to American radicals for inspiration—even in his darkest moments with HUAC. But in Vietnam, Pete Seeger found little room for patriotism. "Pete's an incredible idealist," Bernice Reagon said, "an optimist throughout the period of the civil rights movement—the struggle was going to win, we're going to fix it. He ran into real trouble handling the United States and the war in Vietnam. He did not sail through it. He took a heavy glimpse of what was happening and got incredibly frustrated and depressed. . . .

"There was one period where I felt Pete was at some base level an American—you know, 'Our fathers bled at Valley Forge' [from "Wasn't That a Time"] and 'This land is your land, this land is my land.' At some point in this Vietnamese war, those things became the issue and the problem—you were no longer working for the dreams of the founding fathers."

Seeger's patriotism was still at issue. *Counterattack*, limping along, now harped on antiwar dissidents, complaining, "American fighting men have one hand tied behind them." Grass-roots anti-Communist groups popped out of the woodwork when Seeger came to town. The Citizens' Anti-Communist Committee of Connecticut called Seeger "Moscow's trained canary." The Committee to Combat Communist Propaganda handed out leaflets with pictures of wounded GIs, captioned:

THE HORRIBLE TRUTH!
THROUGH THE ADMISSION CHARGE
YOU ARE FINANCING COMMUNISM
. . . THROUGH PETE SEEGER

A California school superintendent asked *Scholastic* for a statement that Seeger wasn't a Communist after the magazine published an interview with him. "Our respect for the dignity of an individual restrains us from asking anyone questions related to his personal convictions or beliefs," responded a brave editor. But these outside forces threatened Seeger less than pressures within.

Seeger had marched, spoken politely, and nothing had changed; the bombers kept rolling out a carpet of death. Seeger was himself stuck in the Big Muddy; he could not avoid his responsibility as an American in the Vietnam War era. His internal conflict surfaced explosively after his return from that painful Middle East trip. He was performing for a group of Arab professionals when, at the end of the evening, he made the mistake of asking one why he hadn't gone back to his Near East home: "He smirked and said, 'Well, there's a lot more money here, after all.' "'But don't the people there need you?'" The man made a derisive remark. Seeger got so mad he lost it. He grabbed the nearest tablecloth, from a table set with fine crystal, and before he knew what he was doing he had wrenched it from the table, causing an awful crash. The Arab sat down astonished. The whole room stopped talking and stared. Toshi hustled him out the door.

Seeger had no more control than in 1949, when he'd thrown a glass of Coke at a woman who'd baited him about Henry Wallace. His anger came from the peculiar passion that makes a performer. "If you are very hot all the time, you have to be able to control it one way or another," Bess Lomax Hawes reflected. "In performance, you can pour out your emotion on the stage. Another way is by finding ways to keep yourself very cool in normal human interaction. I've seen Pete just walk away and then put his fist through something."

Seeger's frustration was also directed at Columbia Records. He had hoped "Big Muddy" would be a breakthrough; after all, Robert Shelton of the *New York Times* had called it a potential smash hit. Throughout the summer of 1967 he waited to see if "Big Muddy" would take off as a single. A few progressive FM stations played it once or twice, and the free-spirited Pacifica stations wore their copies out, but commercial stations ignored the song. Without radio play, sales lagged. Still, Seeger reasoned, he should have word-of-mouth success; at concerts the crowd wouldn't stop applauding the antiwar songs. Something funny was going on at Columbia.

Of course, Pete Seeger had never been a record executive's dream. He had as many records as any singer alive, but only one solo "hit": "Little Boxes." He toured constantly. Anyone who gave as many concerts as Seeger should have sold a lot of records. Yet his first record companies had gone out of business or fallen to conglomerates. The music business had become the music industry, with multinational companies controlling publishing, distribution, and TV and radio stations. Gross album sales surpassed a billion dollars annually.

Pete Seeger was the animal that zoologists of the music world couldn't classify. He didn't know a Buying Power Index from a Weekly Sales Net. No half-ton of amplifiers, instruments, and road managers arrived with The Pete Seeger Show. He had no private bus with wraparound stereo and hot and cold running drugs. He refused to plug his records. In fact, he rarely listened to them or to the radio; he owned a fifty-dollar record player.

Seeger inhabited a world of song that record companies visited only occasionally. They came looking for folk tunes as if on a French country picnic, bringing their own cutlery and tablecloth, to make sure the fare was served to their taste. Then, at a hint of controversy or gravity, they fled; Seeger—and his friends—were left to tend folk music until the next visit.

In 1965, Seeger had let his contract lapse at Columbia Records. He'd quietly returned to Folkways until John Hammond demanded CBS renew Seeger. Then he'd optimistically re-signed, waiting to use Columbia's well-oiled distribution system for something he really cared about. Now, with "Big Muddy," he had his chance—but nothing had come of it. "Columbia dropped the ball," Judy Collins reflected. "I just don't think they put enough money, time, and effort into Pete's records."

Midway through the summer after "Big Muddy" came out, Seeger met a man working in Columbia's distribution agency in Denver. "Pete, I have to tell you that record of yours arrived a few months ago. My boss just laughed: 'They expect me to get this sold? They're nuts.' He didn't even ship them out of the delivery room, they just stayed on the shelves." After going along with Columbia for so long, he'd expected better.

Seeger was furious but could do nothing; he set off on another tour with Bernice, traveling to Texas, where he visited his brother

Charles. On the five-day tour Seeger finished writing one of his only original blues, "False from True," an extraordinarily personal song for him.

When my song turns to ashes on my tongue
And I look in the mirror and see I'm no longer young
Then I got to start the job of separating false from true
And then I know I need the love of you.

The lyrics so disturbed Charles's wife, Judith, that she told a reporter that she hoped "everybody who loved Pete would come and tell him that the world was not hopeless" and that "False from True" was a symbol of his depressed mood. The newspaper printed her comments. "She shouldn't have said that," Seeger angrily told Bernice.

"That song seemed a very internal and personal statement," Reagon remembered. "He was saying that stuff was not working out the way he thought it should. . . . I thought it was good that he put it out; I'd never seen him do that, because all his stuff is always so high level. It's a blues, you know. And he sings other people's blues, but I'd never heard him sing his own. I remember feeling he must really be in bad shape now."

He was. Pictures of burned children haunted him; in page after page of his journal, he searched for a solution. His characteristic seriousness became anguish. Married to an Asian American, his children a mix of Japanese and American, Seeger took the destruction of Asian children personally. He wrote a poem about a baby in North Vietnam whose mother gave birth during an American air raid. The child, Bao Ngac, was wounded before she was born, when shrapnel pierced the mother and tore into the baby's cheek.

You will bear the scar all your life long
And I, whose only scars are mental ones,

Must stagger out and tell my countrymen
What happened.

The weeks passed and with them an endless stream of concerts: short intermissions and long encores. At first, it was his core fans who noticed a change in Seeger, the ones who came to every concert, who knew by his introductions what the song would be. Then, gradually, the casual listener sensed the difference. Had Seeger been quite so somber the last time? As strained and stark?

His columns in *Sing Out!* also had a new grimness, and he needed more and more space for what he had to say. He wrote endlessly of television, which came as no surprise to anyone reading the papers, for his television appearances had become a national controversy.

Seeger's long-range strategy was succeeding, he thought. In August 1967, the producers of *The Smothers Brothers Comedy Hour* received word that Seeger could finally appear in prime time on CBS. The *Los Angeles Times* broke the story, calling it an "important event," and "the glimmer of light at the end of what must seem to Seeger like an endless black tunnel." Tom and Dick Smothers had stuck their necks out. They wanted him on, but after a while they started to get nervous and asked him for a list of songs.

The *New York Times* and the *Delaware County Daily Times* ran editorials praising CBS's heroism. The network received more publicity for breaking its blacklist than they did for maintaining it for seventeen years. Among the Smothers Brothers' sponsors were Procter & Gamble, a major advertiser on *Hootenanny.* "Presenting Seeger," said the Smothers Brothers' producers, "is the most significant thing we'll do all year."

On September 1, Seeger flew to Hollywood with Harold Leventhal, quietly jubilant: "Pete's not the kind of guy to jump up in the air," Harold laughed. "He was reserved, but plenty glad to be back." All summer he'd joked about buying time on TV to sing "Big Muddy"; now he wouldn't have to take out ads.

"I was on my mettle as much as I've ever been in my life," Seeger said in recalling the taping. "I felt history was being made. And when you stop to realize—it was. The more President Johnson got into the war, the more opposition there was, far beyond the narrow Left or pacifist wing. . . . All of a sudden here was a breach in the wall of prime time, a very dangerous thing as far as the establishment was concerned." If Seeger exaggerated the importance of "Big Muddy" and TV's power, this only indicated how seriously he took this opportunity.

Yet, excited as he was, Seeger had a hard time singing. The television studio inadvertently robbed him of his sounding board: the audience. Lights, boom stands, cameras—they all got in the way of the songs. The acoustically deadened walls kept the crowd from hearing themselves sing and frustrated him. His twenty-minute segment didn't give him time to build up momentum. Despite these problems, he left feeling victorious.

"We're going to have to face TV for the good of the world, not just for the good of a small number of people," he told an interviewer. "There's a hell of a lot of things TV isn't showing."

Afterward, when the editor of a small folk song magazine criticized him for lending his talent to TV, Seeger defended himself: "I am no expert at stractics and tategy [*sic*]. I think all of us who love music and love America and the world must figure out how we are going to take the next steps. Unless we prefer to get off in a corner by ourselves and congratulate each other on our exclusiveness."

On September 10, 1967, Tommy Smothers smiled nervously and introduced Pete Seeger to millions of American households. He began with "Wimoweh"; then Tommy asked Seeger, who was holding a twelve-string guitar and fingering the strings, if he was going to sing "that song." The camera closed in on Seeger's face for a moment. When it moved back, Seeger was holding a banjo and "Big Muddy" had vanished into the ether.

Watching at home, Seeger muttered curses at the TV set. They'd been had.

"It's perfectly possible that some clever person at CBS said 'No, don't let him sing his song now,'" Seeger speculated later. "'Let's build up publicity and let him sing it in January.' It's theoretically possible. On the other hand I think more likely they said, 'That's just the kind of goddamn song we knew he'd try and sing. Well, we've got to stop it somehow—scissor it out.' The editor said 'How do I do it?' 'Oh,' they said, 'find a way.' So the poor editor might have said, 'Well, I'll do it the most awkward way, so everybody knows it's been scissored out.'"

Censoring Seeger provoked even more attention than the original decision to broadcast him; once again censorship gave him free publicity. On September 13, *Variety* ran one of its inimitable front-page headlines: "BIG MUDDY" IN CBS-TV'S EYE: SLIP SEEGER'S NUMBER FOR ANTI-LBJ SLANT. The network weakly replied that they didn't want "political controversy on entertainment programs." Exercising mammoth self-restraint—perhaps in hopes of a second chance—Seeger refused public comment. Nevertheless, the *New York Times* headlined SEEGER ACCUSES CBS OVER SONG, asserting that Seeger had been told he could sing "Big Muddy" only if he dropped the last verse ("Every time I read the papers . . ."). Seeger telegrammed Michael Dann, a CBS vice president, that he hadn't "accused" CBS of anything; he denied leaking the story, but concluded, "Do feel strongly that radio and TV communications should allow audiences to judge for themselves. The best censor is that little knob on the set."

The *Honolulu Star-Bulletin* asked, "Is the presidency so teetery that it cannot withstand the musical barbs of a folk singer? And is our democracy so fragile that songs of social protest must be stricken from the public airwaves? We think not." *Newsweek* pointed out that CBS records already featured the song on Seeger's current album. The September issue of the *National Catholic Reporter*—with its premature praise of CBS's "courage"—remained on the stands for two weeks after CBS censored Seeger.

Tommy Smothers told the press, "We definitely plan to have

Seeger back and he's probably gonna want to sing 'Big Muddy' again. Maybe we'll sing it with him." Only Pennsylvania's *York Gazette* grasped how uncomfortable and out of place Seeger appeared. He might *never* be content on soap-selling, mass-merchandising shows; television was not fit for Seeger, the *Gazette* concluded, rather than the other way around.

Two weeks later, after all the flutter had died down, Seeger performed in San Jose, California; a writer there noted he sang "Big Muddy" "with an aggressiveness that was out of character."

THROUGHOUT THE CRISIS of what Seeger could or could not sing on TV, one of his favorite causes had floundered. *Sing Out!*'s circulation was dropping with each issue, and the magazine was mired in infighting, with attacks both by and against Pete Seeger. From three hundred in 1950, the circulation of *Sing Out!* had risen to a thousand in 1955; by 1965, they were mailing almost twenty thousand copies. The folk song boom had seemed unending and, as editor of *Sing Out!*, Irwin Silber took credit for the magazine's success. Then, in 1966, the magazine's attempt at newsstand sales proved a disaster; they printed truckloads of copies that went unsold and lost twelve thousand dollars. As the commercial folk song revival faded, *Sing Out!* couldn't retrench fast enough. In 1966, Seeger had worried that the magazine was too fat and slick; a year later, the magazine was nearly bankrupt. The shrinking circulation opened the magazine to charges of irrelevancy, which came, strangely enough, from its editor of fifteen years.

Since Irwin Silber first became editor, Seeger had tried to put aside his differences. He appreciated Irwin's dedication, but he worried that the magazine was pandering to the star system. And Silber's self-righteousness had always bothered him: "When he thinks he's got the answer it doesn't bother him at all if he had a different opinion a while before, or that he was illogical." Irwin somehow managed to be both the major critic of commercialism in folk music and co-owner of the largest folk music publishing house, Oak Publications. But when Irwin bitterly denounced commercialism at the 1967 Newport Folk Festival and then sold the magazine to the editorial board and departed, that was the last straw. Bitterness against Silber grew until the magazine rocked like an overloaded ship on an uneven keel. On November 13, 1967, Seeger's nonpartisanship broke. He wrote Irwin a fierce and bitter letter: "I feel if you are trying to kill *Sing Out!* . . . you are doing a good job. For 15 years, I've defended you against all attacks. . . . If I have been a blind King Lear, I probably have been most blind about your own failings." Irwin eventually gave up his editorship, and the magazine struggled along on handouts from Moe Asch, the Seegers, and its many friends.

On October 3, 1967, one of *Sing Out!*'s oldest friends, Woody Guthrie, died. He had been in the hospital for thirteen years and, in the end, had little control over his body. Seeger heard the news while on tour in Japan; *Life* asked him for a eulogy, and he obliged, asserting that Woody would have been disgusted by the war in Vietnam.

On the campuses, where Guthrie was best known, frustration with the war in Vietnam grew daily. Some burned their draft cards or fled to Canada to avoid fighting. Seeger's college-age followers felt pressured to shut down the machinery of war—throw rocks through windows, pour glue in the locks at the draft board. For some, irrevocable acts were called for—going to jail or arming for guerrilla warfare. Local police forces, used to panty raids rather than sit-ins, overreacted and broke students' heads. Vietnam had become, as the *Washington Post* observed, "a generation-wide catastrophe." Seeger felt street fighting and yelling "pig" at the police were self-defeating: "My own tactic was to isolate the potential fascist and see if I could turn him into a potential human being."

Everywhere he looked, a new culture spread among young people, one he barely understood. He questioned why anyone would want to take LSD. Why was the Monterey Pop Festival out-drawing Newport five to one? Why had Abbie Hoffman left civil rights for *Revolution for the Hell of it*? When people came up to him at concerts and handed him flowers and beads, Seeger didn't know what to do.

"All You Need Is Love" wasn't going to heal America, that much Seeger knew—particularly in the long hot summers of the mid-1960s, when arson left Detroit and Newark looking like Bristol after the German bombings. Jimmy Collier had written a song justifying the riots, "Burn Baby Burn."

Seeger's "children" were spending more time getting high and listening to Cream and Jefferson Airplane than to him. His music was "right on" but dated, and for many it lacked the rhythmic release of the Rolling Stones or the Temptations. Seeger kept his distance from marijuana and talk of free sex; he didn't get it. A dream in his journal reveals how out of touch he felt: He was performing at a boys' school, similar to Avon, but the students wouldn't sing. In the middle of his concert, the audience filed out one by one to smoke grass on a darkened balcony—and Seeger didn't even realize they had gone.

"Pete Seeger is getting old," wrote a student in the *Daily Pennsylvanian*. "His voice cracks and he is no longer the best five-string banjo man around." The same reviewer pointed out how Seeger used to flourish a crimson bandanna, but now his shirt was dull red. "Times have passed him by, and he is now a respected member of society." A young English journalist pronounced him "lamentably and typically middle-class" and "the reverse of hip." Seeger believed in learning from young people, but he was forty-eight, and communes and psychedelics were not for him.

At the end of 1967 folkies and war resisters packed Carnegie Hall for Pete Seeger's annual Christmas concert. At the Fifty-seventh Street entrance, a woman in army fatigues and a "Dump Johnson" button passed out leaflets for a demonstration at the 1968 Democratic Convention in Chicago. Twenty-year-olds in first beards exchanged stories about Timothy Leary's latest cross-country stump.

The crowd disagreed on whether Seeger was still radical. He'd aged. He'd come to symbolize the union, peace, and civil rights movements; but symbols fade. Seeger represented their parents' generation, the bureaucratic "Old Left," as opposed to "Student Power."

After the crowd filed into their seats and the lights dimmed in the gilded hall, Seeger strode on stage with his banjo, wearing a turquoise shirt. He stood out even from the distant third balcony, a stick figure with his musical wand. "It's Christmas and Hanukkah. I've got a wish for the New Year. Let's get America to wade out of the Big Muddy." The audience laughed, relaxing in his resonant, sing-song voice. Genial, with no hint of the tension in his journals, he resembled a favorite uncle back from vacation. He played a nameless lick on the banjo and ended suddenly, catching the audience off guard. It may have been Christmas, but he was not jolly.

Next came his banjo tunes: "Old Joe Clark" and "Darling Corey." Seeger paced them too fast. When people applauded, he played right over them. "We were really on edge the first part of the concert," his friend Josh Dunson wrote afterward. "It seemed for the first twenty minutes or so, you were trying desperately to relax, to get absorbed in the music."

Then Seeger played "Jacob's Ladder," and for one minute the clear arpeggios mounted in silver rungs. The sound spread like mortar, clean and solid, and he trimmed it into place before the ear could notice. Yet he seemed ready to break off at any time, unsure whether to release this perfection or cover it up.

"A real performer just puts everything out of his mind and concentrates," Seeger once said: "Family, friends, everything just goes by the boards and he just concentrates on not being second-best but that you're the best. And I've been distracted all my life by a little of this and that."

Seeger started a civil rights hymn. People stirred uncomfortably—here comes the nostalgia. But Seeger presented the songs as music, not solutions, and got the crowd singing without having to acknowledge that the black-and-white-together era had ended. In the balcony, a few freedom riders—blacks who had ridden in the front of southern buses to integrate them—began to rock and clap to "This Little Light of Mine." The rest of the audience followed.

"Pete steps out of the wings, walks on stage, and he takes it over," Judy Collins said. "It looks like that stage is too small for him. . . . What makes his voice so marvelous is really what makes all the greatest singers marvelous—you understand every word. He has a miraculous gift for phrasing. It wouldn't matter if he was singing Rigoletto; he would still mesmerize."

Next he sang a somber song, his "Letter to Eve," and his voice colored with a personal note. "If you want to have great love, you've got to have great anger. . . . If music could only bring peace, I'd only be a musician."

At intermission, the balconies were awash with remembered causes. SNCC stories tumbled out so fast, a motion from the orchestra seats might have resurrected the moribund organization. "If music could only bring peace . . ." echoed in the halls. When the lights blinked, people streamed back for more.

"Say, those old Christmas songs sound fine when you sing them in harmony." For once, Seeger's joviality rang false. The audience again shifted in their seats: Christmas songs weren't going to save the Vietnamese. Ignoring the mood, Seeger divided the crowd in thirds for "We Wish You a Merry Christmas" and amazed the audience by fitting the pieces together like doweled pine. A few carols and environmental songs later, Seeger sang "False from True." "Musicians are supposed to cheer people up," Seeger said in introduction, "but who's going to cheer up the musician?"

When I found tarnish on some of my brightest dreams
Yes, and when some people I trusted turned out to be
not what they seemed
Then once more I have to start the job of separating
false from true.
Then I know I need the love of you.

He did not ask the audience to come in on the chorus.

When Seeger sang "No song I sing will change Governor Wallace's mind," the audience was as fascinated and shocked as if he'd opened his shirt to show a wound. For the first time, he sang about *his* life, rather than serving the world. The crowd almost didn't want to see this anguish—it was too intense, like gazing in a teacher's face and seeing corruption there.

"I was most concerned by that song you sang—the new one with 'My dreams had been tarnished,'" a fan wrote after the concert. "There was so much real pain in that song. If you despair, what happens to the many, many people like myself who look to you constantly for hope and the bliss of spirit which you bring to our lives?"

Seeger picked up the tempo with an antiwar song, but the crowd remained behind. A few moments before he'd made himself vulnerable; was that the performance, or this? He pounded out "Support our boys in Vietnam, bring 'em home," forcing the audience to drop their individual thoughts and share his anger. One by one they sang, overlooking his intimations of mortality. At the end of the song, he applauded the audience. With a quick "Thank you, Merry Christmas," he was offstage with his instruments. Restrained feeling broke out with a roar. The audience wanted its optimist back.

An encore, and the crowd left warmhearted. Something in the group singing—a roomful of strangers reverberating together, their ears filled with a communal resonance—renewed community. He had broken down the barrier between performer and audience. Though the *New York Times* called his performance "distracted," Seeger had held his core audience—barely. As his belief in song wavered, his step became less sure. Some listeners left wondering how much longer Seeger could keep going.

THROUGHOUT 1968, which Seeger called "the year of revelations," images of Vietnam pursued him, robbing him of his moments of quiet, resisting his attempts to pound them out at the woodpile.

In February, he received the call he'd been waiting for: He had six hours to fly cross-country and tape "Big Muddy" on the Smothers Brothers' program. The triumph was anticlimactic. Only the CBS affiliate in Detroit had censored the song—and then only the pointed last verse. (Citizens of Detroit didn't want to hear criticisms of the president, according to Lawrence Carino, an executive of Storer Broadcasting.) The following year, CBS canceled *The Smothers Brothers Comedy Hour.* When the entertainers sued, this same Lawrence Carino testified that the show caused him "problems" in Detroit, citing Pete Seeger's appearance.

Carino's protectiveness was unnecessary, for on March 15, Lyndon Johnson announced a pullback of troops and his decision not to run for reelection. Seeger took some of the credit for this, calling the *Smothers Brothers* appearance "one of the high points of my life; I probably reached seven million people all at once."

Seeger had always believed that the right song at the right moment could change history. He used to argue this point with Bess Hawes and her husband: "Butch felt art came out of events and didn't make them. Pete never thought that was true," Bess said. "There was a line from Engels we discussed: 'Art is the spume of history,' what flies off the top. Pete was convinced songs had helped start the civil rights and union movements; Butch felt songs appeared only when events provided the material."

"Big Muddy" was Seeger's case in point, but in an electronic age, folk songs didn't seem to have the punch they'd had earlier. In

Sing Out!, Seeger shared his favorite story about how a song had stopped a war by reminding soldiers of their kinship: "In 1758, an English force attacked at Brittany. Local militia advancing to battle were astounded to hear a local song. It was Welsh mountaineers, singing an old Celtic melody, older than their estrangement. French officers commanded the militia to fire, but the troops would not."

A touching story, certainly; but in the 1960s, army bomber pilots couldn't hear the songs of the Vietnamese as they were sighted with infrared scopes. Seeger tried to sing his way to peace: "My songs must be so good that they reach out to 190 million Americans," he wrote the organizer of a festival in Japan. "I have not succeeded yet, but I must keep trying, as long as I have breath in my body. I need songs with melodies so unforgettable that listeners will be humming them at their work. The words of some songs must be so well put together that even those who disagree will want to hear them again. Songs must be so funny that even the stony-faced will break into a grin. And we need songs with strength to make cowards stop fleeing, turn around, and face the future with a breath of courage."

ON APRIL 4 Martin Luther King Jr. was assassinated. Seeger received an emergency call from poet John Beecher.

"Pete, you've got to come down here. I've never seen anything like it on any southern campus. After King's assassination, about two hundred white students [at Duke University] decided they must do something, not just talk. They went to the million-dollar home of the president. . . . He refused to talk further with them. They refused to leave. After two days he went to the hospital with a breakdown. They moved their vigil to the quadrangle. Their numbers grew to five hundred, to a thousand, to fifteen hundred. I've been reading poems to them. Will you come down and sing for them?" Seeger agreed to come two days later, but his conjuring was in short supply. He was more in the mood for a public burning than reasoned discourse.

Duke University, in Durham, North Carolina, is set amid the rolling Piedmont hills where the Seegers had once been accosted as gypsies. When he arrived, he found two thousand disturbed collegians waiting for someone to explain the America of 1968. They were seated on the grass at the center of the campus, listening to an improvised P.A. system; the stage was lit by a lone lightbulb hung from a tree. Poet John Beecher read, and the president of the maintenance union of black workers spoke: "I have a vision that I'd like to pick up after black boys here, as well as white boys."

Facing the crowd that night, Seeger's mood was dark and fiery. King's assassination, the end of the civil rights era, youth culture, Vietnam—all these had pushed him to the edge, judging from his journals. Graceful songs and witty quotations disappeared from his music notebooks, replaced by song fragments that slid off the staff lines. Phrases like "peace of the graveyard" kept returning to his thoughts; a few days before visiting Duke he had written:

Go tell White America
If he wants his cities to burn
Three hundred years is long enough
Both cheeks have been well turned.

Go tell every light-skinned face
I'm not a violent person
But there's one thing I've learned
If you want freedom you got to fight for it.

Despite these dark reflections, Seeger's songs stirred hope in the students, hope he could barely give himself. The crowd applauded for his personal authenticity; Seeger's embodiment of his music had become his stock in trade. Before closing his part of the concert, Seeger lined out a hymn or two and talked to the students.

"Why hasn't there been more publicity about this nationally?"

"Oh, the local papers have been full of it," a student replied, "but the wire services hardly mention it. When we called up the TV networks, they said they didn't have any cameramen to spare, 'but let us know if there is any violence—we'll send someone down.'"

"I felt a deep rage boil in me," Seeger wrote, "as though all the experiences with TV censorship and misrule had suddenly come to a head. When my turn came to sing again, I found myself speechifying—probably a dangerous thing for any singer.

"'You read today about crime in the streets! I say there's crime in the New York offices of CBS and NBC! Crime! I'd like to make a pledge to you here tonight. . . . Before I leave Duke I'm going to take a stone with me, and put it in my banjo case, and if I ever meet a TV man up there who says he won't cover a story like this because there's no violence, some*thing* is going to get hurt.'"

PREOCCUPIED AS HE WAS, a part of him kept imagining ways life could be improved on a small scale. There was always something positive to be done. If teenagers burned up the cities in the summer, why not set up block parties to cool the tension, he wrote Thomas Hoving, New York's imaginative parks commissioner. On one page of his notebook he would speculate how to set up free outdoor movie showings—paint walls white in vacant lots and bring in mobile projectors; on the next, he would plan allegorical dramas of the end to the human race, such as the *500-Mile Bookshelf*, where various creatures evolved and became extinct; it could happen to humans too. These zany ideas were his way of reminding himself that too often people live their daily lives inside an immense wall, which cuts us off from any really different future and which isolates us from our past. Seeger wanted people to scale the wall, to address a better future. This was the vision behind "Tomorrow Is a Highway": Seeds of the future exist in the present. Children and other idealists must still tend these and themselves for a battle to rebuild and purify, to keep the best stuff of humanity alive during troubled times. For revolutionists have to say they will overcome, even when they know they may not.

Not everyone was ready to listen to such lofty sentiments. In the spring of 1968, Jerry Rubin and Abbie Hoffman—Hoffman had previously written Seeger, signing himself "a devoted fan"—met with Seeger and Leventhal to fill them in on demonstrations planned for the Democratic National Convention in Chicago. Seeger was the only adult they were inviting. He listened thoughtfully but urged them "to represent all the different kinds of human beings in the U.S.A; because there's all kinds of people that are against the war. It's all right if we have long hair there and pot smoking," he said magnanimously, "but if we don't include short-haired people as well, old people alongside the young people, we'd be making a mistake."

"You're not going to have a revolution with a bunch of short-haired older people!" said the founders of the Yippie Party.

An Oberlin College student sensed the distance Seeger felt from his former audience: "The war had left him wounded and scarred, internally bleeding, like the abominably infected knife of an incompetent surgeon, poisoning by its touch what it did not cut entirely away. . . . His songs grew harder and more cutting. Perhaps something in his voice when he sang 'Letter to Eve' ['If music could only bring peace . . .'] gave subtle hints of a new urgency that had not been there before." Seeger could remain youth's fellow traveler only so long.

In *Sing Out!* he quoted Thoreau: "Is there not a sort of bloodshed when the conscience is wounded? Through this wound a man's real manhood and immortality flow out and he bleeds to an everlasting death. I see this blood flowing now."

MORE THEN EVER Seeger sounded like a preacher, disdainful of wealth and worldly vanities: "What is right and what is wrong in the world?" he wrote. "The most truthful answer I know comes from that hard-boiled section of the Bible, Ecclesiastes." Years before, Seeger had turned a passage from Ecclesiastes into a song, adding a final couplet and a refrain that titled the song: "Turn! Turn! Turn!" In this chapter of the Bible, a worldly preacher traveled with his gospel, preaching rectitude: Dead flies cause the ointment of the apothecary to send forth a stinking savor: so doth a little folly him that is in reputation for wisdom and honor.

In the sixties, this seemed out of place; people wanted a little folly. Seeger understood this better now than when he had complained about Woody buying a pint on the sly, but he demanded moral consistency in an inconsistent time. Seeger seemed to be asking, in the words of an old country song: "Do you preach what you live/Would you live what you preach?"

Seeger's songwriting had by this point grown apocalyptic. He borrowed a line from Uncle Alan's most famous poem, "I Have a Rendez-vous with Death" for his song "The Torn Flag":

At midnight in a flaming angry town
I saw my country's flag lying torn upon the ground
I ran in and dodged among the crowd
And scooped it up to safety.

And then I took this striped old piece of cloth
And tried my best to wash the garbage off,
But I found it had been used for wrapping lies.
It smelled and stank and attracted all the flies.

Then, in May 1968, he confided a dreamlike parable to his journal and to his friend Bess: "I feel like I'm on a ship and we're going down the river. There's a big crew and we're having a party. Everybody is singing and dancing and having a marvelous time. And the word comes in that there is a huge waterfall ahead. I go up and try to tell everybody that we had better stop and get the ship turned around before we go over the falls. But everybody is so busy singing and dancing that they won't listen to me." The only way to make the crowd listen, Seeger concluded, was to drill holes and sink the ship.

A CHILLY RAIN drenched the ground outside the Seegers' tent in Resurrection City in June 1968. Toshi and Pete had come to Washington to support the encampment that Martin Luther King had been organizing before his death—gathering America's poor together in the nation's capital.

Cold wet weather had spread mud and mosquitoes throughout the campsite. Rows of battered and hastily constructed plywood houses stood leaking and abandoned. Kids from the streets of Detroit and Chicago had just been sent home for harassing visitors and the whites in the campsites. As the Seegers arrived, police threatened to bulldoze the campsite. People walked through the puddles of Resurrection City without shoes because they'd worn out their only pair marching. Others sat in groups huddled under blankets and stared up at the gray sky.

The Poor People's Campaign hadn't started out this way in March, when Dr. King had sent out the call. Presidential candidates Robert Kennedy and Eugene McCarthy had endorsed his plan. Richard Nixon tellingly responded that America couldn't afford to fight a war on poverty while it fought in Vietnam.

On dedicating Resurrection City—three weeks before the Seegers arrived—Reverend Ralph Abernathy had said the poor would "plague the Pharaohs of this nation. . . . We'll stay here until 'We Shall Overcome' becomes 'We Have Overcome.'" Andrew Young, one of the campaign leaders, declared, "If they close down the City, they have to close down America." Reading all this in the papers, Seeger had been glad to be going. He could not bear the America he saw, but he could not stop himself from looking.

Before he'd left for Washington, he appeared on Steve Allen's popular TV show. He'd started to sing "It Takes a Worried Man." About two verses into the song, he'd stopped, saying, "I can't sing this song." When Lee Hays later asked what happened, Seeger answered that the spirit just went out of him. "The idea of the spirit going out of that man is very, very unusual," Don McLean reflected.

On June 6, Robert Kennedy was assassinated in Los Angeles. America seemed infected with violence. "Don't be afraid of death," Seeger had written in his journal. "And when you finally take his hand, death will be no stranger."

THE SEEGERS CAMPED in the section where the Appalachian people were staying, Jimmy Collier remembered: "Pete just showed up one day with a tent and his wife and kid. Everything was wet. The mud was two feet thick and for the whole camp, all we had was a couple of portable showers. Pete and Toshi and Tinya wandered around, going from one campfire to another. At nighttime, people sat down in the mud and sang. There was urgency and real seriousness in the atmosphere: King had been *killed*!"

The residents of the lean-to city were determined to stay, despite nearby bulldozers. Their resolution was strengthened by a demonstration on June 19 of fifty thousand people from across the country. The crowd booed Vice President Humphrey and cheered Seeger and Gene McCarthy. The *New York Times* found a quiet desperation in the speeches. A little girl carried a sign: THIS IS THE LAST CHANCE FOR NONVIOLENCE. That night, when the Seegers returned to their tent, they found few white people left.

Pictures show Seeger sitting in the mud, a hat covering his wispy hair. Gaunt with fatigue, his angular, white, New England features and his clean shirt give him the air of a tired clergyman. One of their last nights there, Seeger helped out on a sing-along. By this time, Resurrection City was out of control. Police were using tear gas against gangs of kids throwing firebombs at passing motorists. What had started as nonviolent was now semiviolent, and heating up by the hour. Garbage had become embedded in the mud, and the acrid smell hung in the tents. Everyone's nerves were on edge. Nobody knew what would happen next, and the people were too tired and too uncomfortable to care.

The encampment depended on music to keep up its spirits. Every night they held programs in a cultural tent led by Jimmy Collier and Reverend Frederick Douglass Kirkpatrick ("Kirk"), a six-foot-three black with a gentle manner and a quick laugh. Kirk managed to be both angry and philosophic at the same time, a quality that later made him Seeger's treasured friend. Amid the tear gas, Kirk and Jimmy would round everyone up for music sessions. They called square dances while Pete Seeger played banjo. To finish off the evening, Seeger asked Collier to lead "This Land Is Your Land." Jimmy hesitated before answering: "Pete, why don't you ask Henry Crow Dog first—ask him if it's all right to sing that song." How could it *not* be all right?

"You have to understand," Collier said later, "sitting with a couple of Apaches in full dress I felt a little silly singing 'This Land Is Your Land.' "

"Reverend Kirkpatrick and Jimmy Collier were saying, 'This land belongs to the Indians! I'm going to sing "This Land," but I've asked Chief Crow Dog's permission,' " Bernice remembered. "That song was the basis of Pete's principles, him and good old Woody. And it's the basis of the American dream—coming in and building a country, freedom, blah, blah. I felt that in '67 and '68, all that got smashed to smithereens." The radical patriotism of the Popular Front era of his teenage years had run its course.

The Seegers packed up and left, before the bulldozers moved in and hundreds were arrested. The gathering storm had hit. Seeger didn't know where to turn. Despite all his efforts to live a good life, he found himself part of a racist system beyond his control. His world looked corrupt, beyond redemption:

If my skin showed an African cast
It would be easier for me to be honest
But as I am I can walk upon the carpeted floor
And only when they find out my name
And only when I won't deny the blame
Will I be finally shown the door.

Seeger wrote these lines in his song notebook, but he could not craft a song from such thoughts. His faith in his music faltered. Eventually, as Bernice said, "the people don't need you to sing their folk songs; they can sing themselves." On his next album, due to be recorded in a few weeks, he decided to have Bernice and Jimmy and Kirk with him.

Pete Seeger Now was as openly incendiary as any record he'd recorded. He sang "False from True," "Letter to Eve," "The Torn Flag," and a bitter talking blues against the war. The whole record is a cry for help, to wake up America before her ship shatters in the falls.

"Pete invited Bernice and me to do this concert," Jimmy recalled. "I think it was in Westbury, Long Island [a largely white, upper-middle-class suburb]. Pete was becoming—and the times were creating a situation where he became—more radical. He was also at the end of his romance with Columbia Records. It didn't feel like an old man singing Burl Ives's songs. You hear that on the record.

"There was a war going on, and this was a battlefield and a sense of danger. It was an intense and personal time. People were having to make decisions. People were beginning to doubt that sweetness and goodness and light would win over. At that concert we were all angry—that was our stance. And Pete, spending that time in Resurrection City, caught that anger," Collier continued.

"I remember *Pete Seeger Now*, him feeling he could no longer stand on the stage alone," Bernice Reagon reflected. "And I remember Pete talking constantly about that exchange with Kirkpatrick and Collier around Chief Crow Dog, and how he then had a hard time doing 'This Land Is Your Land.' It felt like he didn't know what to sing . . . he was not sure what his function was."

After finishing the record, Pete Seeger decided to give up singing.

Chapter 12

Golden River

PETE SEEGER HAD RESOLVED TO QUIT SINGING BEFORE. HE'D make the threat when his life reached an impasse, musically or politically, when he couldn't "see how to grow." In the summer of 1968, he looked back on his life with dark reflection. He'd started singing to organize unions—and wound up isolated from self-serving institutions that had no place for him or their radical heritage (with some exceptions). He'd restocked America's repertoire with songs from the reservoir of folk tradition—and others had created *Hootenanny*, which also had no place for him. "Maybe I felt I'd shot my wad, and there wasn't much more to do."

After the death of Dr. King and the debacle at Resurrection City, Seeger's hopes for integration lay in ruins. His friend Julius Lester again tore holes in liberal ideals: "Yet while black anger increases, whites remain only concerned and deeply disturbed. . . . This is why the black radical reserves his greatest anger for the white who, to all appearances, is most sympathetic to him."

Then that same summer, on July 30, his daughter Mika was arrested and jailed during student demonstrations in Mexico at the 1968 Olympics; ironically, he'd been asked to write a song celebrating the games. There were rumors of CIA involvement in the arrest, for police were waiting for her when she returned from a demonstration. Mika was in jail for six months. Initially she refused aid from her parents, Seeger wrote Moe Asch. "But in jail she learned Spanish and argued politics," Seeger reflected optimistically. "That's why she'd gone."

Others were less nonchalant. On a news clipping of her arrest, in Seeger's file in the Senate Internal Security Subcommittee, a note reads: "Get this girl on a list of second generation Commies! [signed] J. [Edgar Hoover]"

Mika was first placed in a jail her father called "very dangerous—when Toshi visited, she was shadowed and her phone tapped." They hired a lawyer: "Who he bribed nobody knows." Mika was abruptly taken from her cell and put on a jet to Houston.

"In Houston, she calls Toshi. She was sent back with no passport, and Toshi sent her some money. It was about Christmas time. They surprised me. I walked in and there was Mika who I thought was in Mexico."

Paradoxically, all these troubles moved him to compose songs like "Old Devil Time" and "Quite Early Morning," in the final phase of a now-familiar creative cycle.

You know it's darkest before the dawn
This thought keeps me moving on.
If we could heed those early warnings,
The time is now, quite early morning. . . .

And so we keep on while we live,
Until we have no, no more to give.
And when these fingers can strum no longer
Hand the old guitar to young ones stronger.

An irrepressible belief in humanity's potential stood at the core of his art; the more defeats he suffered, the more resilient his music. Seeger didn't follow through on his decision to stop singing, at least not in 1968. Instead, in the last decades of his middle age, the forty-nine-year-old set out to find a cause worth singing about, something positive to inspire a nation divided and a people numbed by war, something close to home.

"What I think I saw in this period was that he didn't know too much what the issues were," Bernice said. "That sloop boat saved his life."

HIS NEED FOR local ties was critical. In 1965 during a boycott of one of his concerts, a few Beacon Ku Klux Klansmen had nearly run him and his family out of town. On September 20, 1965, at the invitation of the Beacon Teachers' Association, Pete Seeger had agreed to give a benefit to endow a scholarship at Beacon High School. For months students and teachers had wanted him to sing, but the principal kept refusing; finally, after threatening a suit, they had their way. On November 26, he was to sing in the high school gym.

"You may get some hassles," Seeger had warned.

"We don't care," his sponsors had told him. "We want to go ahead."

Seeger had put the date out of his mind until, returning from a tour of the Soviet Union, the Seegers had read that headline in the *New York Times*: SEEGER SONG IN MOSCOW IS ANTI-U.S. It had surprised neither of them to reach home and find conservatives attempting to cancel the Beacon concert.

The Right Reverend Monsignor Hubert Beller, pastor of St. John's Church in Beacon, objected to having Seeger perform on school property; recent headlines, he'd written to the *Beacon Evening News*, "give positive proof of his [subversive] views." For the next two weeks, Beacon's papers headlined the controversy. The community was finally taking note of its most famous resident. One local conservative called Seeger "an American who bites the hand that feeds him."

Three weeks before the scheduled concert, Pastor Beller handed out anti-Seeger leaflets in church, based on information from HUAC and John Birch Society files. A Stop Pete Seeger Committee formed, sponsored by the Veterans of Foreign Wars, the Knights of Columbus, and the Catholic Daughters of America. Even the local fire department joined the boycott; luckily, nothing caught fire at the Seegers'.

At ice-cream parlors and gas stations on Main Street, people signed petitions to deny Seeger the school gym. "Who's behind the Seeger show?" one letter in a local paper had asked ominously. Neighbors asked each other who this guy was; few had ever met him in town. Beacon's professionals refused to speak out; one doctor told him, "Pete, you know this is fascism. You know perfectly well what it is, and you are going to be run out of town if you don't cancel this."

At first, Seeger hadn't known how seriously to take the challenge. It seemed absurd: He could sell out concert halls across the country, but in his home town, he wasn't considered patriotic enough to donate his services. Once his music was called anti-American, few in Beacon would listen long enough to judge for themselves. It was like fighting HUAC all over again. As the number of signatures on the petitions mounted to seven hundred, Seeger realized this was seriousness. "If somebody balked at signing, they'd look at him and say, 'Well what kind of a Commie are you?'" he wrote Rockwell Kent.

Neighbors on the hill were asked to sign the petition, people who had known Pete and Toshi for over fifteen years. They signed. By challenging Seeger in his own town, right-wingers sought to humiliate him: keeping him from the high school he paid taxes to support, defaming and endangering his family.

Relations with his neighbors had barely improved since Peekskill. The trees he had chopped down for the nearby school were long forgotten; Toshi's PTA work had ended years ago. Seeger's HUAC appearance and trial, on the other hand, were still talked of in town. "A few brave people did stand up. Not the few intellectuals or liberals, but ordinary working people, mostly Catholics, who knew us from the PTA."

At a boycott-Seeger meeting, Seeger's supporters were ruled

out of order. They had brought a record player and records, but no one wanted to listen.. "Such things are not important," the Reverend Beller said. "I know enough about the man's background."

"He doesn't even deserve to live here," one shopkeeper said. "If he likes Russia so much, why doesn't he go there? Why don't the people in this town just ship him there?

"I don't know the man myself. They tell me he's a great artist—maybe he is . . . but that doesn't matter, I can tell about him. His wife's half-Jap, but I guess that doesn't matter either. But you should see the people who go to visit him. They look like queers and beatniks, you know. Why, the other day there was a man going out there I could have sworn he was a spy. You could tell by the way he looked, with his shifty eyes. You can tell about Seeger from the way he lives, way off in Beacon like some crazy hermit."

Beacon's hermit had his break when a conservative doctor, one of the town's biggest taxpayers, decided to support him, writing in the *Beacon Evening News*, "It seems to me that American democracy is big enough to encompass all opinions. Why all this fuss about Mr. Seeger's singing?" Then the teachers' association renewed its invitation, and the school board finally voted to allow him to sing. Some of the petitioners retreated. "All of a sudden the liberals realized they didn't need to be so scared. Every day in the paper there were more letters in favor of me and fewer against me."

When the concert finally took place at the end of 1965, a few cars had cruised past the sold-out gym, with people hollering and spitting at concertgoers. The Beacon police had expected trouble. They advised Pete and Harold to come in different cars, which the officers checked for bombs. Harold stood backstage through the whole concert, "worried sick," in his words. Midway through the sold-out concert, he thought he saw a gun protrude from the curtains, pointed straight at Seeger. Harold ran on stage and knocked over what must have been a very surprised photographer with a telescopic lens.

In 1968, as Seeger was contemplating quitting music, he mulled over the incident in a letter to his friends, black actors Ossie Davis and Ruby Dee: "One of the weaknesses in my own work, and probably the work of many an intellectual, is that I may have friends all around the world, but in my own neighborhood, I am in a very weak position, and can be knocked down by anyone who wants to tell a few lies about me."

The Beacon concert was a real victory, but he might not get off so easily a second time. Ten-year-old Tinya still attended the local public school. He was also heeding the advice of black friends in the civil rights community: "Work in your *own* community."

THE ARENA SEEGER had chosen for linking himself to his community was the relatively new cause of environmentalism. Seeger had been moved by reading Rachel Carson's *Silent Spring* in 1961 during a visit to Cape Cod, where he performed at George Wein's Club, Storyville. (The man introducing him said, "Next we have Pete Seeger, out on bail.")

A friend of a friend had taken him sailing near Chatham, Massachusetts. That's when he realized why people loved to sail. He'd been hooked: "I'm sure wind and waves must be in our genes."

He'd lived by the Hudson for fifteen years. Often from his perch overlooking the river, he'd seen the faint white specks of sail and how they'd skate like water bugs across smooth, brown water. In 1959, he'd bought his first sailboat, a seventeen-footer the kids could sleep in. He was no expert sailor; he'd sometimes capsize and paddle for shore. But he enjoyed skimming along the water and hearing the slap of wind-filled canvas as the boat lurched forward. Seeger sailed the Hudson because it was convenient, but when he looked in the water he saw raw sewage. He did his best to keep the boat upright. On his English tour in late 1959, he'd heard an audacious idea. The

Committee on Non-Violent Action were building a flotilla on the Thames to block nuclear submarine production there. They were building a twenty-three-foot sloop, the *Satygraha* (Gandhi's term for nonviolence), and a rowboat, *The Thoreau.*

Whether or not the Clearwater project was a direct descendent of those boats, in 1963, a neighbor, Vic Schwartz, had lent him a history, *Sloops of the Hudson.* Written in 1908, the book contained beautiful drawings of old-time sailing ships—sloops, the name derived from the Dutch *sloep*—with masts a hundred feet tall. "It wasn't great literature, but it was full of love. I wrote the man who'd lent me the book. 'Why don't we get some people together and build a replica. . . . If we get a thousand people together and if everybody chipped in, we could do it.' "

Before long he was telling friends, "Wouldn't it be fun to build one of these sloops?" Why not build a community boat, get to know people, and clean up the river? Clearly this was another of Seeger's crazy ideas, an impractical one for someone who'd just weathered an attack from his neighbors. Yet the more he heard of local history and the more he sailed, the more excited about the idea he became. Probably only a project that touched his earlier, naturalist side could have inspired Seeger so deeply. He remembered building wooden boats with the tools in his father's home in Patterson.

"I think he wanted to be involved in an actual Movement again. He wanted to see the singing and the spirit happen right there on the Hudson River. He wanted to be a part of that community," Jimmy Collier said later.

"Most people who dream those kinds of things never put it together, because you don't have the money: Who the hell do you contact to even start to build a boat, and if you did, what makes you think they would listen to you anyway?"

IN THE DAYS of the sloops, the Hudson River had been alive with commerce and marine life: "Ice cut near Kingston tinkled in the glasses of New York restaurants. Sturgeon were common; the packing of this fish was an important industry. They called them 'Albany Beef,' and America exported caviar to Europe," Seeger wrote in *Look*. Tourists came to sail and even to drink the Hudson. "Said river water is far from being dirty," a nineteenth-century traveler wrote. "Rather remarkable for its purity, it is a pleasant, wholesome beverage." From Lake Tear of the Clouds high in the Adirondacks, Seeger learned, the river had flowed through a densely wooded Hudson Valley. Shad, bass, clams, and oysters were abundant.

The Iroquois and the Algonquin Indians had once inhabited the river's shore, and Seeger learned of a local Indian legend that enchanted him, "of a river that went to hear a fountain sing. The song was so beautiful that the river decided to sing it to the ocean. All the way to the shores of the ocean, the river sang. Soon, the mountains heard of the river's song and came from all over the land to listen. And because the song was so beautiful the mountains settled down and stayed to listen forever."

When Seeger started talking like this, Toshi could do little but throw up her hands. Anyone could see the river was filthy—coated with an oily slick and lined with old tires and junk. Every time they drove near the shore, they smelled chemical waste. One night Pete sailed off on his own. Toshi was worried: "You mean you're going out all by yourself, overnight?" she asked.

On the water, he peered at the skies for signs of a summer storm, prepared to race the thunder that often crashed down the rugged alley made by the river's cliffs. Then he relaxed, savoring his first time out alone. He drifted silently with the current and had the river to himself. The sail flapped lightly, and the boat tipped to the water: "The sun was first golden, and a few minutes later it was orange and a few minutes later it was beet red, and then the sky was all purple and finally it got dark." As he floated across the rainbow-colored reflections, he imagined what the river would look like if it were clean. He could see the beaches cleaned up and full of children wading in this golden river and fishermen hauling in nets of sturgeon.

Tacking his way back through the glowing darkness, he made up "Golden River":

Sailing down my golden river
Sun and water all my own
Yet I was never alone
Sun and water, old life-givers
I'll have them where e'er I roam
And I was not far from home.

Sunlight glancing on the water
Life and Death are all my own
Yet I was never alone.

Life to raise my sons and daughters
Golden sparkles in the foam
And I was not far from home.
Sailing down my winding highway
Travelers from near and far
Yet I was never alone.

Exploring all the little byways
Sighting all the distant stars
And I was not far from home.

"Like 'Where Have All the Flowers Gone?' I wrote it and didn't think it was such a good song. I never sang it. Then I was quite taken with surprise when Don McLean and Bill Spence were singing it once in harmony, backstage. I said, 'Where did you learn that?' They said, 'We heard you sing it.' 'Well, gee,' I said, 'that's beautiful. . . . I was too embarrassed to sing it.'"

Building a giant sloop was a huge, dreamy symbol. The destruction of the river concerned everyone along the Hudson, from conservative Upstaters to the crowded millions who lived in New York City. He hoped the as yet unnamed boat would unite "wealthy yachtsmen and kids from the ghettos, church members and atheists"—the new Popular Front he had hoped to reach on TV. If song brought people together, a sailboat might too.

Among his friends, reactions were mixed. Jack Elliot called his plans totally impractical: "The boat would cost $100,000 at the minimum, and require a large crew. Where are you going to get that kind of money?"

"Pete, there's a war on! You're out of your mind," Mary Travers told him flatly. Others pointed out—as if Seeger needed reminding!—how conservative local townsfolk were. Within New York's folk music community, people wondered if Seeger was off balance: Did he have a new hobby, playing with yachts?

"I remember he was criticized about that sloop project," said Bernice Reagon. "Once I said that ecology is racism coming into your own front yard, as far as I was concerned. . . . We were dealing with it all the time and all of a sudden, it was 'clean it up!' "

" 'Is this all you're going to do?' " I said to Toshi.

"Toshi said, 'It's not true that we are just doing this for ecology.'

"They had been attacked about this; with the sloop they were evading the issues of the day. That's what I said. But he was going to find a movement that no one could take him out of because that was *his* movement."

Such talk forced the Seegers to think seriously about the project. His followers had high expectations of him. Yet as Seeger neared fifty, it grew harder to keep not only his performances, but his life in inspiring form. Over the years he'd joined many movements—racial and economic equality, freedom of speech—but none was as locally rooted. None started from his own home. Much as the word conjured up the leisure class and bird sanctuaries, conservationism was not foreign to Seeger. This was Seton's spirit, crunching through the snowy woods to sketch animal prints.

As Seeger later expressed it, "The whole idea was to reach out to rank-and-file people of all sorts and tell them, 'This is our river. Who's going to save it if we don't? Can't leave it to the scientists, they're too busy researching. Can't leave it to the politicians, they're too busy getting elected.' "

Implicit in his hopes for restoring the river was a notion of environmental memory. Each generation risks having its sons and daughters forget the taste of woods-scented water, the sight of a shimmering mountain lake, just as succeeding waves of people arriving at a lawn concert cannot imagine what it was like to be surrounded by empty space.

As early as November 1958, Seeger had commented to an interviewer, his voice rising with emotion, "Look at the waste we make of our rivers, beautiful clear streams like the Hudson which flows past my door—an open sewer! . . . A river which was once clean and clear—Indians speared fish twenty feet down—is now an open sore. Nobody swims in it; you go on a boating trip, you just don't look down." Now he meant to do more than sing about it.

HE AND TOSHI didn't know how to start. Then a wealthy environmentalist on the board of Scenic Hudson asked Seeger for a benefit concert. But when the man took the idea to his board of directors, they said, "Oh, don't touch Seeger with a ten-foot pole. If we have anything to do with him, we will be tarred with the same brush!" So he came back to his friend: "Sorry they turned me down, but I'd like to hear some music so maybe we can raise money for something else." And that's when Vic Schwartz said, "Pete and I are talking about trying to raise money to build a Hudson River sloop." A month or two later, on Alexander Saunders's lawn, Seeger sang for 160 people, and they passed the hat and took in about $160. "We voted to start an organization that at that time was called the Hudson River Sloop Restoration, Inc. One of the members was a lawyer and got us non-profit status," Seeger recalled.

The Seegers built up funds as they had their house, one bag of cement at a time. Seeger had to sing three and four times a day to raise half the cost: about $140,000.

To assemble this much cash, they and their friends canvassed wealthy sailors and local historians with estates on the Hudson. This was not Seeger's favorite audience, but he gritted his teeth and attended barbecues and cocktail parties. Once he met with a Hudson Valley millionaire who had reservations about the *Clearwater.* "It's a beautiful boat all right," the millionaire said, looking over the drawings. "But what do you want to sail the Hudson for? I do my sailing around the Virgin Islands."

Seeger had scarcely contained himself: "I felt my fingers clenching in anger, but I didn't say anything. Unwittingly, he had given us our best reason for building the boat. . . . We had allowed some people to make a good profit along the Hudson, and then go somewhere else to enjoy clear water."

Having an enemy had made it easier to keep going. Local residents—who stood to benefit the most—had been hostile or indifferent in the beginning. Conservatives among them assumed Seeger was up to his old tricks. Perhaps he planned to use the boat for something sinister, like ferrying in undesirable aliens.

An arsonist took these sentiments further and tried to burn the Seegers out in 1967.

> There was a guy who worked for the city of Beacon and came up the road every day to chlorinate the reservoir. And he was a cynical guy, in a cheerful sort of way.
>
> When the first fire was started, up about a quarter mile north of us, the fire department came up and put it out. He was there. I thought it perfectly normal for him to be there. And he was kind of smiling, didn't seem worried about it.

A week later, another fire was set by my house, about a hundred yards away; and he was also there, smiling. Now, my neighbors who are in the fire department got to him. They said, "You trying to burn the mountain down because you don't like Seeger?"

Why did he do it? Well to show this guy Seeger that we don't like him.

Seeger was learning a great deal, watching in admiration as Jimmy Collier, who'd now moved to the Beacon area, drove around town with a big smile, waving to people on the sidewalks, and saying, "Hi. Come on down to the waterfront tomorrow night. Don't forget." Collier excelled at what Seeger had the hardest time doing: dropping in at the local pool hall to drink beer and shoot the breeze.

"It was a real lesson," Seeger said. "Here I thought of myself as somebody who knew political organizing, but I didn't know it at all. In the past, all I had to do was come in and sing a song. Other people had to do the dirty work." Toshi must have smiled to see her husband enroll in Organization 1 under Professor Collier, for Jimmy had learned much of what *he* knew from Toshi: "It was most assuredly Toshi who kept things together . . . calling on the phone, getting people together at night, knowing who the right people were and making sure they showed up." As with many husbands, Seeger had a hard time learning from his wife.

"The *Clearwater* project—so many times—was almost a failure." Jimmy continued, "Through sheer guts and power—financial power and contacts—Peter kept it together with his spiritual ability to motivate people. . . . He goes into these projects with the same attitude you or I might have: frustrated, not knowing whether things will come out right. But somehow he could hold on long enough, till the tide would turn."

Between fund-raising concerts, Seeger helped out at the shipyard in Maine. He enjoyed the manual labor, painting red lead on the boat's weights, thirty thousand pounds of iron. At the end of a day carrying weights into the bilge, Seeger ached, but the pain was a fulfillment and the salty mists bracing. The labor tightened his lean frame and tanned him evenly, as he worked shirtless alongside college-age volunteers. To celebrate his fiftieth birthday, he did something he'd never dared before. He grew a beard.

"It's hard to believe that a beard could be such a big thing," Collier said. "But for years he kept promising himself he was going to do it."

Pete Seeger had always taken pains to appear sober and upstanding. "You're singing enough strange stuff," his manager in the Weavers had told him, "you might as well look conventional." Working on the ship had loosened him up: "'Now's my chance,' I said to myself. 'Nobody is around to say no, so I'll try it.' . . . I stopped shaving and the workers in the boat yard couldn't dig it. They said, 'These young people are one thing, but you!' I told them I was going up to the shop to pick up a wrench and one said, 'Better pick up a razor too.'"

Seeger had expected problems in accommodating wealthy donors, but not the jeers of left-wing friends. "In my mind," Gordon Friesen of the Almanacs and *Broadside* said, "the *Clearwater* is probably the closest thing in recent years to Don Quixote tilting at the windmills. It's a diversion. Pete's a playboy with a yacht."

Seeger had alienated some radicals by approaching the financiers who traditionally underwrote conservation, such as Laurence Rockefeller, who equated environmental preservation with "efficient management" and called conservation "essential to any national defense program"—at the same time he made a fortune selling uranium for nuclear reactors. The *Clearwater* brought Seeger strange bedfellows.

Some orthodox Marxists had difficulty understanding arguments for a separate "ecology" movement. In Marx's time, progress seemed to require expanding industry; Marx assumed that once the profit motive faded, people would minimize waste through social planning. Radical hostility to conservationism partly originated in the 1920s from the Soviet Union's struggle to industrialize. In the futurist era, belching smokestacks were understood as a sign of progress and an end to exploitation. To some, Seeger was playing the banjo while corporations burned the land. Nonetheless, the *Clearwater*, as she was now called, was finally finished, with a 108-foot mast of Douglas fir. She stood ready for her maiden voyage and for the first bottle of Hudson Valley champagne to break on her hull.

ON JUNE 27, 1969, the *Clearwater* slid quietly toward the Atlantic, the first boat of its kind to be built in eighty years. She floated 106 feet long from stern to bowsprit. The deck was twenty-four feet wide, and the boat had bunks for fifteen, plus a captain's cabin, storage, and the ship's mess. The *Clearwater* was outfitted 95 percent in the traditional manner; the major improvements from the twentieth century were invisible from a distance: Dacron sails, electricity, and an engine. She was a vision of the past.

The first crew was an odd bunch, all musicians. Even the captain, Alan Aunapu, played guitar. Some had never been on a sailboat before. The crew would have filled a folk festival: Len Chandler, Jimmy Collier, Kirk, Pete's friend from Resurrection City, Jack Elliot, Don McLean, Fred Starner, and Lou Killen, who played the concertina like an old tar. First mate Gordon Bok, a singer of ballads from his native Maine, was the only sailor in the lot. Fitting thirteen landlubbers into the small hold was a challenge—particularly when it rained. The first night out, they sailed through forty miles of ocean fog, cold and clammy. "We slept under there and we ate under there. It was pretty uncomfortable, on a boat that really wasn't built for the ocean. On top of everything, these were all musicians, with musicians' egos," Jimmy Collier chuckled.

As pleasant as it might sound to skip across the waves with a boatload of musicians, the sloop was so far in debt (fifty thousand dollars, which Toshi'd borrowed from musician friends in a week) that fund-raising concerts were scheduled the length of the journey, each a day's sail from the next. The crew was expected to perform every night and sail all day. Seeger had the most at stake, having personally guaranteed the loans.

The first *Clearwater* concert took place in Portland, Maine. The great ship swooped into dock from the fog, and then, like the Magical Mystery Tour, out popped the musicians. Seagulls swooped overhead in the breeze. Seeger's new beard was stubbly and gray; he wore a watch cap, and a bright red handkerchief dangled from his jeans.

His mood expanded like a sail in good wind. Eyes bright from the sea air, the woodsman in him joined the organizer and the musician. Lou Killen would lead off "In South Australia I Was Born," as they raised the main sail: "To me heave away, to me haul away." Seeger learned to keep a weather eye for changing winds, and when to rig up the tiller tackle for better leverage. There were quiet times, too, perfect for singing "Golden River" or for pausing to listen to the waves thump against the bow when everyone was below deck. In such moments an eerie stillness settled on the sea, and the water slid by like memories, under the sparkling velvet of night. Seeger peered out into the darkness: a New England salt steering a ship through the ocean.

Thirty-seven days after launch, the *Clearwater* swooped into the murky East River. She had earned twenty-seven thousand dollars on her first cruise. In New York Harbor, the *Clearwater* amazed traffic on the Triboro and Queensboro bridges. Tugboats jockeyed alongside, sounding their horns. Mayor John Lindsay welcomed the *Clearwater* to Manhattan Island and took a turn at the tiller. Helicopters swooped low, and TV news crews appeared with shotgun microphones—high technology in an old-fashioned setting. Crew mate Collier called it "one of the happiest days of Seeger's life." Pete Seeger had the "Quote of the Day" in the *New York Times*: "The price of liberty is eternal publicity. And we're getting it."

"Well, if he doesn't know what kind of press he gets and what it means, Toshi does for sure. She knows who the reporter was who wrote it and probably what his motivation was," Jimmy reflected.

"They've always been uptight about the kind of image that Peter presents to the press. I've been at the house when *Wall Street Journal* reporters and people from *National Geographic* show up. Sometimes Toshi's way of handling it is to have someone there; so that what is happening is not what Peter is saying, but what is actually happening around the writer while he's there. If they think it's going to be tough, that they're going to be interviewed by someone they thought would be really critical and say Peter lives up on this nice hill and makes a lot of money, they'd make sure there was an activist there that could tell the reporter about Peter's contributions."

The twenty-year-old Almanac singer, writing songs of class struggle, could hardly have imagined a glowing tribute from the *Wall Street Journal*, but there was something about resurrecting an old ship that conservatives admired. It would have been easier on Seeger if he could have relaxed with the *Clearwater*'s triumphant entry: but *his* aims were so high that he spent his life tracking behind them. "I wish I could give [Pete] the gift of goofing off," Lee Hays once wrote.

IN THE COMING MONTHS, just as in the Weavers, some of Seeger's severest criticisms came from former colleagues, such as the ubiquitous Irwin Silber, who called the *Clearwater* "antiseptic" in a contemptuous letter to Seeger: "Being who you are, you have the ability to involve many others in your schemes—for a variety of reasons. And this means you are capable of wasting a huge amount of effort, energy, time, and funds on hare-brained, diversionary projects. . . . I wish I could believe that these undertakings and the philosophy behind them were leading us to fundamental change. . . . But I don't believe it. And if you think they are, I think you're kidding yourself. Perhaps it's easier that way."

It wasn't so much the political philosophy behind the *Clearwater* that disturbed radicals as the company Seeger kept. When Allan Young, writing for the *Liberation News Service*, discovered that a conservative founder of *Reader's Digest* had contributed to the boat, he concluded the project was "hardly militant." Compared to Black Panther shootouts with the Oakland police or the bombing of Cambodia, Seeger's talk of bringing people together at the waterfront seemed Pollyanna-ish. Many who had followed him from disarmament to civil rights to antiwar demonstrations hesitated at the *Clearwater*. "At some point around this time, I began to get the feeling Pete was no longer on the cutting edge of the movement," Bernice Reagon said.

"What can a song do?" Seeger answered his critics, reverting to his favorite passion. "What can a sailboat do? Some would say music exists just to soothe or distract people from their worries. Some say sailboats are just rich men's toys. Wrong, wrong. In the summer of 1969, they helped clean up a river."

"There's as much of a relation between the *Clearwater* and socialism as there is in putting out a book on how to play the banjo," Seeger said another time. "[Both] are part of a continual struggle to oppose the inhumanity of the technology which capitalism foists on people: 'Don't do anything creative yourself, just do your job, and let the machine do the rest for you.' But you play a little music yourself, you start making up songs for yourself, and next thing you know, you'll be thinking for yourself. Maybe voting for yourself."

Seeger had more difficulty answering local conservatives, including a few on the *Clearwater*'s governing board.

In 1970, midway through the *Clearwater*'s second season, the boat docked for a songfest at the town of Cold Spring, once a stronghold of Ku Klux Klan activities. A year before, the *Clearwater*'s first appearance had caught conservatives unawares, but afterward, they were outraged. "So when we came in 1970, they were prepared," Seeger said. "There had been rumors somebody was going to cause trouble, but I said, 'Well, we got away with it last summer . . . let's not back out now.'" The Mid-Hudson Philharmonic played a Haydn symphony for five hundred people. Then Pete Seeger appeared on stage before the last piece to thank the crowd for coming.

"At that moment," Seeger continued, "fifteen or more drunken people stood up waving little American flags and saying 'Throw the Commies out.' They stood in front of the stage and unrolled a banner: STOP POLLUTION, GET RID OF PETE. The conductor decided to ignore it and started to play Mozart. They stayed there, waving the little flags. After the short piece was played, the conductor quickly said, 'Star-Spangled Banner in B-Flat.'

"They did the most rousing rendition I ever heard an orchestra do. . . . I stayed behind to see that everything was going okay.

"The conservatives came up to me and said, 'Seeger, why don't you sing some American songs?'

"'What songs do I sing that aren't American?' I said.

"'Oh, you know, all those songs you sing aren't American. Why don't you sing "In the Good Old Summertime"?'"

Finally one of the policemen suggested he leave. There were threats to dump gasoline on deck and set the boat afire. That night someone cut the sloop's mooring. While everyone agreed that none of this was Seeger's fault, these weren't the pleasant outings board members anticipated, and a sharp tension broke out within the *Clearwater* organization.

"As the boat became more and more of a reality," explained Jimmy Collier, "problems of priorities came up—who was going to get the boat? Is it going to be allied with schools or with hippies?" After initially pulling together to fund the boat, the sailors, historians, and community activists each developed separate agendas. The tenuous coalition—based on Seeger's charisma—foundered, and the five-person board wished the boat's reputation was less tied to Seeger's.

His 1970 testimony on behalf of the Chicago Eight didn't make this group any happier. When the government tried to impugn Seeger by bringing up his experience with HUAC, he was ready. With a twinkle in his eye, he offered to sing "Wasn't That a Time," the song mentioned by the prosecution. Judge Hoffman refused. Seeger recited the words, but at the last stanza, he couldn't help himself; he started singing. "It was just a lilt, your honor," said Bill Kunstler for the defense. "I'm afraid I'm a better musician than you," Hoffman told Kunstler in reprimanding Seeger. "That was no lilt."

However much Seeger's conservative colleagues disapproved of his politics, they knew the *Clearwater* needed him badly. "Toshi and Peter know how to write grants," Collier pointed out. "And they have many admirers. . . . The old rich people like these replicas of boats that sail up and down. 'We can go have cocktail parties on it,' they thought, 'and invite our friends.'" The Seegers, on the other hand, wanted the ship to be a public boat, to stop at the Harlem docks. At one point, a conservative board member asked Seeger not to sing "Big Muddy" at any *Clearwater*-sponsored event: "We're singing about the water. Can't you stay away from all that Vietnam stuff?"

"Look," Seeger replied, "all these subjects are tied together. You know why we don't have money to clean up this river? Guess who takes the big bite out of the tax dollar?"

It dawned on his opponents that there was no changing Seeger; he intended to sing whatever and whenever he wanted. The disenchanted sailors and historians, anxious about their investment in the *Clearwater*, decided Seeger had to go. Fights left Seeger with a bad taste in his mouth. This time he was particularly upset, sensing that if he won, he would owe his victory to Jimmy's and Toshi's effective organizing, rather than to his own ability.

IN THE LATE SIXTIES, Toshi Ohta Seeger found herself simultaneously organizing her husband's life and complaining about it. Her husband's domestic consciousness-raising had now progressed to where he wrote, with that uneasy humor men often adopt in answering feminist challenges, “Most men only chain their wives to a sink. I’ve chained mine to a desk as well.” Because Toshi was a woman, and because she disliked spotlights, she never received her due. She had her own humorous rejoinder: “If only Peter would chase women, I would have had an excuse to leave him. But chasing good causes . . .”

He knew what Toshi did for him and the debt he owed her. “Is it really necessary to have a Personal Manager, Publicity Agent, a Road Manager, and an Accountant? Where is it all going to end? Perhaps what I should do is make seven carbon copies of myself . . . and thereby afford the vast organization, the Empire that revolves around me.”

His words had a bitter ring; he had been hearing complaints about his “inaccessibility.” Toshi and Harold had become Seeger’s gatekeepers. If Toshi and Harold took this role, however, it was he who abdicated it. He needed them, but his dependence cut two ways, as a comment of Irwin Silber made clear: “I guess that all of us who have dealt with you over the years as publishers, editors, producers, managers are all participants in a similar kind of deception. . . . I’m sure you are aware how almost all the people in your life are constantly trying to manipulate you—just as I’m sure you’re working on them in turn—yours perhaps with a ‘larger’ purpose, theirs for more mundane, private purposes.”

Toshi Ohta rarely talked to reporters, but when she did, her remarks were certainly original. “I hate it when people romanticize him,” she told a surprised reporter from the *Chicago Tribune*. “He’s like anybody good at his craft, like a good bulldozer operator.” Another time, asked why Seeger had remained popular over the years, she answered that his fans were “nuts.” Did Seeger ever give a bad concert? “When he talks too much—when he doesn’t sing,” she said. Discussing male chauvinism, she teased her husband, “I should write ‘pig’ on the back of your shirt”; the interviewer had obviously hit a sore spot.

“You have the right to extricate yourself from the painful pressure," Seeger wrote his wife. "In spite of our occasional blow-ups this family has accomplished much in the world."

Leaving aside her rare barbs, the partnership worked well. "Toshi's been a partner, not a closet partner, but a real partner," Judy Collins said. "The fact that he's on the stage—and she isn't—doesn't make that much difference."

But when duty was involved, there was just no arguing with Peter. And he was not the easiest man to live with: He didn't drink coffee or liquor, he didn't smoke, and he disliked listening to records or going to the movies. Attending concerts with him could be aggravating; he'd grimace when the performers' timing was off or when they misread their audience. Despite his hopes for TV, it was all he could do to sit silently for a half hour; he kept getting up to turn the set off. Nonetheless, he wrote Silber about plans to organize a People's Television Conference.

IN THE FALL of 1970 the confrontation between Pete Seeger and the *Clearwater*'s directors finally came to a head. Jimmy Collier remembered people insulting Seeger to his face in the meetings. "Toshi would sometimes organize another little meeting afterwards; Pete wouldn't get involved," Jimmy recalled. "When we started to do our little caucusing, we'd never tell Peter; we just did it, because his attitude was: 'If you'd tell people about things, they'd do what was right.'"

On September 27, at the conclusion of a particularly acrimonious meeting, Seeger's opponents made their move. One stood up and said, "Pete, we can't clean up the river by ourselves. We need the establishment to do it. They are the ones with the power. If you antagonize them, we'll never clean up the river."

"They're never going to clean up the river, period," Seeger answered tartly. "You've got to get a new establishment before this river's going to be cleaned."

"As long as Seeger is connected with this organization, we'll never get far," board member Donald Presutti declared, introducing a resolution calling for Seeger to resign. It failed by only one vote. Then Presutti resigned, later telling a *New York Times* reporter that he no longer wanted to be associated with the "hippie types" attracted by Seeger's involvement with the boat.

THOUGH HE'D WON his battle, Seeger gradually withdrew from the *Clearwater*. He had a right to stay and wouldn't be driven out, but he sailed less. He and Toshi were ready for the rank-and-file to take over their boat. He still longed for a chance to make his voice heard widely, and for this, he still looked to reforming television: "I used to be snobbish about TV; I am no longer. Anyone who says, 'Slobs can watch the boob tube, I prefer to read books,' is like someone who says, 'I don't care who swims in the polluted river; after all, I have a swimming pool.'"

Seeger still hadn't received many TV offers; the reasons for this were obvious, as one incident showed. Pete Seeger was invited on the *Today* show, one of the most popular morning programs on television.

"Pete," he was asked on arriving in the studio, "what do you have for us?"

"Well, I have two songs, but one's very short, so I'm sure there's time."

"You have five minutes."

"Fine," Pete answered. "The first is a nice cheerful banjo piece, the second is kind of a satire, in contrast." He played a banjo tune, then sang "Garbage," with a new verse about "financiers and other crooks . . . Nukes and other knavery." He had expected a protest, and he got it.

"Pete! It's kind of early in the morning for that. Do you have anything else?" the producers asked.

"Well, how about this?" Seeger said, singing "Walking Down Death Row."

"Do you have anything else?"

He sang "If a Revolution Comes to My Country."

"Well, I guess we better stick to 'Garbage,'" the producers agreed. At that the whole studio broke up with laughter. The cameramen and directors agreed, "Yeah, we'll stick with 'Garbage'!"

Seeger wasn't as naïve as his critics made him out to be. No one had to tell him why he wasn't flooded with invitations: He would not sing what he was told. "Tell a man what he may not sing," Mary Renault has written, "and he is still half free; even all free, if he never wanted to sing it. But tell him what he must sing, take up his time with it so that his true voice cannot sound even in secret—there, I have seen, is slavery."

SEEGER HAD TRIED TELEVISION, without much luck; he had tried folklore, but lacked the patience for scholarship. Now he decided to try his hand at writing: If he couldn't make himself heard on TV, he could at least publish his thoughts.

That Seeger chose, among his many interests, to write about aesthetics in his first article published in the *New York Times* is instructive: "For Art's Sake," 1971.

Of course, Seeger had already been widely published, in *Saturday Review*, *Life*, *Look*, and in scholarly journals. And in between contributing over two hundred pieces to People's Songs *Bulletin*, *Broadside*, and *Sing Out!* (and editing a half-dozen song and instruction books), he had composed over a hundred songs.

It wasn't enough. He had more to say, and in the early seventies, he worked on five books, completing two of them. The best known of these (and the most ambitious) is a collection of writings brought out as *The Incompleat Folksinger* in 1972. Publishing anything autobiographical was a departure for Seeger. In his journals, however, Pete Seeger imagined the day when his biography would be written: "The cult of the personality needs to be fought every step of the way. It leads to a dead end trap. If, in the future, anyone pores through these notebooks with biography in mind, please be hardheaded. . . . Think of the really great artists and thinkers whose reputation has been well-nigh ruined by unthinking adulators."

A strange note for a man to leave historians, but true to character. This same distrust of individual achievement hamstrung *The Incompleat Folksinger*, where he summed up his career in twelve pages: He wanted to be known only as "a link in a chain" of singers. The book's title reflected his assuming modesty. He tried to persuade his publishers to display the name of the editor, Jo Metcalf Schwartz, in the same size type as his; he even tried to restrict the advertising, a request editors at Simon and Schuster rarely received from authors. The book that emerged from Seeger's renunciations was an almanac, a disarming hodgepodge of favorite recipes (cheddar rarebit and strawberry shortcake), songs, and homespun philosophy. The perfect book for anyone who ever wondered how to carry a banjo, two guitars, and a recorder at the same time (answer: Sew your own banjo case, instructions provided).

After *The Incompleat Folksinger*, he published *Henscratches and Flyspecks* ("How to read melodies from songbooks in twelve confusing lessons"), a guide to sight-reading for those who like to sing but distrust music teachers. Next he wrote down his favorite stories and anecdotes. He did this with reluctance, convinced that good storytellers retell freely rather than read stories aloud. In 1973 Macmillan made a children's book out of his father's *Foolish Frog* story, but the bulk of Seeger's stories lay buried in a typescript, "Stories for Retelling."

Perhaps the most revealing work was his unpublished *Fantasies of a Revisionist*, the story of an invalid with half-baked, half-visionary ideas for saving the world. In his isolation, the hero ruminates on opening a storefront "Freedom of the Press" reading room (featuring Seeger's favorite quote from Jefferson: "We have nothing to fear from error as long as reason is free to oppose it").

In the end, Seeger wanted something more dynamic in his life than a typewriter; he needed a fight closer to the barricades. He decided to visit the countries forbidden to U.S. citizens: Cuba,

North Vietnam, and China. In 1971, a few months after the showdown with the *Clearwater*'s board, Pete Seeger flew to Cuba by way of Spain, accompanied by Mika and her Puerto Rican photographer partner, Emilio Rodriguez.

The Seeger party received VIP treatment, with a twenty-fourth-story suite in the former Havana Hilton and a chauffeured car taking them around—just what Seeger didn't want. His greatest disappointment was his lack of contact with the Cuban people. He'd looked forward to cutting cane, but his schedule allowed him only two hours in the field. Riding in a car with a former prosecutor of Batista's allies, he was told, "It was a pleasure to execute them." Seeger listened silently. "I have reservations," he confided to his journal. "What happened to their families? Should one shoot them too? Where did they draw the line?" Seeger would have made a mediocre Robespierre; this was a country surrounded by enemies, he rationalized, including CIA operatives.

Pete Seeger always had a blind spot to the excesses of socialism-in-the-making. In the 1970s, he refrained from criticizing the Soviet Union even when groups of musicians, such as the Czech Plastic People ensemble, were tried and jailed under Russian pressure. About the only thing Seeger objected to in the USSR at this point was polluted lakes. Criticisms were for renegades and right-wingers. (This would change.)

Returning to Spain on the way home from Cuba, the musician found himself with a censorship battle surpassing anything on American TV. Spanish government censors forbade him to sing three songs: Country Joe McDonald's "The Fish Cheer: What Are We Fighting For," "Bring 'Em Home," and, inexplicably, "Sally Racket," a chantey sung on the *Clearwater* (perhaps the chorus, "Haul 'Em away," suggested Franco's street arrests). By knocking on enough doors, though, Seeger's supporters received rulings that counteracted each other. He knew he couldn't sing—and didn't try—the songs of the Spanish Civil War, which he had recorded for Moe Asch back in 1944. As it was, he broke Spanish law by singing Basque separatist songs at a party.

His moods were mercurial. When Seeger failed to get an audience singing in Seville, he plunged into self-doubt, as confused about his art as he had been in 1963, when he noted in his journal on his world tour, "I seem to stagger about this agonized world as a clown, dressed in happiness, hoping to reach the hearts and minds of the young. When newspaper reporters ask me what effect my songs have, I try and make a brave reply, but I am really not so certain."

When he arrived in Barcelona, he discovered the police had canceled his concert at the university, fearing a left-wing riot. Seeger's mood picked up. He went anyway. As he drove up he could see a traffic jam near the theater, and thousands of students standing at a distance. Near the university building, mounted police patrolled. Seeger decided to go around to the back door. The head of the engineering school met with him in the corridor, but as hundreds of students crowded around, they heard pounding feet. The police broke in, and the director moved off in one direction and Seeger went the other way. Being back on the battle lines was a tonic; a government genuinely feared his songs.

"I am sorry that the concert could not have been held," the dean told Seeger an hour later. "It is out of my hands. The governor of Barcelona says that he personally ordered the police to stop it, and he did so on orders from Madrid." Seeger left, vowing to sing in Barcelona another time.

In the spring of 1972 he set out on a marathon tour of forbidden Asia, North Vietnam, and China, with Toshi and Tinya. Before he left, a documentary about him premiered at a New York cinema, *Pete Seeger: A Song and a Stone*, directed by Robert Elfstrom. (The stone was the one he carried in his banjo case since the 1968 incident at Duke.) The film turned out to be a minor disaster: Seeger was disappointed at its hero worship, and the *New York Times* called it "perfectly dreadful, ranging from merely inept . . . to openly offensive." While *Cue* and *New York* were mildly impressed, the *Times*'s comparison with Leni Riefenstahl's pro-Hitler documentary *Triumph of the Will* sank the film. (Here was the "unthinking adulation" he'd hoped his biographers would avoid.)

In March he and his family arrived in North Vietnam. Their plane circled Hanoi, and below them lay the small land, about the size and population of New York State, that had held its own against Uncle Sam. Palm trees and rice fields stretched off on all sides. He had no idea how his family would be received here; the Vietnamese had good reason to hate Americans. At the airport, though, the Seegers were greeted with hugs and bouquets of flowers.

His emotions continued at a peak throughout his stay. Preoccupied by his responsibility as an American, he watched the Vietnamese carrying fuel and live chickens on their bicycles, gardening, and rebuilding bombed-out structures. He'd arranged to meet Seymour Hersh, then a correspondent for the *New York Times*. Hersh brought out the journalist in him; in two weeks, he wrote fifteen thousand words about the visit, sitting down to work after Toshi fell asleep. He strolled the streets of Hanoi with his notebooks and banjo, dressed in rubber-tire sandals like those worn by Uncle Ho. Children would stop and point at the tall, fair-skinned musician, and Seeger would open his banjo case on the sidewalk and play for the amazed youngsters.

The Seegers again received VIP treatment. Despite requests to travel like fellow workers, not diplomats, they were given a fancy car and a driver who honked bicycles and pedestrians out of the way. Once, unable to communicate his discomfort to their driver, he jumped out and walked alongside. Reminders of U.S. bombings surrounded him. One afternoon the family visited an exhibit of "bombs and devices to carry on computerized electronic warfare from the air. Enough to give anyone nightmares." That night he shut his eyes and saw shrapnel and platoons burned alive; he wrote that he "didn't sleep—not a wink all night."

Their two weeks ended momentously. After a farewell concert, Pete Seeger heard a comment that stopped him cold, one he'd later repeat hundreds of times. He'd ended his concert with songs of the Hudson Valley. Afterward, a Vietnamese novelist and war veteran came up. "When you sing songs of the Hudson Valley, where you live, that was when I decided I could believe you. Only when Americans realize that they too must stay home and fight to free their corner of the world—as we are fighting for ours—can the world live with America."

Seeger had traveled ten thousand miles to be reminded of the importance of community organizing. "That was a very important story for Pete—for all of us," Arlo Guthrie said. "It became his way of saying: 'It's not a bad idea to go out and see the world, but you also have to do things at home.'" He carried the Vietnamese writer's speech like a medal. It took foreigners, searching for something positive in America, to call him a patriot.

After all this excitement, China proved anticlimactic. Seeger gave only one major performance, a concert in Peking that he called one of his "signal failures" (along with the Albany, Georgia, concert). It was the same throughout China: "They were so busy analyzing me that they couldn't join in one little bit. Analyzing this song, analyzing that one . . . they didn't even tap their feet."

SEEGER RETURNED FROM his trip—as he had so often returned—brimming with enthusiasm. Out in his yard, he surveyed the water and heard the river's song afresh, echoing as it flowed to the sea. The projects piled on his desk now seemed more manageable. The vindication carried from Vietnam eased his mind. The Hudson even looked cleaner, and he worked on the *Clearwater* with new vigor. Then, in 1975, a state conservation pathologist discovered contamination from PCB (polychlorinated biphenyl). This industrial chemical, used by General Electric and others, was colorless, odorless—and an extremely toxic carcinogen. GE had dumped one and a half million pounds of PCBs into the river, according to the *New York Times.* While the *Clearwater* project had been winning advances in sewer treatment, the lethal chemical had been slowly seeping into the river bottom, lodging in the mud and entering the food chain; the fish ate it with their food, which poisoned them for humans. Seeger was furious. He considered visiting General Electric and dumping PCBs on their desks. "The people of America must realize we've got to organize a defense against these chemical companies—they're getting away with literal murder."

After this, he continued to raise funds for the *Clearwater* and sailed occasionally but didn't connect with the project as before. He had a ready answer when old friends asked what he was up to, but he could not shake the association with yachtsmanship or his frustration over the PCBs.

The *Clearwater* also hadn't caught on with local unions, who feared the loss of jobs and industry from environmental regulation. This effectively put Seeger on the opposite side from labor. Environmentalism already had a reputation—often ill-deserved—as a middle-class, white cause; if union organizers had written topical songs in the seventies, they might have satirized environmentalists. Sympathizing with both sides threw Seeger into a mild political paralysis.

The *Clearwater* had fulfilled his initial hopes; it had brought him closer to his community and politicized the Hudson's pollution. But publicity was not the same as social change, as Seeger would admit, quoting Lenin's statement that change comes not in thousands but millions. When those millions failed to materialize in the 1970s, Seeger endured. Without a movement for change, Seeger resembled the pagan gods who became mortal once their last follower disappeared.

"Pete's always looking for the excitement of song and the movement," Jimmy Collier said. "When he can't find it, he addresses the young people and uses everything he has to make it happen. . . . And because he has money and success—well, no one's asked him to justify this, but it didn't happen that way with Woody."

Seeger was admitted to the Songwriters' Hall of Fame, alongside Gershwin and Berlin, but few writing on popular song paid him attention. Rarely, if ever, did his name appear in scholarly works on American music, and when mentioned, it was his politics, rather than music, that attracted attention.

He also continued to have troubles with Columbia. In 1973 Columbia turned him over to Bob Johnson, Dylan's former producer. Lester Flatt, Earl Scruggs, and others played behind Seeger, but for some reason the tapes were never released, except for a few cuts on *Rainbow Race* (which finally included a moving rendition of "Golden River"). The song Seeger most wanted to record was Joe McDonald's antiwar "The Fish Cheer: What Are We Fighting For?" When Columbia refused to distribute this as a single (it was released as a single to deejays), Pete Seeger decided he was through with the company and returned to Folkways. "The need to make records had gone out of him." Don McLean commented, "Something's gone from Pete's performing: It's gone perhaps because he let it go. Or it may have slipped away without him being able to retain it."

IN THE WINTER of 1971, Pete Seeger began feeling noticeably ill.. He kept postponing a hernia operation. His sun-sensitive skin, with rosacea, flared up. And to his considerable distress, he found he couldn't sing as often or as long.

In the Almanacs, he could play at parties and come home singing. Now he worried about losing his voice. He'd never taken voice lessons; his father hadn't want him to sound "trained." What Seeger knew about preserving his voice had come from trial and error.

Tiredness overtook him, perhaps the absence of a reason for his art. Seeger didn't want people attending his concerts to remember how it used to be. He tried to point ahead: Why sing, if people came only for nostalgia?

"Political artists are big, empty shells," reflected singer-activist Holly Near, who would perform with Arlo, Ronnie, and Pete as Harp. "It's what they notice that fills the void. When there's nothing going on to do that, to stimulate concern, that's trouble."

Seeger decided to take a year off from singing. He wanted to see if he could do it, and he had a lot to heal. For 1973, he told Harold not to accept paid bookings and to cut down on benefits. The hernia operation laid him up for two months, and his skin problems took another couple to clear. He stayed at home, playing banjo or writing, the first time he'd stopped singing professionally since 1939.

This wasn't the first time he had *considered* stopping, of course. In 1949, before Peekskill and before the Weavers entered nightclubs, he had thought about giving up performing. Then, after the Weavers had been blacklisted, he'd tried to teach or to do research; instead, he and Toshi had created a college music circuit. In 1968, after Resurrection City, he had felt little impetus to sing, except for the *Clearwater*. But only when no social movement called to him did Seeger actually stop.

The first change he noticed was that his health deteriorated: "As long as I have to perform, I can't get hoarse. Got to get sleep. The minute I don't have to perform, I say, 'Well, it doesn't matter if I catch a cold.' And one thing leads to another." It wasn't clear which was worse: the operation or not singing. "It was a year before I got back into the swing of things. I was very weak and out of condition. My voice got weak, my legs were weak, my hands were weak."

Seeger discovered he needed his audience more than they ever could need him. For his concertgoers, singing meant a pleasant evening; for Seeger, it was a matter of survival: "For my health I know I've got to keep singing. I don't think I'll live long if I don't."

AT LEAST THE *Clearwater* was having success. But even after the group (and New York State) took GE to court over the PCBs and won—a multimillion-dollar penalty—some of his friends still scorned the project, jibing, "How long will it take to get the last beer can out of the Hudson?" Nor was criticism limited to radicals: Seeger received one of his worst concert reviews in 1978, when Robert Palmer of the *New York Times* wrote, "He has lost the ability to provoke. . . . Much of his political material has begun to sound unappetizingly shrill." In 1975, performing in Berkeley, tremors in his hands led him to throw down his flute on the stage after messing up a tune.

Since the late seventies audiences come to hear Seeger the living legend, flocking to a *Clearwater* festival, such as one in 1976, where the crowd spread over a grassy amphitheater sloping down to the Hudson. As the day turned to dusk, Pete Seeger played "Kisses Sweeter Than Wine" on his twelve-string guitar, and the audience relaxed together. The fading rays of the sun rested for a moment on the vibrating strings, then spread out across the river's surface in a carpet of reflections. His seadog beard was untrimmed. His lumber jacket, a few sizes too large for his slim, muscular arms, bunched up in the valley of his arm, beneath the guitar. His bushy eyebrows puckered like tiny wings taking flight when he sang. At the concert's end, his voice soared into the starry sky with a song about the sleeping lion who will someday return. Out across the river the harmony floated, a warm melodic wind on a cool summer evening.

Chapter 13

TURN! TURN! TURN!

—

IN THE 1980S, PETE SEEGER BEGAN AGAIN, WITH THE FIRE OF late middle age boiling over. He appeared on five albums in 1980 alone, beginning with his poignant song, "One Grain of Sand," which rehearses his recurrent metaphor for social change, the "teaspoon brigades": "Environmentalists are like a few guys putting sand on one side of a scale with teaspoons, while on the other side of a lot of industrialists are loading boulders with dump trucks. . . . You can never tell what might work if we had enough people with teaspoons."

The sense of not having forever drove Seeger forward into the new decade. As he turned sixty in 1979, he began planning a new kind of record, one documenting his techniques for group singing. Later, Arlo Guthrie, his performing partner, would wonder if this came about from Seeger's fear of losing his voice.

"In some sense, I did predict that loss when I did the Sing-Along record. As far as I was concerned, it would be the last real record I'd make."

Starting in 1980, at Harold Leventhal's suggestion, Pete Seeger began to tour more often with Arlo Guthrie's band Shenandoah. He'd finally found a rock band with whom to harmonize. He and Arlo would alternate sets, with the band growing adept at following Seeger's lead. Having a Guthrie as his traveling partner again calmed the worries about his voice.

After decades of struggle, Seeger had made a separate peace with pop music, still recording for Folkways but trying out a more commercial sound on Warners in the *Circles and Seasons* LP produced by Fred Hellerman—his third recording with electric backup.

There was time now to pursue cherished projects, such as the centennial of the 1886 Haymarket Square demonstration, and the construction of two small versions of the *Clearwater* boat, the *Sojourner Truth*, and the *Woody Guthrie.* His relaxation revealed itself in small, light-hearted gestures; once, smiling at the way people plunged through a revolving door in midtown Manhattan, he drew himself up to his full height and turned a pirouette inside the revolving door.

In his sixties he was at the top of his game, no longer buffeted by protests and lawsuits. Many recordings were in the works. An album recorded at the *Clearwater*'s Great Hudson River Revival came out, with Seeger leading the Sloop Singers in a sea chantey. A few months later another live recording appeared, with Seeger joining Joan Baez, the Chambers Brothers, and the Roches with an audience of ten thousand in the open-air Greek Theater on the Berkeley campus. Then, just after Thanksgiving 1980, he appeared in a documentary commemorating twenty-five years since the Weavers' 1955 reunion, "The Weavers at Carnegie Hall": *Wasn't That a Time.* (The Weavers' final performance took place six months later, at the Great Hudson Revival, June 21, 1981. Lee was ailing.)

Yet this list of recordings does not capture the rhythm of his day-to-day activity in a period when rallies and benefits outnumbered his concerts. He sang for five thousand antinuclear demonstrators in Harrisburg following the Three Mile Island nuclear disaster and yet made time to play banjo to raise money for the roof of a school near home.

Fairly typical was the last week of March 1981, when he performed with Tom Paxton to benefit the *Clearwater*, at the Rockland County Mental Health Association, and at the Ethical Culture

Meeting Hall in New York City. All these events were in New York, but with the drive to and from Beacon and time to sleep, change clothes, and restring instruments, he was always on to the next gig, hurrying to sing as much as he could, while he could.

To his core audience, the college graduates who support community radio, independent publishers, and nonchain bookstores, Seeger was omnipresent. A monthly program guide of Pacifica station WBAI-FM in New York City made this clear in a cartoon.

Two organizers of a demonstration are talking, and one asks the other, "Where's Pete Seeger?"

"I don't know. Did you invite him?" the other answers.

"No, did you? He always shows up at demonstrations. I didn't know we needed to ask him!"

The pendulum in Seeger's life that had always swung between individual and collective work now slanted toward organizing with an enthusiasm unmatched since the 1940s. He and Toshi decided to build a network of support groups for the *Clearwater*, such as the River Lovers in Croton and a half-dozen others.

Of all these clubs, none was as dear to them as their local, the Beacon Sloop Club. In an indication of its growing prominence, the local cable access station shot a program on it—then twelve more shows, including some out on the boat. The Sloop Club itself underwent a transformation. It had started out as an abandoned diner in a little tin building, damp, cold, and dark. In summer, the tin siding used to heat up enough to be uncomfortable but not enough to dry the place out. In winter, river breezes blew through it. Its old, broken-down couch and a refrigerator listed to one side, and the only places to sit were wooden boxes. Sunday afternoons, a dozen or so would gather in this heap to plan a future with a cleaner river. Phyllis Newham, later a club president, remembers her first meeting.

"I'd gone down to the Sloop Club because I had seen a poster on the wall of the A & P that read, 'Pumpkin Festival!' I couldn't imagine what people did at a pumpkin festival, so I went down to find out. Here was Pete sitting inside the Sloop Club with a little group of people gathered around him, talking about what a big job it would be to save this river. At the end of the afternoon I said to myself, 'My goodness, these people are going to need all the help they can get.' So I signed up for everything."

"Pete had realized that he could not just use his town like so many commuters do, as a bedroom community," said club member David Bernz, "people sleeping in a condominium, where they get into a gas-guzzling car in the morning, they go to the city and go into a tall building to work, and they put it in reverse at night. The Beacon Sloop Club reminds people that they're connected to their environment. That they live on a beautiful river. That there are farms along the shores that grow things. So when the strawberries get ripe in June, we have a Strawberry Festival. When the corn gets ripe in August, we have a Corn Fest, and when the pumpkins are in season in October, a Pumpkin Festival. The people come to the river, the produce is there, and it somehow reconnects people to the world they live in."

For the Strawberry Festival, Sloop Club members would gather a few days beforehand to pick. If people joined the club in awe of Pete Seeger, they ended up thinking differently, Sue Altkin reflected: "You're on your knees in a strawberry field with the likes of Pete Seeger, and he'd tell stories. I mean a lot of people work side by side and they're quiet, but if you're working next to Pete or in the row across from Pete, you hear stories—his memory of history, not just of his own life. I'd be in the strawberry field listening to him recite poems by Alfred Whitehead."

There is a strawberry tent where people chop berries and another for buttering shortbread and whipping cream. The first batch of shortcakes is mushy, the second slightly burned.

"IF PEOPLE CAME UP from the train station and crossed over to the front of the Sloop Club when he was working, they'd say, 'Are you Pete Seeger?' He'd say, 'Yes. And this is Phyllis and Sue and Dave,'" Altkin recalled. "It was charmingly democratic. And not for show, not false humility." This was the Pete Seeger who'd sung, forty years earlier, "I'm an ordinary guy, worked most of my life, sometime I'll settle down with my kids and wife" in "Dear Mr. President."

"Sometime" had finally come, but as to settling down? His decision to stop accepting paid performances—except with Arlo—meant he'd perform for anyone whose cause he and Toshi liked. He loved it.

The benefits, the *Clearwater* festivals, the new recordings—all this seems rooted in Seeger's complex reaction to the emotional and professional dilemma of losing his voice. If he couldn't sing, what else would he do?

At home in the barn, he finished books he'd started a decade before: Children's books (such as an illustrated version of Abiyoyo) poured out of him; five of his songs were illustrated for children in the 1980s. Then he turned to a musical autobiography, *Where Have All the Flowers Gone*, which took him five years.

In *Where Have All the Flowers Gone*, Seeger tells his sources for songs, his tunings, tunes, even the hand gestures and the jokes he tells. The non-song-leader will find here more than he or she wants to know; the mix is very like Seeger's pocket notebooks, or what it must be like in his cerebellum, where fragments of song lyrics bounce up against a remembered tune—and come out as songs.

In 1986 another of his books, *Carry It On*, became a square in the patchwork quilt of the alternate patriotism he'd woven. Written with Bob Reiser, it offered a tour through America's labor history via song, complete with poignant quotes: "I can employ one half of the working class to kill the other half" (Jay Gould); "The strike breaker is the hero of the American industry" (Charles Eliot, president of Harvard).

Even topical song made a comeback in his life. In 1979, singer

Charlie King founded the Peoples' Music Network, a biannual gathering of songwriters and performers using music in social action. "We often meet backstage at peace rallies," King wrote to twenty-five people. "Why don't we get together?" He rented a summer camp, and seventy-five showed up. They debated the best way to lead songs and how to write and perform inspiring music, an end-of-the-century People's Songs.

Then there was *Sing Out!*, the magazine Pete Seeger had started a lifetime ago. The Great Folk Boom of the 1960s had waned and with it, *Sing Out!*'s finances. Coffeehouses were shuttered. It was Disco Time, and young people seemed more interested in John Travolta's white suits than in musicians reminding them of history. Sunday afternoons, Washington Square Park was left to the pigeons.

Yet almost unnoticed, this period was the beginning of a *third* folk revival, carrying forward the collectors of the '30s and the strummers from the '60s. Now in the '80s, many quietly played their homemade music at home, at pancake breakfasts, and at informal dances. None of this flashed on the screen of popular culture, but baby boomers starting families would dust off old Pete Seeger records for the kids or grandkids. But they'd let their subscriptions to *Sing Out!* lapse.

The cover of *Sing Out!*'s thirtieth anniversary issue, 1980, pictured Seeger by the Hudson River. Inside, Seeger wrote, "Commercial publishers are not interested in the songs that might be controversial. Progress is made by controversy. We believe in controversial songs!"

But controversy requires a response. And that *Sing Out!* was not getting. So he and Toshi turned their energetic selves to helping its revival.

Sing Out! now managed to be simultaneously diverse and obscure. Jewish klezmer, Louisiana zydeco, and Mexican American norteña music appeared. Losing its focus, it had also lost its audience. Some now read it only for Pete's column, "Appleseed." Subscriptions dwindled as articles favored the current over the timely, the esoteric over the popular. Its editorial collective of three women kept on as if there was no problem. The next issue was billed as a "Teach-in Issue: All You've Ever Wanted to Learn . . ." But all anyone ever wanted to learn from *Sing Out!* had to wait two years for its next issue.

Mark Moss, leader of a fund-raising group called Friends of *Sing Out!*, one day visited the magazine's office in lower Manhattan. "When I went there to take subscription forms up to the Hudson River Revival, they told me not to take any new subscriptions."

"We're out of here. We haven't been paid in a while, we're giving up. If you can raise some money," they told Mark Moss, "that's great. We have bills we have to pay."

Moss sadly loaded up back issues to sell and then sat down with Seeger. "What are we going to do?" he asked.

"Even if we have to mimeograph *Sing Out!* in someone's basement, like we did in the very beginning of Peoples' Songs, we should try to keep the magazine," Seeger replied.

The next Monday, before *Sing Out!* could be evicted, Moss rented a U-Haul truck, drove to New York City, cleaned out the office, and took its records to Easton, Pennsylvania, where, in frustration, he stored everything in the basement of a bicycle shop. Figuring out what to do took a while. When Moss asked Seeger what they'd do for seed money, Seeger told him a tea company had offered him two thousand dollars for the right to use "If I Had a Hammer" in an ad. Seeger promised Moss that money to get started again. By the spring of 1983, they'd found an office space and a new issue. Everything was ready to go, Moss thought. It was then he learned a crucial lesson about working with Pete Seeger.

"We were getting together to do the layout, and Toshi and Harold showed up toward the end of the afternoon to pick Pete up."

"So where do you think you're getting the money to print this thing and mail it out?" Toshi asked.

"Well, Pete said he had some money coming in from a tea commercial," Mark answered, somewhat confused.

"Mark, I'm going to tell you something just once. If you want to talk to Pete about songs or music, that's all good; but if you're talking to him about money, you have to talk to either me or Harold. I've been living with this guy for thirty-five years, and he's yet to learn how to defrost the refrigerator." Seeger sat next to her, looking down at the floor.

"Okay. Pete said we were going to do it, so I guess we'll do it," Toshi finished. Then Moss learned a second lesson about working with the Seegers: Don't count on thanks.

"Pete hated that first issue. He thought it was amateurish, and that it looked like crap. And he told me so. He was 150 percent right. After all, I was a construction worker, I was a fan, I didn't know anything about magazines."

Here was a contradiction typical of Seeger: first saying, "Oh we can mimeograph it in someone's basement like we used to," then, when an issue finally appeared, complaining that it was amateurish. One day Seeger walked into a *Sing Out!* board meeting with one of those far-out ideas of his.

"Pete came in and said, 'Here's what I think we ought to do. We ought to rent a truck and put the office in the back of the truck and Mark can drive from city to city. At each city, he can roll up the back of the truck and people will say, "What are you doing in there?" Mark can say, "I'm making a folksong magazine. You want to help?" Then, everybody will participate, and we'll make the magazine together.' "

"Pete, if you want to get into a truck and drive around and do that," Moss answered, "you go do it. But I'm not doing that."

The other people on the board supported Moss, saying it was his first issue and that he was doing good work.

"Well, I quit," Pete Seeger said. "I'm going home."

"Pete had realized he likes to be in day-to-day control of things," Moss later reflected. "From then on, he would threaten to quit every few years—even participated in a campaign to get rid of me. But there was no way I was going to drive around in that truck!" What does this incident say about Seeger's family priorities, that he imagined Moss giving up his family and personal life to drive the magazine around in a truck?

With *Sing Out!* foundering, and some on the *Clearwater* board still complaining about Seeger, he was busy but isolated. It was a time for mending fences. As always, Seeger turned to his resident fence mender, outreach coordinator, and festival organizer, Toshi. And as always, she responded. But now there was a distinct edge to her comments. Toshi's quiet role was beginning to change.

IN 1980, SHARP-EYED READERS of the *New York Times* discovered an unfamiliar name in an ad for the Women's Strike for Peace: Toshi Seeger. What did she play?

When reporters talked to Pete Seeger, Toshi was largely invisible. (On Arlo and Pete's second record, *Together*, Toshi appears as a "production assistant," with her name misspelled.) To Seeger's fans, she was equally invisible. Few noticed her in the crowd, leaning up to whisper in her tall husband's ear: He should sing a few slow ones, and not forget to talk about next week's demonstration.

Back in 1959, when Seeger had recorded "Singing in the Country" on *Nonesuch*, he prefaced it with, "Toshi is washing the dishes; Mika is out playing with Danny; and I'm goofing off." Here was an introduction that did not play well on phonographs of the 1980s.

"She is the yin to his yang that allows Pete to be who Pete is," Mark Moss said, "and makes sure that he remembers to eat and sleep and get stuff done. In my estimation, without Toshi, Pete would have been dead a long time ago."

Toshi's stick-to-itiveness is remembered with awe by those who worked with Seeger. After *Carry It On*, Bob Reiser reflected, "Pete really doesn't like the idea of carrying a grudge against somebody.

People over the years will say and do things that really hurt him. Toshi will remember. She reminds him. Pete will purposely forget it." Reiser wrote another book with Seeger, *Everybody Says Freedom*, on the civil rights movement. He remembers when the book was finished, right after the 1988 election: "A bleak day for every Democrat or liberal. Reagan's protégé, Bush, was going to be president now. It was a hopeless election. As I was talking, Pete said this: 'Change doesn't happen in a second. We get so impatient; we think things are going to change right away. They *do* change, but they just never happen as fast as we want them to.' Then he started talking about all the good things he'd seen going around.

"Their relationship is something I've thought a lot about. She makes him possible. She's extraordinary; she's also a tough cookie. She allows Pete to be really sweet and nice all the time, and she does all the dirty work. She makes it possible for him to live in his imagination when he needs to and wants to dream. She'll do whatever's necessary."

Every day held a bushel basket of mail to be sorted, bills paid, and requests. Toshi didn't usurp Pete. She rarely wrote no to anyone. That was Pete's job. Hers was addressing the envelopes afterward and stamping and mailing responses by the hundreds. Another day, another bushel of mail. If she took a day off, there was just twice as much mail the next day; so she didn't.

Few musicians said no to her phone calls to join the Revival, fast becoming as large as the Newport Folk Festival was in its early years: "She had all the contacts, arranged for transportation, for housing people," said their friend David Bernz. "The thing about Toshi is how very detail-oriented she is. Where Pete is the broad stroke of the idea, Toshi can work out all the details. She can calculate exactly how many rolls of toilet paper fifteen thousand people will use in forty-eight hours."

"Toshi pretends she's not leading things, she's very subtle,"

Phyllis Newham of the Sloop Club says. "But she gets her point across, and she gets people together to do things. She buttonholes people and tells them, 'You're going to come and do this' or 'You better do this.' You want to help her, so you just do it."

By the '80s and '90s, a woman whose full-time job was standing by her man did not play well. Sensitive about this, Toshi nevertheless persisted. She was known for being the wife who'd allowed Pete Seeger to take stands on principle—such as intentionally driving with his kids into the Peekskill riots and refusing to take the Fifth Amendment.

"Any other wife in that situation might say, 'Let's take the easy road, let's not fight this battle now,'" reflected record producer Jim Musselman. "They always took the harder road.

"When you're fighting the world you need love at home. You also need support, and you need a rock. Pete was the rock to so many people, but Toshi was the rock to Pete."

Jim Musselman was in law school in the early 1980s when he read a book about Seeger's life and decided against being a corporate executive. He ended up as one of "Nader's Raiders" for eight years and eventually participated in the lawsuit against General Motors to place airbags in cars. In an indirect way, Pete Seeger is responsible for the airbags Americans drive around with.

In time, Musselman tired of the law. He started a record label devoted to songs of social change, named Appleseed Records after Seeger's column. One of its first releases was a double CD of Seeger's songs performed by others, *Where Have All the Flowers Gone?* Bob Dylan was going to contribute; Musselman paid for the performers' studio sessions but quickly ran out of funds. He mortgaged his house. He sold some things. Then Bob Dylan changed his mind about the project, leaving Musselman mildly hysterical.

Then he had the inspiration of contacting Bruce Springsteen. But Springsteen knew very few of Seeger's songs. So Musselman researched a dozen in Seeger's biography and mailed them to the Boss.

"Outside of one or two songs that Seeger asked me to withdraw, he basically kept his hands off. What did he dislike? He liked it when people could hear the words." Finally, he sent Pete and Toshi the CD—and worried because he knew Seeger didn't want more publicity.

"When I did the CD, people said that Pete wasn't going to be happy with that. I said, 'My responsibility is not to Pete, my responsibility is to history and to music and to the musicians who want to thank Pete.' I think many times people don't want to upset Pete, but he has to be put in some sort of historical context. It's the bigger picture. Seeger finally understood that he's bigger than himself."

This did not stop the Seegers from hauling him over the coals for an hour on first hearing the CDs.

"First, they said the CD was not good quality acoustically—they were playing it on a battered old player, which was out of alignment. I told them to pull it out of that damn thing and listen to it on a better CD player before they made up their minds."

Then, they criticized the liner notes: "There was a typo on page thirteen, and they didn't like the drawings on another page."

This was a familiar syndrome for anyone who worked closely with Seeger. His initial enthusiasm was followed by Toshi's down-to-earth practicalities: the logistics, the financing, the publicity. Once finished, the project, whether a new issue of *Sing Out!* or a CD devoted to his songs, is found wanting. Disappointment and anger follow until, finally, acceptance and the possibility of another project.

Musselman's CD collections (eventually, there were three) had two other effects: reminding people (musicians in particular) of the value of Seeger's songs and arrangements, and kindling the fire of Springsteen's later *Seeger Sessions* album and tour.

Though both these effects were important, more publicity

meant more mail and more work for Toshi. By the late 1980s, Toshi's periodic allergic reaction to being Pete Seeger's caretaker reemerged. "The feminist movement affected Toshi in ways she will deny if you ever ask her about it. In these years she was really after Pete a lot," noted John Cohen, fellow musician and brother-in-law.

Arlo Guthrie, who's known Toshi all his life, commented, "I can tell you that in my life it takes about twelve people for me to be me. It takes *hundreds* of people for Pete to be Pete. Toshi does that well. She's the fulcrum. Pete is on one side; she is in the middle; and there are hundreds of people on the other side.

"What you really need to be free to be yourself are people who are willing to not only put up with you, but support you. Toshi's decision at some point along the way was to not only allow Pete to be Pete, but to rein him in when she thinks he's not being Pete."

One time Pete and Toshi had dinner at the home of John McCutcheon, a talented musician who'd followed Seeger into social song leading: "'Boy, she sure does give him a lot of shit,' my kids told me afterwards."

They tried having an assistant for the mail. It never worked out, and soon Toshi was back at the helm. Many wondered how Seeger was able to keep on being Pete all these years, but the real question was how Toshi kept on being Toshi. And now she had another problem. The inevitable had occurred. Her world-famous singer finally lost his voice.

IT HAD ALL STARTED around the time Seeger turned sixty and planned that sing-along record. He remembered the warnings heard when he'd begun singing with the Almanacs, that he'd lose his voice if he didn't get training, that he should relax his throat and tense his stomach muscles as he sang. He ignored all this. If he'd known what would happen, would he have done it differently? Would he have worked his falsetto less hard on songs like "Wimoweh"? Or stopped throwing his head back so violently that in his early concerts it seemed as if his Adam's apple would leave his neck and shoot out into the crowd?

"Before my voice and memory, and sense of rhythm and pitch were too far gone I decided, at age sixty, to document one of my two-hour concerts such as I've given for over twenty-five years," he'd written in the liner notes to that sing-along album. "In January, my wife Toshi once again put aside her own work to help me drive to Cambridge, Massachusetts. Sanders Theater, on the Harvard University campus is one of our best small auditoriums. Lots of wood paneling with wonderful live acoustics for singing.

"It's one of the better records, maybe *the* best record I ever made. I said to Moses Asch, 'Let me give a two hour concert and put out the whole concert.' I figured it would take 2 LPs. . . . But I got somebody to put sixteen microphones around through the audience so you could really hear the audience singing and then I sat at the side of the engineer when we were mastering it. Funny, I wanted to have some bass singers so I got together with a Harvard choir. Just before the concert started, a whole batch of little kids came in. We couldn't find room for them so they sat them right next to the basses. I couldn't turn up the basses without turning up the little kids."

If the recording was not quite the success he'd hoped for, neither was his voice.

"Toshi noticed my voice wobbling in 1980," he remembered twenty-five years later. "As long ago as that! She said, 'You used to have a steady tone, a contralto, but now it's wobbling like this.' There were songs I wanted very much to sing, but I couldn't lead them anymore.

"It happens to every singer, sooner or later. The vocal chords tire and stretch after a lifetime of singing and performing. Many great singers lose their voice at forty. They can no longer hit the high notes and they don't have the volume or control.

"I can't hit the high notes, and I can't hit the low notes. When my voice is warmed up I can squeak by. But when it's not warmed up it's almost pitiful it's so bad." And it would get worse.

SEEGER HAD SCALED BACK to captaining the *Clearwater* one day a week. With no phone ringing, no mail to answer, he could enjoy the silent wind. He'd stand with one hand on the wheel, looking out across his golden river as the wind pulled the ship from shore, its bronze and purple reflections sliding across the water's surface in the last light of day. At times he too seemed made of wood, tall and straight like the mast.

Always, there was a creek-full of ideas and new projects: "Board members learned to look the other way when they heard Pete bringing up some new idea," one *Clearwater* volunteer remembered: an oar boat, capable of carrying a dozen rowers at once; a raft from driftwood. Then Seeger decided what they really needed was a giant dugout canoe, constructed the old way, by burning and carving a log. A power company brought down the log for him.

"He'd found out about this tulip tree twenty feet or more in length, and they cut it down and brought it to the riverside. People worked on that dugout canoe for nearly a year," Betty Harkins of the Sloop Club remembered.

"I was in the canoe when we paddled up to the Newburgh-Beacon Bridge and then turned around and paddled back—in this log!" Then, because it wasn't well tended over the winter, it rotted and sank the next time out. Like his father, Seeger was always best at starting projects.

The Beacon Sloop Club was vulnerable to right-wingers getting at Seeger. One day a man named Rich showed up. "He began hanging around the Sloop Club and taking on so many jobs that they said he practically lived there," David Bernz remembers. Once someone heard him muttering something under his breath that was violent, and members began to worry.

"You can't be here anymore," they told him. "A few weeks

later there was a drug raid in Newburgh with FBI agents storming into a bar—and Rich was one of those FBI agents," Bernz recalls.

"In the early days, we were often perceived as troublemakers," recalled David O'Reilly, a reporter who'd crewed the *Clearwater*. "While I was on board, somebody was coming on and cutting the dock lines at night, so the boat would drift off. And these expensive dock lines were about one and a half inches thick!

"It was at night and we were in Garrison's Landing, directly across from West Point. I remember someone calling out that we were swinging away, drifting down—maybe a hundred feet off shore. We fired up the engine to get back in."

GRADUALLY, ALL THIS began to change. It was hard to dismiss the *Clearwater* as a Communist yacht when local children went out for a day on the river or when kids baked cupcakes for their local Sloop Club.

A bus with up to fifty-five kids would arrive from a school for a couple of hours in the morning and another in the afternoon. "Once they'd get out onto the river, they'd line the kids up on both sides with the line that pulls the peak and sing a sea chantey and pull in time until the sails are all the way up. And then they drop a net into the river and fish out some fish," said David Bernz. "Students see there's still life in the river.

"Somewhere near the end, the organizers say, 'Now that we're in the middle of the river, let's just be totally silent so you can hear the sounds that sailors would hear two hundred years ago when this river was clean and undisturbed.'

"And then they listen to the water lapping to the side and the sails, and the mast creaking, and after a few minutes of this, one of the crew will come up from the bottom with a guitar and lead the kids in song."

The formula was successful and self-sustaining, and as local and sweet as the Seegers' maple syrup production. March, when the Seegers finished the taps on the maple trees, brought hand labor, though not as labor-intensive as when native settlers had to drop hot rocks into raw sap. Family, visitors, all get involved in the glorious mess of turning sap to sugar.

YET, AS SWEETLY as the syrup trickled down his throat, it did little to salve his voice.

"I had known that my abilities would go down. My sense of timing, my sense of pitch, and my energy. But I didn't know it would go down so quickly," Pete Seeger reflected in 2006. "By 1985, when I was sixty-six, I had to face the fact that I could no longer sing 'Wimoweh,' and I could no longer sing a whole bunch of songs that had long, held notes. Instead of holding a steady note it came out 'eeeeee' with big quavers in it."

He and Toshi decided something had to be done. They visited a string of doctors. Some cultured his throat, others discussed surgery. Physical therapy didn't help. Seeger was given two rules by his voice doctors: first, at public gatherings, no talking before a concert; second, keep his head down when singing. One specialist isolated the problem. Besides singing too many times in the same day, and singing too loudly to drown out traffic on a picket line, Seeger's head-up style had abused his vocal chords. By singing with his face lifted to the sky, Adam's apple pointing straight ahead, over the years he had torqued and overstretched his vocal cords. It was hard to face, but he was going to have to give up solo performances. "My voice lasted longer than I'd thought," he consoled himself.

In a new song at the beginning of the century, "Arrange and Rearrange," he sang:

There's a time to laugh, but there's a time to weep
And a time to make a big change.
Wake up you bum,
The time is come to arrange and rearrange.

—

IF THAT LINE, "A time to laugh, but there's a time to weep" sounds familiar, it's probably because it's from "Turn! Turn! Turn! (To Everything There Is a Season)," a powerful melody whose lyrics Seeger chose from Ecclesiastes.

The song had been composed in 1959, during Seeger's peak songwriting years. One of his peaceful songs built of anger. His normally kind and patient music publisher, Howie Richmond, had written him, "Pete, can't you write another song like 'Goodnight Irene'? I can't sell or promote these protest songs."

"You better find another songwriter," Pete Seeger had replied tartly. "This is the only kind of song I know how to write."

Nevertheless he'd pulled out that pocket notebook and found verses jotted down the previous year. Verses by, as he put it, "a bearded fellow with sandals, a tough-minded man called Ecclesiasties who lived in Judea, three thousand years ago. I added one line ('A time of peace, I swear it's not too late'), omitted a few lines, and repeated the first two as a chorus (plus one new word repeated three times). Taped it. Mailed it in the morning."

His publisher was elated. "Wonderful; just what I hoped for."

To everything (turn, turn, turn)
There is a season (turn, turn, turn)
And a time for every purpose under heaven.

A time to be born, a time to die
A time to plant, a time to reap
A time to kill, a time to heal
A time to laugh, a time to weep.

A time to build up, a time to break down
A time to dance, a time to mourn.
A time to cast away stones
A time to gather stones together.

A time of war, a time of peace
A time of love, a time of hate
A time you may embrace
A time to refrain . . . from embracing.

A time to gain, a time to lose
A time to rend, a time to sew
A time of love, a time of hate
A time of peace . . . I swear, it's not too late.

When he published "Turn! Turn! Turn!" in his 1964 songbook, *The Bells of Rhymney*, he added a verse of Toshi's—a verse to be sung to children:

A time for dirt, a time for soap.
A time for tears, a time for hope.
A time for fall, a time for spring.
A time to hear the robin sing.

In the early 1960s, Roger McGuinn, a young Seeger fan, was forming a band and asked to record it. The Byrds' version of "Turn! Turn! Turn!" became an FM hit, Seeger's first widely played tune since the Weavers. Was this because the lyrics were unexceptionable, directly from the Bible?

"Myself, I was delighted by the version of The Byrds: all those electric guitars. Like clanging bells." A time to sing . . . and a time to be silent.

AFTER MUCH SEARCHING, Seeger decided that one solution to his declining voice lay with his grandchildren.

His oldest, Tao Rodriguez-Seeger, was born to his daughter Mika, the ceramacist once arrested in Mexico. Four days later Danny had a girl, Cassandra (Cassie) Seeger. Tinya's firstborn was a boy, Kitama, then a girl, Moraga. Then Mika adopted a girl, named after Pete's youngest half-sister, Penny. Of his five grandchildren only one became a musician, though all are involved with art, from ceramics to film. (And his nephew Nick has made two records.)

Though Seeger had largely missed out on fathering during his solo journeys of the 50s, he was determined that wasn't going to happen with his grandchildren. Mika and Tinya had made interracial marriages, like their parents. And so in the '80s and '90s the Seeger house was joyously filled with part-Hispanic, part-African American, part-Japanese American grandkids.

It was to Tao that Seeger turned as his voice weakened.

"I had to stop singing *this* song and stop singing *that* song and stop singing another song." Enough already. He asked Tao, with whom he'd sung informally, to go on stage with him, singing the high notes his voice could no longer reach. This began a shift in his performances, moving from performing to song leading, and then from song leading to directing choruses. Afterward, he'd almost always work with Tao or Arlo, or with backup singers, such as Jane Sapp or Kim and Reggie Harris. As African American performers, working with living oral traditions, they were impressed with how he taught people songs. "He knows when the song could derail. He has a very particular mind for process in working with people of color. He listens. He gets it," Reggie Harris said.

"Did I notice his vocal capacity decreasing?" Arlo Guthrie reflected. "Sure, but it didn't matter. It was always more important to Pete than anyone. I think at some point you just can't hit those high notes or you can't sing that long.

"Plus his memory: 'Did I already sing that verse?' or 'How does that song go?' All of these are real factors for somebody who had been the tinkerer he was. [As a performer] he was starting to feel as though it was getting tougher and tougher. He just applied that practical common sense to the situation that he did to everything else: 'I can't sing as well as I used to, but I can teach other people to sing together.'

"It's plan B. Nothing wrong with that."

Over a fifteen-year period, Arlo and Pete worked on a half-dozen albums: *Pete and Arlo Together* (1975), *Precious Friend* (1982), *More Together in Concert* (1984), *HARP* [Holly Near, Arlo, Ronnie Gilbert, and Pete]; (1985), *More Together Again* (1986). Over this span, the careful listener can hear a shift, from the soloist Seeger (since leaving the Weavers in 1958) to a song leader for whom voice and instruments seem to recede.

"There were certain moments in the songs where he was playing the banjo, he would really hammer out a few notes here and there," Arlo said. "Or stop playing and let people sing. He had this wide range to play with. He might have lost some of the middle ground, but the extreme ends are still there."

The Guthrie-Seeger concerts continued to be a success, whether on the summer playhouse circuit or in large halls such as Wolf Trap, near DC. "Here people were saying, 'Folk music is dead,' and Arlo and I were performing to the largest audiences of my life."

But not without some changes, Arlo remembers. "The first thing was to get Pete to use a monitor. That was the first big crisis. So that he could hear us and he could hear himself over us. Then the next phase was to get Pete to glue up some pick-ups on his banjo and guitar so that we could hear what he was playing. The next thing was to actually rehearse a couple of the songs for over five minutes. Pete has just gone along with this: kind of hesitant, but smiling.

"We'd fly to these different events, and I don't think we ever rehearsed anything," Arlo said. "It was all right before sound check or right after sound check and Pete would say, 'Oh, let me run this over, I'm going to sing this song tonight, this is how it goes.'"

For Arlo, the decade they performed regularly (1975–85) were great years. "I learned all kinds of little things—not making them necessarily sing along with *you*, but have you sing along with *them*. It seems like the same thing, and there are a lot of people that get up there and sing their songs and if the audience sings along, that's great. It's not something that's unique to folk; there's probably a dozen glam-rock singers who understand the same principle. When you get a couple hundred thousand kids out there waving lighters in the air—they're all in it together. How do you keep that, and have that feeling, and also sing a song that's more than in the key of Me?"

What Arlo ended up learning most was Seeger's timing: "You learn to anticipate what he's going to do so you can be a worthy accompanist, so you're not dragging the event down by your inability to keep up." Pete and Arlo and Tao would watch each other's lips to see where they were in a song.

Sometimes Tao would attempt to straighten out a song's rhythmic irregularities. They'd argue about that, grandpa and grandson, because Seeger had a very precise notion of where he wanted to slow down or add a grace note.

For about a dozen years, up until 2000, when he and friends formed their own band, The Mammals, Tao literally gave Pete a voice. "Tao is in a long tradition of people who are giving people who normally don't have a voice, not just a voice, but a song to sing," Arlo Guthrie said. "That's what Pete's been doing for his whole life. That's what my dad Woody was doing."

Tao was picking up the techniques and pacing, "not outrunning the audience, not getting too far behind either." With Arlo's daughter Sara Lee Guthrie and his son Abe Guthrie, another generation was taking the stage. "You pay attention to how to sing the song, how you play it, how you emphasize it, where you breathe, where you don't. All these little things audiences don't think about," Arlo said.

Seeger would point, nod, swing the guitar or banjo neck toward the audience when it was their turn to join in. They complied willingly, parents and grandparents introducing a new generation to Pete Seeger.

David O'Reilly is the author of "The Fathers We Choose," a lengthy and moving feature on Seeger for the *Philadelphia Inquirer.*

He's one of the hundreds of thousands who listened to Seeger's albums of children's music in elementary school, who played a few licks on the guitar or banjo during the folk musical revival. By the time they were of draft age, they might have heard "Bring 'Em Home" or "Waist Deep in the Big Muddy." They've been called "Pete's Children," ages fifty to seventy.

Freud writes of the "family romance," a domestic legend that, when it goes awry, sends individuals searching for alternative mothers and fathers. It was Seeger's fate to be implicated in many such searches.

O'Reilly's article hints at the role of Pete Seeger for this cohort: "a man who showed me a way to live at a time, and in ways, my own father could not." O'Reilly and his two brothers were shaped in the mysterious ways sons emulate and challenge their fathers. But entering adulthood, he wanted a new model. "I supposed I was merely stepping onto a quaint, old-fashioned sailboat, but in truth I was stepping into the moral universe of Pete Seeger, one more reminiscent of the utopian Shaker, Hudderite, and Oneida religious communities than of Marx and Lenin.

"He was essentially a private man," O'Reilly continued. "Someone who gave off more light than warmth. I understood this: a lot of people asked a lot of Pete."

David O'Reilly was with Pete Seeger on the *Clearwater* on September 11, 2001. That day Seeger had been scheduled to sing at a conference on music and politics at Wesleyan College. Instead, he went down to the waterfront, sorrowing over a friend who worked on the 102nd floor of the World Trade Center.

"We took out a group of kids, on one of the most beautiful days I'd spent on the *Clearwater*: blue sky, warm, and there was something profoundly serene," O'Reilly mused.

"Then someone came on board and said 'The World Trade Center's been bombed.' The Coast Guard told the *Clearwater* not to come down. The fourth-graders were scared—and Pete showed up."

—

PETE SEEGER WAS NOT a standard role model for boys growing up in the 1950s. He was not Buffalo Bob of *The Howdy Doody Show.* Not Charles Atlas, the fellow whose ads for exercise equipment appeared on the inside covers of comic books. Getting along in life has always meant compromises too grim for youth to consider. Instead, Seeger was uncompromising—and fun in a picking-and-singing, let's-sing-something-silly way.

For a fraction of a generation, Seeger was that father or uncle they hoped they'd have. There are perfectly respectable accountants, lawyers, dentists who live with a small terror that they'll open the newspaper one day and discover Pete Seeger has died, and a little bit of their own best hopes will have gone with him. These children played his music over and over, as kids will, until they could tell why Jimmy cracked corn and why Michael rowed the boat ashore.

"He was kind of like an uncle when I was young," Bob Reiser said. "A favorite uncle. Pete's coming meant like Uncle Joe is coming and he's going to sing to us and we're going to have a great time."

"It's scary," Jim Musselman said. "Musicians run from [this surrogate fatherhood] because they don't want the responsibility; that's what Dylan did. It's hard because you don't *want* people to be looking up to you."

One fifty-something mused, on pulling out an old Pete Seeger record, "The intervening years of much louder, more elaborate popular music, far from making Seeger seem quaint, actually make his sound miraculous."

Other listeners tired of Seeger's rustic image: "Sullenly I mumbled 'blue overalls,' 'disingenuous,' 'archaic aesthetic,'" wrote Jesse Lemisch in *The Nation*, complaining of Seeger's unwillingness to criticize the Soviet Union—a sprinkle in the coming storm of attacks from former fans on this issue.

—

SEEGER HAD DRIFTED OUT of the Communist Party early in 1950, after moving to Beacon, when he discovered only two or three members in his new area. His reexamination of the Party, however, really began in the mid-1950s, as documented in a poem he gave to one of his grandchildren with the note, "This is about the U.S. Communist party. Date March 1, 1958." In this, he characterizes his involvement in the Party as "a long love affair." "Now—well, let's just say we're mostly separated."

Could the CP revive itself? If so, he might again join, but "here I am a balding forty and could I ever be so ardent? (Some would say so 'blind'—they lie!)" He didn't regret "the books we wrote, the melodies we composed, lines written on the page of history." The poem ends with a line his father had written at the time of a personal tragedy: "A good thing that has happened cannot be made to unhappen."

Some will conclude that Seeger was a hypocrite. Here he was, nostalgic for the Soviet Union following Khrushchev's denunciation of Stalin and following the repression of Hungarian democracy. But which Communist Party had Seeger treasured? Not the "shreds of mind and body" he noted in 1958, but a vital, patriotic movement of the Popular Front thirties.

Seeger's *public* reexamination of the Soviet Union probably began in 1982, when he performed at a benefit concert for Solidarity, the Polish resistance movement. By the late 1980s, as the Soviet Union disintegrated, "I can't say I was very surprised," he reflected. "I felt Gorbachev's mistake was trying to change everything all at once. It's hard enough to change one at a time, but all at once was a traumatic thing. I'm really in favor of incremental change, otherwise it's like Judy Collins singing from the famous musical, *Marat/Sade*, 'We Want a Revolution Now! I don't want to wait until tomorrow; I want it today!' I'm convinced now that the lasting revolutions are those that take place over a period of time."

Perhaps the hundreds of interviews in which he was asked about his contemporary feelings about the Soviet Union weigh on him. In 1997, in the first edition of his musical autobiography, *Where Have All the Flowers Gone*, he wrote, "Today I'll apologize for a number of things, such as thinking that Stalin was simply a 'hard-driver' and not a supremely cruel misleader.

"I guess anyone who calls himself or herself a Christian should be prepared to apologize for the Inquisition, the burning of heretics by Protestants, the slaughter of Jews and Muslims by Crusaders. White people in the U.S.A. could consider apologizing for stealing land from Native Americans and for enslaving blacks . . . for putting Japanese-Americans in concentration camps—let's look ahead."

By 2000, Seeger's comments on the failure of Russian Communism became more pointed: "For many decades I felt that the mistake made over in Russia was Lenin's mistake. If it hadn't been Stalin, it would have been somebody else. It was a failure of Communists and Socialists to work together that enabled Hitler to take power, after all. They could have stopped him immediately but they were too busy fighting each other: 'We will lead the revolution!' 'No, WE will lead the revolution!'"

Or, in 2006, at another interview: "In 1919 Rosa Luxemburg wrote a letter, 'Comrade Lenin, I hear you have censorship of the press and you restrain the right of people to peaceably assemble. Don't you realize in a few years all the decisions in your country are going to be made by a few elite, and the masses will only be called in to dutifully applaud your decisions?' Is that a wonderful sentence! It's exactly what happened. I quote this to millions of people."

Surprisingly, Seeger and his right-wing critics actually agree. He sees the problem with Communism as systemic: Not the ideology of Marxism, but the structure for sharing power and wealth was wrong; the withering away of the organs of the state never took place. Now he advocated an E. F. Schumacher, small-is-beautiful approach. "Big things tend to attract power-hungry people. What makes me optimistic now is that there are not thousands but millions of little organizations springing up all over the place. They don't all agree with each other, but at least they agree it's better not to shoot each other."

THESE DAYS, PETE SEEGER is still asked if he's a Communist. "Yes," he answers, but with a proviso: "I am a Communist with a small 'c.' Like the Native Americans, who shared resources and took care of everyone in the tribe." Some will read this answer as disingenuous. Yet for anyone who remembers Seeger's early passion for Ernest Thompson Seton—his first ideology—this remark might seem consistent and full-circle. For the negative comments lobbed at Seeger accused him of inconsistency: that he was for peace and then suddenly for fighting Hitler once the Soviet Union was attacked; that he claimed to be a pacifist, but supported World War II and not the Vietnam War; that he was for democracy yet was willing to accept the Party's coercive demands for discipline.

Seeger acolytes who became anti-Communists and neoconservatives, such as Ron Radosh (author of a 2007 article, "Time for Pete Seeger to Repent"), find such contradictions galling—because by merging his music with his life Seeger presented himself as a man of his word, a dangerous promise by any entertainer. For performers stand up on a stage before us not as people but as entertainers: characters providing a service. No one expects the dry-cleaner to be involved in saving whales or the baker to serve Martin Luther King cookies. In the end, Seeger's contradictions are pretty much like our own. As Walt Whitman, nineteenth-century poet and patriot, wrote, "Do I contradict myself? Very well then, I contradict myself. (I am large, I contain multitudes.)"

By presenting his ideals to the public as he performed for them, Seeger raised the bar on himself. Newspaper accounts praise him for precisely this: for ardently recycling every scrap of waste, for driving a modest car and living in a modest home built with his own hands and his own lumber.

—

IS THERE A new generation listening to Pete Seeger? David O'Reilly's son Chris spent a week crewing on the *Clearwater.* He didn't like the hippie food, but he loved floating on the river in the dark, singing folk songs. Teenage Chris is the only one of his crowd to listen to folk music of the '60s.

"The appeal of Seeger's music is the melody; I just like that better than what's being done now. Then after listening to it more closely, I realized that the people singing these songs had something to say, they were trying to make a statement—not just that they're mad at the world, and they want to scream their way out of it."

Perhaps from Generations X, Y, or Next there will be a folk music boomlet, from children of the '90s and '00s who grow up listening to the folk music their parents heard at their age. They will not be uncritical of the tradition they inherit.

"My generation needs Seeger badly," said a twentysomething woman in 2007. "We've grown up on sterile, mass-produced tunes; it's cut the legs off music, for many bands in their twenties are apolitical and retro.

"But we also don't have much use for the self-satisfied baby boomers who grew up on Seeger: Despite all their protests, why aren't things better? The right-wingers are taking over environmentalism to win votes. You guys from the '60s made my generation cynical: What did you accomplish? Where was your staying power?"

By the time Pete Seeger turned seventy in 1989, his staying power was clear: He was meeting the grandchildren of people who'd heard him in the '30s, and he took being a grandfather seriously.

A friend of Seeger's, Oren Lyons, of the Onondaga tribe in upstate New York, once attended a World Economic Conference in Switzerland. There he met the CEOs of billion-dollar corporations. "I asked them," said Lyons, "if they realized that the way they were using up the world's resources, in a sense they were headed for a brick wall.

"They said to me: 'Yes, Mr. Lyons, of course we realize that, but you should realize that we have been put in our jobs to make as much money as we can for our stock holders. If we don't do that we're out of a job.'

"I asked, 'Are any of you grandfathers?' And a number of them readily said yes.

"I then asked them, 'When do you stop being a CEO and start being a grandfather?'"

Seeger loved to tell that story to his foster grandchildren at summer camps and progressive schools, and to those who formed the core of the New Left. "My guess is they're still around and doing good things in some corner of the world," he said. "A great many of them are already gone . . . and they've got their own jobs to do. They may still play my records—who knows?"

At the website peteseeger.net, one finds their words. "Please get me these words by Tuesday, because I have a report to give," one young woman asks. Others say, "I heard you back in 1942." Another site, mudcatcafe.com, has forty-nine different threads with nearly a thousand comments on Seeger: an electronic laying-on-of-hands via the Internet.

"That may be," Seeger said. "But I already can't answer the mail I get now. I had to write the webmaster, Jim Capaldi, 'Jim, please put on an extra line that people should not write me because I don't see the letters.'"

A MAJOR TASK for the last chapter in his life is shaping his legacy and finding a way to put down or pass along the burden of being Pete. In the midseventies a slavish film, *A Sword and a Stone*, had adulated him, to his disgust; a few years later Seeger had cooperated with an unauthorized biography. Later, he'd distanced himself from it, writing in *Sing Out!* that the book was about why he didn't brush his teeth every morning. He was done with documentation, he told people.

Throughout the '80s and '90s, however, filmmaker Jim Brown

(who'd helped Harold Leventhal produce the Weavers reunion film *Wasn't That a Time*) had followed Seeger with a movie camera. Three times Brown tried to mount a documentary; three times Pete and Toshi had withdrawn from the project, sometimes after Brown had received funding. He was patient. He went on to work on other films, such as *We Shall Overcome*, and a filmed concert tribute to Leventhal at the end of 2003. But he could not get permission to finish his documentary.

"Make your film after I'm gone," Seeger would say. "Publish that book or article after I'm dead." But at the beginning of the new century, he and Toshi decided to cooperate. Pete sat down with the biographer to review the work and comment. Toshi decided that she'd better be a consulting producer on the film, *Pete Seeger: The Power of Song*. (Toshi had been a frustrated filmmaker since their around-the-world tour in 1963, when they'd shot so much film and stills. She'd passed this cinematographic impulse to their son Dan, who worked as an editor.) By the end of the first decade of the 2000s, the Seegers' public reticence had begun to thaw. The Library of Congress acquired those films and showed them publicly at a sold-out Seeger Symposium in 2007. And for once, *Toshi* had the ovation.

PETE SEEGER WAS FEELING swamped by his public, according to Musselman. "People pour their hearts out to him—and they mean it. Pete just doesn't have the time to respond to everybody. He pulls out so many emotions in public. Of their childhood or social justice or that sense of hope. At times it's a burden."

Mark Moss noticed this when traveling to *Sing Out!* benefit concerts with Seeger.

"We'd be staying at a hotel, and people would come up to him in the lobby and the elevator—there was no barrier. It was 'Hey, you're that Seeger guy!' They would immediately start talking to him. Anybody in that kind of bubble—where everybody thinks you're famous and great and wonderful—you start to believe it.

There's a certain amount of that there for Pete. Even at the same time that he hates that. He's repulsed by the cult of personality.

"Unlike most of these other celebrities out there, who really start to buy into the 'I'm really cool, you do whatever I say,' Pete's really about, 'I'm going to be part of the garbage crew! I'm going to pick up the garbage.'"

IN THE TWENTY-FIRST CENTURY much of our art, popular and esoteric, is not complete when the listener/viewer/reader makes a purchase. There's a need for a direct connection to the artist in a world where letters are e-mails and concerts so expensive and so huge that the performer seems no bigger than an insect. This hunger for connection falls particularly hard on figures like Seeger, who still performs the ideals offered to a generation in its youth.

"I'm fairly good at relaxing," Seeger said in 2006, "but the pressure, it's not easy. There's too many letters, too many autographs, and it's no longer as much fun to be in a crowd because you get stopped all the time. I don't want to hurt people's feelings so I sign, but it leaves me without a day I might have enjoyed. When I go to a festival I have to limit the hours I'm there, because I'm just talking and talking. At the end of the day I have no energy left."

This vulnerability was accentuated as a string of awards arrived, starting in 1991. He flew to Havana to accept the Felix Varela medal, the highest honor awarded by the Cuban government. The New York Civil Liberties Union gave him a medal in 1994. Then Seeger, whom Bill Clinton called "an inconvenient artist" when they met onstage, received the National Medal of the Arts and the Kennedy Center Award (alongside Aretha Franklin). The televised awards show brought more offers. He was inducted into the Rock and Roll Hall of Fame in 1996.

"In Garrison, New York, 1994, Toshi and Pete were being honored," David Bernz remembered. "Toshi spoke first: 'Well you know, most people work five days a week, eight hours a day with two weeks vacation. Well, in my job I work twenty-four hours a day, seven days a week, fifty-two weeks a year with *no* vacation. I want to introduce my husband, Pete, you know, the guy who goes around the country singing for the eight-hour day!'" The audience just laughed.

"I foolishly accepted a lot of awards, and they have made it much more difficult for me, with all the publicity." As the new century opened, he stopped accepting awards the same way he stopped accepting payment for concerts.

"All this publicity. And I allowed myself to get in for it. Funny things happen. Paul Winter wanted me to record some songs I had never recorded, with the help of a chorus and very good sound engineers." The album, *Pete*, won Seeger his first Grammy. His laconic response to the recording industry's highest honor was in character: "There's some nice things in it, but my singing didn't carry the record, the chorus did."

He kept trying to give up the limelight for a quieter life. One of the Sloop Club founders sensed this. "Pete, could I paint a saying on your barn?"

"Yes. If I don't like it I can paint over it."

"They painted a picture of the *Clearwater* and mushrooms and flowers. Then these lines: 'I am done with great things and big success and I am for those tiny, invisible, molecular, moral forces that work from individual to individual, creeping through the crannies of the world like so many rootlets or like the capillary oozing of water. Yet which, if you give them time, will rend the hardest monuments of man's pride. William James.'"

When Seeger asked the fellow where he'd heard this quote, he said that he'd read it in some magazine. That it was folklore—passed along with variations—made it even more attractive to Seeger.

"I put it on my stationery. This is what's going to save the world," Seeger said. "It's too easy to say there's no hope for this community, let me go somewhere else. I mistrust the mobility of modern times. It's too easy to leave where you are, instead of sticking it out and making the place better.

"This is the same lesson of the American Revolution where King George's soldiers were defeated by stubborn farmers who refused to give up, and a few stubborn middle-class people and upper-class people, too. It's a lesson of Hitler's defeat. He couldn't get soldiers to win in the Stalingrad siege because they were tied up, trying to keep control of France and Italy and so on. It's a lesson of the Vietnam War. The Vietnamese people stubbornly, in the face of overwhelming odds, refusing to give up. And I think it's the lesson of the Green Guerillas [urban gardeners], the *Clearwater.* The world is going to be saved by people who fight for their homes."

Seeger huffed as he split a log. "A person my age should get out of breath once a day." Once, when Arlo was trying to persuade Seeger to drive up north to Massachusetts for a recording session, he told him, "Pete, I've got to get the wood in. There's a lot of it; so bring your own ax." He was there in a flash.

"Playing with Arlo's band was awfully loud," said Seeger, the author of "My Get Up and Go Has Got Up and Went." "My hearing started getting worse and worse. I now have to wear hearing aids when I perform, even while I'm talking. My eyes are going, I'm blurry when I'm trying to read things. So when people ask, 'Pete, how are you?' I say, 'From my shoulders on down, I'm about 60 or 70 percent here, but from my shoulders on up, 20 or 30 percent here.

"I'm having to learn how to say no. It's hard. I write, 'I'd love to come to sing for you but at the time I do not have the time. I've got some jobs I have to complete; I don't have forever to complete them.'" It's the octogenarian's complaint. In 2000, he even managed to lose his banjo.

"I needed to take a nap in the car and so I rearranged the banjo and guitar and clothing so I could put my seat way back. So I took the banjo out and put it on the roof. I woke up and drove off."

The story made the national news. A fellow in Chicago called and said he had it; Pete sent him six hundred dollars but never heard from him again. Eventually a house painter called to say he'd found it in a ditch. He returned it, unharmed. The incident reinforced his and Toshi's second thoughts about traveling far from home.

SO HE STOPPED touring with Arlo.

"That was Pete's decision," Arlo reflected. "I think Pete didn't want to be away from the Hudson River as much. I think it's just a practical response to getting older. It's harder and harder to travel. You have to carry all these instruments, you have to get to the plane on time and now, with all this security, it's easier to stay at home. Plus, I think he's earned the right at this point. He realized that *he's* earned the right; we all knew that forty years ago.

"He got to the point where he realized that if you're going to work on your garden, if you're going to get the wood in on time, if you're going to do all the things he wants to do, he has to make the time to do it. I think he just made that decision. I think it was the right one. I hope I'm smart enough to make it at some point. It's one thing singing about the average guy, it's another thing to enjoy *being* the average guy. (He was never average, but you know what I'm saying.) There's time to be the people you're singing about."

He has come full circle, starting out in Patterson and traveling around the world to Beacon, fifty miles away. For most of these years he followed the two paths of his childhood, his woodsy soul and his worldly duties. One led him to sketch, then become a musician; the other to journalism and community organizing. He tried to combine both paths in the *Clearwater*, not always successfully. Even after the *Clearwater* took GE to court over the PCBs and won one of the largest environmental penalties awarded, some old friends still scorned the project, asking, "How long will it take to get the last beer can out of the Hudson?" Probably never, but why not try? Clean water is destined to be the major resource battle of the twenty-first century.

In his late eighties, people ask Pete Seeger if he's discouraged, just as a few keep asking if he's a Communist. He has a half-dozen ways of saying no. The most common is the metaphor of the "teaspoons brigades," or he'll admit uncertainty about whether the world and humanity will continue. A third answer is brusque: "Do I get discouraged? Yes, every night around nine-thirty and then I call it a day and go to sleep. But there's always the next morning."

IN 2006 PETE SEEGER was reintroduced to the American public. The occasion was Bruce Springsteen's decision to put out his first-ever cover record, *The Seeger Sessions*, followed by two lengthy tours of Europe and the United States. In Paris, he sang Seeger's antiwar song "(If you love our boys) Bring 'Em Home." With this came a barrage of interviews, as if the national media had just waited for an excuse to rediscover Pete Seeger, and Springsteen provided one. In a one-week period in June, both *Billboard* and the Associated Press trekked to Beacon. A long and thoughtful profile appeared in the *New Yorker*. Staff writer Alec Wilkinson quotes a man driving along when he recognized a tall, slim figure in the rain—it was Pete Seeger.

> He's standing here all by himself and he's holding up a big piece of cardboard that clearly has something written on it. Cars and trucks are going by him. He's getting wet. He's holding the homemade sign above his head—he's very tall and his chin is raised the way he does when he sings—and he's turning the sign in a semicircle so that drivers can see it as they pass, and some people are honking and waving at him and some are giving him the finger.
>
> He didn't call the newspapers and say, "I'm Pete Seeger and here's what I'm going to do."

> He's just standing out there in the cold and the sleet like a scarecrow. I go a little bit down the road so that I can turn and come back, and when I get him in view, the solitary and elderly figure, I see that what's written on the sign is "Peace."

A touching anecdote, but Pete Seeger had kept a monthly vigil against the war in Iraq for years, rain or snow or sunshine. To him, the point is to ask people to consider the terrible situation the human race has drifted into, one in which war and genocide appear as rational, strategic choices.

"Nobody really knows what the world's going to bring. I tell people I think there's a fifty-fifty chance. Some think they're certain the world will end. We always find solutions, we're an intelligent race. Some of us are very pessimistic, saying, 'We could have been able to save it if we hadn't made such big mistakes.' But as long as I've got breath, I'll keep on doing what I can."

EPILOGUE

—

"Today I look upon myself as Old Grandpa. I'm very proud to see not dozens, not hundreds, but thousands of young people, and some middle-aged, and some elderly now, carrying on," Pete Seeger said recently.

"Now I'm trying to reach people who think they disagree with me strongly. They are devout churchgoers, for example, and they've heard that I'm not. I am not so eager to make people angry. I want to make them laugh and think."

BY 2008, THE STRANDS OF PETE SEEGER'S LIFE HAVE WOVEN together into a carpet of music and old acquaintance. A new generation hears his voice on his 150+ CDs and records. The songs he sang and arranged moved out into the world, notably via recordings of Bruce Cockburn and Bruce Springsteen. "I wasn't aware before of the vast library of music Pete helped create and collected," Springsteen told CNN. "'Mrs. McGrath' is an Irish antiwar song, but it's ripped right out of the headlines of today."

"I would have liked it if he'd included at least one of my more serious songs, like 'Walking Down Death Row,'" Seeger says. "The human race is on Death Row. We've *got* to straighten up and fly right."

"Big Muddy" has found its way into dictionaries of slang as a reference to the war in Vietnam—and now, perhaps, Iraq and Afghanistan. "If I Had a Hammer" floats up from elevators and hotel lobbies; musicians as different as Perry Como, Aretha Franklin, and Trini Lopez sang the song. "Where Have All the

Flowers Gone?" has been recorded by everybody from rockers to Marlene Dietrich. And, after many decades, Seeger finally learned "John Henry" to his satisfaction, pitching it in a key where he could get a bell-like ring. Once, asked his message, Seeger quoted two lines from the song:

And before you let that steam drill beat you down
Die with that hammer in your hand.

"We Shall Overcome" belongs to the world. Danes and Greenlanders together sing it by torchlight in independence parades. Hindus in India sing it as a patriotic song; Taiwanese sing it to resist a Chinese takeover. The song's world royalties are donated to the We Shall Overcome Fund.

Not only his songs persist. Seeger's life is today filled with ghosts—people from his past who reappear in the headlines or backstage. Bascom Lamar Lunsford, who first played the five-string for Seeger, told a mutual friend that Seeger could have gone a long way with his banjo playing if only he hadn't fooled around with unions.

In 2001, Ronnie Gilbert of the Weavers had once again caught the attention of the FBI, this time in connection with the Bureau's investigation of Women in Black, a group that stands in silent vigil against war and violence. She suspects that had the Weavers not been so popular, they'd have been under the blacklist's radar. Lee Hays kept writing and gardening avidly until his death in 1981. Fred Hellerman produces CDs and film scores. "Nowadays being blacklisted is a badge of honor," he told an interviewer. "Ring Lardner Jr. recently told me 'the Hollywood Ten has somehow become the Hollywood ten thousand.'"

Bernice Reagon formed and retired from a political-gospel group, Sweet Honey in the Rock. Irwin Silber left *Sing Out!* to edit the ultra-left *Guardian* and then *Line of March*. Seeger's family attenuated. When Charles Seeger died at age ninety-two, on his desk was a sheaf of papers for a talk at Yale the following week.

Harvey Matusow, who'd testified against the Weavers—and 240 others in 1952—received a four-year prison sentence after recanting his false testimony. He married eleven times, suggesting he was as true to his marriage vows as he was to Joe McCarthy. Behind him, he left a wake of ruined lives; his biography is titled *Deadly Farce*. Irving Younger, the attorney who prosecuted Pete for contempt of Congress, ran into the Seegers at a party. "I wasn't doing anything wrong," Younger volunteered. "I'd be willing to prosecute you again."

NO ONE WAS GOING to prosecute Seeger any longer; like an old song, he was parodied rather than banned. *National Lampoon* had Seeger revising "Frog Went A-Courtin'" into a class-conscious ballad.

Seeger's reputation has been not only transformed, it's been studied by scholars: "Resurrecting the Red" concludes, "He is not dangerous. . . . [He is] free to sing whatever he likes because this saintly old man can hardly be seriously reprising rebellion. His reputation traps him."

His shelf-full of medals and plaques—even from the government that once investigated him—is a mixed blessing. Just as at the ending of "Abiyoyo," when the town's elders couldn't remember why the boy and his father weren't heroes.

"I'm no longer a pariah," he admits, "except to a very few John Birchers.

"Why? Partly because the cold war is over; partly because I'm so frank about my politics. The way I put it now, I've blown my cover. My radical reputation saved me [from too much attention] most of my life, and now I've blown it. Telephone calls every day: Can I interview you? Can I interview you? The latest is *Der Spiegel* magazine in Germany and *The Guardian*." Because using the media's power, like music's power, is his forte, he answers questions, though he'd rather be ice-skating.

In the *New York Times*, a talented songwriter, Christine Lavin, reported an impromptu testimonial: "I put my purchases on the counter, gave my cashier my credit card, and she asked for ID. No ID.

"The woman in line behind me had obviously looked over my shoulder and saw that I was mailing something to Pete Seeger. Without any prompting, she said: 'Come on! Look—she's mailing something to Pete Seeger. He's the most honest guy in America. He cleaned up the Hudson River. I'm sure her credit card is good.'

" 'Who is Pete Seeger?' he asked.

"I explained that he'd written the song 'Turn! Turn! Turn!' and that he had helped popularize the South African hit 'Wimoweh' many years ago. I sang a bit of it.

"The manager smiled and said, 'Yes, I know the song.' To the cashier he said, 'Her credit card is good.' "

SEEGER'S FASCINATION WITH TELEVISION has dimmed. A quarter-century ago, he'd sought an ideal television program, "using inobtrusive video equipment to record music in homes around the world." When German television expressed an interest, he confessed he'd "even give up the *Clearwater* to work on 'Songwriters Against the World.' " It didn't pan out. Today the medium only depresses him; he calls it "the plug-in drug." He's not up to date technologically, but although he rarely uses a computer or e-mail, he has seventy-seven clips posted by others on YouTube.

POLITICAL SONGS STILL kindle his flame, but without the social movements that inspire them, they're less widely sung.

"Contemporary protest songs have purpose but not function," writes David Hadju. "Pete Seeger used to say 'It's not how good a song is that matters, it's how much good a song does.' What good is the most impassioned challenge to the Iraq war in the face of public indifference? The protest singers of the 1960s acted out of belief that a song could change the world. Their children have taken note that wars are raging in the same old way. It is 'Where Have All the Flowers Gone?' that seems different now."

"Music's modes of persuasion have also changed, from a strum-and-sing to stomp-and-shout," according to Jon Pareles, music critic of the *New York Times*. "Now a song with a political message is more likely to reach a broad public if that message is slipped into a rhythm-and-blues or hip-hop song."

Hip-hop and rap are today as controversial as Seeger's labor songs in the 1940s. Ice-T's "Cop Killa," for example, was withdrawn by Time Warner Records. This is political music for an audience Seeger and Guthrie never thought of singing to: Hispanic and African American youth in cities.

Just as political songs persist, so do their critics. In the fifties, Seeger was assailed by Billy Joe Hargis's Christian anti-Communists; today, it's Pastor Fletcher Brothers of "Freedom Village" who complains, "Pop music is the single most powerful tool with which Satan communicates." Or George W. Bush's State Department: "There are many people in the world who will take advantage of something like music or performing and use it for their own sinister purpose. . . . It's the new reality and the arts world has to adjust."

Such threats were not idle. In 2005, Mufid Abdulqader of Dallas was indicted for "conspiracy to fund [a] designated terrorist organization." "Defendant performed skits and songs which advocated the destruction of Israel," read one of the charges in his indictment.

In this never-ending War on Terrorism, there's no danger of music losing its edge. In 2006, British police stopped a plane and pulled a man off after a taxi driver complained the man was singing "Now war is declared . . . and battle come down." (The guy had "London Calling" by The Clash in his MP3 player.) Once released, he told London's *Daily Mirror*, "I like Led Zeppelin, too. I was singing that. I don't think there was any need to tell the police."

Today, the only time most Americans sing is in church or synagogue or at birthday parties. They're members of the audience, not singers; they'll try a lullaby, or the first few verses of the national anthem. But Pete Seeger had larger hopes for us.

Perhaps Seeger's ultimate message is not political, but cultural: he urged Americans to make their own home-grown music.

"The artist in ancient times inspired, entertained, educated his fellow citizens," Seeger wrote. "Modern artists have an additional responsibility—to encourage others to be artists. Why? Because technology is going to destroy the human soul unless we realize that each of us must in some way be a creator as well as a spectator or consumer." Make your own music, write your own books, he fairly shouted, if you would keep your soul.

What became of Seeger's audience? Its core in the '50s and '60s, alongside the baby boomers raised on Seeger's two-dozen records for children, was folkies and politicos, in '60s slang. For a brief time in American history, these two groups combined.

For folkies, this was "when we were good," as Robert Cantwell titled a book on the folk music revival: "Folk was the living prayer of a defunct [Popular Front] movement . . . gingerly holding the place of a Left in American culture."

For the politicos of the New Left, Seeger was just always there. Hold a rally; call Pete Seeger (and talk to Toshi). As Paul Cowan wrote, "Whenever I attended one of Seeger's concerts, I felt the belief, nearly religious, that there was a generation like myself preparing to help America break free."

To teenagers, Pete Seeger's appeal was a hunger for independence and self-reliance, the kind of man who builds a cabin in the woods, who follows the ideals of Ernest Thompson Seton, "with its basic analogy of physical fitness and cleanliness, to moral rigor and purity." These twin struggles, for social justice and moral rigor, defined him.

This coalescence of moral politics, group singing, and religion is deeply rooted in America's religious traditions, including Congregationalism and Methodism. It's there in the hymnals the Puritans brought.

In the twenty-first century, the appeal of Pete Seeger is akin to that of a nineteenth-century Romantic figure, the rustic innocent with the magic flute, who appeals to all those unable to live fully for the frantic quality of their lives.

At a dinner party in San Francisco, thirtysomethings were trying to pick ten living people they most admired; Seeger's name came up often. Pete Seeger's "children" have not vanished, though some think him as old-fashioned as Dickens's Christmas Past. "Pete Seeger—I remember singing those folk songs," said one woman, lounging in a hot tub in Colorado with a sweet, stoned smile. "That was before dope and the Rolling Stones and all that." Perhaps Seeger has known, like the farmer who toiled on difficult soil, that most of his seeds will die, but the ones growing to maturity will seem the sweeter for that struggle. And perhaps he has been awaiting not his "children," but his "grandchildren" before evaluating the fruit of his labors. Maybe this is what *Rolling Stone* called, in its 2007 "hot" list, the "YouTube Folk Revival": people who aren't performers strumming in living rooms, and sharing music the only way they know by uploading files.

In the '60s, when a generation was feeling good about themselves because they'd figured out those chord changes and let their hair and fingernails grow, an extraordinary confluence emerged: teenage idealism and the noncommerciality of traditional music, which anybody could sing or record without asking permission. The obstacles of adulthood and of sustaining political opposition appeared to this generation late: "The New Left took to heart those lessons that in the short-run allowed them to grow spectacularly; but not the lessons that in the long-run might have allowed it to survive fruitfully," historian Todd Gitlin wrote.

Today that core audience comes back to hear another chorus of the ancient song about a world without war and a planet whose people are trying hard not to damage it further. They're seeking

Hope and think this singer might remember something they don't. The old songs melt hearts hardened by the marketplace, the courts, or by a life in retail selling goods people don't really need.

And not all of the campers are happy ones. Ron Radosh (who did attend a camp where Seeger sang) went from being Seeger's banjo student and thinking of him as "the man who inspired virtually everyone—our Elvis Presley," to thinking of him as "the Karl Marx of the teenagers."

In his autobiography, *Commies*, Radosh replays the classic criticisms of Seeger: for peace songs after the Nazi-Soviet pact; for singing about happy Jewish farmers amid Russia's anti-Semitism; for not denouncing misdeeds in Cuba and other Communist governments long ago. Then in 2007, to his surprise, Pete sent him a new song, "Big Joe Blues": "He had a chance to make a brand new start for the human race, instead he set it back right in the same nasty place." Seeger wrote Radosh, "I think you're right—I should have asked to see the Gulags in the USSR."

"You want to criticize Seeger for not demonizing Stalin?" novelist John Nichols asked. "Get in line!"

Today anti-Stalinists tracking Seeger (and others who took too long to repent earlier beliefs) have a new battle cry, "In Denial," the title of a book about radical historians, whose authors assert, "The number of apologists for the former Soviet Union and its mass murders dwarfs the handful of aberrant pro-Nazi academics in the U.S."

But right-wing critics are arguing over a corpse. The Left culture they attack, with its Socialist summer camps and progressive schools, has largely vanished (and with it, its minstrels). What's left are dissertations and nostalgia.

And lessons learned. Instead of hate mail on peteseeger.net, the visitor finds adults still connected: "Thanks for teaching, by example, how to fight darkness with a song." "I could not have thought that what entered my ears went to my soul, till I heard your music."

Mudcatcafe.com lists forty-nine threads for comments on

Seeger, everything from "Pete Seeger's last concert" (175 posts) to his use of a pseudonym, sixty-five years ago.

"It all ends in forgetting, whatever we wish," one contributed. "Pete's done more than most to ensure and justify remembrance, and to his credit, seems never to care about any of that."

Former fans joked about his optimism, so out of fashion today. Still others shook their heads and sighed when Seeger, in later years, missed a verse or a beat; he wasn't the musician they remembered him to be.

Indeed he was not. He had lost some dexterity—and changed his musical focus. Seeger simplified his art to the point of being almost minimalist: Instead of playing chords, he sounded selected notes to remind the audience of the melody as they sang, a twang on the guitar instead of a loud strum. He focused attention back on the audience and withdrew from the music until only the skeleton of the song remained, alongside a transparency in which he and the song and the audience connected.

His music has a way of making people feel more musical. Audiences either join in the music or sit silently, impressed; Seeger prefers the former. In *Rolling Stone*, Gene Marine summed this up well: "Many performers can turn on an audience as well as Pete can. What they can't do is turn on *any* audience the way Pete can. . . . In Moscow, Pete had 10,000 people who didn't speak English singing four-part harmony to 'Michael Row Your Boat Ashore.' I doubt whether Barbra Streisand and Mick Jagger together could do that."

As Bob Dylan reflected, "Pete Seeger makes an orchestration out of a simple song and the whole audience sings it . . . even the ones who had *no* intention of doing it."

ONE REASON FOR this success was the way his life corresponded to his songs; as Colman McCarthy wrote in the *Washington Post*, he wouldn't have the same magic "were he a flashier fellow who would get out of his workshirts when he gets onstage or were he a singer who wouldn't clear his throat for less than $10,000 a performance." Or as Jimmy Collier put it, "He's one of the few performers who has to live his songs. Other people sing nice songs, but you don't expect them to live that way. Somehow Peter creates the image that if he sings a song about turning the other cheek, that's the way he is."

But this integration of art and life had a price. The pressure of public scrutiny was enormous. Instead of having a refuge in his art, Pete Seeger has wondered if he couldn't have led a happier life had he not been in show business. If he could have been a writer and hidden behind a nom de plume, say, Papa Banjo or Uncle Zeke. "Then I could be Pete Seeger/Uncle Zeke," he said. "The posters would say Uncle Zeke, and everybody would know Uncle Zeke is Pete Seeger; still, the posters wouldn't say Pete Seeger."

SINGING ON HIS TERRACE by the river or hauling trash to the dump, Pete Seeger has cultivated his own garden, as Voltaire advised. His life flowed from one cause to another, threading through the city and the woods. Like his golden river, his music joined upstaters and downstaters, city folk and farmers. "I feel like the revival preacher who led a wild youth," he joked, reflecting on how, after traveling the world, he could sit contentedly around the stove at the Beacon Sloop Club, telling stories and picking on his banjo.

It has been a long time since Pete Seeger stepped out from behind the Vagabond Puppeteers' curtain to play his banjo in public. He never succeeded in persuading the world to take songs as seriously as he did—not the Communist Party, who considered music as icing on a determinist cake; not the FBI, who heard only plots in his music. Nevertheless, he dragged his banjo into battle in Peekskill and Mississippi, into Henry Wallace's campaign and HUAC's courtroom, onto prime-time TV during the war in Vietnam—and his music helped win a few battles.

Two qualities protected him from his attackers: hope and endurance. With enough of these, people can move mountains. Perhaps he oversimplified his life when he wrote, "All you need to be a modern Johnny Appleseed is a guitar and some sticktoitiveness." But that was where Seeger started, at age sixteen.

IN THE TWENTY-FIRST CENTURY, the old contradictions stand out more clearly than ever. Here was a man who contributed his art to every social movement of his time, even when activists dismissed his work; who thought himself a patriot despite a thousand attacks for subversion; who set out to promote union singing and ended up with unison singing, where each voice adds to the whole. Songs were Seeger's gifts, and many outlasted their recipients, as fine gifts do. It might be said of him what conductor Michael Tilson Thomas said of Aaron Copland: "His great insight is that he could rouse and unite people not by scaring them, or making them angry, but by helping them to find a sense of ownership and pride in a mythical heritage that they, as Americans, all shared."

Future generations will judge the *Clearwater*'s importance in restoring the earth's environment—and, ironically, in raising property values and improving train service along the Hudson.

"We need people who still believe in what we once thought we were certain of," John Leonard wrote of Seeger in the *New York Times*. "Even the fish in the sea and the birds in the air would thank him if they knew," wrote Mike Cooney in *Sing Out!* "He is our music teacher. Any of us who were so carefully taught to hate music in school then learned to appreciate and understand what it is for with Pete Seeger. He is one of the greatest of American patriots."

Patriots and nationalists from the Grimm brothers to Mao Tsetung have used folklore and folk songs to bolster their cause. The most lasting contribution of Pete Seeger may come from his musical populism. His was not the first make-America-musical movement, but it was the most nonelitist. He was, it will be remembered, a great believer in the moral, magical powers of song.

"He could create songs with messages that penetrated people's minds in a lyrical way, even sort of mythical way," David O'Reilly suggested. "So he was doing something more than, maybe, Judy Collins or people of that ilk. Pete has a Daniel or Jeremiah view of the world, hammering out a warning. He was a prophet and a scold who could sing and write songs. Not very many people carry that load on their shoulders the way Pete Seeger does. And I think he feels if he ever slows down, if he doesn't keep doing it, he's not going to get there. We're not going to. So he's going to keep on doing it."

"I think he's aware that his time left is finite. I think he's concerned that certain things might not get done within his lifetime," filmmaker Jim Brown reflects. One of these was Brown's film, *Pete Seeger: The Power of Song*. "A terrific, multi-layered portrait," according to the paper that once headlined "Weavers Deny Commie Link," *Variety*.

"I think he will be remembered for one of the extraordinary examples of cultural workers who struggle across issues," Bernice Reagon said. "He's one of the few people who was with us in the sixties who talked about the thirties. And the level of pain he went through at different stages: He didn't always hold a safe position, and so could smoothly move from one to the other. I felt like in most of these situations he took stances that really put him on some kind of line. And stood on it."

"Songs won't save the planet," Seeger once wrote. "But then, neither will books or speeches. . . . Songs are sneaky things. They can slip across borders. Proliferate in prisons. Penetrate hard shells." Seeger also used to paraphrase an admonition of Plato: "Watch music. It's an important art form. Rulers should be careful about what songs are allowed to be sung." He believed these teachings. All his life he labored under the impression that the right song at the right time could work wonders. "If rulers really knew how important songs can be," he once said, looking back on his life, "they would probably have done something to Woody Guthrie and me and other people long ago."

ONCE, SOON AFTER SEEGER had been sentenced to a year in jail, he told an audience in Providence his thoughts on why humans sing: "Some people sing because they're so happy they just can't stop. Some sing to keep their spirits from going five miles below Hell. And some sing just to keep their courage up." Then Seeger said he wanted to sing them a hymn "made up years ago when people were getting thrown in jail for their beliefs." The lyrics summed up his life as well as any could:

My life flows on in endless song,
Above earth's lamentation.
I hear the real, though far-off hymn,
That hails a new creation.
Through all the tumult and the strife
I hear that music ringing
It sounds an echo in my soul.
How can I keep from singing?

What though the tempest round me roars,
I know the truth, it liveth.
What though the darkness round me close,
Songs in the night it giveth.
No storm can shake my inmost calm
While to that rock I'm clinging.
Since love is lord of Heaven and earth,
How can I keep from singing?

When tyrants tremble, sick with fear
And hear their death knells ringing;

When friends rejoice both far and near,
How can I keep from singing?
In prison cell and dungeon vile
Our thoughts to them are winging.
When friends by shame are undefiled,
How can I keep from singing?

ACKNOWLEDGMENTS

—

BOOKS ARE COOPERATIVE UNDERTAKINGS, AS WRITERS MUST often point out in thanks. My first debt is to the people I spoke and corresponded with, including Pete Seeger's associates, relatives, and friends. A hundred or so allowed their interviews to be tape-recorded, and many more contributed guidance and materials. (Interview credits are included in the notes.)

I particularly thank the musicians for their patience with an untrained strummer: Oscar Brand, Guy Carawan, Norman Cazden, John Cohen, Jimmy Collier, Judy Collins, Mike Cooney, Sis Cunningham, Barbara Dane, Rambling Jack Elliot, Ronnie Gilbert, Arlo Guthrie, Bess Lomax Hawes, Lee Hays, Fred Hellerman, Wally Hille, Si Kahn, Reverend Frederick Douglass Kirkpatrick, John McCutcheon, Country Joe McDonald, Don McLean, Holly Near, Bernice Reagon, Malvina Reynolds, Earl Robinson, Charles, Peter, Mike, and Peggy Seeger, and Mary Travers.

I thank Harold Leventhal for his cooperation; Marjorie and Nora Guthrie for helping me explore the Woody Guthrie Archives in New York City; Chelsea Hoffman, for helping track down pictures, and Howie Richmond and his associates at TRO for their patient assistance in tracking down copyrights. And thanks to Toshi, without whom Seeger's "sun would not shine and the stars not turn."

I thank the researchers whose insights and discussions have been invaluable: Richard Reuss, Archie Green, Ron Cohen, Norman Studer, Robert Rosenstone, Ron Loewinsohn, Alan Dundes, Jon Schneer, and Willa K. Baum. Any errors or omissions are my responsibility and not the fault of these thoughtful, generous advisers.

I thank those who volunteered their comments on the manuscript, particularly Angus Cameron, Steve Mayer, John Berger, Nancy Guinn, Kim and Reggie Harris, and my editor at Villard, Ryan Doherty. I owe a special debt to Ellie Shapiro and those who helped in the research: Abbey Asher, Molly Beer, Ellen Campbell, Jack Liederman, Bobbie Raymond, Whitney Brown, Felicia Karas, and Deena Nez. My thanks to the photographers for their work; to the typists, typesetters, printers, graphic artists, sales staff, booksellers, and all who labor anonymously to bring the public its reading matter. To my agent, Loretta Barrett, and her associates Gabriel Davis and Nick Mullendore, I'm truly grateful. The work of so many people goes into a book, yet only the author has a byline.

Finally I thank my community of old and new friends and particularly my parents and Nina Wallerstein—my doctor and companion in the book's dark hours.

David King Dunaway
Albuquerque, New Mexico
December 2007

NOTES

The major sources for this work are a set of 110 interviews conducted by the author from 1976 to 1982 (now housed at the American Folklife Center, Library of Congress), and twenty conducted in 2006–2007; the writings and recordings of Pete Seeger (published and unpublished); and the articles and books listed in the bibliography that follows these notes. At this writing, no collection of papers or letters of Pete Seeger exists, other than those compiled by the Seegers in their home office in Beacon, New York (which the author reviewed). Harold Leventhal, Seeger's manager, also maintained scrapbooks and files, which he graciously opened to me. The author conducted ten oral-historical interviews with Pete Seeger over the period of April 1976 to August 1978, and six more, from July 2000 to September 2006, yielding approximately 1,200 pages of transcript. Also valuable were Seeger's collection of journals and unpublished notebooks, amounting to another 1,000 pages, and the 1,600 documents released under a Freedom of Information Act suit, *Dunaway v. Kelley et al.*, U.S. District Court, San Francisco, over the singing groups with which Seeger was affiliated. In 2000, Seeger and the author reviewed the manuscript of the first edition, referred to here as "manuscript comments."

D.K.D.

The numbers to the left of each citation refer to the page numbers of text on which the relevant passages appear. Each passage is identified by its key words. Unless otherwise identified, all letters are unpublished. In a very few cases—fewer than a half-dozen—interviewees furnished information with the request of confidentiality. Names of interviewees are listed in the order used in chapters; when directly quoted, sources are listed by name and interview date in specific notes. Titles included in the bibliography have shortened citations.

CHAPTER 1: HOLD THE LINE

Author's interviews with Pete Seeger, April 15, 1976, March 6, 1977, May 23, 2006; Bess Lomax Hawes, August 28, 1977; Mario Cassetta, September 26, 1976; Howard Fast, January 15, 1977; and Ronnie Gilbert, January 14, 1977, December 21, 2006.

page/reference

5 *The preconcert parade:* See Fariello, *Red Scare,* pp. 74–80.

6 "*We'll finish Hitler's job!*": Howard Fast, *Peekskill USA* (New York: Civil Rights Conference, 1951).

8 *The special agent in charge:* Documents released after a 1976 request under the Freedom of Information Act and a subsequent suit, *Dunaway v. Kelley et al.,* U.S. District Court, San Francisco.

8 *"If the police:* Quoted in Richard Reuss, "The Peekskill Riots: Domestic Cold War in Action," unpublished seminar paper, 1962.

9 *"Our objective was:* Clipping in the Peekskill Public Library collection.

9 *The day before:* Letter dated September 3, 1949, from the Ku Klux Klan to People's Artists, in the possession of Pete Seeger.

10 *"There'll be no problem:* Pete Seeger, manuscript comments, 2000.

10 *"Don't be naïve,":* Pete Seeger, May 23, 2006.

12 *Up ahead a state trooper:* These two incidents reported in *Eyewitness: Peekskill USA* (New York: Civil Rights Conference, 1951) section 5, p. 2. T. C. Boyle fictionalized this scene in *World's End,* pp. 80–97, with Pete Seeger called "Will Connell."

15 *"Hold the Line.":* As recorded by Pete Seeger on *Gazette, Vol. 2,* Folkways FN 2502.

15 *Which line:* Richard Reuss to author, January 16, 1980.

CHAPTER 2: WASN'T THAT A TIME

Author's interviews with Charles Seeger III, October 10, 1977; John Seeger, August 29, 1977; Pete Seeger, April 15, July 19, October 10, 1976, August 8, 1978; and Charles Seeger, April 6, 7, 8, 1976. Information on Charles Seeger's background also comes from his *Reminiscences of an American Musicologist*, a memoir in the UCLA Oral History Office, 1972, and from Pete Seeger's family papers.

page/reference

17 "*enormously Christian:* Pete Seeger, 1961 concert in San Francisco, broadcast over KPFA-FM, Berkeley, California.

18 "*The nerve:* Pete Seeger, August 8, 1978.

20 "*You don't live:* Charles Seeger, *Reminiscences of an American Musicologist*, p. 114.

20 *She communicated:* Charles Seeger III, October 10, 1977.

21 "*We talked:* Charles Seeger, April 7, 1976, p. 115.

21 "*Deeply shocked:* Pete Seeger, "Charles Seeger: A Man of Music," *Sing Out!*, May 1979.

23 "*of mixing my bourgeois:* Charles Seeger, *Reminiscences*, p. 130.

23 *To escape:* Charles Seeger, *Reminiscences*, pp. 134–35.

25 *Thin, effusively idealistic:* William Archer, "Introduction," *Poems by Alan Seeger* (New York: Scribner's, 1917).

26 *In one camp:* *Reminiscences*, p. 136. A contemporary of Seeger's, Harold Story, tells a similar experience in a memoir in the UCLA Oral History Office, 1967, pp. 280–84.

CHAPTER 3: ABIYOYO

Author's interviews with Charles Seeger, April 6, 7, 8, 1976; Charles Seeger III, April 6, 1976; Pete Seeger, April 15, October 6, 1976; Don McLean, November 10, 1976; Bob Claiborne, December 13, 1977; George Draper, September 22, 1976; John Seeger, August 9, 1977; Dan North,

May 23, 1977; Bill Leonard, December 9, 1977; Dr. David Boyden, July 14, 1976; Bess Lomax Hawes, August 28, 1977.

page/reference

28 *Pete Seeger was born:* Samuel Eliot Morrison, *The Oxford History of the American People*, vol. 3 (New York: NAL, 1972), p. 2.

28 *Charles hit on:* Charles Seeger, April 6, 1976.

30 *"She wasn't enthusiastic:* Pete Seeger, manuscript comments, 2000.

30 *The failure at Pinehurst:* Charles Seeger, April 6, 1976.

31 *his brothers and father slept:* Charles Seeger III, October 10, 1977; Pete Seeger, October 6, 1976; Charles Seeger, April 6, 1976.

32 *"We're having such:* Pete Seeger, manuscript comments, 2000.

32 *Peter's musical education:* Charles Seeger III, October 10, 1976.

33 *"Charles was no longer tied:* John Seeger, August 27, 1977.

33 *Years later, Seeger made up:* The original "Abiyoyo" melody and story as Seeger learned it is on *Bantu Choral Folk Songs*, Folkways FW 6912; the story appeared in *African Folksongs*, J. N. Maselina and H. C. N. Williams, editors (Cape Town, South Africa: St. Mathews College, 1947). It's published as *Abiyoyo* (New York: Macmillan, 1985).

33 *A close friend:* Don McLean, November 10, 1976.

34 *Ernest Thompson Seton:* Pete Seeger, October 6, 1976: Ernest Thompson Seton, *Two Little Savages* (New York: Doubleday, Page, & Co., 1903).

35 *Another friend held:* Bob Claiborne, December 13, 1977; Pete Seeger, October 6, 1976.

36 *He had arranged to meet:* Pete Seeger, October 6, 1976.

36 "*his education:* *The Education of Henry Adams* (Boston: Houghton Mifflin, 1918), p. 26.

40 *Peter didn't understand:* This evening is described in Charles Seeger's obituary by Archie Green, *Journal of American Folklore*, October 1979, and by Charles Seeger, April 7, 1976.

42 *"Please, mother:* Correspondence reported by Toshi Seeger, October 6, 1976.

42 *"I liked rhythmic music.:* Pete Seeger, October 6, 1976.

44 *unfriendly witnesses:* Frank Donner, *The Un-Americans* (New York: Ballantine, 1961).

45 *"But, Peter,":* Pete Seeger, July 19, 1976; letters from Adrian and Arthur Kantrowitz to author confirm this in part.

45 *"a lack of political intransigence.":* Irving Howe and Louis Coser, *The American Communist Party*, 2nd edition (New York: Praeger, 1962), p. 278. Praeger was a publisher secretly affiliated by the CIA.

45 *"I guess the Communists mean it.":* Howe and Coser, *The American Communist Party*, p. 280, criticized the belief "in some ultimate reality that the Communists alone had been able to penetrate."

49 *"Well, father,:* Charles Seeger, April 6, 1976. Had Seeger's father been involved with radical groups less enthusiastic about New Deal folklore—the Trotskyists, for example—Seeger might never have developed an interest in American folk music.

50 *In England:* Maud Karpeles, *Cecil Sharp: His Life and Works* (Chicago: University of Chicago Press, 1967), p. 25. Virtually every article written on Pete Seeger mistakenly places his visit in 1935; the sequence of festivals that summer and Charles's reports to the Resettlement Administration date the summer Seeger discovered the five-string banjo to 1936.

50 *"Lunsford's style—:* Michael Cooney, self-interview, May 11 and June 21, 1978.

51 *Buell Kazee,:* Seeger learned the banjo from recordings, not oral (from the mouths of others) but aural (by listening) transmission. Folkways Records recorded and reissued many of Seeger's inspirations, among them Pete Steele (FS 3828), Dock Boggs (FH 5458, FA 2351), and Uncle Dave Macon (RF 51). Bascom Lamar Lunsford is on Rounder Records 0065. Additional sources are Bill Malone, *Country Music, U.S.A.* (Austin: AFS University of Texas Press, 1968). A partial list of Seeger's musical sources is found in *The Incompleat Folksinger* and *Where Have All the Flowers Gone*, 2nd edition, 2008.

52 *the thunder of the stadium:* Robert Rosenstone, *Romantic Revolutionary* (New York: Knopf, 1975), p. 48.

53 *John Reed:* Rosenstone, *Romantic Revolutionary.*

54 *'They're obviously tortured:* Pete Seeger, November 19, 2006.

55 *"It's impossible to explain:* Pete Seeger, October 6, 1976.

CHAPTER 4: 66 HIGHWAY BLUES

Author's interviews with Charles Seeger, April 6, 1976; Pete Seeger, April 16, 1976, March 6, 9, 10, 1977, August 8, 1978, July 26, 2000; Jerry Oberwager, April 3, 1977; Gordon Friesen, April 14, 1976; Bess Lomax Hawes, May 6, 1977; Lee Hays, May 25, 1977; Mike Seeger, December 7, 1977; Mrs. Joe Gelders, December 8, 1979.

page/reference

57 *A small crowd gathered:* Information on Seeger's New York life comes from his journals and interviews with John Seeger, August 27, 1977, and Charles Seeger III, October 10, 1977.

59 *Huddie Ledbetter:* Biographies of Huddie Ledbetter include *The Midnight Special* by Richard Garvin and Edmond Addeo (New York: Bernard Geis Associates, 1971), a "biographical novel." The Lomaxes' book, *Negro Folk Songs as Sung by Leadbelly* (New York: Macmillan, 1936), was partially repudiated by Ledbetter. See also Frederic Ramsey Jr., "Leadbelly, A Great Long Time," *Sing Out!*, January 1965, a chapter of Seeger's *Incompleat Folksinger;* Kip Lornell and Charles Wolf, *The Life and Legend of Leadbelly* (New York: Harper, 1992).

60 *"Huddie was not:* Pete Seeger, manuscript comments, 2000.

61 *"Well, I play the banjo,":* Gordon Friesen, April 14, 1976, p. 26.

61 *"Pete had a single-mindedness:* Mary Jimenez, letter to the author, November 30, 1979.

62 *He fumed:* Jerry Oberwager, April 3, 1977. Information on the Puppeteers comes from "The Vagabond Puppeteers," a memo Pete Seeger wrote on February 6, 1940 (seventeen pages), and Warren Gardner (who wrote about the Puppeteers for the Federated Press Syndicate), on March 1, 1979.

64 *"Alan was only:* Pete Seeger, manuscript comments, 2000.

67 *"I was a bust,":* Bess Lomax Hawes, May 6, 1977.

69 *"Go back to that night:* David De Turk and A. Poulin, editors, *The American Folk Scene* (New York: Dell, 1967), p. 214.

69 *"Pete, you want to come West:* Cray, *Woody Guthrie,* p. 185.

70 *"Ya got me plumb on fire,":* Woody Guthrie, *Seeds of Man* (New York: Dutton, 1976), p. 100.

71 *The countergirl avoided them:* "Low Levee Cafe," manuscript in the Woody Guthrie Archives in New York, dated May 28, 1947.

72 *"Now Pete thinks:* Lee Hays, May 25, 1977. Hays probably included Seeger's later performances with the Weavers in this assessment.

75 *"Aw, he just stole:* Pete Seeger epigraph, *The Incompleat Folksinger.*

75 *Seeger looked to Guthrie:* Lee Hays, May 25, 1977.

76 *"Grass Roots:* Charles Seeger, "Grassroots for American Composers."

76 *As one folklorist:* Lawless, *Folksingers and Folksongs in America,* p. 211.

78 *"too American":* Waldemar Hille, September 23, 1976.

79 *"An old man came:* "Pete and His Banjo Meet Some Fine Mountain Folks," Birmingham *Southern News Almanac,* 1940 (undated).

80 *"There is something too slow:* Woody Guthrie, *Born to Win* (New York: Macmillan, 1965), p. 29. When Guthrie wrote this, he was himself halfway through the long novel eventually published as *Seeds of Man.*

81 *"We had a cow:* Quoted in Willens, *Lonesome Traveler,* p. 122.

CHAPTER 5: TALKING UNION

Author's interviews with Pete Seeger, March 9, 10, December 14, 1977, August 8, 1978; Lee Hays, May 25, 1977; Mill Lampell, October 29, 1979; Gordon Friesen, April 14, 1976; Bess Lomax Hawes, May 6, 1977; Earl Robinson, March 18, 1976; Dorothy Millstone, December 29, 1977; Irene Paull, September 7, 1976; Peggy Seeger, August 29, 1977.

page/reference

84 *'I like Churchill!':* Pete Seeger, interview with Richard Reuss, April 9, 1968.

87 *"My contribution was:* Pete Seeger to Mill Lampell, October 1, 1987, p. 18.

87 *"When Woody and I:* Lee Hays, May 25, 1977.

87 *"Talking Union":* In *Talking Union,* the Almanac Singers, Folkways Records, FA 5285. The original version includes the phrase "God-damned Reds," later deleted.

88 *"Talking Management Blues":* *Bosses Songbook,* Richard Ellington, Dave Van Ronk, and Roy Berkeley, eds., 2nd edition (New York: Self-published, 1959).

88 *His zeal for unions:* This proved too much for his college roommate, Holland Willard, who chided him, "Pete, I think I'll go into labor unions—that's where the real power's going to be in this country." Pete Seeger, March 9, 1977.

89 *"Even at that early age:* Gordon Friesen, April 14, 1976.

89 *"the original of the fresh:* Cantwell, *When We Were Good,* p. 255.

89 *"Pete was superb:* Earl Robinson, March 18, 1976.

89 *"Inspired by the Anonymous movement":* By its nature, this group was not well-known. See Richard and Joanne Reuss, *American Folklore and Left-Wing Politics: 1927–1957* (Lanham, MD: Scarecrow Press, 2000).

89 *newspaper writers spotlighted:* *New Masses,* May 27, 1941; *Time,* September 15, 1941.

90 *"Lanky Pete Bowers:* The group followed Party procedure by taking pseudonyms. "Butch Hawes said he'd be 'Joe Bowers' [after a folk song.] I said, I'll be 'Pete Bowers,'" Manuscript comments, 2000.

90 *"Anyone could write:* Quoted in Tony Palmer, *All You Need Is Love* (New York: Penguin, 1977), p. 107.

91 *"There were those who said,:* Frank Donner, *The Un-Americans* (New York: Cameron Associates, 1957).

91 *"I scratched my head:* Pete Seeger to Mill Lampell, October 1, 1987, p. 4.

93 *'On Account of That New Situation':* Bess Lomax Hawes, May 6, 1977. Prior to World War I, many Leftists made an equally abrupt switch to support the government's war effort.

94 *These were one of the few sessions:* There are, curiously enough, few songs released on which Guthrie and Seeger play together. Either

because both singers were rarely in the same place for long or because, with Guthrie's disease developing in the late forties, they were rarely at equal levels of instrumental skill. See "The Soil and the Sea," "Dear Mr. President," and "Folksay," vols. I–V in the discography.

95 *"The FBI is worried:* FBI documents released under a Freedom of Information Act suit, *Dunaway v. Kelley et al.*, 1975–80.

95 *One host described the pair:* Esther McCoy, *Los Angeles Times*, March 27, 1977.

99 *"That was when the Communist Party:* Pete Seeger, manuscript comments, 2000.

100 *Seeger loved the echoey:* Klein, *Woody Guthrie.*

101 *"Bosses have hired:* Quoted in *People's World*, October 28, 1941.

102 *"The idea of plucking up:* Mike Cooney, self-interview, March 11, 1978.

103 *"Jim Crow":* Reuss, *American Folklore and Left-Wing Politics.*

106 *"We were struggling,:* Pete Seeger, manuscript comments, 2000.

111 *"There was big drops of sweat:* Woody Guthrie, *Bound for Glory* (New York: E. P. Dutton, 1943). In Woody's account, he was alone.

113 *The way they got on radio:* Background is from Palmer, *All You Need Is Love.*

115 *"I'd been knocking myself out:* Pete Seeger to Mill Lampell, October 1, 1989.

119 *he worried that he might not live:* "Soldier's Diary," journal in the possession of Pete Seeger.

CHAPTER 6: UNION MAID

Author's interviews with Pete Seeger, October 6, 1977 (with Toshi Ohta Seeger), March 6, 10, 1977, August 8, 1978; Charles Seeger, April 8, 1976; Alan Lomax, December 27, 1977; Jimmy Collier, July 10, 1978; Mario Cassetta, September 22, 1976; Bess Lomax Hawes, May 6, 1977; Wally Hille, September 23, 1976; Leo Christiansen, September 22, 1976; Earl Robinson, March 18, 1976; Irwin Silber, May 26, 1977; Margaret Gelders Frantz, June 21, 1978.

page/reference

122 *"You want to know:* Jimmy Collier, July 10,1978.

123 *three recording sessions:* These were "Lonesome Train," 1943, Decca 29139–41; "Songs of the Lincoln Brigade," 1943, Asch 330 (reissued as Folkways 5436); "Solidarity Forever," 1944, Stinson 622.

126 *Or they sang about:* Songs collected by Pete Seeger, catalogued in *Notes from the Marianas,* manuscript in the Library of Congress.

127 *By the 1940s,:* Author's correspondence with Malvina Reynolds (an early People's Songs member) and Richard Reuss.

128 *in his isolation on Saipan:* Pete Seeger, March 10, 1977; August 8, 1978.

128 *The Communist Party U.S.A.:* Material for this section was drawn from *American Communism in Crisis, 1943–1957* by Joe Starobin (Berkeley: University of California Press, 1975); *The Autobiography of an American Communist* by Peggy Dennis (Westport, CT: Lawrence Hill, 1978); *A Long View from the Left* by Al Richmond (New York: Dell, 1972); *The Decline of American Communism* by David Shannon (Chatham, NJ: Chatham Bookseller, 1971); and *If I Had a Hammer* by Maurice Isserman (Chicago: University of Illinois Press, 1993). For the Communist Party's self-history, see "Fifty Years of the Communist Party U.S.A.," a special issue of *Political Affairs,* September–October 1969.

128 *"Marxism was the transforming:* Quoted in Vivian Gornick, *The Romance of American Communism* (New York: Basic Books, 1978).

131 *one legendary incident:* Author's correspondence with Felix Landau, September 2, 1976, and Pete Seeger, March 10, 1977, December 14, 1977.

131 *All he wrote in his journal:* This emotional distancing was so striking that years later, as Seeger reread his journals, he noted in the margin, "No mention of Pitou's death?"

132 *"back from the war party,":* Guthrie, "People's Songs and Its People," ten-page manuscript in the Woody Guthrie Archives, New York City.

133 *"Toshi played:* Wally Hille, September 23, 1976.

133 *Playing the banjo or hiking:* Leo Christiansen, September 23, 1976.

134 *The meeting disappointed him;:* Pete Seeger, August 8, 1978.

135 *"Pete, here in New York:* Pete Seeger, August 8, 1978. The Party may have been out of date, for the big bands so popular in New York in the 1930s were now disbanding; in 1946, Tommy Dorsey and Woody Herman both split up their groups. Seeger himself had periodic doubts about using folk music for the new "people's music," as he wrote the Almanacs during the war. "I wonder if we really have the right slant on the future of American music—us using so much folk music when jazz is so popular. But Kentucky would reaffirm anyone's faith."

135 *This cheeky comment—:* Pete Seeger, August 8, 1978. After the criticism Seeger received, the *Bulletin* actually did print several jazzy tunes.

136 *The FBI notwithstanding:* *Dunaway v. Kelley et al.*, U.S. District Court, San Francisco. Through the Freedom of Information Act some six hundred documents on People's Songs have been released or declassified. An additional two thousand were released on the Almanacs, the Weavers, and People's Artists. These were deposited in the American Folklife Center.

136 *as even Earl Browder predicted:* Starobin, *American Communism in Crisis.* Earl Browder's thinking was accurate but prematures.

138 *Union leaders were unenthusiastic.:* From newspaper clippings and PS's list of bookings, its union activities peaked in mid-1947 (during a filmstrip for the CIO Political Action Committee) and had largely faded a year later. Among those with repeated contact were United Auto Workers; radio workers in the United Electrical Workers; the Oilworkers' International; United Office and Professional Workers; the National Maritime Union; the Transport Workers' Union;. the International Typographers' Union; the Mine, Mill and Smelter Workers' Union; and the Newspaper Guild. Ads for People's Songs appeared in the *Trade Union Service Newspapers*, the *Department Store Employee*, the *N.Y. Teachers News*, and the *C.I.O. Bulletin.*

139 *One West Coast member:* Leo Christiansen, September 22, 1976.

140 *He complained to Alan Lomax:* Pete Seeger, July 16, 1946.

141 *Well, they gave him his orders:* *Bosses' Songbook.*

141 *"trim, slim Sinatra:* *Billboard*, December 21, 1946. On March 15, *Billboard* was less enthusiastic: "Seeger should make an effort to acquire

more polish and smoothness. In addition, he should either wear make-up or the Vanguard should spotlight him with a diffused light."

142 *To Hear Your Banjo Play:* The film on YouTube includes footage of Woody Guthrie playing guitar, among the only motion pictures of him performing. The pair reportedly performed in a CBS experimental telecast in 1943, according to Cray, *Woody Guthrie.*

143 *Domestic Intelligence Summary:* Some idea of the accuracy of this report can be gleaned from this excerpt: "Communism in the United States is no longer confined to the fellow with the thick-lensed glasses and tieless shirt preaching on a soapbox. Communists are now operating a section whose representatives wear full dress suits and top hats for the men and silver and gold spangled evening gowns for the fairer sex." People's Songs belonged to the workshirt-and-jeans set.

145 *A VISIT WITH HARRY:* *Songs for Wallace,* August 1948, song folio printed by People's Songs.

146 *Then Wallace decided:* Material on Wallace comes from *Gideon's Army* by Curtis MacDougall (New York: Marzani and Munsell, 1965), particularly pp. 712–17, and Margaret Gelders Frantz, June 21, 1978.

148 *"The man was absolutely furious,":* Manuscript comments 2000.

148 *"We knew the price:* Irwin Silber, May 26, 1977.

151 *"Union Maid":* Headnotes from *Hard Hitting Songs for Hard Hit People,* compiled by Alan Lomax, notes by Woody Guthrie, music edited by Pete Seeger (New York: Oak Publications, 1967), p. 324. Words from *Talking Union,* Folkways Records FH5285.

151 *had a percussive effect:* Klein, *Woody Guthrie,* p. 180.

152 *a parody:* Ellington, et al., *Bosses' Songbook.*

153 *"Even unions with left-wing leadership:* "Whatever Happened to Singing in the Unions," *Sing Out!,* May 1965.

155 *Duncan Emrich:* The Seeger-Emrich correspondence is in the Archive of American Folk Song in the Library of Congress; the Emrich-FBI contacts are detailed in FBI memoranda, *Dunaway v. Kelley et al.*

155 *One day a friend stopped by:* Klein, *Woody Guthrie.*

156 *"Tomorrow Is a Highway":* *Gazette Volume 2,* Folkways FN 2502.

CHAPTER 7: IF I HAD A HAMMER

Author's interviews with Pete Seeger, March 6, 9, 10, October 9, December 14, 1977, August 8, 1978, March 26, 1980, September 6, 2006; Lee Hays, February 11, 1977; Fred Hellerman, March 3, 1977; Ronnie Gilbert, January 14, 1977, December 20, 21, 2006; Gordon Friesen, December 21, 1977; Arlo Guthrie, November 5, 1978; Mario Cassetta, September 26, 1976; Oscar Brand, March 27, 1980; Dave Garroway, January 14, 1977; Don McLean, November 10, 1976; Bess Lomax Hawes, May 6, 1977; Peggy Seeger, August 29, 1977; Charles Seeger, April 8, 1976; Pete Kameron, September 11, 1980.

page/reference

158 *With an ax:* Jonathan Kwitny, "Timeless Troubadour," *Wall Street Journal*, June 12, 1973.

159 *Going around the room:* Actually, the group had considered other members, including two young black singers, Hope Foye and Bill Dillard.

160 *"This is where we're abandoning:* Reuss, *American Folklore*, p. 336.

160 *"We had never intended:* Seeger, *Incompleat Folksinger*, p. 22.

161 *"If I Had a Hammer,":* This song was first issued as Hootenanny Records 101 (A), and first performed on June 3, 1949, at a testimonial for the Foley Square Twelve.

162 *"When the song was first published:* Pete Seeger in Fariello, *Red Scare*, p. 364.

164 *"Lee kept complaining:* Doris Wilens, *Lonesome Traveler* (New York: Norton, 1988), p. 120.

165 *"short, a bit round:* Wilens, *Lonesome Traveler*, p. 125.

165 *At a typical Weavers show:* This description is a composite of some of the Weavers' best-known performance pieces.

168 *"We may have to take:* Wilens, *Lonesome Traveler*, p. 122.

169–70 *"I don't mind wasting my money,":* At this Reno engagement, the Weavers felt direct censorship, the manager telling them, "Cut that political stuff out." The Weavers self-censored. Ronnie Gilbert, December 20, 2006.

173 *Ed Sullivan:* This anecdote and much supporting information comes from an excellent history of blacklisting in the media, *A Journal of the Plague Years* by Stefan Kanfer (New York: Atheneum, 1973).

174 *" 'chasing the bitch goddess Success:* Quoted in Wilens, *Lonesome Traveler*, p. 133.

175 *The spirit of People's Songs:* The FBI was asked by the Department of Justice to prepare a full-scale report for prosecution of People's Artists before the Subversive Activities Control Board.

177 *Decca liked Gordon Jenkins's sound;:* A number of orchestras recorded with the Weavers, though Jenkins did the most. For background, see David Samuelson, editor, "Goodnight Irene," Bear Family 2000.

178 *When Seeger answered:* Pete Seeger, March 6, 1977; March 26, 1980.

178 *"The Communists are hell-bent:* Spector, "The Weavers," pp. 115–16.

179 *one researcher points out:* Koppelman, *Sing Out Warning!*, p. 21.

179 *cold clinical but deadly bureaucratic repression":* David Caute, *The Great Fear* (New York: Simon and Schuster, 1979).

179 *Dave Garroway:* In 1971 Seeger appeared on Dave Garroway's comeback show in Boston. His previous rejection may have smarted; Seeger was so outspokenly opposed to the war in Vietnam, the local RKO station regretted the spot, and eventually canceled Garroway's show. Interview with Dave Garroway, January 14, 1977.

179 *A slick NBC release:* Wilens, *Lonesome Traveler*, p. 142.

180 *"walking down the street:* Fariello, *Red Scare*, p. 372.

180 *"I'll take it now":* Ronnie Gilbert, December 21, 2006.

180 *The McCarren Committee:* *Dunaway v. Kelley et al.*, U.S. District Court, San Francisco, 1975–80.

181 *two men, two women:* Reuss, *American Folklore*.

181 *"Irwin's a literary figure:* Ron Radosh, March 24, 1980.

181 *he received word:* Walter Lowenfels to Pete Seeger, February 26, 1951.

181 *"Keep working:* This quote is sometimes attributed to Walter Lowenfels. "If the Party liked what we did," Lee Hays cavalierly wrote, "that was their good luck." Koppelman, *Sing Out Warning!*, p. 51.

182 *Seeger hedged:* *Variety,* August 29, 1951.

182 *"I'll go along with it:* Koppelman, "*Sing Out Warning!,*" p. 104.

184 *An eight-year-old visitor:* Author's correspondence with Jill Reidel, September 11, 1979.

185 *Harvey Matusow:* See Cohen and Lichtman, *Deadly Farce* (2005)

185 *"It was there that:* Harvey Matusow, *False Witness* (New York: Cameron and Kahn, 1955). See also Ron Cohen, *Rainbow Quest.*

187 *"It was like one of these movies:* Fariello, *Red Scare,* p. 372.

194 *"Pete created his own style:* Mike Seeger, recorded self-interview, March 29, 1978.

196 *"I was interested in ethnomusicology:* Pete Seeger, manuscript comments, 2000.

197 *Yet evading questions:* Pete Seeger, December 14, 1977.

197 *"Seeger is probably:* *New York Herald Tribune,* March 20, 1955.

203 *In 1953 I. F. Stone:* I. F. Stone, *The Haunted Fifties* (New York: Vintage, 1963).

CHAPTER 8: WHERE HAVE ALL THE FLOWERS GONE?

Author's interviews with Pete Seeger, October 6, 1976 (with Toshi Seeger), October 9, December 14, 1977, August 8, 1978, July 26, 2000; Bess Lomax Hawes, August 28, 1977; Moe Asch, May 8, 1977; Harold Leventhal, June 9, 1977; Lee Hays, May 25, 1977; Peggy Seeger, August 24, 1977; Don McLean, November 10, 1976; Ron Radosh, March 24, 1980; Myles Horton, May 2, 1980; Norma Starobin, January 20, 1980.

page/reference

204 *"What's so dangerous:* From the author's personal recollection.

207 *"I want to get up there,":* Pete Seeger, October 9 and December 14, 1977.

207 *"It all took:* Pete Seeger, manuscript comments, 2000.

208 *a new generation of fans:* At a 1977 reunion of the Students for a Democratic Society, someone asked, "How many of you were 'red-diaper babies'?" Three-quarters raised their hands.

208 *He fit an American mold:* Thoreau was the Romantic godfather to this

heroism-in-principle. David Mairowitz, *The Radical Soap Opera* (New York: Avon, 1974), pp. 150–54.

208 *Including progressive social clubs,:* In the fifties Seeger sang regularly at approximately fifty camps and fifty schools; together their enrollment might add up to thirty thousand people. A hundred or so colleges hired him, particularly after the headlines of his HUAC testimony; fans from these might amount to another thirty thousand.

208 *One teenager who took banjo lessons:* Ron Radosh, March 24, 1980. On visiting Highlander for its twenty-fifth anniversary in 1957 (alongside Martin Luther King and other luminaries), Pete Seeger wandered off from the stage area to play banjo for the kitchen help while they worked (Myles Horton, May 2, 1980).

209 *Harold Velde:* Walter Goodman, *The Committee* (New York: Farrar, Straus & Giroux, 1968).

211 *"amid the popping:* Donner, *The Un-Americans.*

211 *Francis Walter:* Charlotte Pomerantz, editor, *A Quarter Century of Un-Americana* (New York: Marzani and Munsell, 1963).

212 *"I make my living:* Seeger's testimony is reproduced in *Thirty Years of Treason,* Eric Bentley, editor. HUAC members did *not* mention Matusow's perjured testimony on Seeger before the committee in 1952.

216 *"he is involved:* Dalton Trumbo, *Time of the Toad* (New York: Harper & Row, 1972).

218 *Walt Whitman's poetry:* *Pete and Sonny at Carnegie Hall,* Folkways FA 2412.

220 *"They caught him,":* Pete Seeger, May 2006.

225 *The* Daily Worker: Peter Fryer, *Hungarian Tragedy* (London: Dennis Dobson, 1956).

225 *"We were still:* Fryer, *The Hungarian Tragedy.*

225 *"betrayed and wondering . . . :* Paul Buhle and D. Georgakis, "CPUSA" in *Encyclopedia of the American Left* (Urbana: University of Illinois Press, 1992), p. 154.

225 *"The niceties:* Peggy Dennis, *The Autobiography of an American Communist* (Westport, CT: Creative Arts Books, 1977), p. 225.

225 *In retrospect,:* Pete Seeger, manuscript comments, 2000.

225 *He did not criticize:* Seeger, though far from Party discipline, arrived at the University of Chicago folk festival in the late fifties telling a student, "Oh good, you have the *Worker*—I'm two weeks behind."

226 *a few sharp choruses:* *Bosses Songbook.*

226 *"I just went to everybody:* Harold Leventhal, June 7, 1977

232 *"Music is the most powerful:* Stephen Spender, "Poetry and Revolution," in *The Thirties and After* (New York: Vintage, 1979).

233 *"He was quite critical:* Pete Seeger, September 16, 2006.

234 *"I still feel I committed no wrong,:* Pete Seeger, circular letter, March 30, 1957; Seeger characterized newspaper reports of his "hassle with the government" as "incomplete, inaccurate, and sometimes downright malicious."

235 *"A Paean to Pete Seeger:* San Francisco *People's World,* February 8, 1958.

235 *The Detroit Arts Commission:* *New York Times,* July 12, 1958.

CHAPTER 9: JOHN HENRY

Author's interviews with Pete Seeger, July 19, 1976, October 9, December 14, 1977, August 8, 1978; Bess Lomax Hawes, August 28, 1978; Malvina Reynolds, September 5, 1976; Jimmy Collier, July 10, 1978; Mike Seeger, December 7, 1977; Peggy Seeger, August 29, 1977; Charles Seeger III, October 10, 1977; Irving Younger, May 24, 1980; Mike Cooney, May 30, 1978; Don McLean, November 10, 1978; Charles Seeger, April 8, 1976; Mary Bernstein, December 29, 1961; Judy Collins, December 30, 1977; Howie Richmond, February 24, 1980; Harold Leventhal, June 9, 1977.

page/reference

237 *"America the Beautiful":* Introductory statement to "America the Beautiful," on *Hootenanny Tonight,* Folkways FN 2311.

239 *"When Pete left:* Wilens, *Lonesome Traveler.*

240 *Charles Seeger had predicted:* "Professionalism and Amateurism in the Study of Folk Music," *Journal of American Folklore* 62 (1949): 112.

Before the Almanacs, Charles Seeger wrote "Grassroots for American Composers"; in the early 1950s he suggested that somebody should revitalize oral communication by getting children and parents singing in their homes and schools. "Folk Music in the Schools of a Highly Industrialized Society," reprinted in *The American Folk Scene,* David De Turk and A. Poulin, editors (New York: Dell, 1967).

241 *"God help Pete Seeger:* Jimmy Collier, July 10, 1978.

241 *The attacks worsened: Great Neck News,* December 11, 1959; *Los Angeles Examiner,* May 15, 1960; *Los Angeles Times,* May 13, 1960; *San Diego Union,* May 14, 1960; *People's World,* May 21, 1960.

242 *Texans for America:* Frances Fitzgerald, "Rewriting American History," *New Yorker,* February 26, 1979, p. 56.

245 *always the last to leave:* Sara Effron to author, February 18, 1980.

247 *"Seeger will be lucky: Harvard Crimson,* March 29, 1961; *New York Post,* March 29, 1961. For coverage of the trial, see also *New York Daily News,* March 30, 1961, *New York Journal-American,* March 30, 1961, and *New York Times,* March 30, 1961.

249 *"Everybody was being so:* Irwin Silber, December 21, 1977.

249 *"'Why can't he: Little Sandy Review,* no.10 (1959): 30–31.

250 *Hammond met with:* John Hammond, *On Record* (New York: Summit Books, 1979), p. 346.

250 *Malvina Reynolds:* Reynolds subsequently left Columbia after being bitterly disappointed by her treatment there.

252 *"Thank you, your honor.:* Seeger's statement to the court is printed in *Sing Out!,* Summer 1961.

254 *Battle of Washington Square:* Oscar Brand, *The Ballad Mongers* (New York: Minerva/Funk & Wagnalls, 1962), p. 159; *New York Times,* April 10, 1961; Peter Tammony, "Hootenanny: Who Invented the Term?," *Hootenanny* 1, no.2 (Oct. 27, 1963).

257 *"I am always uncomfortable:* Gus Hall quoted in Pamela Allara, *Pictures of People: Alice Neel's Portrait Gallery* (Waltham, MA: Brandeis University Press, 1998), p. 124.

257 *"Seegers take mainly":* Ron Cohen, *Rainbow Quest,* p. 128.

258 *"Seeger's puritan lifestyle:* Archie Green, January 14, 1976.

260 *Instead, the court found:* *U.S.A. v. Pete Seeger,* Second Court of Appeals, N. 27, 101; *New York Times,* May 19, 1962.

262 *terrific new song: "Guantanamera.":* Author's recording at Camp Woodland, July 15, 1962, which he forwarded to Seeger so that the song could be first published in *Sing Out!*

263 *"Seeger walked down the aisle":* Lyon, "The Ballad of Pete Seeger."

265 *'Look, we have Pete Seeger.':* Pete Seeger, August 8, 1978.

267 *Joan Baez refused:* *Billboard,* March 30, 1963. Other boycotters included Ed McCurdy, the Greenbriar Boys, and Erik Darling.

268 *I told my brother:* Pete Seeger, manuscript comments, 2000.

268 *"Pete Seeger just can't hold":* Lyon, "The Ballad of Pete Seeger." The original source for this quotation is a file of letters and notes on conversations about *Hootenanny* in the possession of Harold Leventhal's office, now the Woody Guthrie Foundation.

268 *"ABC made its position:* Dave Van Ronk, *The Mayor of MacDougal Street,* Elijah Word, editor (New York: DaCapo, 2005), pp. 198–99.

269 *"What a mistake":* Pete Seeger, manuscript comments, 2000. In a 2002 movie, *Confessions of a Dangerous Mind,* this conversation occurs: "Chuck, they didn't go for 'The Dating Game,' they went for 'Hootenanny.'" "Hooten-fucking-nanny?" Chuck Barris answers.

269 *"The ABC network:* Seeger gave his most vivid description of *Hootenanny* years later to a British interviewer: "The show was only a bunch of white college kids all clapping inanely, no matter what song was sung, big smiles all over, and never a hint of controversy or protest." Palmer, *All You Need Is Love.*

CHAPTER 10: WE SHALL OVERCOME

Author's interviews with Mary Travers, January 19, 1977; Harold Leventhal, June 7, 1977; Pete Seeger (with Toshi Seeger), October 6, 1976, December 14, 15, 1977, August 8, 1978; Bernice Reagon, December 7, 1977; Jimmy Collier, July 10, 1978; Mike Cooney, May 30, 1978; Irene Paull (Calamity Jane), September 7, 1976.

page/reference

273 *Among black churchgoers the banjo:* Dena Epstein, "The Folk Banjo—A Documentary History," *Ethnomusicology,* September 1975.

273 *If he had known that Guy Carawan:* The story of Seeger's difficulties in Albany is from *The Incompleat Folksinger;* Bernice Reagon discussed the problems Carawan had in her unpublished PhD dissertation, Howard University, 1975.

275 *"We Shall Overcome":* Bernice Reagon dissertation and Pete Seeger, August 8, 1978.

278 *Weavers' fifteenth anniversary:* Vanguard issued two records from the May 2 and May 3, 1963, reunion concerts (VSD 215Q, Part I; VSD 79161, Part II).

278 *A fellow organizer:* Jimmy Collier, July 10, 1978.

278 *"Toshi is probably:* Jimmy Collier, July 10, 1978.

280 *Bernice is one of those:* Hajdu, *Positively 4th Street.*

280 *they were madly in love:* Dave Van Ronk in Martin Scorsese's film, *No Direction Home,* 2006.

282 *"If you want to get out of:* Notes taken by author.

283 *"When I got that* We Shall Overcome *album:* John McCutcheon, August 6, 2006.

284 *His mind continued to dwell:* Journal in the possession of Pete Seeger, edited for publication by Joe Berger.

284 *"Do books pose danger?":* Pete Seeger, manuscript comments, 2000.

284 *the government would have tried harder:* Seeger used virtually these words in an interview printed in *Outside,* May 1979.

285 *"We earned in each country:* Pete Seeger, manuscript comments, 1981.

285 *Gandhi, like Seeger:* Both believed, as Seeger had written at Harvard, that no person is greater than his spiritual repute. Gandhi is reported by his biographer, Erik Erikson, to have led strikers in processions singing improvised lyrics that showed "a transfer of traditional religious feeling to the new kind of social experience." *Gandhi's Truth* (New York: Norton, 1969).

287 *Forced to rely on musicianship:* A Soviet magazine later headlined

SEEGER GOOD FOR FLU, after a number of people reported being cured by an evening of singing with Seeger. Reported in *New York Times*, April 11, 1964; *New York Post*, April 12, 1964. Interestingly, on his Russian tour, Seeger was told to sing only in formal concerts and eschew informal sing-alongs. He answered that his voice was tired, but he would try to sing where he wanted.

287 *"The U.S. seems very big,:* Letters in possession of the author; see also Seeger's correspondence with S. Cunningham and G. Friesen, American Folklife Center, Library of Congress and Southern Folklore Collection, University of North Carolina–Chapel Hill.

288 *One Freedom Summer volunteer:* Paul Cowan, *The Making of an Un-American* (New York: Viking Press, 1970).

288 *"We've been told over and over: Letters from Mississippi*, edited by Elizabeth Sutherland (New York: McGraw-Hill, 1971).

289 *"They were a group of people:* Bernice Reagon, December 7, 1977.

292 *"In this movement:* Jimmy Collier, July 10, 1978.

292 *"I'm studying Russian:* Pete Seeger to Rockwell Kent, November 19, 1964.

293 *Bernice Reagon, who pointed out":* Pete Seeger, December 15, 1977. Reagon has no copy of this correspondence.

293 *Lyndon Johnson addressed Congress:* Francis Fox Piven and Richard Cloward, *Poor People's Movements* (New York: Pantheon, 1977).

294 *"It was very well organized..:* Jimmy Collier, July 10, 1978.

294 *'I Love Everybody.':* This and subsequent songs are from a documentary with Pete Seeger, *WNEW's Story of Selma*, produced by Jerry Graham and Mike Stein, 1965, Folkways FH 5595.

294 *Sheriff Jim Clark:* Reverend James McGraw, "Footnotes of a Marcher," *The Realist*, May 1965. In New York, a Selma support march took many whites to Harlem for the first time. Sheriff Jim Clark was the diehard segregationist who later guarded three tons of marijuana.

297 *"There were people getting shot:* Jimmy Collier, July 10, 1978.

298 *Two shots traveled:* Fifteen years after Liuzzo's death, FBI files revealed that after the accident, FBI director J. Edgar Hoover began a

campaign to vilify her, ordering anonymous letters sent that asserted that she was a drug addict and "necking" with a black man at the time of her murder.

300 *"The tone of the movement:* Jimmy Collier, July 10, 1978.

301 *Julius Lester:* "The Angry Children of Malcolm X," *Sing Out!*, October 1996.

CHAPTER 11: WAIST DEEP IN THE BIG MUDDY

Author's interviews with Bernice Reagon, December 7, 1977; Harold Leventhal, June 8, 1977; Pete Seeger, March 6, 1976, December 15, 1977, August 8, 1978; Danny Kalb, March 24, 1980; Gordon Friesen, December 27, 1977; Jack Elliot, August 27, 1978; Don McLean, November 10, 1976; Judy Collins, December 30, 1977; Bess Lomax Hawes, August 28, 1977; Country Joe McDonald, March 30, 1978; Reverend Frederick Douglass Kirkpatrick, December 21, 1977.

page/reference

303 *"Tonight let's sing:* Background on the events at Newport comes from many sources: Hajdu, *Positively 4th Street; Bob Dylan: A Retrospective,* Craig McGregor, editor (New York: William Morrow, 1972); "Folk Rock: Thunder without Rain," by Josh Dunson, in De Turk and Poulin, editors, *The American Folk Scene;* Anthony Scadato, *Bob Dylan* (New York: Grosset & Dunlap, 1971), and author's interviews with Bernice Reagon (Dec. 7, 1977); Pete Seeger (Dec. 15, 1977); and Harold Leventhal (June 8, 1977); Marine "Guerrilla Minstrel."

304 *"the most written-about performance:* Clinton Heylin, *Bob Dylan: Behind the Shades Revisited* (New York: Morrow, 2001), p. 206.

304 *"The myth of Dylan's:* Hajdu, *Positively 4th Street.*

305 *"folk music's stodgy right wing.":* At least according to Spitz, *Dylan*, pp. 302–10.

305 *"I think he's prostituting himself;:* *No Direction Home,* Martin Scorsese, 2006; these comments are from interviews at his next British tour.

306 *"Play folk music!:* Richard Farina quoted in Hajdu, *Positively 4th Street.*

306 *"Pete Seeger towered over us:* Ron Cohen, *Rainbow Quest,* p. 236.

309 *"He said he was just in a lot of pain:* Bernice Reagon, December 7, 1977.

310 *A* New York Times *editor:* Pete Seeger, August 8, 1978. *New York Times,* October 25, 1965. The second edition headline read "Seeger Critical in Moscow." The apology was printed in the *Beacon Free Press,* November 18, 1965.

310 *"Not publicly:* Toshi Seeger, written manuscript comments, 1981.

311 *"If we'd had 20:* Siminoff and Kissil, "Pickin', Workin' at the Other End: A Conversation with Pete Seeger."

314 *"Pete didn't take the session:* Danny Kalb, March 24, 1980.

315 *When he finally sang in East Meadow:* "American Minstrel's Song of Success," *New York Times,* January 23, 1966. The East Meadow case is best reported in *Newsday,* April 12, 1966, and *New York Times,* July 8, 1966. *Who's Who* listed Pete Seeger as editor of *The New Lost City Ramblers Songbook.*

316 *eerie interior monologues:* These notebooks run from March 1966 through summer 1969 in possession of Pete Seeger, roughly corresponding to one per month. These quotes from #4 and #3.

319 *"Pete bitterly blames himself:* Si Kahn, April 21 and November 6, 2007.

320 *"In future years:* Extended letter, Pete Seeger, May 10, 1967; "Lebanon/Israel, the Coin Has Two Sides"; and *The Incompleat Folksinger.*

320 *Seeger sang "We Shall Overcome":* Pete Seeger, *Where Have All the Flowers Gone?,* pp. 32–35.

321 *his rejection of pacifism:* "A Portfolio on War," *Sing Out!,* December 1966. There was a strong pacifist tradition in the Seeger family: Charles Seeger had declared himself a conscientious objector in World War I; so had his son John, in World War II, and Mike Seeger during the Korean War period.

322 *A California school Superintendent:* Cliff Jordan (superintendent of schools, Coronado, California) to *Scholastic Magazine;* reply undated.

325 *"That song seemed:* Bernice Reagon, December 7, 1977.

327 *"We're going to have to face TV:* Siminoff and Kissil, "Pickin'."

328 *"It's perfectly possible:* Pete Seeger, December 15, 1977.

330 *He wrote Irwin:* Pete Seeger to Irwin Silber, November 13, 1967; letter in possession of Irwin Silber. Seeger's attack overlooks the significant work Silber did in editing such folk music books as *Songs of the Civil War, Songs of the Great American West, Songs America Voted By,* and *The Folksinger's Word Book.*

331 *"the reverse of hip.":* Jeff Nuttall, *Bomb Culture* (London: MacGibbon and Kee, 1968); "Players and Seeger," *Daily Pennsylvanian,* April 4, 1966.

332 *"A real performer:* Siminoff and Kissil, "Pickin'."

336 *"My songs must be so good:* Seeger to a Mrs. Seki, undated.

338 *These zany ideas:* *Sing Out!,* December 1967; Charles Seeger to Pete Seeger, March 17, 1967.

339 *An Oberlin college student:* Steven Mayer, "Seeger."

339 *"What is right:* Head notes from "Turn! Turn! Turn!" in Pete Seeger, *Bells of Rhymney;* Ecclesiastes 3:1–8 (King James version).

341 *sink the ship:* Bess Lomax Hawes, August 28, 1977. Notebook #17, in Seeger's possession. Seeger wrote a song, "All My Children of the Sun," based on this vision.

341 *"plague the Pharaohs:* *New York Times,* May 14, 1968. Background here is from *New York Times,* March 20–June 25, 1968.

343 *"You have to understand,":* Jimmy Collier, July 10, 1978. Seeger now tells the story differently. *Where Have All the Flowers Gone?* p. 144.

344 *"I remember* Pete Seeger Now,: See "Resurrection City Reminiscences," in Pete Seeger's column in *Sing Out!,* October 1968; Jimmy Collier; July 10, 1978; Bernice Reagon, December 7, 1977.

CHAPTER 12: GOLDEN RIVER

Author's interviews with Harold Leventhal, March 28, 1977; Jack Elliot, August 27, 1978; Jimmy Collier, July 10, 1978; Gordon Friesen, April 14, 1976, December 27, 1977; Bernice Reagon, December 7, 1977; Don

McLean, November 10, 1976; Bess Hawes, August 28, 1977; Peggy Seeger, August 29, 1977; Judy Collins, December 30, 1978; Pete Seeger, December 14, 15, 1977; August 8, 1978; Charles Seeger, April 7, 1976.

page/reference

346 *Julius Lester:* Julius Lester, *Revolutionary Notes* (New York: Grove Press, 1969).

346–47 *she learned Spanish:* Pete Seeger, manuscript comments, 1999.

347 *On a news clipping:* National Archives, Senate Internal Security Committee, Seeger file, 1968.

347 *"In Houston, she calls Toshi.:* Pete Seeger, manuscript comments, 2000.

348 *For months students and teachers:* The episode at Beacon is covered by *The Village Voice*, "Non-Confrontation in Beacon, N.Y.," December 16, 1965. Pete Seeger, August 8, 1978; manuscript comments, 2000.

348 *Beacon's papers headlined:* The *Beacon Evening* News printed letters almost daily for three weeks beginning November 6, 1965. See the *Poughkeepsie Journal* on November 11 and 18; the *Beacon News* and *Beacon Free Press.*

352 *building a flotilla:* *New York Times,* August 26, 1960.

352 *"I think he wanted:* Jimmy Collier, July 10, 1978.

353 *"Said river water:* Excerpts from the 1826 travel journal of John Maude, reprinted in *Hudson River Sloops* (Dobbs Ferry, NY: Morgan and Morgan, 1970).

353 *a local Indian legend:* "The Hudson," *Parade,* November 26, 1978.

354 *Tacking his way back:* Pete Seeger, September 19, 2006.

356 *"The whole idea:* Pete Seeger, October 6, 1976.

356 *"Look at the waste we make:* Interview broadcast over WPM-AM in Cleveland, November 12, 1958.

357 *"I felt my fingers clenching:* Quoted in Marty Gallanter, "Can Music Save a River?," brochure for the 1979 Hudson River Revival.

357 *"There was a guy:* Pete Seeger, May 23, 2006.

359 *Laurence Rockefeller:* Peter Collier and David Horowitz, *The Rockefellers* (New York: Holt, Rinehart, and Winston, 1976).

360 *On June 27, 1969, the* Clearwater*:* Details on the *Clearwater*'s first cruise are from *Songs and Sketches* and "The Launching of the *Clearwater.*" *A Hudson Slooper's Handy Guide* (Poughkeepsie, NY: Hudson River Sloop Restoration, 1975) has the *Clearwater*'s specifications.

362 *"Well, if he doesn't know:* Jimmy Collier, July 10, 1978.

363 *"At some point around this time:* Bernice Reagon, December 7, 1977.

364 *His 1970 testimony:* *New York Times,* January 31, 1970.

366 *Toshi Ohta rarely talked:* *Chicago Tribune*, March 3, 1974; *Denver Post*, August 15, 1974.

366 *"You have the right to extricate yourself:* Pete Seeger to Toshi Ohta, March 1, 1967.

367 *Nonetheless, he wrote Silber:* Pete Seeger to Irwin Silber and Joe North, May 25, 1972.

367 *"Pete, we can't clean up:* Pete Seeger, September 19, 2006; manuscript comments.

368 *the* Today *show:* When he said, "Mutter along with me for your mutter country," Barbara Walters danced across the set, saying, "Well, Mr. Seeger, we really are a country of mutterers, aren't we?"

369 *"Tell a man what he may not sing,":* Mary Renault, *The Praise Singer* (New York: Knopf, 1979).

370 *"Stories for Retelling.":* Pete Seeger and Paul Dubois Jacobs (Walter Lowenfels's grandson), *Pete Seeger's Storytelling Book*.

376 *few writing on popular song:* In Alec Wilder's *American Popular Song* (New York: Oxford University Press, 1972) of the eleven songwriters discussed in depth, not one has roots in folk music. Arguing either by sales volume or by influence, Seeger (and Guthrie) had considerable impact on American popular song.

377 *Seeger decided to take a year off:* The exact dates of this sabbatical are uncertain. According to *Sing Out!* (November 1972), 1973 was to be the year; yet on April 15 Seeger sang at Paul Robeson's seventy-fifth birthday; his operations took place at the beginning of 1974, and Seeger's first commercial booking of the year was probably on March 10, 1974, at the Opera House in Chicago.

CHAPTER 13: TURN! TURN! TURN!

page/reference

379 *Later, Arlo:* Arlo Guthrie, May 19, 2006.

379 *"In some sense:* Pete Seeger, May 23, 2006.

382 *"You're on your knees in a strawberry field:* Sue Altkin, Beacon Sloop Club, May 21, 2006.

395 *"My voice lasted longer:* Pete Seeger, July 26, 2000.

397 *"Myself, I was delighted:* Pete Seeger, *Where Have All The Flowers Gone*, pp. 172–73; Seeger, *Bells of Rhymney*, p. 122.

398 *"He knows when the song:* Reggie and Kim Harris, July 1, 12, 2007.

399 *"The first thing:* Arlo Guthrie, November 6, 1978.

401 *"We took out a group of kids:* David O'Reilly, June 5, 2006.

402 *"The intervening years:* David Fine, August 17, 2006 to author.

406 *"My generation needs Seeger badly,":* Molly Beer, August 26, 2006.

407 *Seeger loved to tell that story:* There are now Ph.D. dissertations and monographs on these petri dishes of the New Left, e.g., Mishler, *Raising Reds*, and Ron Radosh, *Commies* (San Francisco: Encounter Books, 2002).

413 *trekked to Beacon.:* Lipp, "Reviving Folk's True Meaning."

EPILOGUE

Author's interviews with Irving Younger, May 24, 1980; Pete Seeger (with Toshi Seeger), December 14, 15, 1977, August 8, 1978; Jimmy Collier, July 10, 1978; Mike Cooney, May 30, 1978; John McCutcheon, August 8, 2006; John Cohen, October 18, 2006; Ronnie Gilbert, December 20, 2006; Holly Near, December 19, 2006.

page/reference

415 "Today I look upon myself: Pete Seeger, May 23, 2006.

415 *"I wasn't aware:* Bruce Springsteen, cnn.com, April 25, 2006.

416 *She suspects that had the Weavers:* Ronnie Gilbert, December 20, 2006.

416 *"Nowadays being blacklisted:* Fariello, *Red Scare,* p. 370.

417 *Irving Younger:* Pete and Toshi Seeger, December 14, 1977; Younger does not recall this incident.

417 *"Resurrecting the Red":* Bromberg and Fine, 2002.

417 *"He is not dangerous":* Jeff Greenfield, "The Party"

417 *"I'm no longer a pariah,":* Pete Seeger, May 23, 2006.

419 *"Pop music is the single:* Denselow, *When the Music's Over.*

419 *Mufid Abduqader:* Filing, U.S. District Court, November 3, 2005.

420 *"The artist in ancient times:* Pete Seeger, liner notes to *Pete,* 1996.

420 *"Folk was the living prayer:* Todd Gitlin, *The Sixties* (New York: Bantam Books, 1987), p. 75.

421 *"The New Left:* Gitlin, 1987.

421 *"with its basic":* Cantwell, *When We Were Good,* p. 251.

422 *"The number of apologists:* John Earl Haynes and Harvey Klehr, *In Denial: Historians, Communism, and Espionage* (San Francisco: Encounter Books, 2003), p. 13.

423 *Instead of playing chords,:* An example of this can be heard on a banjo solo on "Shenandoah," playing a passage of thirty-nine notes, more like a classical guitar than a five-string banjo: *Clearwater,* Sound House Records PS 1001.

423 *"Pete Seeger makes an orchestration:* Bob Dylan, in Jim Brown, *Pete Seeger: The Power of Song,* 2007.

425 *"All you need to be a modern:* Pete Seeger, "Johnny Appleseed" column, *Sing Out!* 4, no. 7 (Fall 1954).

425 *"His great insight:* M. T. Thomas, in *Keeping Score,* a PBS documentary broadcast November 2006, minute 34.

426 *"I think he's aware:* Jim Brown, May 16, 2006.

426 *"Songs won't save the planet":* Foreword, *Sierra Club Survival Songbook.*

427 *"If rulers really knew":* Quoted in *Outside,* May 1979.

427 *"Some people sing because: Providence Evening Bulletin,* September 6, 1961; "How Can I Keep from Singing?" new words by Doris Plenn, from Seeger, *The Bells of Rhymney.*

BIBLIOGRAPHY

—

BOOKS AND PAMPHLETS WRITTEN, EDITED, OR WITH CONTRIBUTIONS BY PETE SEEGER

(arranged chronographically)

Hard Hitting Songs for Hard Hit People. Compiled by Alan Lomax. Notes on songs by Woody Guthrie. Music transcribed and edited by Pete Seeger. Originally compiled in 1940. New York: Oak, 1967. 368 pages. [Songbook] 2nd. ed. 1999.

The People's Songbook. Pete Seeger, associate editor. New York: Boni and Gaer, 1948. 128 pages. [Songbook]

How to Play the 5-String Banjo, third revised edition. Mimeographed edition, 1948. New York: Oak, 1962, 1996. 73 pages.

The Weavers Sing. With Ronnie Gilbert, Fred Hellerman, and Lee Hays. New York: Folkways, 1951. 48 pages. [Songbook]

The Carolers' Songbag. Pete Seeger, editor, with the Weavers. New York: Folkways, 1952. 40 pages. [Songbook]

"How to Make a Chalil." May 1955. 12 pages. Self-published (third edition, 1968).

The Folksinger's Guitar Guide, by Jerry Silverman. New York: Oak, 1967. Originally a booklet to accompany Seeger's instruction record, Folkways FI 8354, 1956.

Choral Folksongs of the Bantu for Mixed Voices. Pete Seeger. New York: G. Schirmer, 1960. 58 pages.

"Foreword." Reprints from *People's Songs Bulletin*. New York: Oak, 1961. 1 page.

American Favorite Ballads. New York: Oak, 1961. 94 pages. [Songbook]

The Goofing Off Suite. New York: Hargail, 1961. [Songbook]

The Steel Drums of Kim Loy Wong. New York: Oak, 1961. 40 pages.

"Leadbelly." In Moses Asch and Alan Lomax, editors, *The Leadbelly Songbook*. New York: Oak, 1962. 1 page.

Woody Guthrie Folk Songs. Edited and compiled by Pete Seeger. New York: Ludlow Music, 1963. 264 pages. [Songbook]

The Bells of Rhymney. New York: Oak, 1964. 128 pages. [Songbook]

Bits and Pieces. New York: Ludlow Music, 1965. 48 pages. [Songbook]

The Twelve-String Guitar as Played by Leadbelly. With Julius Lester. New York: Oak, 1965. 80 pages.

Pete Seeger Singers Popular American Songs. Compiled by Grigory Schneerson. Translated into Russian by Samuel Bolotin and Tatiana Sikorskaya. Moscow: State Publishers Music, 1965. 32 pages. [Songbook]

We Make Our Tomorrow. Beacon, NY: Glasco Press, 1965. Drawings by Anton Refreiger, verse selected by Pete Seeger. 22 pages.

Songs for Peace. Jeff Marris, Cliff Metzler, Pete Seeger, editors. Introduction by Seeger et al. New York: Oak, 1966. 112 pages. [Songbook]

Oh Had I a Golden Thread. New York: Sanga Music, 1968. [Songbook]

"Foreword." In Don McLean, editor, *Songs and Sketches of the First Clearwater Crew*. New York: North River Press, 1970. 1 page.

Pete Seeger on Record. New York: Ludlow Music, 1971. 40 pages. [Songbook]

The Sierra Club Survival Songbook. Collected by Jim Morse and Nancy Matthews. Introduction by Pete Seeger. Sierra Club, 1971.

The Incompleat Folksinger. Edited by Jo Metcalf Schwartz. New York: Simon and Schuster, 1972. 596 pages.

Henscratches and Flyspecks: How to Read Melodies from Songbooks in Twelve Confusing Lessons. New York: Berkeley Books, 1973. 256 pages.

Foolish Frog. With Charles Seeger. New York: Macmillan, 1973. Unpaged.

A Hudson Sloopers Handy Guide. With Tom Allen and Rita Hurault. New York: Huson River Sloop Restoration, Inc., 1974.

"4 Devils." Santa Barbara: Mudbarn Press, 1982 [Songbook].

Abiyoyo. Pete Seeger. New York: Macmillan, 1985. [1994 Aladdin] 48 pages.

Everybody Says Freedom. Pete Seeger and Bob Reiser. New York: Norton, 1989, 1991.

Carry It On: The Story of America's Working People in Story and Song. Pete Seeger. New York: Simon and Schuster, 1985. Bethlehem, PA: Sing Out! Publications, 1991.

Where Have All the Flowers Gone: Songs, Seeds, Robberies. Bethlehem, PA: Sing Out! Publications, 1993, 2007.

Rise Up Singing. Edited by Peter Blood and Annie Peterson. Introduction and afterword by Pete Seeger. Sing Out! Publications, 1999. 4 pages. [Songbook]

Pete Seeger's Family Sing-a-Long. Video. Mike Seeger and Peggy Seeger. 1999. 35 min.

"Hobo's Lullaby." Pete Seeger and Robert Santelli. In *Hard Travelin': The Life and Legacy of Woody Guthrie.* Robert Santelli and Emily Davidson. Hanover, NH: Wesleyan University Press, 1999.

Pete Seeger's Storytelling Book. With Paul DuBois Jacobs. New York: Harcourt, 2000.

Pure Pete Seeger. McGraw Hill Video. 1996. January 2001. 60 min.

Pete Seeger's Abiyoyo Returns. With Paul Dubois Jacobs. New York: Simon and Schuster, 2001.

I Had a Rooster (Laura Vaccaro Seeger). New York: Viking, 2001.

One Grain of Sand: A Lullaby. Pete Seeger. Boston: Little, Brown, 2002.

Turn! Turn! Turn! W. A. Halperin, ed. New York, Simon and Schuster, 2003.

The Ageless Spirit. Connie Goldman, editor. Minneapolis: Fairview Press, 2004. 251–258.

Some Friends to Feed: Stone Soup. With Paul Dubois Jacobs. New York, Putnam Juvenile, 2005

The Deaf Musicians. With Paul Dubois Jacobs. New York: Putnam Juvenile, 2006.

INTRODUCTIONS, PREFACES, AND FOREWORDS BY PETE SEEGER

(arranged chronologically)

Guthrie, Woody. *California to the New York Island.* New York: Oak, 1958. "An Introductory Note about the Man and His Music." 2 pages.

Lomax, J., Leadbelly, A. Lomax, and H. Wood. *Leadbelly: A Collection of World-Famous Songs*. New York: Folkways Music Publishers, 1959. "Note on Lead Belly's 12-String Guitar." 1 page.

Asch, Moses and Alan Lomax, eds. *The Leadbelly Songbook*. New York: Oak, 1962. "Leadbelly."

McLean, Don, ed. *Songs and Sketches of the First Clearwater Crew*. New York: North River Press, 1970. "Foreword." 1 page.

Vishner, Mayer. *When the Mode of Music Changes*. New York: War Resisters League, 1970. "Foreword." 1 page.

Morse, Jim and Nancy Matthews. *The Sierra Club Survival Songbook*. San Francisco: Sierra Club, 1971. "Introduction." 1 page.

Rogovin, M., M. Burton, and H. Highfill. *Mural Manual*. Boston: Little Brown, 1973. "Introduction."

Robbins, Ed. *Woody Guthrie and Me*. Berkeley, CA: Lancaster House, 1979. "Introduction." 2 pages.

Knud-Hansen, Erik. *Pumpkin Happy*. Camptonville, CA: Aniccha Press, 1979. "Introduction."

Renehan, Ed, ed. *The Clearwater Songbook*. New York: G. Shirmer, 1980. "Introduction." 1 page.

Ramsey, Frederic. *Leadbelly: A Great Long Time*. [S.I.]: Serpent & Eagle Press, 1982 [1965]. "Introduction."

Guthrie, Woody. *Bound for Glory*. New York: New American Library, 1983 [1943]. "Foreword."

Rosenbaum, Art and Margo. *Folk Visions and Voices*. Athens: University of Georgia Press, 1983. "Foreword."

Segal, Edith. *A Time to Thunder*. New York: Philmark Press, 1984. "Introduction."

Verplanck, W., M. Collier, and G. Woolsey. *The Sloops of the Hudson*. Fleischmonns, NY: Purple Mountain Press, 1984 [1908]. "Introduction"

Pietzner, C., C. Pietzner, and W. Root. *Village Life: The Camphill Communities*. Boston: Neugebauer Press, 1986. "Foreword."

Caplan, Ruth. *Our Earth, Ourselves*. New York: Bantam, 1990. "Foreword."

Stavis, Barrie. *The Man Who Never Died: Joe Hill*. South Brunswick, NJ: 1992. "Introduction."

McLaren, Jen and Heide Brown, eds. *The Raging Brownies Songbook.* Gabriela Island, BC: New Society, 1993. "Foreword."

Benincasa, Janis. *I Walked the Road Again: Stories of the Catskill Mountains.* Fleischmanns, NY: Purple Mountain Press, 1994. "Foreword."

Get America Singing—Again. Vol. 1. Milwaukee: Hal Leonard Publishing, 1996. "Foreword." 72 pages. [Songbook]

Guthrie, Woody and Kathy Jakobsen. *This Land Is Your Land.* Boston: Little Brown, 1998. "Preface." 1 page.

Kayton, Brice. *Radical Walking Tours of New York City.* 2nd ed. New York: Seven Stories Press, 1999. "Foreword."1 page.

Cunningham, Agnes "Sis" and Gordon Friesen. *Red Dust and Broadsides.* Amherst: University of Massachusetts Press, 1999. "Foreword."

Fisher, Harry. *Comrades! Tales of Brigadista in the Spanish Civil War.* Lincoln: University of Nebraska Press, 1999. "Foreword." 1 page.

Get America Singing—Again. Vol. 2. Milwaukee: Hal Leonard Publishing, 2000. "Foreword." 72 pages. [Songbook]

Benson, John L. *The Hudson.* Hensonville, NY: Black Dome, 2000 [1866]. "Foreword."

Hoose, Philip. *It's Our World, Too: Young People Who Are Making a Difference.* New York: Farrar, Strauss, Giroux, 2002. "Foreword."

Truesdale, Hardie, and Joanne Michaels. *Hudson River Journey.* Woodstock, VT: Countryman Press, 2003. "Foreword."

Adler, Cy. *Walking Manhattan's Rim.* New York: Green Eagle Press, 2003. "Foreword"

Marti, José. *Versos Sencillos.* Jefferson, NC: McFarland, 2005. "Foreword."

Robeson, P., D. Murphy, and S. Turell. *Paul Robeson: Portraits of the Artist.* Irvington, NY: Criterion Collection, 2007. "Note."

MAGAZINE AND NEWSPAPER ARTICLES, REVIEWS, AND ALBUM NOTES BY PETE SEEGER

(arranged chronologically)

"Brookwood Chautagua Songs." New York: Brookwood Labor College, 1939. Poetry/Songs, 8 pages.

"Pete and His Banjo Meet Some Fine Mountain Folks." *Southern News Almanac*. Birmingham, AL, October 1940. 1 page.

People's Songs Bulletin. January 1946–April 1949. Pete Seeger, principal editor. (Unsigned articles, letters, and notes, published monthly)

"People's Songs and Singers." *New Masses,* 44 (July 16, 1946): 2–3, 9.

"A Menace to the Nation's Songs" (letter to the editor). *Daily Worker,* May 31, 1948.. 1 page.

"Library of People's Music." *Sing Out!* July 1950, pp. 6–7, 16.

Review of *Ngoma: An Introduction to Music from South Africans* (by Hugh Tracey). *Music Library Association Notes,* 11, no. 2 (March 1951): 314.

"The Weavers" (record review). *Sing Out!* September 1951, p. 16. By "Nathan Charliere" (pseudonym).

"Sea Song Paperback." *Sing Out!* 6, no. 4 (Winter 1952): 21.

"A Contemporary Ballad-Maker in the Hudson Valley." *New York Folklore Quarterly* 10, no. 2 (Summer 1954): 133–34.

"Johnny Appleseed, Jr." Column of 100–200 articles, in *Sing Out!*, beginning with vol. 4, no. 7 (Fall 1954). (ran until 2004)

"The Coal Creek Rebellion." *Sing Out!,* summer 1955, pp. 19–20.

"Introductory Notes." Album notes to *Bantu Choral Folk Songs*. Folkways Records, 1955. 6 pages.

Testimony before HUAC, 1955, reprinted in Eric Bentley, editor, *Thirty Years of Treason*. New York: Viking, 1971, pp. 686–700.

"Introduction." Album notes to *Negro Prison Camp Work Songs*. Ethnic Folkways Library, FE 4475, 1956. 2 pages.

"Introductory Notes on Community Singing." Album notes to *With Voices We Sing*. Folkways Records, FA 2452, 1956. 2 pages.

Review of *Sea Songs* (by Burl Ives). *Sing Out!,* winter 1957, p. 21.

"The Steel Drum: A New Folk Instrument." *Journal of American Folklore* 71, no. 279 (January–March 1958): 52–57.

"Too Many People Listen to Me—and Not to the People I Learned From." *Caravan,* May 1958, pp. 13–14.

"Notes on Background of Songs." Album notes to *Pete Seeger at Carnegie Hall with Sonny Terry*. Folkways Records FA 2412, 1958.

"Play Parties." Album notes to *American Play Parties.* Folkways Records, FC 7604, 1959.

"On Singing Folk Songs in a Night Club." Album notes to *Pete Seeger at the Village Gate*, with Memphis Slim and Willie Dixon. Folkways Records, FA 2450, 1960. 1 page.

"Statement to the Court" (contempt of Congress case). *Sing Out!*, summer 1961, pp. 10–11.

"Letter from the Editors." *Sing Out!*, April–May 1962, pp. 59–60.

"The Folk Process in Albany, GA." *Sing Out!*, October–November 1962. 1 page.

"The American Folk Music Revival." In H. Grafman and B. T. Manning, *Folk Music U.S.A.* New York: Citadel Press, 1962, pp. 8–15.

"Remembering Woody." *Mainstream* 16, no. 8 (August 1963): 27–33.

"The Integration Battle: A 'Singing' Movement." *Broadside*, no. 30 (August 1963).

"In My Opinion." *Seventeen*, November 1963, pp. 27–33.

"Pete Seeger's Farewell." *Hootenanny* 1, no. 1 (December 1963): 15, 73–74.

"The Country Washboard Band." Album notes to *Washboard Band Country Dance Music*. Folkways Records, FA 2201, 1963. 1 page.

"The Copyright Hassle." *Sing Out!*, December–January 1963–64. 2 pages.

"The Guitar Improvisations of Mwenda Jean Bosco." *Sing Out!*, April 1964. 2 pages.

"Woody Guthrie—Some Reminiscences." *Sing Out!*, April 1964. 4 pages.

"Footloose in Asia and Africa." *Hootenanny* 1, no. 3 (May 1964): 20–21.

"Long Live Plagiarism." *Broadside*, no. 49 (August 1964): 1–2. (Followed by a letter to the editor of *Broadside*, October 20, 1964.) 1 page.

"Record Review: Pete Seeger." *Sing Out!*, March 1965, pp. 85–87.

"Some Songs of the Selma Marchers." *Broadside*, no. 57 (April 1965). 3 pages.

"Whatever Happened to Singing in the Union?" *Sing Out!*, May 1965, pp. 28–31.

"How Can People Talk to Each Other?" (letter to the editor). *American Dialog* 2, no. 2 (May–June 1965): 31.

"You Can't Write Down Freedom Songs." *Sing Out!*, no. 15 (July 1965): 7–10, 16–18, 11.

"A Challenge to Our Readers from Pete Seeger." *Sing Out!*, no. 16 (February–March 1966). Inside front cover.

"Folk Songs and the Top 40." *Sing Out!*, February–March 1966, pp. 13–14.

"On Protest Songs." Album notes on *Dangerous Songs!?* Columbia Records, CS 9303/CL 2503, 1966. 1 page.

"Why Folk Music?" In David A. De Turk and A. Poulin Jr., *The American Folk Scene: Dimensions of the Folksong Revival*. New York: Dell, 1967, pp. 44–48.

"So Long Woody, It's Been Good to Know Ya." *Life*, November 10, 1967, p. 8.

"Sleep-time Stories and Songs." Album notes to *Abiyoyo and Other Songs for Children*. Folkways, FT 1500, FTS 31500, 1967. 1 page.

"Vietnam" (letter to the editor). *Harvard Alumni Bulletin*, March 16, 1968, p. 1.

"This Paleface Does a Double Take (Confessions of an American History Buff)." *Daily World*, July 4, 1968. 1 page.

"Let the Children Paint the Walls." *Daily World*, July 17, 1968, pp. 4–7.

"Lebanon/Israel: The Coin Has Two Sides." *Sing Out!*, June–July 1968, p. 37.

"TV: A Variety of Cream Puffs." *Daily Variety*, 35th Anniversary Edition, 1968. 1 page.

"Your Own Thing." *Seventeen*, August 1968, p. 92.

PS Sings and Answers Questions. Interview with Pete Seeger at Ford Hall Forum. Broadside Records, BRS 502, 1968. 8 pages.

"Woody Guthrie, Songwriter." *Ramparts*, November 30, 1968, pp. 29–33. (Excerpt from *The Incompleat Folksinger*).

"Parable of Uncle Sam." Album notes to *Young vs. Old*. Columbia, CS 9873, 1968. 1 page.

"The Air Belongs to Everyone." *Harvard Alumni Bulletin*, April 28, 1969, pp. 53–57.

"To Save the Dying Hudson: Pete Seeger's Voyage." *Look*, August 26, 1969, pp. 63–66.

"Sequoia: The Story of the Talking Leaves." *Sing Out!*, September–October 1969, pp. 9–10, 12–13.

"This Land Is Your Land." *Village Voice*, July 1, 1971, p. 5.

"The World Flood of U.S. Pop Music Culture." *American Dialog* 6, no. 1 (Autumn 1971): 5–6, 36–38.

"For Art's Sake." *New York Times*, December 1, 1971, op-ed page.

"Hanoi Dairy." *Eastern Horizon* 11, no. 4 (1972): 26–32.

"Pete's Pie." *Win*, December 15, 1972, p. 20.

"Strumming the Banjo in North Vietnam." *Saturday Review*, May 13, 1973, pp. 28–32.

"Teach-In: Tuning the Steel Drums." *Sing Out!*, July–August 1973, pp. 23–25.

Untitled (on Walter Lowenfels). *Small Press Review* 6, no. 2 (November 1974), 1 page.

"Songs of Labor and the American People." *Sing Out!*, January 1976, p. 1.

"How the *Clearwater* Got Started." *North River Navigator*, 6-part series, Summer 1975–April 1976. 10 pages.

Review of *The Poverty of Power* by Barry Commoner. *New York Daily World Magazine*, May 29, 1976, pp. 4–9.

"A Thumbnail History of *Sing Out!*" *Sing Out!*, May 1978, p. 33.

"Why We Must Save the Hudson." *Parade* (*Washington Post*), November 26, 1978, pp. 5–7.

"Charles Seeger, a Man of Music." *Sing Out!*, May 1979, pp. 18–19.

"Singalong." Album notes on *Pete Seeger Demonstration Concert*, Folkways Records, FXM 6055, 1980.

"A Note on Studs, Chicago, and City Folk." *Come for to Sing* 6, no. 2 (Spring 1980): 5.

"Want a *Clearwater* of Your Own?" *Clearwater Navigator*, April 1980, 2 pages.

Review of *Joe Scott: Woodsman-Songmaker* by Sandy Ives. *Ethnomusicology* 24, no. 2 (September 1980): 3 pages.

"What's Happening with *Sing Out!*?" *Come for to Sing* 8, no. 4 (1982): 5.

"A Letter from Pete Seeger: Pop, Rock, and Coca-Colonization." *Canadian Folk Music Bulletin* 29, no. 4. (December 1995).

"Love It or Lose It," in Dr. Seuss, *Your Favorite Seuss*. New York: Random House Children's Books, 2004.

SELECTED BOOKS AND THESES WITH REFERENCES ABOUT PETE SEEGER

(by author)

Beer, Molly, and David Dunaway. *Folk Music: More Than a Song*. New York: 2008.

Boyle, T. Coraghessan. *World's End*. New York: Penguin Books, 1987.

Buhle, Mari Jo, Paul Buhle, and Dan Georgakas, eds. *Encyclopedia of the American Left*. Chicago: University of Illinois Press, 1992.

Burns, Kate. *Fighters Against Censorship*. "Pete Seeger." San Diego: Lucent Books, 2004.

Cantwell, Robert. *When We Were Good: The Folk Revival*. Cambridge, MA: Harvard University Press, 1996.

Cohen, Ronald D. *Rainbow Quest: The Folk Music Revival and American Society, 1940–1970*. Boston: University of Massachusetts Press, 2002.

———, ed. *"Wasn't That a Time!" Firsthand Accounts of the Folk Music Revival*. Metuchen, NJ: Scarecrow Press, 1995.

Cohen, Ronald D., and Dave Samuelson. *Songs for Political Action*. Battle Ground, IN: Bear Family Recordings, 1996. (book released with Bear Family box set)

Cray, Ed. *Ramblin' Man: The Life and Times of Woody Guthrie*. New York: Norton, 2004.

DeLeon, David, ed. *Leaders from the 1960s: A Biographical Sourcebook of American Activism*. Westport, CT: Greenwood Press, 1994.

Denisoff, R. Serge. *Great Day Coming*. Urbana: Univ. of Illinois Press, 1971.

Denselow, Robin. *When the Music's Over: The Story of Political Pop*. Boston: Faber and Faber, 1989.

Dunaway, David King. *How Can I Keep from Singing: Pete Seeger*. New York: McGraw Hill, 1981, 1982; Da Capo, 1990. Harrap (London), 1982; Jucar (Spain), 1985; Shakai Shisosha (Japan), 1985.

Dunson, Josh. *Freedom in the Air*. New York: International Publishers, 1965.

Ellington, Richard and Dave Van Ronk. *The Bosses' Songbook: Songs to Stifle the Flames of Discontent*. 2nd ed. 1959. Self-published.

Elliot, Marc. *Death of a Rebel*. New York: Anchor/Doubleday, 1979.

Eyerman, Ron, and Andrew Jamison. *Music and Social Movements: Mobilizing Traditions in the Twentieth Century*. Cambridge, UK: Cambridge University Press, 1998.

Fariello, Griffin. *Red Scare: Memories of the American Inquisition: An Oral History*. New York: Avon Books, 1995.

Fast, Howard. *Being Red*. Boston: Houghton Mifflin, 1990.

Filene, Benjamin. *Romancing the Folk: Public Memory and American Roots Music*. Chapel Hill: University of North Carolina Press, 2000.

Goldman, Connie, ed. *The Ageless Spirit*. Minneapolis, Fairview Press, 2004, interview, 251–58.

Hajdu, David. *Positively 4th Street: The Lives and Times of Joan Baez, Bob Dylan, Mimi Baez Farina and Richard Farina*. New York: Farrar, Straus and Giroux, 2001.

Harker, Dave. *One for the Money: Politics and Popular Song*. London: Hutchinson, 1980.

Hatch, Robert. *The Hero Project*. Seeger interview. New York: McGraw Hill, 2006.

Kaplan, Judy, and Linn Shapiro, eds. *Red Diapers: Growing Up in the Communist Left*. Urbana: University of Illinois Press, 1998.

Klein, Joe. *Woody Guthrie*. New York: Knopf, 1980.

Koppelman, Robert S. "*Sing Out, Warning!, Sing Out, Love*": *The Writings of Lee Hays*. Amherst: University of Massachusetts Press, 2003.

Lankford, Ronald D., Jr. *Folk Music USA: The Changing Voice of Protest*. New York: Shirmer Trade Books, 2005.

Lichtman, Robert and Ronald Cohen. *Deadly Force: Harvey Matuson and the Informer System in the McCarthy Era*. Urbana: Univ. of Illinosis Press, 2004.

Lieberman, Robbie. *"My Song Is My Weapon": People's Songs, American Communism, and the Politics of Culture, 1930–1950*. Urbana: University of Illinois Press, 1989.

Mishler, Paul C. *Raising Reds*. New York: Columbia University Press, 1999.

Noebel, David. *The Marxist Minstrels*. Tulsa, OK: American Christian College Press, 1974. Originally issued as *Rhythm, Riot, and Revolution*, 1966.

Pescatello, Ann M. *Charles Seeger: A Life in American Music*. Pittsburgh: University of Pittsburgh Press, 1992.

Reuss, Richard, and JoAnne C. Reuss. *American Folk Music and Left-Wing Politics, 1927–1957*. Lanham, MD: Scarecrow Press, 2000.

Santelli, Robert, and Emily Davidson. *Hard Travelin': The Life and Legacy of Woody Guthrie*. Hanover, NH: Wesleyan University Press, 1999.

Scarborough, Elizabeth. *The Songkiller Saga: Phantom Banjo Vol. 1*. New York: Bantam Books, 1991.

Schultz, Bud, and Ruth Schultz, eds. "Thou Shalt Not Sing." In *It Did Happen Here: Recollections of Political Repression in America*. Berkeley: University of California Press, 1989.

Seeger, Charles. *Reminiscences of an American Musicologist*. Los Angeles: UCLA Oral History Project, 1972.

Spector, Bert Alan. *"Wasn't That a Time?" Pete Seeger and the Anti-Communist Crusade, 1940–1968*. Dissertation, University of Missouri, Columbia, 1997.

Spitz, Robert. *Dylan: A Biography*. New York: McGraw Hill, 1989.

Stanfeld, Brian J. *Pete Seeger and the Folk Process*. MA thesis, Northwest Missouri State University, 1999.

Taylor, Lori. "The Politicized American Legend of the Singing Hero." M.A. thesis, George Washington University, 1990.

Terkel, Studs. *Hope Dies Last*. New York: New Press, 2003. Seeger interview.

Vassal, Jacques. *Electric Children*. New York: Taplinger Press, 1976.

Weissman, Dick. *Which Side Are You On? An Inside History of the Folk Music Revival in America*. New York: Continuum, 2006.

Wilens, Doris. *Lonesome Traveler: The Life of Lee Hays*. New York: Norton, 1988. 2nd ed. (with Seeger foreward), Lincoln: Univ. of Nebraska Press, 1994.

Wolfe, Charles, and Kip Lornell. *The Life and Legend of Leadbelly*. New York: Harper Collins, 1992.

Zollo, Paul. *Songwriters on Songwriting*. 4th ed. New York: Da Capo Press, 2003.

SELECTED ARTICLES AND ESSAYS ON PETE SEEGER

(by author)

Alarik, Scott. "Pete Seeger in Concert." *Sing Out!* 49, no. 2 (Summer 2005): 57–67.

Allen, Henry. "Pete Seeger after All These Years." *Washington Post*, August 17, 1980.

Auletta, Ken. "None Dare Call It Liberty." Syracuse University *Daily Orange*, November 18, 1964.

Baggelaar, Kristin, and Donald Milton. *Folk Music: More Than a Song*. New York: Thomas Crowell, 1976, pp. 344–48.

Barden, J. C. "Pete Seeger." *High Fidelity*, January 1963.

Barron, James. "Decades Later, '60s Icons Still Live by Their Message." *New York Times*, March 30, 2003.

Barthel, Joan. "American Minstrel's Song of Success." *New York Times*, January 23, 1966.

Beacon News. "Seeger Indicted in Contempt Case." March 27, 1957.

Bell, Carol. "Pete Seeger: An Ideal to Cling to." *Denver Post*, August 15, 1974.

Bogdanovich, Peter. "Notes." *Story Songs*, Columbia Records CL 1668, April 1961.

Bracker, Milton. "Six More Witnesses Back Red Inquiry." *New York Times*, August 19, 1955.

Bromberg, Minna and Gary Fine. "Resurrecting the Red: Pete Seeger and the Purification of Difficult Reputations." *Social Forces* 80, no. 4 (June 2002): 1135–55.

Bruning, Fred. "Voice of Hope, Pete Seeger: 'It's Worthwhile Struggling Even If the Odds Are Against You.'" Newsday.com, September 20, 1998.

Callaghan, J. Dorsey. "Folk Singer Boasts Revival-Tent Fervor." *Detroit Free Press*, April 11, 1955.

Cantwell, Robert. "He Shall Overcome: Pete Seeger." *New England Review* 15 (Winter 1993): 205–19.

Capaldi, James. "Weavers Reunion," *Folkscene*. 9, no. 1 (March/April 1981): 16–21.

Chartock, Alan S. "Fire Still Burns in Seeger." *Troy Record*, May 9, 2007.

Churchill, Michael. Series on Pete Seeger's Contempt of Congress trial. *Harvard Crimson*, March 28, 29, 30, April 14, 1961.

Cooney, Michael. "Pete Seeger: In His Own Words." *Mariposa Notes* 3, no. 3 (Winter 1983): 1.

Corn, David. "Springsteen Does Seeger" (blog). *The Nation*, March 6, 2006.

Cory, Christopher. "A Worried Man Sings." *Providence Bulletin*, September 6, 1961.

Cowan, Paul. "Non-confrontation in Beacon, New York." *Village Voice*, December 16, 1965.

Dallos, Robert. "Pete Seeger Gets New Chance on TV." *New York Times*, August 25, 1967.

Erwin, Michael. "Pete Seeger's Homemade Music." *The Progressive* 50 (April 1980).

Estrin, Kari. "From Haymarket Square to the Hudson: An Informal Talk with Pete Seeger." *Black Sheep Review*, November/December 1984: 12–15.

Folk Songs and the Top 40. "Pete Seeger." February/March 1966: 13.

Forbes, Linda. "Pete Seeger on Environmental Advocacy, Organizing, and Education in the Hudson River Valley: An Interview." *Organization and Environment* 17, no. 4 (December 2004): 513–23.

Friesen, Gordon. Series on life with the Almanac Singers. *Broadside* (New York), June 1, 30, November 1, 1962.

Gleason, Ralph. "Pete Seeger." *San Francisco Chronicle*, May 7, 1963.

Gold, Mike. "A Paean to Pete Seeger." *Daily Worker*, February 8, 1958.

Gould, Jack. "TV: Pete Seeger Makes Belated Debut." *New York Times*, November 15, 1965.

———. "The Little 'List' Still Exists." *New York Times*, April 2, 1967.

Greenfield, Jeff. "The Party." *National Lampoon*, March 1976.

Grossman, Ron. "The Troubadour of Lost Causes." *Chicago Tribune*, April 6, 1994.

Hajdu, David. "Pete Seeger's Last War." *Mother Jones* 29, no. 5 (September/October 2004).

Harris, Scott. "Pete Seeger: Folk Music's Granddad Plays It Green." *E: The Environmental Magazine* 5, no. 6 (November/December 1994).

Hentoff, Nat. "That Ole McCarthy Hoot." *Village Voice*, March 14, 1963.

Hilmore, Edward. "Bruce Blew My Cover." *The Guardian*, February 1, 2007.

Hindustan Times. "Seeger's Folk Songs Charm." December 9, 1963.

Hoekstra, Dave. "Seeger Still a Force of Nature." *Chicago Sun Times*, April 22, 2002.

Husock, Howard. "America's Most Successful Communist." *City Journal* 15, no. 3 (Summer 2005).

Kempton, Murray. "The Minstrel Boy." *New York Post*, March 29, 1961.

Krajnc, Anita, and Michael Greenspan. "Singing Together for Social Change." *Peace Magazine*, July/August 1976.

Kwitny, Jonathan. "Timeless Troubadour." *Wall Street Journal*, June 12, 1973.

Labor's Daily. "Pete Seeger Owes Much to Trade Union Members." December 14, 1957.

Lawless, Ray. *Folksingers and Folksongs in America*. New York: Duell, Sloan and Pearce, 1960, pp. 210–12.

Lemisch, Jesse. "I Dreamed I Saw MTV Last Night." *The Nation*, October 18, 1986, pp. 374–76.

Leonard, John. "From Pete Seeger to the Sex Pistols." *New York Times*, December 6, 1978.

Life. "Minstrel with a Mission." October 9, 1964.

Lipp, Marty. "Reviving Folk's True Meaning." *Associated Press*, July 23, 2006.

Little, Paul. "Seeger Helps Restore American Folk Heritage." *Downbeat*, May 30, 1956.

Lyon, Peter. "The Ballad of Pete Seeger." In David De Turk and A. Poulin, editors, *The American Folk Scene*. New York: Dell, 1967.

Marine, Gene. "Guerilla Minstrel." Rolling Stone, April 13, 1972.

Mayer, Steve. "Seeger." *Oberlin Review*, March 13, 1969.

McCarthy, Colman. "Pete Seeger Sings for the Folks." *Arizona Star*, June 19, 1978.

Muns, Monty. "Pete Seeger: An Appreciation." *Sing Out!*, February 1961.

Nelson, Paul. "Newport Folk Festival, 1965." *Sing Out!*, November 1965.

New Yorker. "Pete Seeger on Vanguard." December 21, 1946.

New York Post. "Dangerous Minstrel Nabbed Here" (editorial). March 31, 1961.

———. "The Return to Reason" (editorial). May 20, 1962.

New York Times. "Seeger Explains Stand at Inquiry." March 15, 1961.

———. Coverage of contempt of Congress trial. March 28, 29, 30, 1961.

———. "Seeger Song in Moscow is Anti-U.S." October 25, 1965.

———. "A Timeless Seeger Gives Concert Here." February 28, 1970.

———. "Planned Songfest for Balmville Tree Has Political Overtones." June 14, 1975.

———. "400 Honor Seeger's Folk Protests." March 19, 1980. (These articles selected from those published 1946–.)

New York World Telegram. "OWI [Almanac] Singers Change Their Political Tune." January 4, 1943.

———. "3 N.Y. Entertainers Indicted for Contempt." March 26, 1957.

O'Hagan, Sean. "The Reluctant Revolutionary: Pete Seeger's Faith in the Song as a Vehicle for Social Change Remains an Inspiration." *The Observer*, April 23, 2006, p. 9.

O'Reilly, David. "The Fathers We Choose." *Inquirer Magazine*, June 21, 1998, pp. 16–26.

Palmer, Robert. "Seeger Sings of Fun and Politics." *New York Times*, August 16, 1977.

Pankake, Jon (with Paul Nelson). "P-for-Protest," In David De Turk and A. Poulin, editors, *The American Folk Scene*. New York: Dell, 1967.

———. "Pete's Children: The American Folksong Revival, Pro and Con." Reprinted in *The American Folk Scene*.

Pareles, Jon. *New York Times*, March 9, 2003.

Philbrick, Herbert. "Red Underground: Pete Seeger." *New York Herald Tribune*, March 1955.

Phine, Ken. "Pete's Eager." *Sing* (London), February 1962.

Pittsburgh Press. "WQED Cancels Leftist Singer." April 13, 1962.

Poughkeepsie New Yorker. "Seeger's Sister in Moscow," July 30, 1957.

Powers, Anne. "No Last Hurrah Yet for Political Rock." *New York Times.* December 31, 2000.

Radosh, Ron. "Time for Pete Seeger to Repent." *New York Sun,* June 12, 2007.

Ranzal, Edward. "Seeger Conviction for Contempt of Congress Voided in Appeal." *New York Times,* May 19, 1962.

Renehan, Edward J., Jr. "Pete Seeger: American." http://renehan.typepad.com (blog), June 22, 2007.

Rosenberg, Ed. "Pete Seeger: People's Artist." *Daily Worker,* June 19, 1949.

Rosenthal, Rob. "Serving the Movement: The Role(s) of Music." *Popular Music and Society* 25, nos. 3–4 (Fall/Winter 2001): 11–24.

Russell, Don. "They Sing the Hard Hitting Songs That Belong to America's Workers." *People's World,* August 8, 1941.

Sacks, Leo. "Q & A: Pete Seeger." www.billboard.com, June 26, 2006.

Schaef, A. Finley. "The TV Blacklist—A Case History." *Concern,* December 1, 1963.

Schanberg, Sydney. "L.I. School's Ban on Seeger Concert Ruled Unconstitutional." *New York Times,* July 8, 1966.

Scheck, Frank. "Pete Seeger: The Power of Song." *Hollywood Reporter,* May 21, 2007.

Schmid, Will. "Reflections on the Folk Movement: An Interview with Pete Seeger." *Music Educators Journal,* vol. 66, no. 6 (February 1980), 42–46, 78–79, 81.

Scholtes, Pete S. "Something about That Song Haunts You." Citypages.com (Complicated Fun blog), July 9, 2006.

Seeger, Charles. "Grassroots for American Composers." *Modern Music,* March 1939.

"Seeger, Pete." *Current Biography* 24, no. 11 (December 1963): 23–26.

Shelton, Robert. "The Weavers." *High Fidelity Magazine,* December 1960, p. 122.

Silber, Irwin. "The Weavers—New 'Find' of the Hit Parade." *Sing Out!,* February 1951.

———. "Pete Seeger, Voice of Our Democratic Heritage." *Sing Out!,* May 1954.

———. "The Incompleat Folksinger." *The Guardian,* August 8, 1973.

Siminoff, Roger, and Don Kissil. "Pickin', Workin' at the Other End: A Conversation with Pete Seeger." www.peteseeger.net, May 1976.

Smucker, Tom. "If Every Concert Were a Benefit, Pete Seeger Would Be Frank Sinatra." *Village Voice*, October 18, 1976.

Soviet Life. "Pete Seeger's Tour—Music Good for Flu." April 1966.

Spector, Bert. "The Weavers: A Case History in Show Business Blacklisting." *Journal of American Culture* 5 (Fall 1982): 113–20.

Terkel, Studs. "Pete Seeger Is 86." *The Nation*, May 16, 2006.

Vanity Fair. "Pete Seeger: The Riverman." November 2001, pp. 357–58.

Variety. "The Weavers." June 28, 1950.

———. "Catholic War Vets and N.Y. Journal Force Weavers' Cancellation." October 10, 1951.

———. "Weavers Deny Commie Link." March 5, 1952.

———. "Talent Boycott Threatened in Ban of Seeger, Weavers on 'Hootenanny.'" March 20, 1963. 86.

Vellela, Tony. "Pete Seeger vs. Pollution." *Christian Science Monitor*, November 3, 1975.

Wakin, Daniel J. "This Just In: Pete Seeger Denounced Stalin over a Decade Ago." *New York Times*, September 1, 2007.

Weissberg, Jay. "Pete Seeger: The Power of Song" (review). Variety.com, April 30, 2007.

Whitehead, John W. "When Will They Ever Learn?" *Rutherford Institute*, January 1, 2006, p. 7.

Wilkinson, Alec. "The Protest Singer." *New Yorker*, April 17, 2006, pp. 44–53.

Woltman, Frederick. "Melody Weaves On, along Party Line," *New York World Telegram*, August 25, 1951.

DISCOGRAPHY

—

This partial listing of Pete Seeger's major recordings on commercial discs is arranged chronologically, in approximate order of the original recordings. A comprehensive work, "The Pete Seeger Discography," which includes searchable song titles, is a forthcoming online publication of the American Folklife Center, Library of Congress http://www.loc.gov/folklife/archive.html. This discography is divided into albums, extended-play discs, singles, foreign releases, anthologies, private pressings, and additional materials. This loc.gov site also houses the author's interviews with Seeger and his associates.

SAMPLE ENTRY

TITLE	RELEASE DATA	PUBLISHER ID#
(Other artists) Songs	(Recording data)	Release and recording information [Rerelease data]

SONGS FOR JOHN DOE (The Almanac Singers: Bess Lomax, Lee Hays, Mill Lampell, Josh White, Peter Hawes; Pete Seeger accompanies and harmonizes throughout)	June 1941 (March 1941)	Keynote 102 (listed as Almanac Records) [October 1996 MCA 11499 reissue of 1941 recordings*]

* Almanacs, Weavers, and People's Songs recordings were rereleased in two Bear Family CD sets numbered BCD 15720 and 15930. Titles are as follows: *American Favorite Ballads 2*; *Folk Music of the World*; *For Kids and Just Plain Folks*; *Greatest Hits . . . Plus*; *The Essential Pete Seeger.*

The Soil and The Sea (The Almanac Singers: Woody Guthrie, Lee Hays, and Peter Hawes; Seeger accompanies on banjo and harmonizes throughout)	1941 (June 1941)	Fontana Mainstream TL 5299 [516005]. Originally issued on General Records and on Commodore BA 20, 21, *Sod Buster Ballads, Deep Sea Chanties* [1964]
Talking Union (Pete Seeger, Lee Hays, Millard Lampell, Josh White, Sam Gary, Carol White, Bess Lomax Hawes)	(July 1941)	Keynote 106 [rereleased as Folkways 52885 in 1955]
Dear Mr. President (The Almanac Singers: Baldwin Hawes, Sis Cunningham, Arthur Stern, Bess Lomax, Mill Lampell, Woody Guthrie, Pete Seeger)	May 1942 (January 1942)	Keynote III
Songs of the Spanish Civil War, Vol. 1: Songs of the Lincoln Brigade, Six Songs for Democracy (with Tom Glazer, Baldwin Hawes, and Bess Hawes)	1943 (August 1942)	Folkways FW05436 (also Stinson SLP 52). Originally released as Asch 330, *Songs of the Lincoln Brigade*, 1961 [reissued on Collectables 5606, 1995 *Songs of Lincoln/ International Brigades and Southern Mountain Hoe-down*]

Songs of Lincoln, Vol. 2/International Brigades and Southern Mountain Hoedown	February 1995	[Reissued on Collectables 5606 compilation of previous recordings]
America's Favorite Songs (with Tom Glazer, Bess Lomax Hawes, Baldwin Hawes)	1943–44	Disc 607 [rereleased, in part on *Asch Recordings 1939–1945, Volume 2, AA*3, 1967]
Darling Corey	1950	Folkways FA 2003 10"
Lonesome Valley—A Collection of American Folk Music (with Tom Glazer, Bess Lomax, Baldwin Hawes)	1951 (recorded 1943–46)	Folkways FA 2010 [FW 2010] 10"
Songs to Grow On, Vol. 2: School Days	1951	Folkways FC 7020 [FW07020] 10"
Songs to Grow On, Vol. 3: This Land Is My Land	1951	Folkways FC 7027 [FW07027] 10" Originally issued on FP 27
Folk Songs of America and Other Lands (The Weavers: Pete Seeger, Lee Hays, Ronnie Gilbert, Fred Hellerman, with Gordon Jenkins and his orchestra)	1951 (1950–51)	Decca DL-5285 10"

BEST OF THE WEAVERS	1959 (1950–53)	DL8893/DXS 7173. [rereleases from the above sessions, including additional songs; also rereleased as DL8909, *Folksongs around the World*, DL4004, *The Early Fifties*, DL7-5169, *The Weavers' Greatest Hits*, DL4485, *All Time Hootenanny*, and *The Weavers' Gold*]
WE WISH YOU A MERRY CHRISTMAS (The Weavers)	1952	Decca DL5373 10"
AMERICAN FOLKSONGS FOR CHILDREN	1953	FTS 31501/FC 7601. Originally issued on Folkways EPC 1–3, extended play (45 rpm) records [FC7001 10"] [1954]
GOOFING OFF SUITE	1954	Folkways FA2045 10" [April 15, 1993 Smithsonian Folkways SFW40018]
BIRDS, BEASTS, BUGS, AND LITTLE FISHES	1954	Folkways FC 7610 [reissued as SFW45039, February 1998]

Frontier Ballads, Vol. 2	1954	Folkways FA2176 10" [some cuts rereleased on *American History in Ballad and Song* FH5801] [FW02176]
German Folk Songs (Seeger accompanies Martha Schlamme on banjo and recorder)	1954	Folkways FW6843 [FW06843] 10"
How to Play a 5-String Banjo (instruction/record)	1954	Folkways FW08303 [FI8303, 1968]
The Pete Seeger Sampler	1954	FA2043 10" [FW02043]
Birds, Beasts, Bugs, and Bigger Fishes	1955	Folkways FC 7611
Bantu Choral Folk Songs (with chorus)	1955	Folkways FW 6912 10"
Folksongs of Four Continents	1955	Folkways FW6911 10"
The Weavers at Carnegie Hall (with the Weavers: Ronnie Gilbert, Lee Hays, Fred Hellerman)	(December 1955)	VSD6533 [1957]

CAMP SONGS (with Erik Darling and the Song Swappers)	1955	Folkways/Scholastic Records SC7628 [FC028] [reissued on Smithsonian Folkways as FW07628]
AMERICAN INDUSTRIAL BALLADS	1956	Folkways FH5251 [reissued on Smithsonian Folkways SFW40058 1992]
LOVE SONGS FOR FRIENDS AND FOES	1956	Folkways FA2453 [FW 2453]
STUDS TERKEL'S WEEKLY ALMANAC: RADIO PROGRAMME, NO. 4: FOLK MUSIC AND BLUES	1956	Folkways FS3864 [FW 3864]
WITH VOICES TOGETHER WE SING	1956	Folkways FA2452 [FW 2452]
AMERICAN FAVORITE BALLADS, VOL. I	December 1957	FA2320 [SFW40150]
JEWISH CHILDREN'S SONGS AND GAMES (Seeger accompanies Ruth Rubin on banjo)	1957	Folkways FC7224 10" [FW07224]
THE WEAVERS ON TOUR (Pete Seeger, Lee Hays, Ronnie Gilbert, Fred Hellerman)	1958 (1956–58)	Vanguard VSD6537/VRS9013

THE WEAVERS AT HOME (Pete Seeger, Lee Hays, Ronnie Gilbert, Fred Hellerman)	August 1958 (1956–58)	VRS9024/VSD2030
AMERICAN FAVORITE BALLADS, VOL. 2	1958	Folkways FA2321 [FW02321]
GAZETTE, VOL. 1	1958	Folkways FN2501 [FW02501]
PETE SEEGER AND SONNY TERRY AT CARNEGIE HALL	July 1958	Folkways FA2412 [FW02412]
SLEEP-TIME SONGS AND STORIES	1958	Folkways FC7525 [reissued as *Abiyoyo and Other Story Songs for Children*, FTS31500, 1967]
TRAVELING ON WITH THE WEAVERS (Pete Seeger sings and plays on five songs)	1958	Vanguard VRS9043 (mono) [VSD-2022 (stereo release)]
AMERICAN FAVORITE BALLADS, VOL. 3	1959	Folkways FA2322 [SFW40152]
HOOTENANNY TONIGHT!	1959	Folkways FN2511 [FW02511]
NONESUCH AND OTHER FOLK TUNES (with Frank Hamilton)	August 1959	Folkways FA2439 [FW02439]

Songs of Struggle and Protest, 1930–50	1959	Folkways FH5233 [FW05233] [rereleased as *Wimoweh and Other Songs of Freedom and Protest*]
Folk Songs for Young People	1959	Folkways FC7532 [reissued as Smithsonian Folkways SFW45024]
Folk Festival at Newport, Vol. 1	1960 (July 11–12, 1959)	Vanguard VRS9062
Champlain Valley Songs	February 1960	Folkways FH5210 [FW05210]
Hootenanny at Carnegie Hall	1960	Folkways FN2512 [FW02512]
Indian Summer (soundtrack)	1960	Folkways FS 3851 [FW03851]
Old Time Fiddle Tunes Played by Jean Carignan (with Jean Carignan, Marcel Roy, Denny MacDougal; Pete Seeger plays banjo)	1960	Folkways FG3531 [FW03531]
Highlights of Pete Seeger at the Village Gate with Memphis Slim and Willie Dixon	1960	Folkways FA2450, FA2451

The Rainbow Quest	July 1960 (1958–59)	Folkways FA2454 [FW02454]
Songs of the Civil War	1960	Folkways FH5717 [FW05717]
American Favorite Ballads, Vol. 4	1961	Folkways FA2323 [SFW40153]
Gazette, Vol. 2	1961	Folkways FN2502 [FW02502]
Sing Out with Pete!	August 1961 (1956–61)	Folkways FA2455 [FW02455]
Pete Seeger: Story Songs	1961 (April 1961)	Columbia CL1668/CS8468 [rereleased as Columbia Folk Odyssey 32-16-0266: *3 Saints, 4 Sinners, and 6 Other People*]
12-String Guitar as Played by Leadbelly (instructional record)	1962	Folkways FI8371 [FW08371]
American Favorite Ballads, Vol. 5	1962	Folkways FA2445 [FW02445]
Pete Seeger at the Village Gate, Vol. 2	May 1962	Folkways [FW02451]

AMERICAN GAME AND ACTIVITY SONGS FOR CHILDREN	1962	Folkways FC7674 [reissued on Smithsonian Folkways SFW45056, January 2000]
BROADSIDE BALLADS, VOL. I	1963	Folkways FH5301 [FW05301]
BROADSIDE BALLADS, VOL. 2	1963	Folkways BR 302 [FW05302]
SING OUT! HOOTENANNY WITH PETE SEEGER AND THE HOOTENEERS	1963 (mid-1950s)	Folkways FN2513 [FW05213] Recorded live at People's Artists hootenannies
CHILDREN'S CONCERT AT TOWN HALL	August 21, 1963 (April 28, 1962)	Columbia 46185 (Columbia CS8747) [reissued as Harmony 30399; released on CD August 21, 1990; Legacy 046185]
THE BITTER AND THE SWEET	January 1963 (May 1962)	Columbia CL1916, CS8716
THE WEAVERS: REUNION AT CARNEGIE HALL	1963 (May 2, 3, 1963)	Vanguard VSD2150
WE SHALL OVERCOME	1963 (June 8, 1963)	Columbia CS8901

NEWPORT BROADSIDE (with Bob Dylan)	1964 (July 1963)	Vanguard VSD79144
LITTLE BOXES AND OTHER BROADSIDES	1963	Verve/Folkways FV/FVS9020
BROADSIDES: SONGS AND BALLADS	1964	Folkways FA2456 [FW02456]
WNEW'S STORY OF SELMA (with Len Chandler and others)	1965 (March 1965)	Folkways FH5595 [FW05595]
THE WEAVERS REUNION, PART 2	1965 (May 2, 3, 1963)	VSD79161
STRANGERS AND COUSINS	June 1965 (1963–64)	Columbia CL2334, CS9134
I CAN SEE A NEW DAY	January 1965	Columbia CL2252, CS9232
GOD BLESS THE GRASS	January 1966	Columbia CL2432, CS9232 [Folkways FW37232, 1982; Legacy 065287 includes three unreleased tracks, May 12, 1998]
DANGEROUS SONGS!?	August 1966	Columbia CL2503, CS9303 [Sony 65261, 1998]

ABIYOYO AND OTHER STORY SONGS FOR CHILDREN	1967	Folkways FC7525 [rereleased in 1989 as SFW45001]
WAIST DEEP IN THE BIG MUDDY	August 1967	Columbia CL2705, CS9505 [January 25, 1994]
PETE SEEGER'S GREATEST HITS	October 1967	Columbia CL2616, CS9416: Releases of previously recorded material for Columbia; some cuts may not be previously issued.
PETE SEEGER SINGS WOODY GUTHRIE	1967 (mid-1950s)	Folkways FTS31002 [FW31002] Probably recorded in the mid- and late 1950s.
PETE SEEGER SINGS LEADBELLY	1968	Folkways FTS31002 [FW31002] Probably recorded in the mid- and late 1950s.
PETE SEEGER NOW (with Frederick Kirkpatrick and Bernice Reagon)	1969 (1968)	Columbia CS9717
PETE SEEGER YOUNG VS. OLD	1971	Columbia CS9873
A TRIBUTE TO WOODY GUTHRIE, VOLS. 1, 2	1972 (1968–69)	Warner Bros. 2W3007

Great Folksingers of the Sixties	1972	Vanguard VSD17/18 rereleases
Rainbow Race	1973	Columbia C30739
Banks of Marble and Other Songs	1974	Folkways FTS31040 [FW31040]
Clearwater	1974 (1969–74)	Sound House Records PS 1001
The World of Pete Seeger	1974	Columbia KG31949. Anthology of previous recordings for Columbia.
Pete Seeger and Arlo Guthrie Together In Concert	1975	Warner Bros. 2R2214
Fifty Sail on Newburgh Bay (with Ed Renehan)	1976	Folkways FH5257 [FW05257]
Clearwater II	1977 (1969–77)	Sound House Records SHRI022
The Essential Pete Seeger	1978	Vanguard 97/98 [rereleases from Folkways Records, 1950–74]
Circles and Seasons	1979	Warner Bros. BSK3329
The Weavers Together Again	1980	Loom Records 10681 [rereleased as Reunion-80]

PRECIOUS FRIEND (with Arlo Guthrie and Shenandoah)	1982 (1981)	Warner Bros. 2BSK 3644
HARP: A TIME TO SING (Holly Near, Arlo Guthrie, Ronnie Gilbert, Pete Seeger)	1985	Redwood Records RR4409 [rereleased in 2001 as Appleseed Records APR CD1054]
A FISH THAT'S A SONG	1990	Smithsonian Folkways SFW45037
DON'T MOURN—ORGANIZE! SONGS OF LABOR + SONGWRITER JOE HILL	1990	Smithsonian Folkways SFW40026
PETE SEEGER'S FAMILY CONCERT	1993 (April 21, 1992)	Sony 48907
PETE SEEGER LIVE AT NEWPORT	(1961–65)	Vanguard 77008 [1993 rerelease of Vanguard Newport series]
MORE TOGETHER IN CONCERT (with Arlo Guthrie)	March 25, 1994	Rising Son 0007/8
PETE—LIVING MUSIC (with Joanie Madden, Howard Levy, Paul Winter, Paul Prestopino, Gaudeamus, and the Union Baptist Church Singers)	April 1996	LMUS 0032

The Weavers: The Best of the Decca Years	1996	MCA 11465. Compilation of previous recordings.
Weavers: Goodnight Irene 1949–1953	2000	Bear Family BCD 15930 EK. Compilation of previous recordings.
The Martins & the Coys	2000 (1944)	Rounder 11661-1819-2
If I Had a Song: The Songs of Pete Seeger, Vol. 2	2001	Appleseed 1055
Seeds: The Songs of Pete Seeger, Vol. 3	2003	Appleseed 1072
The Weavers: Rarities from the Vanguard Vault	2003 (1957–58)	Vanguard Records 79707-2
My Name Is Buddy (Ry Cooder; Pete Seeger plays on title track)	October 2007	Nonesuch B000MDH8E6

This discography was originally prepared by David Dunaway in 1980 with the assistance of Eleanor Shapiro. It was revised in 2007 with the assistance of Whitney Brown and Felicia Karas. Subsequently, it was reviewed by experts familiar with Seeger's recordings: Ron Cohen, Dave Samuelson, and Jim Capaldi. My thanks to all of these associates and reviewers. In addition, I would like to thank the staff of the American Folklife Center at the Library of Congress—particularly Todd Harvey, David Taylor, Michael Taft, and Peggy Bulger—for their encouragement and enthusiasm for this effort.

PERMISSIONS

The Almanac Singers collectively produced "Ballad of October 16," "On Account of That New Situation," "Jim Crow," "Arctic Circle," and "Dear Mr. President." All are on file at the Library of Congress.

"A Visit with Harry," "The Same Merry-Go-Round," and "Swinging on a Scab" were first printing in the pages of *People's Songs*, as was "Wallace the Man" by Woody Guthrie.

"Ballad of a Party Singer" and "Talking Management Blues" were written and composed by Roy Berkeley and appeared in *Bosses' Songbook*, uncopyrighted, edited and published by Dick Ellington.

"Oh, Wallace" was communally composed by members of the Civil Rights Movement and published in *We Shall Overcome and Freedom Is a Constant Struggle*, edited by Guy and Candie Carawan, Oak Publishers, 1963 and 1968.

Grateful acknowledgment is made to the following for permission to reprint previously published material:

"Union Maid," words and music by Woody Guthrie, TRO-copyright © 1961 (renewed) and 1963 (renewed) by Ludlow Music, Inc., New York, N.Y. Used by permission.

"If I Had a Hammer (The Hammer Song)," words and music by Lee Hays and Pete Seeger, TRO-copyright © 1958 (renewed) and 1962 (renewed) by Ludlow Music, Inc., New York, N.Y. Used by permission.

"De Grey Goose," words and music by Huddie Ledbetter, collected and adapted by John A. Lomax and Alan Lomax, TRO-copyright © 1936 (renewed) by Folkways Music Publishers, Inc., New York, N.Y. Used by permission.

"Waist Deep in the Big Muddy (The Big Muddy)," words and music by Pete Seeger, TRO-copyright © 1967 (renewed) by Melody Trails, Inc., New York, N.Y. Used by permission.

"Sailing Down My Golden River," words and music by Pete Seeger, TRO-copyright © 1971 (renewed) by Melody Trails, Inc., New York, N.Y. Used by permission.

"The Torn Flag," words and music by Pete Seeger, TRO-copyright © 1970 (renewed) by Melody Trails, Inc., New York, N.Y. Used by permission.

"Tomorrow Is a Highway," words by Lee Hays, music by Pete Seeger, TRO-copyright © 1950 (renewed) by Folkways Music Publishers, Inc., New York, N.Y. Used by permission.

"If You Love Your Uncle Sam (Bring Them Home)" by Pete Seeger, copyright © 1966 by Stormking Music, Inc. All rights reserved. Used by permission.

"False from True" by Pete Seeger, copyright © 1968 by Sanga Music, Inc. All rights reserved. Used by permission.

"King Henry" by Pete Seeger, copyright © 1965, 1966 by Sanga Music, Inc. All rights reserved. Used by permission.

"Letter to Eve" by Pete Seeger, copyright © 1967 by Sanga Music, Inc. All rights reserved. Used by permission.

"Abiyoyo" by Pete Seeger, copyright © 1963, 1964 by Sanga Music, Inc. All rights reserved. Used by permission.

"Where Have All the Flowers Gone?" by Pete Seeger, copyright © 1961 by Sanga Music, Inc. All rights reserved. Used by permission.

"Joy Upon This Earth" by Charles Seeger, copyright © 1979 by Sanga Music, Inc. All rights reserved. Used by permission.

"66 Highway Blues" by Woodie Guthrie and Pete Seeger, copyright © 1966 by Stormking Music and Woody Guthrie Publications, Inc. All rights reserved. Used by permission.

"Talking Union" by Pete Seeger, Lee Hays, and Millard Lampell, copyright © 1947 by Stormking Music, Inc. All rights reserved. Used by permission.

"How Can I Keep from Singing?" adapted with additional words by Doris Plenn, copyright © 1964 by Sanga Music, Inc. All rights reserved. Used by permission.

"Quite Early Morning" by Pete Seeger, copyright © 1969 by Sanga Music, Inc. All rights reserved. Used by permission.

"Wasn't That a Time?" by Lee Hays and Walter Lowenfels, copyright © 1957, 1960, 1966 by Sanga Music, Inc. All rights reserved. Used by permission.

"Turn! Turn! Turn! (To Everything There Is a Season)," words from Book of Ecclesiastes, adaptation and music by Pete Seeger, TRO-copyright © 1962 (renewed) by Melody Trails, Inc., New York, N.Y. Used by permission.

"Hold the Line," words by Lee Hays, music by The Weavers, copyright © 1950 by Sanga Music. All rights reserved. Used by permission.

"We Shall Overcome," musical and lyrical adaptation by Zilphia Horton, Frank Hamilton, Guy Carawan, and Pete Seeger. Inspired by African American gospel singing, members of the Food & Tobacco Workers Union, Charlotte, S.C. and the Southern Civil Rights Movement. TRO-copyright © 1960 (renewed) and 1963 (renewed) by Ludlow Music, Inc., New York, N.Y. International copyright secured. Made in the USA. All rights reserved including public performance for profit. Royalties derived from this composition are being contributed to the We Shall Overcome Fund and The Freedom Movement under the Trusteeship of the writers. Used by permission.

Excerpt from "The People, Yes" from *The People, Yes* by Carl Sandburg, copyright © 1936 by Harcourt, Inc., and copyright renewed 1964 by Carl Sandburg. Reprinted by permission of Harcourt, Inc.

INDEX

—

ABOUT THE AUTHOR

—

David King Dunaway was born in Greenwich Village in New York City. He attended the Universities of Aix-en-Provence, France, Wisconsin, and California, where he received Berkeley's first Ph.D. in American studies. At the University of New Mexico, Dr. Dunaway has taught biography and broadcasting, and he has been a Fulbright Senior Lecturer at the University of Nairobi, Copenhagen University, and the National University of Colombia. Author and editor of a half dozen volumes of history and biography, he consults on and produces national radio series for public radio.